Experiencing the Hebrew Bible

Baron Lectures.
Studies on the Jewish Experience

Editors

Armin Lange, Kerstin Mayerhofer

Advisory Board

Elisheva Carlebach (Columbia University of the City of New York),
Judith Olszowy-Schlanger (University of Oxford),
Dina Porat (Tel Aviv University / Yad Vashem),
Lawrence H. Schiffman (New York University)

Vol. 2

Alina L. Schittenhelm, Amy Fedeski,
Kerstin Mayerhofer (Eds.)

Experiencing the Hebrew Bible

Spotlights on History and Tradition

BRILL | SCHÖNINGH

Published with the support of the University of Vienna (Project Baron Awards), funded by the Salo W. and Jeannette M. Baron Foundation and the Knapp Family Foundation.

 This is an open access title distributed under the terms of the CC-BY-NC-ND 4.0 License, which permits any non-commercial use, distribution, and reproduction in any medium, provided no alterations are made and the original author(s) and source are credited.

Further information and the complete license text can be found at
https://creativecommons.org/licenses/by-nc-nd/4.0/

The terms of the CC license apply only to the original material. The use of material from other sources (indicated by a reference) such as diagrams, illustrations, photos and text samples may require further permission from the respective copyright holder.

DOI: https://doi.org/10.30965/9783657796946

Bibliographic information published by the Deutsche Nationalbibliothek

The Deutsche Nationalbibliothek lists this publication in the Deutsche Nationalbibliografie; detailed bibliographic data available online: http://dnb.d-nb.de

© 2025 by the authors and editors. Published by Brill Schöningh, Wollmarktstraße 115, 33098 Paderborn, Germany, an imprint of the Brill-Group (Koninklijke Brill BV, Leiden, The Netherlands; Brill USA Inc., Boston MA, USA; Brill Asia Pte Ltd, Singapore; Brill Deutschland GmbH, Paderborn, Germany; Brill Österreich GmbH, Vienna, Austria)
Koninklijke Brill BV incorporates the imprints Brill, Brill Nijhoff, Brill Schöningh, Brill Fink, Brill mentis, Brill Wageningen Academic, Vandenhoeck & Ruprecht, Böhlau and V&R unipress.

www.brill.de
E-Mail: info@schoeningh.de

Brill Schöningh reserves the right to protect the publication against unauthorized use and to authorize dissemination by means of offprints, legitimate photocopies, microform editions, reprints, translations, and secondary information sources, such as abstracting and indexing services including databases.
Requests for commercial re-use, use of parts of the publication, and/or translations must be addressed to Brill Schöningh.

Cover illustration: *Salo W. Baron*. Głos Gminy Żydowskiej: organ Gminy Wyznaniowej Żydowskiej w Warszawie 10–11/1938. Wikicommons, public domain. Adapted by Kerstin Mayerhofer.
Cover design: Evelyn Ziegler, Munich
Production: Brill Deutschland GmbH, Paderborn

ISSN 2750-7599
ISBN 978-3-506-79694-3 (hardback)
ISBN 978-3-657-79694-6 (e-book)

Table of Contents

Experiencing the Hebrew Bible: Introduction VII
Alina L. Schittenhelm, Kerstin Mayerhofer, Amy Fedeski

PART I
Text

1 The Many Faces of the Bible: The Pre-History of
   Our Modern Bibles 3
   Emanuel Tov

2 Divergent Versions of *Habakkuk 3*: From the Desk of the
   Hebrew University Bible Project 17
   Michael Segal

3 Ladino and Spanish Bibles: Different Traditions 37
   Ora (Rodrigue) Schwarzwald

4 Textual History as Reception History: Rabbi Meir's Text of
   Isa 21:11 61
   Armin Lange

PART II
Reception

5 Memory, Orality and Textuality in the Reception of the
   Biblical Text in Rabbinic Literature 83
   Lawrence H. Schiffman

6 Converts' Souls in the *Zohar*: A Reception History 101
   Yuval Katz-Wilfing

7 Examples of Medieval Judith Midrashim: The Reception of the
   Pre-Modern Niddah 121
   Rosalie Gabay Bernheim

PART III
History

8 Strengthening the Faith of the Ex-Conversos: Karaites, Translation, and Biblical Exegesis in Northwest Europe 145
   Benjamin Fisher

9 A Profoundly Religious Expression: The Role of Scripture and Ritual in the American Campaign for Soviet Jewish Emigration, 1964–1974 167
   Amy Fedeski

10 The Discipline of Textual Criticism as Experienced in 1970–2020 179
   Emanuel Tov

PART IV
Modern Culture

11 The Gendering Garden: Narrative Creations of Adam and Eve as Cisgender Prefiguration in Biblical, Rabbinic, and Contemporary Young Adult Literature 209
   Daniel Vorpahl

12 Disturbed Depths: The Aquatic Otherness of the Leviathan in *From Dust, A Flame* 233
   Marissa Herzig

13 Beyond Religious and Secular: Biblical Intertextuality in Modern Mizrahi Literature 253
   Alina L. Schittenhelm

   List of Contributors 277

Experiencing the Hebrew Bible: Introduction

Alina L. Schittenhelm, Kerstin Mayerhofer, Amy Fedeski

It is a great pleasure to present the second volume of the Baron Lectures series to the public. This volume is once again a tribute to Salo W. and Jeannette M. Baron, whose research spanned multiple continents—Europe, North Africa, America, and the Middle East—and extended across centuries. Similarly, this volume encompasses a diverse range of topics in various academic fields, including Biblical studies, literary studies, and history. Contributors from around the globe present work that crosses both geographical and temporal boundaries. As such, the contents of this volume reflect the interdisciplinary nature of Salo W. and Jeannette M. Baron's scholarship, as well as the spirit of the Baron Awards, to which this book series is connected.

The *Salo W. and Jeannette M. Baron Awards for Scholarly Excellence in Research of the Jewish Experience* were established in 2020, commemorating Salo W. Baron's 125th birthday. Administered by the University of Vienna and funded by the Knapp Family Foundation, alongside the Salo W. and Jeannette M. Baron Foundation, these awards honour distinguished and aspiring scholars whose research is connected to the Jewish experience. The awards aim to recognise groundbreaking research and studies in this field, acknowledging scholarly excellence in memory of Salo W. and Jeannette M. Baron. Additionally, these awards serve as an incentive for future scholars to follow in the Barons' footsteps, reassessing and exploring Jewish history.

As with the previous volume, the second volume of the Baron Lectures brings together current research related to the 2023 Baron Awards. Emanuel Tov, recipient of the 2023 Baron Senior Award, is an expert in the textual history of Judaism's foundational text—the Hebrew Bible. Like Salo W. Baron, Emanuel Tov has not only contributed to a new field of research but has also played a significant role in organising research and science.

Born in Amsterdam, the Netherlands, Tov emigrated to Israel in 1961. He studied Bible and Greek literature at the Hebrew University of Jerusalem and furthered his education in the Department of Near Eastern Languages and Literatures at Harvard University. He earned his PhD from the Hebrew University of Jerusalem and has served as a professor in its Department of Bible for over twenty years. Tov has specialised in various aspects of the textual criticism of Hebrew and Greek Scripture, as well as the Qumran Scrolls. He has written and edited numerous books and articles, including two textbooks, most notably *Textual Criticism of the Hebrew Bible*. Since the 1990s, Tov has been a leading figure in the Dead Sea Scrolls Publication Project, under whose guidance more than thirty volumes were published between 1992 and 2010 in the *Discoveries in the Judaean Desert* series. Emanuel Tov remains deeply engaged with the Hebrew Bible, its text, evolution, and tradition. This volume not only pays tribute to his expertise but also highlights the ongoing importance of the Hebrew Bible in Jewish life, religious practice, and scholarly research.

The *Baron Young Scholars Awards* are presented alongside the Senior Award to honour exceptional scholarly work conducted by postgraduate students and early career researchers. These awards recognise research focused on the relationship between Jews and non-Jews, as well as perceptions and understandings of Judaism within broader societies. This encompasses the history, culture, religion, and institutions of the Jewish people, including their persecution. In 2023, Amy Fedeski and Alina L. Schittenhelm received the Young Scholars Awards for their outstanding proposals. Each was granted a three-month research stay in Vienna to advance their work on current research topics.

Amy Fedeski is Alfred and Isabel Bader Postdoctoral Fellow in Jewish History at Queen's University in Kingston, Ontario. She completed her PhD at the Corcoran Department of History, University of Virginia in 2022 with a dissertation entitled *"What We Want To Do As Americans": Jewish Political Activism and United States Refugee Policy, 1969–1981*. Her doctoral research, which she is currently writing up as a book, argues that Jewish American Non-Governmental Organisations fundamentally remade American refugee politics in ways which still resonate today. Amy Fedeski's wider research interests focus on transnational Jewish migration politics during the Cold War. Amy Fedeski is working on her second project, *"All Doors Are Closed to Us": Soviet Jewish Returnees from Israel in Cold War Europe.* This research examines the experiences of Soviet Jewish migrants who, after first settling in Israel, returned to Europe seeking resettlement elsewhere. These migrants found themselves in legal and social limbo, unwilling to return to Israel and unable to claim refugee status in third countries. This project explores how returnees moved across Europe, engaging with national and international legal regimes, NGOs, and Jewish communities across Europe and on the global stage, in search of stability and status.

Alina L. Schittenhelm is a PhD candidate at the University of Potsdam and has been an ELES research fellow since April 2022. In May 2021, Schittenhelm completed her Master of Arts in Jewish Studies at the University of Potsdam, following a Bachelor's degree in Jewish Studies and Philosophy. From February to October 2023, she undertook a research stay at the Department of Literature at Tel Aviv University, funded by the German Academic Exchange Service. Her areas of interest include Hebrew language and literature, as well as Israel and Mizrahi Studies. Her PhD project focuses on topographies and gender in modern Mizrahi literature. The study aims to bring to light counter-narratives and nuances in the image of Jewishness through voices from the spatial and social margins of Israeli society. She examines the works of authors such as Ronit Matalon, Dorit Rabinyan, Sami Berdugo, and Sara Shilo, analysing both their content and language. This research is situated within the discipline of Israel Studies and addresses the artistic processing of history, memories, and society.

The two projects, which may initially seem unrelated to the Hebrew Bible, nonetheless contain strong Jewish references that are intricately tied to their textual foundations. Upon closer inspection, both research projects reveal that the Hebrew Bible deeply influences Jewish life in many aspects, from migration history to contemporary discourses. Fedeski's and Schittenhelm's articles engage in an intriguing dialogue with the Hebrew Bible, applying its timeless themes and moral issues to modern contexts. As one of the most important religious texts in the world, the Hebrew Bible has undergone numerous interpretations, translations, and adaptations over the centuries. This volume is dedicated to the diversity of these traditions, examining how they manifest in different Jewish cultures, times, and contexts. From theological reflections to historical analyses and literary interpretations, the volume offers a multifaceted insight into the rich and complex world of biblical traditions.

The authors in this volume are as diverse as their research approaches. We have gathered academics at different stages of their careers to share their perspectives, both individually and collectively. The volume includes contributions from participants in the second Baron Young Scholars Workshop in 2023, as well as papers by invited authors. Given the interdisciplinary nature of their research and their varied academic advancement, the papers in this volume are quite diverse. However, all the articles address topics related to senior laureate Emanuel Tov's research on the Hebrew Bible and highlight its history and tradition.

This spotlight on the Hebrew Bible is further emphasised by the variety within the contributions, which may differ significantly in subject area, period, tradition (Sephardic or Ashkenazi), method, or interpretation. Despite these differences, the volume as a whole illustrates the rich array of research that the Hebrew Bible continues to inspire. It showcases the diverse backgrounds and research focuses of scholars who delve into this foundational text, highlighting its enduring significance and complexity.

This diversity of perspectives, voices, and approaches in the contributions to this volume also posed a challenge in determining the right order for the book. The volume is now divided into four equal parts, each examining different facets of the Hebrew Bible. The book opens with a microlevel analysis of the biblical text and its reception, then broadens to explore historical contexts beyond antiquity, and finally concludes with modern cultural references, depicting both direct and indirect influences of the Hebrew Bible in contemporary society.

The first part focuses on the text of the Hebrew Bible. The textual history of the Hebrew Bible, also known as the Tanakh in Jewish tradition, spans over millennia, with its development, transmission, and reception playing a foundational role in Jewish culture until the present day. An investigation of the biblical text, its original form(s) and numerous extant variants is the subject of textual criticism, strongly influenced by Emanuel Tov. Textual criticism works on intra- and intertextual levels as well as on factors implicating the fashioning and evolution of the biblical texts from the outside world. Material to work with to shed light on the development of the Hebrew Bible and to support exegesis of its content include textual variants from various geographic areas as well as translations. This first part of the book therefore brings together articles that closely examine the biblical Hebrew text, reflecting a broad range of research approaches. These contributions explore the history of our modern Bibles, engage in detailed analysis of specific biblical texts, and investigate the numerous translations the Bible has undergone throughout history.

In his opening article, *The Many Faces of the Bible: The Pre-History of Our Modern Bibles*, senior laureate Emanuel Tov explores the sources we rely on for consulting the Hebrew Bible. He argues that, given that most people today access the Hebrew Bible through translations, it is crucial to understand what these translations are based on—the Hebrew text itself. Tov provides an overview of the evolution of the Hebrew text, tracing its development from the earliest documentation in the Dead Sea Scrolls to medieval redactions and modern-day translations. He asserts that, although we can never fully reconstruct the original text, the Hebrew Bible had already undergone numerous changes and redactions in ancient times. These ancient variants are "still visible in the text forms that have been accepted in the various religious communities" (13), and they can offer valuable insights into what ancient religious life might have looked like.

Michael Segal, in his contribution *From the Desk of the Hebrew University Bible Project: Divergent Versions of Habakkuk 3*, explores the textual variations of Habakkuk 3. His study is based on the research and formulation of Apparatus I to Habakkuk 3 in the HUBP edition, with a particular focus on the Greek evidence for this poetic section. While the apparatus system allows for detailed analysis, Segal's current study aims to synthesize this complex data to shed light on the broader implications for understanding textual dynamics, which are crucial for grasping the development of biblical literature. Segal examines the versions of Habakkuk from the Masoretic Text, the Septuagint, and the so-called Barbarini version, seeking to delineate the different literary editions of Habakkuk 3. Although his study does not yet provide a definitive answer, Segal demonstrates that "the dynamic aspects of growth" (32) in texts like Habakkuk 3 must be considered both in this specific instance and more broadly in discussions about the contribution of textual versions to the literary evolution of biblical books.

In her article *Ladino and Spanish Bibles: Different Traditions*, Ora (Rodrigue) Schwarzwald investigates the variations between medieval Spanish Bible translations and Ladino translations from the sixteenth century. Her linguistic analysis highlights lexical and syntactical differences, as well as distinct features related to Jewish usage, such as the treatment of names, including the name of God. Schwarzwald finds that medieval translations tend to reproduce the content of the Hebrew text, whereas Ladino translations adhere more closely to its structure. This distinction underscores the influence of oral traditions on Ladino translations and their role in preserving linguistic practices. Her study provides insights into Jewish cultural and religious life over the centuries, illustrating how Ladino translations maintained the resilience of oral traditions and the uniqueness of Judeo-Spanish. This emphasises the significance of community practices in preserving language and tradition through religious texts.

Finally, Armin Lange demonstrates how textual history and reception history of the Hebrew Bible are closely connected. In his article *Textual History as Reception History: Rabbi Meir's Text of Isa 21:11*, Lange analyses one particular variant reading of the book of Isaiah attributed to Rabbi Meir (second century CE). Rabbi Meir copied what the scribal tradition had transmitted as a scribal error: the toponym *dumah* that, by confusing the Hebrew characters *dalet* and *resh*, had changed for *romah* to refer to Rome. However, in Rabbi Meir's version of the relevant text, he chose to render *romah* for *romi*, in accordance with contemporary rabbinic practice. Influenced by Koiné-Greek and contemporary cultural developments, this rendering does not only reflect the continuation of a scribal error, but, as Lange argues, a particular interpretive process. Lange's article ends with the claim for acknowledgment of the textual history of the Hebrew Bible as "an important part of its interpretative history." (76) It is the bridge to the second part of this volume.

The second part of this volume focuses on the reception of the Bible. The Hebrew Bible's reception in Jewish culture has been foundational, shaping religious, legal, and ethical life across millennia. Its texts have been studied, interpreted, and expanded upon by rabbinic authorities in works like the Talmud and Midrash, providing deeper insights and practical applications for

Jewish life. Throughout history, the Hebrew Bible has influenced Jewish liturgy, festivals, and communal identity, remaining a central reference for spiritual, moral, and legal guidance. Its ongoing interpretation continues to sustain its relevance in Jewish tradition and scholarship. Extending beyond the original Hebrew text to explore issues of interpretation and practice, the articles in this section address classical rabbinical exegesis, Kabbalistic interpretations, and the medieval transmission and re-appropriation of non-canonical books. This section delves into how the Bible has been understood and (re-)interpreted throughout history, reflecting its evolving impact on religious thought and practice.

Lawrence H. Schiffman's article, *Memory, Orality, and Textuality in the Reception of the Biblical Text in Rabbinic Literature*, opens this section by examining the transmission of the biblical text through both oral and written channels. Schiffman argues that both modes played crucial roles in shaping cultural and religious memory within rabbinic literature. He explores how rabbinic efforts to standardise and correct the text were driven by a concern for textual accuracy, while also recognizing the dynamic nature of oral tradition, which allowed for expansions and developments. Schiffman details how the interplay between oral and written elements in the public reading of Scripture helped preserve variants, errors, and anomalies. He concludes that the integration of orality and textuality is a defining characteristic of rabbinic practice.

Yuval Katz-Wilfing's article, *Converts' Souls in the Zohar*, delves into the concept of soul transmigration within the context of medieval Kabbalah. Although this concept is not explicitly found in the Hebrew Bible, it held significant importance for Kabbalists. Katz-Wilfing explores the central dilemma faced by the Kabbalistic tradition: How can one become a Jew if being Jewish is associated with possessing a unique type of soul? In addressing this question, the Kabbalistic tradition posits that righteous figures like Abraham and Sarah can generate souls, including those of converts, from Heaven. This interpretation challenges earlier teachings regarding the nature and creation of the soul. Katz-Wilfing examines various interpretations of how a Jewish soul is imparted to a convert, noting that one approach suggests converts acquire their Jewish soul at the moment of conversion, while another posits that converts are endowed with Jewish souls from birth. He concludes that these ideas represent a profound shift in the understanding of the Jewish soul, akin to a Copernican revolution in traditional thought.

In her article, *Examples of Medieval Judith Midrashim: The Reception of the Pre-Modern Niddah*, Rosalie Gabay Bernheim explores not only the tradition of the Book of Judith as a non-canonical work but also, more specifically, the concept of *niddah*, or menstrual impurity. She examines the reception of medieval midrashim on Judith, focusing particularly on *Megillat Yehudit*. Medieval

Judith midrashim depict the eponymous heroine in a strategic light, using her menstrual cycle as a symbolic tool of triumph for the Jewish people against non-Jewish adversaries. In response to the Christian tradition that had incorporated Judith into its canon, medieval Jewish texts reframe the concept of niddah to reassert the Jewish identity of Judith and her story. Bernheim argues that, from the tenth century onward, the portrayal of Judith as niddah served both to distinguish Jewish tradition from Christianity and to strengthen Jewish identity and self-perception.

Part III of the volume gathers historical approaches to the Hebrew Bible, showcasing exemplary research that examines this important text from a historical perspective. The contributions aim to provide a glimpse into how the Hebrew Bible has served as a historical reference point across various places and societies. This section illustrates the text's influence and significance in different historical contexts, highlighting its role in shaping and reflecting historical narratives.

In his article, *Strengthening the Faith of the Ex-Conversos: Karaites, Translation, and Biblical Exegesis in Northwest Europe*, Benjamin Fisher examines the Hebrew Bible's role among Karaites, Sephardic diaspora communities in Amsterdam and Hamburg, and Conversos in the sixteenth and seventeenth centuries. He focuses on Isaac ben Abraham of Troki's *Hizzuk Emunah*, a 1593 anti-Christian treatise later translated into Spanish by Isaac Athias for ex-Conversos in Hamburg. Fisher explores why these groups engaged with, translated, and expanded upon each other's works. He argues that Athias' translation, despite his scepticism towards Karaism, was intended to help ex-Conversos reconnect with the Bible from a Jewish perspective. Fisher's analysis underscores the fluid nature of medieval Hebrew manuscript culture and the significance of translation in religious and cultural exchanges.

Amy Fedeski's article, *The Role of Scripture and Ritual in the American Campaign for Soviet Jewish Emigration, 1964–1974*, explores the impact of the Hebrew Bible and Jewish symbolism in the activism of the Student Struggle for Soviet Jewry (SSSJ). Founded in 1964, the SSSJ used biblical stories, holiday observances, and religious rituals in their campaigns to advocate for Soviet Jewish emigration. Fedeski's analysis of campaigns and flyers reveals how the organisation employed biblical and religious symbols to engage both non-Orthodox Jews and Christians effectively. She argues that this strategic use of religious symbolism made the SSSJ a prominent advocate for Soviet Jewish emigration rights, demonstrating the enduring influence of the Hebrew Bible even in secular political contexts.

Emanuel Tov's second article in this volume, *The Discipline of Textual Criticism as Experienced in 1970–2020*, concludes the third part by tracing the evolution of textual criticism from a nascent discipline to one increasingly integrated with Biblical exegesis and literary criticism, particularly following the discovery of the Dead Sea Scrolls. These documents, first uncovered in the late 1940s and studied into the twenty-first century, have significantly reshaped our understanding of the Hebrew Bible's textual tradition. Tov highlights how the recognition of "textual plurality" (187) has transformed scholarly approaches and led to the development of new printed and digital editions of the Hebrew Bible since the 1950s. Institutional projects like the Hebrew University Bible Project and various online resources have broadened access to the text for both academics and the public. Reflecting on the progress made over the past fifty years, Tov concludes that the field has greatly advanced but underscores that much remains to be explored, emphasizing the need for continued scholarly inquiry.

The fourth and final part of the volume continues the exploration of the Biblical text from a different angle, focusing on its motifs in literary works across various contexts. This part of the volume demonstrates how, throughout history and bridging various forms of art, the Bible has been a source of Jewish identity, inspiration, and resilience. Its stories and symbols appear in literature and visual arts likewise, reflecting ongoing engagement with its themes of faith, justice, and identity. They also encourage reconsiderations of human life and nature, of gender constructions, and questions of identity and otherness. The articles in this part reflect this diverse engagement in using theoretical approaches different from that of traditional reception history represented in part III of this volume. The first two articles in this part examine children's and young adult literature through a feminist lens, while the third article explores adult fiction within the Israeli setting. Together, these contributions not only provide a feminist perspective but also introduce a Mizrahi viewpoint, enhancing the volume's intersectional approach.

In their article, *The Gendering Garden*, Daniel Vorpahl examines the creation narrative in Genesis and its influence on gender roles across biblical, rabbinic, and contemporary young adult literature, including Genesis Rabbah and Deborah Bodin Cohen's 2006 work *Lilith's Ark*. Vorpahl argues that while the Genesis narrative initially appears to support a binary gender structure, a deeper analysis reveals complexities that challenge this view. Vorpahl critiques the traditional binary interpretation for reinforcing heteronormative and androcentric gender hierarchies. In contrast, *Lilith's Ark* reimagines Eve as an empowered figure who defies conventional gender norms. Vorpahl uses poststructuralist theory to critique these binary patterns and challenge prevailing heteronormative and androcentric interpretations.

In her article, *Disturbed Depths: The Aquatic Otherness of the Leviathan in From Dust, A Flame*, Marissa Herzig employs a literary and feminist lens to analyse Rebecca Podos' young adult novel *From Dust a Flame* (2022). Herzig explores how the novel incorporates contemporary references to Biblical motifs, particularly focusing on the biblical Leviathan and various Jewish interpretations of water. She argues that both the Leviathan, as a representation of water, and water itself symbolise otherness in the novel. Herzig suggests that the protagonist's nonhuman transformation challenges human and Jewish societal norms, offering a post-humanist and queer reinterpretation of traditional images.

In her concluding article, *Beyond Religious and Secular: Biblical Intertextuality in Modern Mizrahi Literature*, Alina L. Schittenhelm examines the role of the Bible in both modern Mizrahi literature and Mizrahi identity. She argues that, unlike Zionist efforts to secularise Hebrew literature, Mizrahi literature preserves Biblical references, blending religious and secular elements. Schittenhelm analyses three contemporary novels—*Tchahla ve-Hezkel* (Almog Behar, 2010), *Shum Gamadim Lo Yavou* (Sara Shilo, 2005), and *Mox Nox* (Shimon Adaf, 2011)—to reveal how Biblical motifs reflect ambivalences in Mizrahi identity. Her study explores questions of Masortiyut (traditionalism) and Mizrahiyut (Mizrahi identity), highlighting the role of Judaism in shaping migrant identities in Israel.

The diverse voices in this volume highlight the significance of the Hebrew Bible for Jewish identity, life, and experience up to the present day as well as the importance of its study through various scholarly lenses, including text-critical, literary, historical, cultural, religious, and political perspectives. Examining the Hebrew Bible as both a foundational religious text and a rich narrative compendium from such varied perspectives underscores its complexity, multiplicity, and the challenges it presents. Therefore, the aim of this volume is to illuminate and shed new light on both old and new questions, demonstrating the enduring interest and challenge of this significant scholarly topic.

PART I

Text

The Many Faces of the Bible: The Pre-History of Our Modern Bibles

Emanuel Tov

The Baron Award commemorates the great scholarship of the late Salo W. Baron in the twentieth century in the field of the history of the Jews as reflected in his *magnum opus*, *A Social and Religious History of the Jews* (2nd ed., 1952–1983). As a student, I read this work and was deeply impressed by the depth of his understanding. Later I turned to biblical studies, and therefore I have not opened his works for many years. I was pleasantly surprised to see that an active academia.edu account is being maintained posthumously in Professor Baron's name. Today Professor Salo Wittmeyer Baron ז״ל has 298 followers on academia.edu, his papers range in the top 0.5% of that website, and they were given 543 public mentions.[1] Modern students of history can benefit from this site as it posts recent volumes that have been published in Baron's honour as well as studies by Baron himself that were published posthumously.

1. Ancient Sources

As a historian, Salo W. Baron analyzed documents in a magisterial way, and based his conclusions on these documents. The written texts, as well as oral reports, spoken and recorded witnesses, serve as sources for modern analyses. Likewise, the study of ancient literatures is based on the analysis of documents, as in the case of the Hebrew Bible, where we are limited to written sources. The Bible as we know it today has many faces for religious Jews, Catholics, Protestants, Roman-Orthodox, Syriac Christians, Samaritans, Mormons, and the modern secular person.

That being the case, I want to examine what exactly are our sources for consulting the Hebrew Bible. In modern times, most people necessarily consult the Hebrew Bible in modern translations such as in English, French, German, and many additional languages. Now, all these modern translations are based on the Hebrew text, in fact on a single form of the Hebrew text, the so-called Masoretic Text created in the Middle Ages. As a result, from the Middle Ages

---

[1] https://columbia.academia.edu/SaloWittmayerBaron, last accessed October 25, 2024.

onward, all Hebrew manuscripts and subsequently all Hebrew printed editions reflect that text, which is only partially ancient since it also reflects elements from the early Middle Ages. The ancient part is the main component of the text—the consonants, while the vowels and additional elements of the text were added in the early Middle Ages.[2] The lack of ancient documentation for the Hebrew text prior to the discovery of the Dead Sea Scrolls did not disturb the users of the Hebrew Bible and its students. They knew that ultimately the Bible reflects an ancient text as it was translated in antiquity into several languages.

If the Bible was not known in the Middle Ages in an ancient Hebrew text form, at least the ancient translations were transmitted to us in manuscripts from the fourth century of the Common Era onwards in the case of the Septuagint. Thus, the famous Sinaiticus manuscript of the Septuagint (LXX) from the British Museum that was copied in the fourth century CE[3] shows not only that the Septuagint was ancient but also that the Hebrew Bible from which it was translated was ancient. This argument is not waterproof since the Septuagint (LXX) differs much from the Masoretic Text,[4] but the Hebrew Masoretic Text was also quoted almost literally in the ancient Hebrew law codes, the Mishnah and Talmud.[5] All these sources added confidence to the general dating of the Hebrew Bible as an ancient document, although until recently we did not have ancient Hebrew source texts in our hands. The oldest available texts were the medieval manuscripts of the Hebrew Bible from between the tenth and the fifteenth centuries of the Common Era. This date was pushed back a little when slightly earlier manuscripts were discovered in a storage room of a synagogue in Egypt, a so-called *genizah*, the Cairo Genizah.[6] Through this treasure trove of manuscripts, we now have Hebrew manuscripts in our hands from between the sixth and the ninth centuries of the Common Era, all belonging to the same tradition of the Masoretic Text.

---

2   See I. Yeivin, *Introduction to the Tiberian Masorah*, trans. and ed. E. J. Revell, (Missoula, MT: Scholars Press, 1980); Y. Ofer, *The Masora on Scripture and Its Methods* (Berlin: De Gruyter, 2019); E. Tov, *Textual Criticism of the Hebrew Bible* (rev., exp., 4th ed., Minneapolis, MN: Fortress, 2022), 35–85.

3   See *Codex Sinaiticus: New Perspectives on the Ancient Biblical Manuscript*, ed. S. McKendrick et al. (London: The British Library, 2015).

4   Tov, *Textual Criticism*, 215–61.

5   This is a fact, although scholars also collect the occasional deviations from MT in the rabbinic literature. See, for example, the second apparatus in the critical edition of the Hebrew University Bible Project of Isaiah: M. H. Goshen-Gottstein, *The Hebrew University Bible: The Book of Isaiah* (Jerusalem: Magnes, 1995).

6   P. E. Kahle, *The Cairo Geniza* (London: Oxford University Press, 1947; 2nd ed. Oxford: Blackwell, 1959).

However, organized religious traditions do not feel the need for ancient documents in order to trust the Bible. Thus, the Jewish, Christian, and Samaritan traditions maintain a belief in the divine origin of the Hebrew text from ancient times. This belief implies that Moses himself received the Torah from the hands of God.[7] Jewish tradition as embedded in the Talmud even holds on to the tradition that the Torah was written by Moses himself,[8] except for the last eight verses of Deuteronomy. All the same, scholarly inquiry proceeds independently of religious beliefs and therefore scholars were looking for the ancient sources of the Hebrew Bible.

2. Dead Sea Scrolls

The situation of the manuscript evidence of the Bible changed drastically in 1947 with the discovery of fragments of the Hebrew Bible in caves in the Judean Desert near the Dead Sea. The discovery of these ancient manuscripts turned out to be the greatest archaeological discovery of the twentieth century. It so happened that a small community lived at a site called Qumran in an arid, desert-like environment that enabled the preservation of scrolls made of skins and papyrus over the course of two thousand years.[9] In the beginning years after the discovery, when some scholars did not want to believe that 2,000-year-old scrolls had been discovered, it was thought that the Bedouin had stumbled upon medieval texts. However, after Professor Eleazar Sukenik from the Hebrew University of Jerusalem had identified the script of the scrolls as ancient (1948), the world started to believe that a real treasure had been found.

The story of the discovery is one of romance, mystery, and intrigue having taken place during a time of war between the just-born Jewish state and

---

7   Within the Jewish context, one of the "Thirteen Fundamental Principles" of the Jewish faith of Maimonides (1138–1204) is that Moses received the Torah from God: Maimonides, *Commentary to Tractate Sanhedrin of the Mishnah*, 10.1.
8   B. b. Batra 14b. The last verses of Deuteronomy could not have been written by Moses as they relate about his death.
9   See the introductions by F. M. Cross, *The Ancient Library of Qumrân and Modern Biblical Studies* (London: Duckworth, 1958); *The Ancient Library of Qumran* (3rd ed., Sheffield: Sheffield Academic Press, 1995); J. C. VanderKam and P. W. Flint, *The Meaning of the Dead Sea Scrolls: Their Significance for Understanding the Bible, Judaism, Jesus, and Christianity* (New York, NY: HarperSanFrancisco, 2013); G. J. Brooke and C. Hempel, *T&T Clark Companion to the Dead Sea Scrolls* (London: T&T Clark, 2019); R. G. Kratz, *Qumran: Die Schriftrollen vom Toten Meer und die Entstehung des biblischen Judentums* (Munich: C. H. Beck, 2022).

its Arab neighbours.[10] The political situation was even more complex since the initial discovery had been made at the tail end of the British mandate in Jewish and Arab Palestine just prior to the War of Independence that followed immediately after the declaration of the establishment of the State of Israel (May 18, 1948). According to the story, one year earlier, in the beginning of 1947, a Bedouin[11] searched in a cave for his goat that had gone astray. In that cave, which subsequently became known as Cave 1, he found to his astonishment several broken jars, some complete jars, and several pieces of skins inscribed in a language that he was not able to read. I don't even know whether he was able to read Arabic. Not knowing what to do with these pieces of skin, quite naturally his first and very practical thought was to make sandals from them. After a while, he had the good insight to contact an antiquity dealer in Jericho,[12] and the remainder is history. Some of the fragments are very tiny but the large Isaiah scroll (1QIsa^a, 8 meters) is almost complete.

We now know much about these finds. Among other things, we know that a community was living there at Qumran, and that this community decided to hide its written documents in various caves when they feared for their lives due to the nearing of the Roman armies around the year 68. Many hundreds of books[13] have been written about these discoveries made between 1947 and 1956[14] and in the meantime all the ancient texts from the Judean Desert caves have been published.[15] At the same time, we continue to improve our understanding of these texts that are sometimes very fragmentary. In recent decennia, various computer technologies and several technologies from the natural sciences have come to our aid.[16]

---

10   W. F. Fields, *The Dead Sea Scrolls, A Full History: Volume One, 1947–1960* (Leiden: Brill, 2009).
11   Muhammad Ahmed al-Hamed (born 1931), better known by his nickname Muhammed edh-Dhib ("Muhammad the Wolf"), from the Ta'amireh clans residing in Bethlehem.
12   Khalil Iskandar Shahin, also known as Kando.
13   For the most recent bibliography, see the website of the Orion Center for the Study of the Dead Sea Scrolls at the Hebrew University: http://orion.huji.ac.il/resources/bib/orionBibliography.shtml, last accessed October 17, 2023.
14   The last cave to be discovered was Cave 11, containing a wealth of inscribed material.
15   *Discoveries in the Judaean Desert (of Jordan)*, vols. 1–40 (Oxford: Clarendon, 1955–2009) as well as several electronic editions.
16   E. Tov, "The Sciences and the Reconstruction of the Ancient Scrolls: Possibilities and Impossibilities," in *The Dead Sea Scrolls in Context: Integrating the Dead Sea Scrolls in the Study of Ancient Texts, Languages, and Cultures*, ed. A. Lange et al. (Leiden: Brill, 2011), 3–25.

3. Documentation

Let us return to the issue of the documentation. Until 1947, scholars and the public at large were using the text of the Hebrew Bible based on manuscripts from the Middle Ages.[17] This may sound incredible, but it is not so unusual because in the study of the classical writers written in Greek and in Latin, we also often base ourselves on medieval traditions, which as far as we can tell have turned out to be rather precise. It so happens that also the text of the Hebrew Bible as transmitted from antiquity to the Middle Ages in the form of the Masoretic Text turned out to be very precise, as I will explain in a while. But scholars prefer to base themselves on early documents, and the medieval texts are late. Of course, we did not know that we were waiting for the Dead Sea Scrolls. But we did need them for a better understanding of all aspects of the background of the Hebrew Bible because they are closer to the time when the books were written.

4. Limited Textual Variety Known before 1947

We already knew prior to the discovery of the scrolls that the text of the Bible as transmitted in the various ancient sources is represented by more than one tradition. Beyond the Masoretic tradition, which was accepted traditionally by the Jewish community, the Christian world adhered initially to the Greek translation of the Hebrew Bible. That translation, named the Septuagint (LXX, "seventy") because according to tradition the Torah was translated into Greek by seventy wise men, was of central importance for Christianity since the New Testament, written in Greek, used that translation for the version of the Hebrew Bible rather than the Hebrew version. That translation remained the holy text of the Christians until it was replaced gradually between the fifth and the ninth centuries of the Common Era by the Latin translation of Jerome named the Vulgate.[18] Actually, the Septuagint (LXX) remains until today the sacred text of the Orthodox churches, while it is still *one* of the accepted texts in the Catholic world. This Greek translation is also held in great esteem among scholars because its underlying Hebrew text differs from the Masoretic Text in important details. It must have been based on ancient and respected Hebrew

---

17 That is, in the editions of the Hebrew Bible, the medieval texts continue to play a key role.
18 M. Graves, "1.2 Latin Texts," in *The History of Research of Textual Criticism*, vol. 3A of *Textual History of the Bible: A Companion to Textual Criticism*, ed. R. E. Fuller and A. Lange (Leiden: Brill, 2022), 231–91.

manuscripts, ones that were at least as respected and ancient as the Masoretic Text of the Hebrew Bible. This fact has been recognized since the seventeenth century. Also before the discovery of the scrolls, the Septuagint (LXX) was used actively in the scholarly investigation of most books of the Bible, especially in that branch that is named textual criticism. The description is a little complicated because, for the Protestants, the Masoretic Text carries more weight than the Septuagint (LXX), and in the seventeenth century they held heated theological discussions with the Catholics for whom the Septuagint (LXX) was more authoritative.[19]

Another source for the knowledge of the ancient text of the Bible and that likewise differed from the Masoretic Text and known in the western world from the seventeenth century onwards, was the so-called Samaritan Pentateuch, the Pentateuch of the Samaritan community.[20] Once a large group in the land of Israel, the Samaritan community has shrunk during its tumultuous history, until only a few hundred Samaritans remain in our days. The Samaritan Pentateuch, covering only the five books of Moses, differed from the Masoretic Text in numerous large details as well as in many small details. This text did not sanctify Jerusalem as the holy city but Mount Gerizim near Schechem (Nablus) and that belief was written up in a special commandment, the Samaritan tenth commandment.[21] The Samaritans practice the biblical customs and religion according to the exact word of the biblical law, without the intervention of rabbinic Judaism. They are presently living at their holy site of Gerizim in Shekhem (Nablus) in Palestine as well as in Holon in the State of Israel.

What *scholars* think of this Samaritan Pentateuch is another story. They often regard the Samaritan Pentateuch as a secondary source when compared with the Masoretic Text. Its secondary character is visible through its many readings that do away with difficulties in the earlier text and through its exegetical additions.[22] Be that as it may, the textual sources of the Samaritan

---

19 See the instructive study by J.-C. Lebram, "Ein Streit um die hebräische Bibel und die Septuaginta," in *Leiden University in the Seventeenth Century*, ed. T. H. Lunsingh Scheurleer and G. H. M. Posthumus Meyjes (Leiden: Brill, 1975), 21–63, as well as the summary of C. F. Keil, *Lehrbuch der historisch-kritischen Einleitung in die kanonischen und apokryphischen Schriften des Alten Testaments* (6th ed., Frankfurt/Main: Heyder & Zimmer, 1859), 605–8.

20 M. Kartveit, *The Origin of the Samaritans* (Leiden: Brill, 2009); Tov, *Textual Criticism*, 171–203.

21 E. Tov, "The Tenth Commandment of the Samaritans," in *Tempel, Lehrhaus, Synagoge. Orte jüdischen Lernens und Lebens. Festschrift für Wolfgang Kraus*, ed. C. Eberhart et al. (Paderborn: Schöningh, 2020), 141–57.

22 S. White Crawford, "The Jewish and Samaritan Pentateuchs: Reflections on the Differences (?) between Textual Criticism and Literary Criticism," *HBAI* 9 (2020): 320–33.

Pentateuch are medieval, the oldest fragment dating to the eleventh century. However, this text is generally believed to have derived from an ancient text penned down more than two thousand years ago, but we were waiting for the Dead Sea Scrolls for actual proof. In short, so-called pre-Samaritan scrolls from Qumran foreshadow the medieval text of the Samaritan Pentateuch.

In short, before the Dead Sea Scrolls were found we could divide the main Bible texts according to the various adherents of world religions. The Masoretic Text, now the major text of the Bible, was accepted in the Jewish and later in the Protestant tradition, the Septuagint was accepted in the Catholic tradition and in the various Orthodox churches, and the Samaritan Torah was accepted by the adherents of the small Samaritan community. In reality, the situation was a little more complex, as the Syriac churches accepted the Peshitta translation in the Syriac language, one of the Aramaic dialects, and there are several additional churches who adhere to their own texts, such as the Ethiopic and Armenian churches.

But one thing is clear: even before the Dead Sea Scrolls were discovered, we were exposed to a picture of textual variety regarding the Hebrew Bible, and that variety was also reflected in the texts accepted by the various belief communities.[23] Accordingly, the views on the sacred text of the Jewish, Christian, and Samaritan communities diverged, but they did not clash since they were organized in different societies. Within their organized religion, the Jews did not consult the text of the Catholics, the Septuagint, and neither did the Catholics consult the Jewish text, and no one consulted the Samaritan Pentateuch. Only scholars took all three texts into consideration. Whether Jewish, Catholic, or Protestant, scholars always turned to *all* the ancient texts. Thus, prior to 1947, scholars worked with a textual picture of the Bible that was based on a reality of three different texts of the Torah, the Masoretic Text, the Septuagint, and the Samaritan Pentateuch, and two different texts of the remaining books for which there was no Samaritan text.

---

23 E. Tov, "A Modern Textual Outlook Based on the Qumran Scrolls," *HUCA* 53 (1982): 11–27; A. S. van der Woude, "Pluriformity and Uniformity: Reflections on the Transmission of the Text of the Old Testament," in *Sacred History and Sacred Texts in Early Judaism: A Symposium in Honour of A. S. van der Woude*, ed. J. N. Brenner and F. García Martínez (Kampen: Kok Pharos, 1992), 151–69; D. A. Teeter, *Scribal Laws: Exegetical Variation in the Textual Transmission of Biblical Law in the Late Second Temple Period* (Tübingen: Mohr Siebeck, 2014), 210–39.

5. Textual Variety at Qumran

With the new discoveries at Qumran, this situation was changed completely. Great parts of the Hebrew Bible were revealed in 1947. Many copies were found of some Scripture books, such Deuteronomy, Isaiah, and Psalms, while only a few copies have been preserved of other Scripture books.[24]

The greatest surprise that was recognized after the discovery of the first scrolls was the multiplicity of biblical texts that were accepted by the ancient Jewish community of Qumran that lived in the desert near the Dead Sea. While the Jewish people have used only one text throughout its history from the first century of the Common Era until today, viz., the Masoretic Text, the reality that was unfolded in front of our eyes regarding the Qumran community was that many different sorts of texts were used by them in the last century before the Common Era and the first century of the Common Era.

I believe that this multiplicity of texts was imported to Qumran from outside the community; the members of that community brought with them different texts when they settled at the site.[25] What do I mean when referring to textual variety? We find many small differences between the Qumran scrolls, and sometimes large ones, while the overall content of the Bible remains unchanged. It is the same Bible, that is, there are not two different books of Samuel or of Isaiah. At the same time, we see important developments and trends in copying the text of the Bible. Mind you, we are not talking about the earlier period of the composition of the biblical books, but rather the period of the copying of the manuscripts in the third, second, and first centuries before the Common Era and the first century of the Common Era as reflected in the scrolls found at Qumran.

Thus, we see linguistic differences between the texts because obviously the Hebrew and Aramaic languages developed over the course of decennia and centuries.[26] Further, and most importantly, scribes took the liberty of inserting their exegesis in the text, explaining Holy Scripture, while changing and adding

---

24   E. Tov, *Textual Criticism*, 109–70.
25   E. Tov, "The Background and Origin of the Qumran Corpus of Scripture Texts," in *Sacred Texts and Disparate Interpretations: Qumran Manuscripts Seventy Years Later: Proceedings of the International Conference Held at the John Paul II Catholic University of Lublin, 24–26 October 2017*, ed. H. Drawnel (Leiden: Brill, 2020), 50–65.
26   E. Y. Kutscher, *The Language and Linguistic Background of the Isaiah Scroll (1 Q Isa)* (Leiden: Brill, 1974); E. D. Reymond, *Qumran Hebrew: An Overview of Orthography, Phonology, and Morphology* (Atlanta, GA: SBL, 2014).

details in the content.[27] In rare cases, they also omitted a detail. In one case, a long stretch of text was omitted in the large Isaiah Scroll from Cave 1, 1QIsaᵃ, and subsequently added in the line and in the side margin.[28] In this case, note the representation of the name of the Lord, יהוה (*yhvh*) with four dots. Further, we find different styles in matters of spelling. Spelling is not an important part of the text and we are talking about a period before spelling was standardized as it is in modern society. For example, when referring to spelling differences between the United States and Great Britain, we see that the former nation uses the spelling "color" while the latter uses the spelling "colour."

Returning to the insertion of changes in Bible manuscripts, you might say that a scribe is not supposed to insert changes in a sacred text. That is true, but we don't know when a reverential approach of not changing the transmitted Scripture text was developed.[29] Alongside the approach of conservative scribes who did not change the transmitted text, there were always scribes who occasionally inserted their own views into the text. When investigating the different types of scribes, we realize that we can sometimes point to a certain group that practiced a precise or traditional approach to the copying of the Scripture text and likewise to other groups that practiced a free approach. Of course, scribes of all types considered the Scripture text sacred, but they expressed their approach towards the sacred status of the text in different ways. As a result of all these aspects, the scrolls differ among each other, and by implication they also differ from the text that we now name the Masoretic Text. The MT is the text we have in our hands in Hebrew or in translation and is the text you know best. It was one of the texts among those found in the Judean Desert that are known as the Dead Sea Scrolls; not the only text, not even the majority text, but just *one* of the texts. The differences between the various texts are sometimes large, for example in Samuel and Jeremiah, and sometimes small.

When the Judean Desert Scrolls provided the first textual evidence from the third pre-Christian century, lifting the veil from the Dark Ages, we see a multitude of textual forms as described above. It is hard to imagine that this textual variety was created only in the third century, and we assume that it

---

27 E. Tov, "Exegesis of the Bible Enriched by the Dead Sea Scrolls," in *Scribal Practice, Text and Canon in the Dead Sea Scrolls, Essays in Memory of Peter W. Flint*, ed. J. J. Collins and A. Geyser-Fouché (Leiden: Brill, 2019), 225–46.

28 1QIsaᵃ col. XXXIII 7 (Isa 40:7–8). See K. De Troyer and D. R. Herbison, "Where Septuagint and Qumran Meet: The Septuagint and Qumran Texts of Isa 40:7–8," *Textus* 29 (2020): 156–67.

29 E. Tov, "Approaches of Scribes to the Biblical Text in Ancient Israel," in *The Scribe in the Biblical World, A Bridge Between Scripts, Languages and Cultures*, ed. E. Eshel and M. Langlois (Berlin: De Gruyter, 2023), 3–21.

existed already at least in the preceding century. It was imported into Qumran, because the differences between readings such as the Masoretic Text and the Samaritan Pentateuch found there are identical to readings of these texts known from outside Qumran, for example, from the Septuagint, the Samaritan Pentateuch, and the Masoretic Text.

We should also remember that the description of the textual situation in ancient Israel as pluralistic does not do justice to the full picture. After all, there were also clusters of textual unity within the Qumran corpus, such as a group of texts reflecting the Masoretic Text, a group of texts foreshadowing the Samaritan Pentateuch, and a group of texts that we would call harmonizing. Thus, within the pluralistic picture there were also clusters of unity. But the most important lesson we should learn from this description is that the Bible has many faces.

6. Practical Implications

If I say that the Bible had many faces in antiquity, is that true also today? I cannot speak like a theologian; I am an exegete and a textual critic. Despite the many internal differences, the Bible, overall, was the same in antiquity and remains so today. I am not belittling the internal differences, but the message of the Bible is the same. Of course, scholars explain these differences today. The Septuagint, and therefore also the Catholic Bible, includes the beautiful Psalm 151 of the young David that is not contained in the Masoretic Text of the Jewish Bible. That psalm was also included in one of the Qumran scrolls, 11QPsalms^a.[30] Those who study the development of the collection of the biblical writings, the canon, are interested in the different versions of this psalm. The short text of Jeremiah, represented by the Qumran scroll 4QJer^d and also by the Septuagint, presents short names where the Masoretic Text has long ones. For example, it has "Nebuzaradan" (Jer 43:6) where Masoretic Text has "Nebuzaradan, the chief of the guards," and other similar examples.[31] There are also theological differences between these two versions. In chapter 10, the prophet mocks the heathen gods, the idols, since they are made of wood and cannot talk or walk. However, the Masoretic Text adds a long praise for the God of Israel who is a real God.[32]

---

30 J. A. Sanders, *The Psalms Scroll of Qumrân Cave 11 (11QPs^a)*, DJD IV (Oxford: Clarendon, 1965), 49–64.
31 Tov, *Textual Criticism*, 234–36.
32 Ibid., 236.

While the general message of the Bible is the same, scholars focus on the textual differences such as just mentioned. Textual critics delve into the details, trying to explain their background. Usually they also express a view on details that seem to them preferable to others and they even risk a view on the so-called original text of the Bible. I might add that I have been thinking for a long time about this so-called original text;[33] I keep changing my mind, and I will probably never have a clear answer. But I do have a view on this topic, namely that we should keep in mind that the Hebrew Bible was known in antiquity in various forms and that these forms are still visible in the text forms that have been accepted in the various religious communities.

Bibliography

Brooke, George J., and Charlotte Hempel. *T&T Clark Companion to the Dead Sea Scrolls*. London: T&T Clark, 2019.

Cross, Frank M. *The Ancient Library of Qumrân and Modern Biblical Studies*. London: Duckworth, 1958.

--------. *The Ancient Library of Qumran*. 3rd edition, Sheffield: Sheffield Academic Press, 1995.

Crawford, Sidnie White. "The Jewish and Samaritan Pentateuchs: Reflections on the Differences (?) between Textual Criticism and Literary Criticism." *Hebrew Bible and Ancient Israel* 9 (2020): 320–33.

De Troyer, Kristin, and David R. Herbison. "Where Septuagint and Qumran Meet: The Septuagint and Qumran Texts of Isa 40:7–8." *Textus* 29 (2020): 156–67.

Discoveries in the Judaean Desert (of Jordan), volumes 1–40. Oxford: Clarendon, 1955–2009.

Fields, Weston F. *The Dead Sea Scrolls, A Full History: Volume One, 1947–1960*. Leiden: Brill: 2009.

Goshen-Gottstein, Moshe H. *The Hebrew University Bible: The Book of Isaiah*. Jerusalem: Magnes, 1995.

Graves, Michael. "1.2 Latin Texts." In *Textual History of the Bible, Vol. 3 A Companion to Textual Criticism, Vol. 3A, The History of Research of Textual Criticism*, edited by Russell E. Fuller and Armin Lange, 231–91. Leiden: Brill, 2022.

Kahle, Paul E. *The Cairo Geniza*. 1st edition, London: Oxford University Press, 1947. 2nd edition, Oxford: Blackwell, 1959.

Kartveit, M. *The Origin of the Samaritans*. Leiden: Brill, 2009.

---

33   Ibid., 338–48.

Keil, Carl F. *Lehrbuch der historisch-kritischen Einleitung in die kanonischen und apokryphischen Schriften des Alten Testaments*. 6th edition, Frankfurt/Main: Heyder & Zimmer, 1859.

Kratz, Reinhard G. *Qumran: Die Schriftrollen vom Toten Meer und die Entstehung des biblischen Judentums*. Munich: C. H. Beck, 2022.

Kutscher, Edward Y. *The Language and Linguistic Background of the Isaiah Scroll (1 Q Is^a)*. Leiden: Brill, 1974.

Lebram, J.-C. "Ein Streit um die hebräische Bibel und die Septuaginta." In *Leiden University in the Seventeenth Century*, edited by Theodoor H. Lunsingh Scheurleer and Guillaume H. M. Posthumus Meyjes, 21–63. Leiden: Brill, 1975.

McKendrick, Scot, et al., eds. *Codex Sinaiticus: New Perspectives on the Ancient Biblical Manuscript*. London: The British Library, 2015.

Ofer, Yosef. *The Masora on Scripture and Its Methods*. Berlin: De Gruyter, 2019.

Reymond, Eric D. *Qumran Hebrew: An Overview of Orthography, Phonology, and Morphology*. Atlanta, GA: The Society of Biblical Literature, 2014.

Sanders, J. A. *The Psalms Scroll of Qumrân Cave 11 (11QPs^a)*. DJD IV. Oxford: Clarendon, 1965.

Teeter, David A. *Scribal Laws: Exegetical Variation in the Textual Transmission of Biblical Law in the Late Second Temple Period*. Tübingen: Mohr Siebeck, 2014.

Tov, Emanuel. "A Modern Textual Outlook Based on the Qumran Scrolls." *Hebrew Union College Annual* 53 (1982): 11–27.

--------. "Approaches of Scribes to the Biblical Text in Ancient Israel." In *The Scribe in the Biblical World: A Bridge Between Scripts, Languages and Cultures*, edited by Esther Eshel and Michael Langlois, 3–21. Berlin: De Gruyter, 2023.

--------. "The Background and Origin of the Qumran Corpus of Scripture Texts." In *Sacred Texts and Disparate Interpretations: Qumran Manuscripts Seventy Years Later: Proceedings of the International Conference Held at the John Paul II Catholic University of Lublin, 24–26 October 2017*, edited by Henryk Drawnel, 50–65. Leiden: Brill, 2020.

--------. "Exegesis of the Bible Enriched by the Dead Sea Scrolls." In *Scribal Practice, Text and Canon in the Dead Sea Scrolls: Essays in Memory of Peter W. Flint*, edited by John J. Collins and Ananda Geyser-Fouché, 225–46. Leiden: Brill, 2019.

--------. "The Sciences and the Reconstruction of the Ancient Scrolls: Possibilities and Impossibilities." In *The Dead Sea Scrolls in Context: Integrating the Dead Sea Scrolls in the Study of Ancient Texts, Languages, and Cultures*, edited by Armin Lange et al., 3–25. Leiden: Brill, 2011.

--------. "The Tenth Commandment of the Samaritans." In *Tempel, Lehrhaus, Synagoge: Orte jüdischen Lernens und Lebens. Festschrift für Wolfgang Kraus*, edited by Christian A. Eberhart, Martin. Karrer, Siegfried Kreuzer, and Martin Meiser, 141–57. Paderborn: Ferdinand Schöningh, 2020.

--------. *Textual Criticism of the Hebrew Bible*, revised and expanded fourth edition. Minneapolis, MN: Fortress, 2022.

VanderKam, James C., and Perter W. Flint. *The Meaning of the Dead Sea Scrolls: Their Significance for Understanding the Bible, Judaism, Jesus, and Christianity.* New York, NY: HarperSanFrancisco, 2013.

Van der Woude, Adam S. "Pluriformity and Uniformity: Reflections on the Transmission of the Text of the Old Testament." In *Sacred History and Sacred Texts in Early Judaism: A Symposium in Honour of A. S. van der Woude*, edited by Jan N. Brenner and Florentino García Martínez, 151–69. Kampen: Kok Pharos, 1992.

Yeivin, Israel. *Introduction to the Tiberian Masorah*, translated and edited by E. J. Revell. Missoula, MT: Scholars Press, 1980.

Divergent Versions of *Habakkuk 3*: From the Desk of the Hebrew University Bible Project

Michael Segal

The Hebrew University Bible Project (HUBP) aims to publish a diplomatic *editio maior* of the text of the Hebrew Bible, based upon the Aleppo Codex (א), with variants from other textual witnesses recorded in a system of apparatuses. The readings collated in the edition are culled from a broad variety of sources, including the ancient translations, Dead Sea Scrolls, biblical quotations in rabbinic literature, and medieval Hebrew manuscripts, all of these covering a period of almost two millennia. Taken together, this extensive record reflects the attested transmission history of the biblical text.

According to the principles of a diplomatic edition, there is no attempt to reconstruct an *Urtext* of the biblical books nor to delineate multiple literary stages within their transmission history.[1] Instead, the exhaustive presentation of textual information, accompanied by explanatory notes, allows the reader to use and assess the data in his or her own research.

To date, four volumes of the edition have appeared (Isaiah; Jeremiah; Ezekiel; Twelve Prophets).[2] The fifth volume, currently in preparation, will contain Joshua.

Due to the particular character of the biblical text and its various witnesses in Hebrew and in translations, the original editors decided against the presentation of all of this data in a single apparatus. Instead, the variants are organized in four separate apparatuses, each one containing a group of sources that can be presented coherently.

The first two apparatuses contain evidence beginning from the earliest attested textual stage, beginning in the third century BCE, on the basis of the

---

1 M. Segal, "Methodological Considerations in the Preparation of an Edition of the Hebrew Bible," in *The Text of the Hebrew Bible and Its Editions: Studies in Celebration of the Fifth Centennial of the Complutensian Polyglot*, ed. A. Piquer Otero and P.A. Torijano Morales (Leiden: Brill, 2017), 34–55.
2 M. Goshen-Gottstein, ed., *The Hebrew University Bible: The Book of Isaiah* (Jerusalem: Magnes, 1995); E. Tov, Sh. Talmon, and C. Rabin, eds., *The Hebrew University Bible: The Book of Jeremiah* (Jerusalem: Magnes, 1997); M. Goshen-Gottstein and Sh. Talmon, eds., *The Hebrew University Bible: The Book of Ezekiel* (Jerusalem: Magnes, 2004); M. Segal and Sh. Talmon, eds., *The Hebrew University Bible: The Twelve Prophets* (Jerusalem: Mandel Institute of Jewish Studies, Hebrew University / Magnes, 2024).

biblical manuscripts discovered in the Judean Desert. The languages of the textual witnesses from this stage serve as the basic criterion for the division of the material in the first two apparatuses: in the first, readings preserved in the ancient translations; in the second, variants collated from Hebrew witnesses. Variants in the different ancient translations, first and foremost in the Septuagint, vastly outnumber those surviving in ancient Hebrew sources, and thus take pride of place in textual criticism. Therefore, priority is given to Apparatus I, the apparatus of the ancient translations, printed directly below the Hebrew text. Whereas Apparatuses I–II pertain to the earliest stage in the written transmission of the biblical text and evidence a degree of textual variety, the other apparatuses (III–IV) reflect a later stage, in which the Masoretic Text (MT) was the essentially exclusive text in Judaism.

The following study emerged from the research for and formulation of Apparatus I to Habakkuk 3 in the HUBP edition, and in particular the Greek evidence for this poetic section. While the apparatus system allows for the analysis of individual details, the current study attempts to synthesize this (at times) complex data in order to illumine the more general contribution of this textual evidence towards understanding the processes of textual dynamics, which are fundamental for understanding the growth of biblical literature.

Habakkuk 3 in Hebrew and Greek

Habakkuk 3 differs significantly from the two previous chapters of the book in terms of both its genre and content. While chapters 1–2 reflect classic prophetic style, the final chapter of the book presents the prayer of Habakkuk, consisting of a psalm-like theophany (vv. 1–16a), which concludes with the recognition that despite the tribulations of the psalmist, he can rely upon God for deliverance and strength (vv. 16b–19). Based upon arguments of language and genre, some scholars have argued for the possibility that the combinations of chapters 1–2 together with 3 are a secondary stage in the development of the book.[3] In addition, the testimony of Pesher Habakkuk from Qumran Cave 1,

---

3 See e.g. B. Stade, "Miscellen," *ZAW* 4 (1884): 157; W. H. Ward, "A Critical and Exegetical Commentary on Habakkuk," in *A Critical and Exegetical Commentary on Micah, Zephaniah, Nahum, Habakkuk, Obadiah and Joel*, ed. J. M. Powis Smith, W. H. Ward, and J. A. Bewer (Edinburgh: T. & T. Clark, 1911), 6: "The third chapter ... may or may not be by one of the authors to whom we owe 1^{12}–2^{20}." See the extended discussion of T. Hiebert, *God of My Victory: The Ancient Hymn of Habakkuk 3* (Atlanta, GA.: Scholars, 1986), 129–136, who argues for a return to the position of earlier scholars, that Hab 3 was by a different author than the preceding two chapters; and especially the list of scholars for and against this position

which interprets only the first two chapters of book, perhaps provides supporting evidence for this claim.[4] While some of the language of the psalm is enigmatic and despite a few interpretive cruxes, it is relatively straightforward to interpret the overall message of the chapter according to MT, based upon parallels to other biblical theophanies.

As noted above, the current study is an outgrowth of the research in the preparation of Apparatus I for Habakkuk 3, which is of particular interest due to the preservation of two Greek translations for this psalm. One is found in both the primary and vast majority of LXX manuscripts, and is therefore referred to as the Septuagint version. The other is generally known as the Barberini version, since it is contained in the Barberini Codex of the Vatican library (Holmes and Parsons, no. 86). This alternate translation is unique, employing some rare vocabulary, and pertains only to this chapter. It does not appear to have any affinities to the Septuagint elsewhere in the Twelve or beyond.[5] This third version of Habakkuk 3 is found in a sum total of six manuscripts (four of which

---

on p. 178, n. 1; Sh. Ahituv, "Habakkuk: Introduction and Commentary," in *Nahum, Habakkuk and Zephaniah* (*Mikra Leyisra'el*; ed. M. Cogan and S. Ahituv (Jerusalem: Magnes, 2006, in Hebrew) 6–7, accepts the claim of the different origins of Hab 3.

[4] Although note the methodological reservations of using Pesher Habakkuk as proof of this claim by W. H. Brownlee, *The Midrash Pesher of Habakkuk* (Missoula, MN: Scholars, 1979), 218–19; R. D. Haak, *Habakkuk* (Leiden: Brill, 1991), 7–8; Sh. Ahituv, "Habakkuk: Introduction and Commentary," 7.

[5] The origins of Barb Hab 3 are unclear, and also relate to the general question of the literary relationship between the different versions. H. St. J. Thackeray, "Primitive Lectionary Notes in the Psalm of Habakkuk," *JTS* 12 (1910/11): 191–213, and ibid., *The Septuagint and Jewish Worship: A Study in Origins* (London: British Academy, 1921), 47–55, was of the opinion that the Barberini text preceded the LXX version, and was created for the purpose of the Jewish lectionary (הפטרה) cycle, to be read on the Festival of Weeks (see b. Meg. 31a). Although the latter theory has never gained much traction due to its speculative nature, the question of the relative priority of the two Greek translations is still of relevance. N. Fernández Marcos, "El Texto Barberini de Habacuc III Reconsiderado," *Sefarad* 36 (1976): 3–36, transl. and slightly updated in ibid., "Der Barberini-Text von Hab 3: Eine neue Untersuchung," in *Brennpunkt – Die Septuaginta; Band 3: Studien zur Theologie, Anthropologie, Ekklesiologie, Eschatologie und Liturgie der Griechischen Bibel*, ed. H.-J. Fabry and D. Böhler (Stuttgart: Kohlhammer, 2007), 151–80, suggested, based upon an analysis of the lexical equivalents and translation technique in Barb Hab 3, that it is related to the revision of Symmachus, and therefore posited that it is the work of a member of his school (including the claim that its origins were in Asia Minor). While I agree that this version of the poem was created subsequent to LXX, it is certainly not a classic case of one of the revisions; see the arguments below. See the reservations against categorizing the Barb text as being related to a specific recension put forth by H.-J. Fabry, "'Der Herr macht meine Schritte sicher' (Hab 3,19 Barb.) - Die Versio Barberini, eine liturgische Sondertradition von Hab 3?," in *Die Septuaginta - Texte, Theologien, Einflüsse. 2. Internationale Fachtagung veranstaltet von Septuaginta Deutsch (LXX.D), Wuppertal 23.-27. Juli 2008*, ed. W. Kraus and M. Karrer (Tübingen: Mohr Siebeck, 2010), 227–28.

also include the Septuagint version), including Codex Venetus, which has only the Barberini version but in a form that seems to have been influenced by the Septuagint version.[6] A critical text of the Barberini version is presented in the Göttingen edition of the LXX to the Twelve Prophets, and is printed following the Septuagint translation of the chapter.[7]

The Septuagint of the Twelve Prophets, which can be attributed to a single translator,[8] is relatively literal, and it can be shown (when possible) that the translator was reasonably faithful to his Hebrew source. Therefore, due attention is given to the possibility that Greek renditions deviating from MT may reflect a variant Hebrew source. However, at the same time, the difficult language found in certain books of the Twelve led to different attempts by the translator to interpret their Hebrew source text. Caution must therefore be exercised when assessing whether a difference reflects a variant Hebrew *Vorlage* or the translator's exegesis.

In the following discussion, I will present a series of examples from Habakkuk 3, that help characterize the web of relationships between three textual versions, the Masoretic text, the Septuagint and the Barberini version, followed by some methodological remarks based upon the analysis. Further detailed text-critical evidence and analysis of Habakkuk 3 can be found in the recently published HUBP Twelve Prophets edition (pp. 138*–144*).

---

[6] See E. M. Good, "The Barberini Greek Version of Habakkuk III," *VT* 9 (1959): 11, who analyzed five manuscripts. A sixth manuscript (Rahlfs 456), which includes the Barberini version of Hab 3, was identified by W. Baars, "A New Witness to the Text of the Barberini Greek Version of Habakkuk III," *VT* 15 (1965): 381–82. He noted its textual affinity with V. J. L. Harper, *Responding to a Puzzled Scribe: The Barberini Version of Habakkuk 3 Analysed in the Light of the Other Greek Versions* (London: Bloomsbury T&T Clark, 2015), 4–6, suggested that MS 456 was perhaps copied from V (preserving a similar mixed text).

[7] J. Ziegler, ed., *Duodecim prophetae, vol. 13 of Septuaginta: Vetus Testamentum Graecum: Auctoritate Academiae Scientiarum Gottingensis Editum* (16 vols., Göttingen: Vandenhoeck & Ruprecht, 1967), 273–75.

[8] See ibid., "Die Einheit der Septuaginta zum Zwölfprophetenbuch," in *Beilage zum Vorlesungsverzeichnis der Staatl. Akademie zu Braunsberg* (Göttingen: Vandenhoeck & Ruprecht, 1934–35), 1–16; T. Muraoka, "In Defense of the Unity of the LXX Minor Prophets," *Annual of the Japanese Biblical Institute* 15 (1989): 25–36; E. Tov, *The Septuagint Translation of Jeremiah and Baruch: A Discussion of an Early Revision of Jeremiah 29–52 and Baruch 1:1–3:8* (Missoula, MT: Scholars 1976), 135–51; B. A. Jones, *The Formation of the Book of the Twelve: A Study in Text and Canon* (Atlanta, GA: Scholars, 1995), 88–90; J. M. Dines, "The Minor Prophets," in *The T&T Clark Companion to the Septuagint*, ed. J. K. Aitken (London: Bloomsbury T & T Clark, 2015), 439.

Examples from Habakkuk 3

1. *The Textual Affiliation of LXX and Barberini*

Following v. 1, which serves as a title, the opening line of the poem is attested in different forms in the Hebrew and Greek textual witnesses:

Habakkuk 3:2

MT: יְהוָ֗ה שָׁמַ֣עְתִּי שִׁמְעֲךָ֮ יָרֵאתִי֒ יְהוָ֗ה פָּֽעָלְךָ֙ בְּקֶ֣רֶב שָׁנִ֤ים חַיֵּ֙יהוּ֙ בְּקֶ֣רֶב שָׁנִ֣ים תּוֹדִ֔יעַ בְּרֹ֖גֶז רַחֵ֥ם
תִּזְכּֽוֹר: (≈ Mur88 XIX, 4–5)[9]

O Lord, I have learned of your renown; I am awed, O Lord, by your deeds. Renew them in these years, Oh, make them known in these years! Though angry, may you remember compassion. (NJPS)

LXX (and Barberini): Κύριε, εἰσακήκοα τὴν ἀκοήν σου καὶ ἐφοβήθην (/Barb: εὐλαβήθην), (Barb: + κύριε,) κατενόησα τὰ ἔργα σου καὶ ἐξέστην. ἐν μέσῳ δύο ζῴων γνωσθήσῃ, ἐν τῷ ἐγγίζειν τὰ ἔτη ἐπιγνωσθήσῃ, ἐν τῷ παρεῖναι τὸν καιρὸν ἀναδειχθήσῃ, ἐν τῷ ταραχθῆναι τὴν ψυχήν μου ἐν ὀργῇ ἐλέους μνησθήσῃ.

O Lord, I have heard of your renown and feared; (Barb: + O Lord) I considered your works and was astonished. You will be known in the midst of two living creatures; you will be recognized when the years draw near; you will be displayed when the right time comes; you will remember mercy when my soul is troubled in wrath. (NETS)

The two Greek versions of v. 2 as reflected in the critical editions are nearly identical, both reflecting a much longer text that MT. As I will demonstrate, this longer version is clearly secondary vis-à-vis MT. Because the Greek versions reflect shared secondary content readings,[10] then one can therefore conclude that one of these versions is textually dependent on the other.[11] The most

---

9   This second-century CE scroll was published by J. T. Milik, "88. Rouleau des Douze Prophètes," in *Les Grottes de Murabba'ât*, ed. P. Benoit, J.T. Milik & R. de Vaux (Oxford: Clarendon, 1961) 1: 181–205, 2: pl. lvi–lxxiii. It is textually very close to the consonantal basis of MT, and has one significant variant in this chapter (v. 10).

10 For the importance of these secondary readings in determining textual affiliation, see M. Segal, "The Text of the Hebrew Bible in Light of the Dead Sea Scrolls," *Materia Giudaica* 12, nos. 1–2 (2007): 7–8.

11 Many scholars assume that this agreement reflects contamination of one of the translations on the other during the Greek *transmission* process; see e.g.: Fernández Marcos, "El Texto Barberini," 9; C. Dogniez, "La version Barberini: éléments pour une étude littéraire d'un autre texte grec d'Habacuc 3," in *Die Septuaginta – Entstehung, Sprache, Geschichte; 3. internationale Fachtagung veranstaltet von Septuaginta Deutsch (LXX.D), Wuppertal 22.–25. Juli 2010*, ed. S. Kreuzer, M. Meiser and M. Sigismund (Tübingen: Mohr Siebeck, 2012),

prominent variants in this verse are translational doublets vis-à-vis MT (or a text similar to MT):[12]

	MT	LXX/Barb
(a)	בְּקֶרֶב שָׁנִים תּוֹדִיעַ	ἐν τῷ ἐγγίζειν τὰ ἔτη ἐπιγνωσθήσῃ
		you will be recognized when the years draw near
(b)		ἐν τῷ παρεῖναι τὸν καιρὸν ἀναδειχθήσῃ
		you will be displayed when the right time comes

Both readings assume a vocalization of the Hebrew text as בִּקְרֹב ("in the approaching") instead of בְּקֶרֶב ("in the midst"),[13] but otherwise reflect synonymous translations. Note that both of the translations of this clause, in both Greek translations, present a passive verb where MT has the *hifil* causative form תּוֹדִיעַ "make (them) known." While it is possible that they both reflect a *nifal* (passive) form תִּוָּדַע,[14] it seems more likely to me that the Greek versions reflect a similar idea to that expressed at the beginning of the verse, in which Habakkuk declares that he has heard of God's renown.

Similarly, at the end of the verse, we find a double translation of the word בְּרֹגֶז:

MT	LXX/Barb
בְּרֹגֶז	ἐν τῷ ταραχθῆναι τὴν ψυχήν μου
	in the angering of my spirit
	ἐν ὀργῇ
	in wrath

The translation ἐν ὀργῇ for ברגז is attested elsewhere in LXX (Job 37:2; cf. also 3:26; 14:1; 39:24) while the phrase "in the angering of my spirit" is an expression found elsewhere in LXX, although translating other Hebrew equivalents (Gen 41:8 [= ותפעם רוחו]; Ps 6:4 [= ונפשי נבהלה]; 41:7 [= 42:7 נפשי תשתוחח]; cf.

299; Harper, *Responding to a Puzzled Scribe*, 54–55 (noting the numerous doublets in this verse). All of the Greek manuscripts are consistent in this reading, and therefore, they are forced to further posit that this is a rather early conflation; see similarly their assessment of vv. 8 and 18, which are additional verses that are very closely formulated in OG and Barb. In contrast, as I suggest below, the relationship of the two versions is of one rewriting the other, in which it is common for there to be both extended shared material, and passages with differences of formulation and content.

12   See M. L. Margolis, "The Character of the Anonymous Greek Version of Habakkuk, Chapter 3," *AJSLL* 24 (1907–08): 78.

13   Contrast the translation of ¹בְּקֶרֶב earlier in the verse by the apt ἐν μέσῳ.

14   Cf. Prov 14:33. Note also the verb γνωσθήσῃ "you will be known," in the previous stich, which is a plus in both Greek versions vis-à-vis MT; see below.

also Judg 14:19).[15] Both are appropriate translations for the Hebrew "in anger/ though angry." It is unclear how both of these doublets were created, whether by the original translator, the combination of two translations, or the interpolation of readings into an existing translation. In any event, they are clearly secondary to MT, and therefore their appearance in both Greek versions demonstrates their literary interdependence.

A further shared secondary reading in this verse is the restructuring and reformulation of the first half of the verse, expanding the two parallel stichs:

Barberini	LXX	MT
Κύριε,	Κύριε,	יְהוָה
εἰσακήκοα	εἰσακήκοα	שָׁמַעְתִּי
τὴν ἀκοήν σου	τὴν ἀκοήν σου	שִׁמְעֲךָ
καὶ εὐλαβήθην,	καὶ ἐφοβήθην,	יָרֵאתִי
κύριε,		יְהוָה
κατενόησα	κατενόησα	
τὰ ἔργα σου	τὰ ἔργα σου	פָּעָלְךָ
καὶ ἐξέστην.	καὶ ἐξέστην.	

The syntactical structure of MT, as reflected in the cantillation marks (טעמי המקרא), presents a parallelism, where each of the two stichs in the first half of the verse opens with a reference to God in the vocative (in contrast to the NJPS translation quoted above, and most modern translations):

(A1) **O Lord**, I have learned of your renown, I am awed;
(A2) **O Lord**, your deeds, renew them in these years, Oh, make them known in these years!
(B) Though angry, may you remember compassion.

However, this division raises certain problems: (i) in stich A1, one expects a conjunctive *waw* before the second verb "I am awed" (יראתי). (ii) In stich A2, the relationship between the object "your deeds" and the verb "renew them" is unclear. In light of these difficulties, some scholars have suggested parsing the text of MT against the division of the cantillation:

(1a) O Lord, I have learned of your renown;
(1b) I am awed, O Lord, by your deeds.
(2a) In these years renew them!
(2b) In these years make (them) known!
(3) Though angry, may you remember compassion.

---

15   Note also the similar expression with πνεῦμα instead of ψυχή in 1Kgs 20:4,5; Isa 19:3.

This arrangement reflects a more balanced parallelism throughout: Both 1a and 1b contain the vocative address to the Lord (although in 1b it is no longer the opening word of the stich), first-person verbs that describe the reaction of the psalmist (I have learned / I am awed), and the object of the verbs (your renown / your deeds). This division solves the questions posed above according to the MT division – there is no need for a conjunction at the beginning of 1b, and the relation between the verb and its object in that stich is clear. This also leads to a classic parallelism between 2a and 2b, both of which open with the same two words, followed by a second-person verb (imperative, or jussive with imperative meaning). This therefore seemingly reflects the original structure of the verse, and the secondary arrangement according to the MT cantillation was probably the result of the desire to place the Tetragrammaton at the initial position of each of the stichs.

The structure of the opening stichs in both Greek versions is similar to MT, but both of the issues raised above are solved. The knowledge of God's renown leads to fear, and the second verb (Hebrew יראתי = Greek: ἐφοβήθην/ εὐλαβήθην) is connected to the previous clause by the addition of a conjunction (καὶ).[16] Moreover, this division of the verse leads to an imbalance in the parallelism, and the following stich was therefore secondarily "completed" in the Greek translations by the addition of two verbs, κατενόησα and (καὶ) ἐξέστην, to parallel שמעתי and יראתי(ו) respectively.[17] This expansion leads to the following structure:

> O Lord, I have heard of <u>your renown</u> and <u>feared</u>;
> (Barb: + O Lord)[18] *I considered* <u>your works</u> *and was astonished*

---

16 The Vulgate and Peshitta, which share the same sense division as MT, similarly reflect a conjunction at this point in the text, solving the first syntactical difficulty identified above. They do not, however, offer a solution to the second, in contrast to LXX / Barberini.

17 It is difficult to know in this instance if the addition of these verbs took place in Hebrew or in Greek. Margolis, "Character," 78, records this as characteristic of Barb; however, it is also in LXX, and therefore cannot be used to uniquely characterize the former.

18 The presence of a second κύριε in Barberini could reflect a secondary addition in the Greek tradition, either completing the parallelism between the two stichs, or a correction towards MT. If this is a correction towards MT, then it was probably already found in the text of LXX used by the Barberini scribe, since this reading is attested in numerous LXX manuscripts (S *L*''-49'-407 *C*'-68-239 La^{S}Syh Arm Or.Eus.dem. p. 270 Cyr. Th. Tht. Hi. Aug. Cant.^{p}). There does not seem to be a clear reason why LXX would have deleted the word if it was original to the Greek tradition.

Here too, the Greek versions are in agreement, and once again reflect a secondary reading, therefore demonstrating their textual interdependence.

A third secondary reading can be identified in the shared translation of the Hebrew clause בְּקֶרֶב שָׁנִים חַיֵּיהוּ "In these years renew them!," where both read ἐν μέσῳ δύο ζῴων γνωσθήσῃ "in the midst of two living creatures You will be known!" This translation reflects an alternate vocalization of the middle word as שְׁנַיִם,[19] and a reading of the verb as a noun ("living creatures").[20] This reading is almost certainly secondary vis-à-vis MT (or at least the alternative division of the Hebrew text proposed above) for two reasons: (i) LXX / Barberini reflect a plus γνωσθήσῃ "you will be known," which was added to compensate for the lack of a verb once חייהו was taken as a noun ("living creatures"). The choice of the specific verb was conditioned by the surrounding context; note especially ἐπιγνωσθήσῃ "you will be recognized" in the following stich, an almost identical form. (ii) The (re-)vocalization of שנים as "two," and the transformation of חייהו to a noun, ruin the parallelism between stichs 2a and 2b noted above, which both share the same opening expression followed by the 2nd person verb.

Taken together, the details analyzed above lead to two interconnected conclusions: (a) OG / Barberini are secondary to MT in Hab 3:2; (b) the agreement between OG / Barberini regarding secondary readings is evidence for the genetic literary dependence of the two Greek versions,[21] although the direction of dependence still needs to be determined, and will be discussed below.

2.   Barberini Independent of LXX, Similar to proto-MT (MT ≈ Barb ≠ LXX)

Other verses suggest the independence of Barberini from LXX, while at the same time one can show that the Barberini translator had access to a Hebrew text similar, yet not identical to, (proto-)MT.

---

19   Interestingly, an alternate vocalization tradition of this word is the basis for a rabbinic *al tiqre* homily in b.Sot 49a, but it is unclear to me if there is in fact a connection between that and the evidence of the Greek versions here (according to the *derasha*, it appears that it is suggested to read the prepositional phrase בְּקֶרֶב as בְּקֶרֶב, in contrast with LXX/Barberini), and they rather probably reflect independent attempts to read the consonants of the Hebrew text.

20   The description of "two living creatures" from the midst of which God will be known is perhaps a reference to the two cherubim on top of the Ark (cf. Exod 25:22; Num 7:89; Ezek 10:15,20). This motif seems foreign to the rest of the theophany, in addition to the rhetorical and syntactical arguments offered above to demonstrate that LXX / Barberini are secondary in this detail as well.

21   See above, n. 10.

Habakkuk 3:4

MT: וְנֹגַהּ֙ כָּא֣וֹר תִּֽהְיֶ֔ה קַרְנַ֥יִם מִיָּד֖וֹ ל֑וֹ וְשָׁ֖ם חֶבְי֥וֹן עֻזֹּֽה׃
And the brightness was like the sun; rays came forth from his hand, where his power lay hidden. (NRSV)

LXX: καὶ φέγγος αὐτοῦ ὡς φῶς ἔσται, κέρατα ἐν χερσὶν αὐτοῦ, καὶ ἔθετο ἀγάπησιν κραταιὰν ἰσχύος αὐτοῦ. And his brightness will be like light; horns are in his hands. And he has established a strong love of his strength.

Barberini: διαύγασμα φωτὸς ἔσται αὐτῷ, κέρατα ἐκ χειρὸς αὐτοῦ ὑπάρχει αὐτῷ. ἐκεῖ ἐπεστήρικται ἡ δύναμις τῆς δόξης αὐτοῦ. The splendor of light shall be his; horns from his hand belong to him. There the power of his glory has been fixed.

I want to focus on the end of the verse, parallel to the clause in MT וְשָׁם חֶבְיוֹן עֻזֹּה "where his power lay hidden," referring to the presence of God's glory in the brilliant light (נגה) at the beginning of the verse:

Habakkuk 3:4

Barberini	LXX	MT
ἐκεῖ	καὶ ἔθετο	וְשָׁם
ἐπεστήρικται	ἀγάπησιν	חֶבְיוֹן
ἡ δύναμις τῆς δόξης αὐτοῦ.	κραταιὰν ἰσχύος αὐτοῦ.	עֻזֹּה:

Analysis of each element of the LXX translation demonstrates how it corresponds to a similar consonantal (unvocalized) basis as that found in MT. Instead of the reading וְשָׁם in MT, LXX can be safely retroverted to a verb וְשָׂם, which differs from MT only in the diacritical marking of a *śin* versus a *šin*. חביון, a *hapax legomenon*, is translated by the Greek ἀγάπησιν "love," an etymological rendering based upon the geminate root ח-ב-ב "love," instead of the III-*heh* root ח-ב-ה "hide."[22] Finally, the word עֻזֹה is doubly rendered by κραταιὰν ἰσχύος αὐτοῦ "strong (love) of his strength." These differences are all based on a reading (or misreading) of a consonantal text that is very close to MT.

In this clause, Barberini is dependent upon a Hebrew text similar to MT, and does not reflect the LXX reading. This can be demonstrated by the translation of the word שָׁם(וְ) as ἐκεῖ "there" matching MT, and deviating from the reading found in LXX.[23] However, although dependent on a Hebrew text, the final clause in the verse demonstrates the paraphrastic nature of Barberini. It

---

22 See BDB, 285; HALOT, 284–285; M. Z. Kaddari, *A Dictionary of Biblical Hebrew: Alef–Taw* (Ramat-Gan: Bar-Ilan University Press, 2006, in Hebrew), 268–69.

23 Theodotion, Vulgate and Targum Jonathan agree with MT; Aquila, Symmachus and Peshitta agree with LXX.

is difficult to know which Hebrew word is translated by the Greek ἐπεστήρικται "fixed, established." Good suggested that this is a double translation of שׁם/שָׂם, in which case this is also based upon the direct translation of a Hebrew text.[24] Alternatively, it could also be a contextual-exegetical translation of the *hapax legomenon* חביון, without a specific philological basis.[25]

The last element in the Hebrew text, עזה "his power," has been expanded in Barberini to ἡ δύναμις τῆς δόξης αὐτοῦ "the power of his glory."[26] A similar minor paraphrastic expansion is found in v. 3, in which Barberini translated הודו "his majesty" as τὴν εὐπρέπειαν τῆς δόξης αὐτοῦ "the splendor of his glory."[27] From this short expression, we can therefore conclude that the Barberini version was created with an eye towards a Hebrew version (in addition to the LXX, as demonstrated above), but the text created was a free translation, tending at times towards paraphrase.

3. *Amplification of the Theophany Motif in the Greek Versions*[28]

All the versions of Hab 3 present a theophany scene, but this literary motif is more pronounced in the Greek versions than in MT. A prime example of this is exemplified by v. 6:

MT: עָמַד וַיְמֹדֶד אֶרֶץ רָאָה וַיַּתֵּר גּוֹיִם וַיִּתְפֹּצְצוּ הַרְרֵי־עַד שַׁחוּ גִּבְעוֹת עוֹלָם הֲלִיכוֹת עוֹלָם לוֹ׃

When he stands, he makes the earth shake; when he glances, he makes nations tremble. The age-old mountains are shattered, the primeval hills sink low. His are the ancient routes. (NJPS)

LXX: ἔστη, καὶ ἐσαλεύθη ἡ γῆ· ἐπέβλεψε, καὶ διετάκη ἔθνη, καὶ διεθρύβη τὰ ὄρη βίᾳ, ἐτάκησαν βουνοὶ αἰώνιοι πορείας αἰωνίας αὐτοῦ. He stood, and the earth shook; he

---

24   Good, "Barberini Greek Version," 13, n. 8. Harper, *Responding*, 213, notes that "ἐπιστηρίζω is not used for שׂים in LXX," but fails to note the equivalent שׂ-י-ם = στηρίζω in Jer 17:5; 21:10; 24:6; Ezek 6:2; 13:17; 15:7; 21:2, 7; 25:2; 28:21; 29:2; 38:2; Amos 9:4.

25   Other scholars suggest that this word is an addition by the translator: Margolis, "Character," 80 ("an amplification"); Fernández Marcos, "El texto Barberini," 20; Harper, *Responding*, 213 ("periphrastic clarification"). But see the discussion of the subsequent expression below.

26   See Dogniez, "La version Barberini," 301–302. Contrast the position of the scholars in nn. 24,25, who take this doubled Greek expression as a translation of the Hebrew expression חביון עזה.

27   This latter reading is also attested in Aquila, Theodotion and the Peshitta. Good, "Barberini Greek Version," 13, n. 1, notes Barberini's "tendency to paraphrase" in reference to v. 3.

28   The presentation of Barb here is far from exhaustive, and other scholars have highlighted additional themes found in Barb Hab 3 (vis-à-vis both MT and OG); see e.g. Fabry, "Der Herr," 228–236; Dogniez, "La version Barberini," 307–309.

looked, and nations dissolved; the mountains were broken to pieces in violence; everlasting hills of his eternal passage melted.

This verse clearly refers to God's appearance in the world, and the accompanying natural fireworks that it creates. Interpreters have debated the meaning of the Hebrew וַיְמֹדֶד and וַיַּתֵּר. One of the pieces of evidence in this discussion (of modern scholars) is the Septuagint translation, which translates: ἐσαλεύθη ... (διε)τάκη "shook ... tremble," two verbs that are frequently used in the context of a theophany. Similarly, the clause שַׁחוּ גִּבְעוֹת עוֹלָם "the primeval hills sink low" (from Hebrew root ש-ח-ח "be bowed down, prostrated, humbled"), is part of this picture. The Septuagint translates the verb שַׁחוּ as ἐτάκησαν "melted, dissolved." This Greek verb τήκω is used in other biblical theophanies, translating various verbs associated with these type-scenes, including Exod 15:15 (נמגו); Isa 24:3 (חפרה); 63:19 (נזלו); Mic 1:6 (יתבקעו); Nah 1:6 (נתכה); Zech 14:12 (המק ...תמק); Ps 75:4 (נמגים). These lexical choices in the LXX translation are intended to clearly place the psalm within the tradition of biblical theophanies.[29]

The theophany motif is emphasized even more heavily in Barberini than in LXX (and *a foritiri* than in MT). New elements are found in the following verses:

Verse 9b:

MT: נְהָרוֹת תְּבַקַּע־אָרֶץ You make the earth burst into streams.

LXX: ποταμῶν ῥαγήσεται γῆ A land of rivers will be torn asunder.

Barberini: ποταμοὺς διασκεδάσεις καὶ γῆν σείσεις. You will disperse rivers, and you will shake the earth.

---

29 Note perhaps similarly the LXX translation of v. 14 יסערו as σεισθήσονται "they shall quake;" cf. Judg 5:4; 2Sam 22:8; Nah 1:5; Ps 68:9 et al. (as an equivalent of ר-ע-ש). Another case of this phenomenon, the amplification of theophany through allusions to similar passages, is found in MurXII (Mur88) to Hab 3:10. While this scroll almost always aligns with MT, and can therefore be designated as proto-MT, see D. Barthélemy, *Studies in the Text of the Old Testament: An Introduction to the Hebrew Old Testament Text Project* (Winona Lake, IN: Eisenbrauns, 2012), 388; R. Fuller, "9.2.1 Ancient Manuscript Evidence," in *Textual History of the Bible: The Hebrew Bible*, vol.1B, ed. A. Lange and E. Tov (Leiden: Brill, 2016), 601–14. Hab 3:10 is exceptional. Instead of MT זרם מים עבר, the scroll reads זרמו מים עבות, based upon the parallel passage from Ps 77:18, within a theophany psalm. Note that (among others) Ward, *Habakkuk*, 21, 23, 26–27, surmised, *before* the discovery and publication of the Wadi Murabaat scroll, that this was the original text in Habakkuk. However, in my opinion, the direction of development is reversed, and it is secondary to the current context.

The verb σείω "shake" was added by Barberini, both accentuating the theophany (cf. the same verb in e.g. Hab 3:14; Nah 1:5), and "completing" the parallelism as seen above regarding v. 2.

Verse 13:

MT: ... יָצָ֙אתָ֙ לְיֵ֣שַׁע עַמֶּ֔ךָ ... עָר֛וֹת יְס֥וֹד עַד־צַוָּ֖אר

You have come forth to deliver your people ... (You will smash the roof of the villain's house,) raze it from foundation to top.

Barberini: ἀνεφάνης ἐπὶ σωτηρίᾳ τοῦ λαοῦ σου ... ἕως ἀβύσσου τὴν θαλάσσης καταδύσονται ... You appeared for the salvation of your people ... they shall sink unto the depth of the sea.

The reference to sinking "unto the depths of the sea" is an allusion to Exod 15:5, a paradigmatic theophany. It is possible that the lexical choice of ἀναφαίνω is directly related to this context (cf. also Targum Jonathan אתגליתא).

Furthermore, Barberini presents God as a warrior as part of this theophany imagery:

Verse 8b:

MT: :כִּ֤י תִרְכַּב֙ עַל־סוּסֶ֔יךָ מַרְכְּבֹתֶ֖יךָ יְשׁוּעָֽה "that you are driving your steeds, your victorious chariot"

Barberini: ἀνέβης ἐπὶ τὰ ἅρματα σου, ἡ ἱππασία σου σωτηρία ὁ προέβης. You mounted on your chariots; your cavalry, before which you advanced, is deliverance.

The addition of ὁ προέβης emphasizes God's role as a warrior leading into battle against Israel's enemies.

Verse 12

MT: בְּזַ֖עַם תִּצְעַד־אָ֑רֶץ בְּאַ֖ף תָּד֥וּשׁ גּוֹיִֽם: You tread the earth in rage, you trample nations in fury.

LXX: ὀλιγώσεις "you will diminish"

Barberini: ἐγερθήσῃ "you shall be awakened/stirred up"

MT already describes God as attacking the nations. LXX here probably reads תצער*.³⁰ The verb chosen in Barberini perhaps reflects the translator's desire to depict God as a warrior stirred up before going out to battle.

> Verse 13bα:
>
> MT: מָחַצְתָּ רֹּאשׁ מִבֵּית רָשָׁע You will smash the roof of the villain's house
>
> LXX: ἔβαλες εἰς κεφαλὰς ἀνόμων θάνατον You cast death on the heads of the lawless
>
> Barberini: κατετόξευσας κεφαλὰς ἀνθρώπων ὑπερηφάνων you shot down the heads of arrogant people with arrows

Both MT and LXX describe God as punishing the villains. However, Barberini chose the specific verb κατατοξεύω "strike with an arrow" as a continuation of the image in v. 11 in which God is described as sending forth arrows. That is a typical element in theophany scenes, referring perhaps to lightning, and it is expanded in Barberini v. 13 to describe how God acts as a warrior defending his people.

Methodological Reflections

(1) One can identify numerous differences between the three textual witnesses, but not all of the differences are of the same significance. Some can be traced to an alternate Hebrew *Vorlage*, while others reflect translation technique or exegesis of the translator(s). There is an inherent difficulty in analyzing all three of these witnesses since there are expressions and clauses in Hebrew and Greek that are extremely difficult to understand, and therefore it is often unclear how to interpret the relationship between the versions.

(2) Despite these difficulties and the many differences between them, I would suggest that both MT and LXX reflect the same literary edition of Habakkuk 3. Many of the potential variants between these two textual witnesses can be traced back to a similar consonantal Hebrew text, and even in those where there seems to be an alternate Hebrew *Vorlage*, it is usually a reading that is related genetically to that of the MT. In a few cases, LXX seems to reflect an alternate Hebrew text, whose relationship to MT is not clear, and it is therefore possible to view them as alternate *Vorlagen*. However, I suggest that they are still not significant enough to speak of alternate literary versions.

---

30 This reading also attested in a quotation in a manuscript of *Mekilta R. Išmael, širta* 5 (134:13).

(3) Although I have suggested that they belong to the same literary edition, one can identify certain secondary trends in the Septuagint of Habakkuk 3, which do reflect minor editorial activity. These include: (a) a literary-poetic sense of parallelism according to which a scribe "completed" the parallelism absent in an earlier version of the text; and (b) slight amplification of the language and motifs of theophany already found in MT. In all of the examples of these phenomena, it can be demonstrated that the LXX is secondary vis-à-vis MT (this does not imply that LXX [or the *Vorlage* of LXX] is secondary in all details to MT). At the same time, they are only found in a few small details, and I find it difficult to make the argument based upon these differences alone that they reflect an alternate literary edition.

(4) According to the evidence provided above (and as already noted by some scholars), the Barberini text and the Septuagint to Habakkuk 3 are clearly related textually, as demonstrated by their overlap in v. 2 and elsewhere (esp. vv. 8, 18). While the direction of dependence could theoretically be debated, it seems to me most likely that the Barberini text is based upon the LXX, since it adopts motifs and literary techniques that are found there, and further develops them. Barberini is further from MT, and at times seems paraphrastic in nature. Some of the readings above seem to provide evidence that Barberini was translating a textually related, yet different, *Vorlage* to what is found in MT and LXX. We are still not certain whether the extent of the differences between Greek Barberini and MT are primarily the result of this alternate *Vorlage*, or whether the Greek translator/reviser is also responsible for some/many of these differences. Due to the periphrastic nature of this translation, I tend towards the latter option.

(5) A comparison of MT and Barberini does in fact seem to suggest that they reflect alternate versions of Habakkuk 3. The differences between them include amplification of the theophany motif, as well as stylistic-poetic changes, including the "completion" and strengthening of poetic parallels. I suggest that these differences qualify as both quantitative and qualitative differences between these two versions, and thus we are perhaps justified in referring to them as alternate editions. However, this is where it becomes complicated methodologically, since these differences between the MT and Barberini are precisely along the same lines as the differences between MT and LXX, yet they appear with much greater frequency throughout the passage and with greater clarity. In light of this, it is perhaps preferable to view the gradual growth of these different versions as a process of *rewriting* or *textual dynamics*.[31]

---

31 I have analyzed and addressed these scribal phenomena in a number of studies, including: M. Segal, "Between Bible and Rewritten Bible," in *Biblical Interpretation at Qumran* (Grand Rapids, MI: Eerdmans, 2005), 10–28; "The Old Greek Version and Masoretic

This leads to a fundamental methodological question, with which I would like to conclude: is there a clear demarcation between the different literary editions of this chapter? When we examine MT and Barberini alone, it seems clear that the answer is in the affirmative. However, if we trace the trajectory of these differences from MT towards LXX and then onto Barberini, we can ask whether and where a line can indeed be drawn. The same scribal and textual phenomena which have led me to view the Barberini text as an alternate literary edition as compared to MT are found in the LXX text in comparison with MT, but are less pronounced and less frequent. Should the recognition that these trends already began in LXX and were then more fully expressed in Barberini change our evaluation of the status of LXX vis-à-vis MT? This of course is not a question to which there is a definitive answer, but I suggest that the dynamic aspects of this growth need to be considered both in this specific case, and more broadly, in discussions of the contribution of the textual versions towards the literary development of biblical books.

Bibliography

Ahituv, Shmuel. "Habakkuk: Introduction and Commentary." In *Nahum, Habakkuk and Zephaniah* (*Mikra Leyisra'el*), edited by Mordechai Cogan and Shmuel Ahituv. Jerusalem: Magnes, 2006. [In Hebrew.]

Baars, Willem. "A New Witness to the Text of the Barberini Greek Version of Habakkuk III." *Vetus Testamentum* 15 (1965): 381–82.

Barthélemy, Dominique. *Studies in the Text of the Old Testament: An Introduction to the Hebrew Old Testament Text Project*. Winona Lake, IN: Eisenbrauns, 2012.

Brownlee, William H. *The Midrash Pesher of Habakkuk*. Missoula, MT: Scholars Press, 1979.

Text of Daniel 6," in *Die Septuaginta: Orte und Intentionen. Proceedings of the Fifth International Wuppertal Symposium on the Septuagint*, ed. S. Kreuzer, M. Meiser, and M. Sigismund (Tübingen: Mohr Siebeck, 2016), 404–28; "Daniel 5 in Aramaic and Greek and the Textual History of Daniel 4–6," in *IOSOT Congress Volume. Stellenbosch 2016*, ed. L.C. Jonker, C. Maier, and G. Kotzé (Leiden: Brill, 2017), 251–84; "Harmonization and Rewriting of Daniel 6 from the Bible to Qumran," in *HĀ-ÎSH MŌSHE: Studies in Scriptural Interpretation in the Dead Sea Scrolls and Related Literature in Honor of Moshe J. Bernstein*, ed. B. Goldstein, M. Segal, and G.J. Brooke (Leiden: Brill, 2017), 265–79; "Reconsidering the Relationship(s) between 4Q365, 4Q365a, and the Temple Scroll," *Revue de Qumran* 30 (2018): 213–33; "Rewriting the Final Apocalypse of Daniel," in *In (Con)textual Perspectives on the Dead Sea Scrolls: The Seventeenth International Orion Symposium* (forthcoming); "From the Jordan to Mt. Ebal and Back – On the Textual Dynamics of Deut 27 and Josh 3–4; 8," *VT* (2024), 10.1163/15685330-bja10185.

Dines, Jennifer M. "The Minor Prophets." In *The T&T Clark Companion to the Septuagint*, edited by James K. Aitken, 438–55. London: Bloomsbury T & T Clark, 2015.

Dogniez, Cécile. "La version Barberini: éléments pour une étude littéraire d'un autre texte grec d'Habacuc 3." In *Die Septuaginta—Texte, Theologien, Einflüsse. 2. Internationale Fachtagung veranstaltet von Septuaginta Deutsch (LXX.D), Wuppertal 23.–27. Juli 2008*, edited by Wolfgang Kraus and Martin Karrer, 295–310. Tübingen: Mohr Siebeck, 2010.

Fabry, Heinz-Josef. "'Der Herr macht meine Schritte sicher' (Hab 3,19 Barb.)—Die Versio Barberini, eine liturgische Sondertradition von Hab 3?" In *Die Septuaginta— Texte, Theologien, Einflüsse. 2. Internationale Fachtagung veranstaltet von Septuaginta Deutsch (LXX.D), Wuppertal 23.–27. Juli 2008*, edited by Wolfgang Kraus and Martin Karrer, 223–37. Tübingen: Mohr Siebeck, 2010.

Fernández Marcos, Natalio. "El Texto Barberini de Habacuc III Reconsiderado." *Sefarad* 36 (1976): 3–36. Translated, and slightly updated in "Der Barberini-Text von Hab 3: Eine neue Untersuchung." In *Brennpunkt—Die Septuaginta; Band 3: Studien zur Theologie, Anthropologie, Ekklesiologie, Eschatologie und Liturgie der Griechischen Bibel*, edited by Heinz-Josef Fabry and Dieter Böhler, 151–80. Stuttgart: Kohlhammer, 2007.

Fuller, Russell. "9.2.1 Ancient Manuscript Evidence." In *Textual History of the Bible: The Hebrew Bible*, vol.1B, edited by Armin Lange and Emanuel Tov, 601–14. Leiden: Brill, 2016.

Good, Edwin M. "The Barberini Greek Version of Habakkuk III." *Vetus Testamentum* 9 (1959): 11–30.

Goshen-Gottstein, Moshe, ed. *The Hebrew University Bible: The Book of Isaiah*. Jerusalem: Magnes, 1995.

Goshen-Gottstein, Moshe, and Shemaryahu Talmon, eds. *The Hebrew University Bible: The Book of Ezekiel*. Jerusalem: Magnes, 2004.

Haak, Robert D. *Habakkuk*. Leiden: Brill, 1991.

Harper, Joshua L. *Responding to a Puzzled Scribe: The Barberini Version of Habakkuk 3 Analysed in the Light of the Other Greek Versions*. London: Bloomsbury T&T Clark, 2015.

Hiebert, Theodore. *God of My Victory: The Ancient Hymn of Habakkuk* 3. Atlanta, GA: Scholars Press, 1986.

Jones, Barry Alan. *The Formation of the Book of the Twelve: A Study in Text and Canon*. Atlanta, GA: Scholars Press, 1995.

Kaddari, Menahem Zevi. *A Dictionary of Biblical Hebrew: Alef–Taw*. Ramat-Gan: Bar-Ilan University Press, 2006. [In Hebrew.]

Margolis, Max L. "The Character of the Anonymous Greek Version of Habakkuk, Chapter 3." *American Journal of Semitic Languages and Literatures* 24 (1907–08): 76–85.

Milik, Józef T. "88. Rouleau des Douze Prophètes." In *Les Grottes de Murabba'ât*, edited by Pierre Benoit, Józef T. Milik, and Roland de Vaux, 1: 181–205. Oxford: Clarendon, 1961.

Muraoka, Takamitsu. "In Defense of the Unity of the LXX Minor Prophets." *Annual of the Japanese Biblical Institute* 15 (1989): 25–36.

Segal, Michael. "Between Bible and Rewritten Bible." In *Biblical Interpretation at Qumran*, edited by Matthias Henze, 10–28. Grand Rapids, MI: Eerdmans, 2005.

--------. "Daniel 5 in Aramaic and Greek and the Textual History of Daniel 4–6." In *IOSOT Congress Volume. Stellenbosch 2016*, edited by Louis Jonker, Gideon Kotzé, and Christl M. Maier, 251–84. Leiden: Brill, 2017.

--------. "From the Jordan to Mt. Ebal and Back—On the Textual Dynamics of Deut 27 and Josh 3–4; 8." *Vetus Testamentum* 2024, 10.1163/15685330-bja10185.

--------. "Harmonization and Rewriting of Daniel 6 from the Bible to Qumran." In *HĀ-ÎSH MŌSHE: Studies in Scriptural Interpretation in the Dead Sea Scrolls and Related Literature in Honor of Moshe J. Bernstein*, edited by Binyamin Y. Goldstein, Michael Segal, and George J. Brooke, 265–279. Leiden: Brill, 2017.

--------. "Methodological Considerations in the Preparation of an Edition of the Hebrew Bible." In *The Text of the Hebrew Bible and Its Editions: Studies in Celebration of the Fifth Centennial of the Complutensian Polyglot*, edited by Andrés Piquer Otero and Pablo A. Torijano Morales, 34–55. Leiden: Brill, 2017.

--------. "The Old Greek Version and Masoretic Text of Daniel 6." In *Die Septuaginta: Orte und Intentionen: Proceedings of the Fifth International Wuppertal Symposium on the Septuagint*, edited by Siegfried Kreuzer, Martin Meiser, and Marcus Sigismund, 404–28. Tübingen: Mohr Siebeck, 2016.

--------. "Reconsidering the Relationship(s) between 4Q365, 4Q365a, and the Temple Scroll." *Revue de Qumran* 30 (2018): 213–33.

--------. "Rewriting the Final Apocalypse of Daniel." In *(Con)textual Perspectives on the Dead Sea Scrolls: The Seventeenth International Orion Symposium*. Forthcoming.

--------. "The Text of the Hebrew Bible in Light of the Dead Sea Scrolls." *Materia Giudaica* 12, nos. 1–2 (2007): 5–20.

Segal, Michael and Shemaryahu Talmon, eds. *The Hebrew University Bible: The Twelve Prophets*. Jerusalem: Mandel Institute of Jewish Studies, Hebrew University / Magnes, 2024.

Stade, Bernhard. "Miscellen." *Zeitschrift für die Alttestamentliche Wissenschaft* 4 (1884): 149–59.

Thackeray, H. St. John. "Primitive Lectionary Notes in the Psalm of Habakkuk." *Journal of Theological Studies* 12 [1910/11]: 191–213.

--------. *The Septuagint and Jewish Worship: A Study in Origins*. London: British Academy, 1921.

Tov, Emanuel. *The Septuagint Translation of Jeremiah and Baruch: A Discussion of an Early Revision of Jeremiah 29–52 and Baruch 1:1–3:8.* Missoula, MT: Scholars Press, 1976.

Tov, Emanuel, Shemaryahu Talmon, and Chaim Rabin, eds. *The Hebrew University Bible: The Book of Jeremiah.* Jerusalem: Magnes, 1997.

Ward, William H. "A Critical and Exegetical Commentary on Habakkuk." In *A Critical and Exegetical Commentary on Micah, Zephaniah, Nahum, Habakkuk, Obadiah and Joel,* edited by John Merlin Powis Smith, William Hayes Ward, and Julius August Bewer, 3–28. Edinburgh: T. & T. Clark, 1911.

Ziegler, Joseph, ed. *Duodecim prophetae.* Volume 13 of *Septuaginta: Vetus Testamentum Graecum: Auctoritate Academiae Scientiarum Gottingensis Editum.* Göttingen: Vandenhoeck & Ruprecht, 1967.

--------. "Die Einheit der Septuaginta zum Zwölfprophetenbuch." In *Beilage zum Vorlesungsverzeichnis der Staatl. Akademie zu Braunsberg,* 1–16. Göttingen: Vandenhoeck & Ruprecht, 1934–35.

Ladino and Spanish Bibles: Different Traditions

Ora (Rodrigue) Schwarzwald

Introduction

One of the fundamental questions raised by Bible researchers is: What are the relations between the Spanish medieval translations and the Jewish Sephardic translations printed from the sixteenth century? This question will be addressed in the following discussion.

The tradition of translating the Bible into the Iberian vernacular languages is well-attested from the thirteenth century by both Jews and non-Jews. In this article, I focus on the Spanish translations while excluding the Catalan and Portuguese ones. Jewish translations of the Bible into Ladino, also known as Judeo-Spanish, are documented in print from the sixteenth century onwards, following the expulsions of Jews from the Iberian Peninsula. These translations are composed in the contemporaneous Spanish, incorporating a unique vocabulary typical of Jewish usage and several distinct linguistic features.

The first section of the article delineates the Spanish medieval translations, succeeded by an exploration of the Ladino translations. A linguistic comparison is conducted between the two types of translations. The concluding section establishes the independence of the Ladino translations from the medieval Spanish ones.

Medieval Spanish Translations

Regarding the Spanish translations of the Bible, it should be emphasized from the beginning that, unlike some other languages which attained canonical status, Spanish translations did not acquire such prestige. The Vulgate of Jerome in Latin, Luther's translation of the Bible into German, and the King James translation of the Bible into English are recognized as canonical translations. Neither the Spanish medieval translations of the Bible nor later well-known translations like *La Biblia del Oso* from 1569 achieved the status of standard Spanish translations.[1] The variations among them are significant and depend

---

1 A. Enrique-Arias, "Traducción bíblica e historia de las lenguas iberorrománicas," ["Biblical Translation and the History of the Ibero-Romance Languages,"] in *Traducción bíblica e historia de las lenguas iberorrománicas*, ed. A. Enrique-Arias (Berlin: De Gruyter, 2022), 3–8.

on reliance on the Latin and Greek traditions of translating the Bible, as well as on Hebrew homiletic interpretations, as will be demonstrated below.

The study of medieval Spanish translations commenced at the end of the nineteenth century and continues intensively to the present day.[2] These translations, known as "las biblias romanceadas," were written from the twelfth century onwards and appear in manuscripts, many of which are incomplete.[3] Some of the translations are extensively described, particularly those found in the Escorial Monastery, marked as "E" below.[4] One of the texts that has received detailed attention is the illuminated Alba Bible, better known as Rabbi Moshe Arragel's translation of the Bible from 1430, commissioned by Grand Master Luis González de Guzmán.[5] Morreale's programmatic article

---

2   See, for instance, S. Berger, "Les bibles castillanes," ["The Castilian Bibles,"] *Romania* 28 (1899), 360–408, 508–567; F.J. Pueyo Mena, and A. Enrique Arias, "Los romanceamientos castellanos de la biblia hebrea compuestos en la Edad Media: manuscritos y traducciones," ["The Spanish-Romance Translations of the Hebrew Bible Composed in the Middle Ages: Manuscripts and Translations,"] *Sefarad* 73 (2013), 165–224; Enrique-Arias, ed. *Traducción bíblica e historia de las lenguas iberorrománicas*.

3   A detailed list of the manuscripts, their dates, and contents can be found in J.F. Pueyo Mena, "Biblias romanceadas y en ladino," ["Romance and Ladino Bibles,"] in *Sefardíes: literatura y lengua de una nación dispersa. Actas del XV Curso de verano cultura hispano-judía y sefardí (Toledo, 5–8 sep. 2005)* [*Sephardis: Literature and Language of a Dispersed People*] ed. E. Romero Castelló (Ciudad Real et al.: Universidad de Castilla-La Mancha, 2008), 193–263.

4   O.H. Hauptmann, *Escorial Bible I.j.4: The Pentateuch*, 1 (Philadelphia, PA: University of Pennsylvania, Press, 1953); S. Berger, *La Bible romane au Moyen Age* [*The Medieval Romance Bible*] (Genève: Slatkine, 1977); O.H. Hauptmann and M. Gibson Littlefield, *Escorial Bible I.j.4* (Madison, WI: Hispanic Seminary of Medieval Studies,1987); M.G. Littlefield, *Escorial Bible I.ii.19* (Madison, WI: The Hispanic Seminary of Medieval Studies, 1992); M. Lazar, ed., *Biblia Ladinada: Escorial I.j.3* (Madison, WI: The Hispanic Seminary of Medieval Studies, 1995); On E5/E7 versions, see J. Llamas, *Biblia medieval romanceada judío-cristiana* [*The Jewish-Christian Medieval Romance Bible*] (Madrid: CSIC, 1950).

5   For example, M. Morreale, "El glosario de Rabí Mosé Arragel en la 'Biblia de Alba,'" ["Rabbi Moses Arragel's Gloss on the 'Biblia de Alba,'"] *Bulletin of Hispanic Studies* 38 (1961), 145–52; A. Keller. "The making of the 'Biblia de Alba,'" in *La Biblia de Alba in the Collection of the Palacio de Liria*, ed. J. Schonfield (Madrid and London: Fundación Amigos de Sefarad, 1992), 147–56; L. Amigo Espada, "El influjo del latín en el vocabulario de la Biblia de Alba: Algunas voces raras," ["The Latin Influence on the Vocabulary of the Alba Bible: Some Rare Words,"] *Helmantica* 46 (1995), 183–200; A. Enrique-Arias. "Texto subyacente hebreo e influencia latinizante en la traducción de la Biblia de Alba de Moisés Arragel," ["Underlying Hebrew Text and Latinizing Influence in Moisés Arragel's Translation of the Biblia de Alba,"] in *Traducción y estandarización: la incidencia de la traducción en la historia de los lenguajes especializados* [*Translation and Standardization: The Impact of Translation in the History of Specialized Languages*] ed. V. Alsina Keith (Madrid: Iberoamericana, 2004), 99–112; A. Enrique-Arias, "Sobre el parentesco entre la Biblia de Alba y la Biblia de la Real Academia de la Historia MS 87," ["On the Relationship between the Alba Bible and the Bible of the Royal Academy of History MS 87,"] *Romance Philology* 59 (2006), 241–64; A. Enrique-Arias and C. Matute,

outlines the issues involved in deciphering the translations within the variety of texts under consideration, and Enrique Arias contributes further insights to these problems.[6] In addition to detailing the existing translations, various issues are raised: their time of publication, the possible translators, the target audience, the included books and their order, the language used—archaic or vernacular—and their reliance on Greek, Latin, or Jewish interpretations.

Andrés Enrique-Arias, the director from the University of the Balearic Islands, and F. Javier Pueyo Mena from Madrid, have collaboratively established an exceptional online collection of medieval Spanish Bibles known as *Corpus Biblia Medieval*.[7] All translations within this corpus are rendered in Latin letters, allowing users to observe the actual form of the text in its manuscript format. The collection encompasses fourteen manuscripts. As previously noted, certain manuscripts exhibit missing sections of the Bible, while others may have blurred scripts.

Within this comprehensive corpus, each verse is presented in all available Spanish translations, its Latin equivalent, the Hebrew original text, the Hebrew lexical entries, and the transcription of the Hebrew text in those translations based on the Hebrew Bible. This remarkable compilation serves as a valuable tool for researchers and investigators of the Bible, providing the capability to examine the texts and explore the translations present in each existing manuscript.

Several of the Spanish translations during the Middle Ages were undertaken by Jews under the supervision of Christian clergymen, though the identities of most translators remained unknown. Some medieval Spanish translations included both the Old and New Testaments. Notably, the translations of the

---

"El estudio morfosintáctico de la lengua de la 'Biblia de Alba': un acercamiento a la variación discursiva y dialectal del espanol en el siglo XV," ["The Morphosyntactic Study of the Language of the 'Bible de Alba': An Approach to the Discursive and Dialectal Variation of Spanish in the Fifteenth Century,"] in *Actes du XXVe congres international de linguistique et de philologie romanes* (Innsbruck, 3–8 septiembre 2007), eds. M. Iliescu, H. Siller-Runggaldier and P. Danler (Berlin: De Gruyter, 2010), 115–23; L.M. Girón Negrón and A. Enrique-Arias, "La 'Biblia' de Arragel y la edición de traducciones bíblicas del siglo XV," ["Arragel's 'Biblia' and the Edition of Biblical Translations in the Fifteenth Century,"] *Helmántica* 190 (2012), 291–310.

6 M. Morreale, "Apuntes bibliográficos para la iniciación al estudio de las traducciones bíblicas medievales en castellano," ["Bibliographic Notes for the Introduction to the Study of Medieval Biblical Translations in Spanish,"] *Sefarad* 20 (1960), 66–109; A. Enrique-Arias, "Dos problemas en el uso de corpus diacrónicos del español: perspectiva y comparabilidad," ["Two Problems in the Use of Diachronic Corpora of Spanish: Perspective and Comparability,"] *Scriptum Digital* 1 (2012), 85–106.

7 A. Enrique-Arias and F.J. Pueyo Mena, *Corpus Biblia Medieval: Biblia Medieval*, http://www.bibliamedieval.es, last accessed December 21, 2023.

Old Testament did not consistently adhere to the book order of the traditional Masoretic Hebrew Bible, despite their partial reliance on Jewish homily.

For instance, the book of Ruth was positioned immediately after the book of Judges rather than among the five Jewish *megillot* ("scrolls"). This deviation was influenced by the opening verse: "Now it came to pass in the days when the judges ruled, that there was a famine in the land" (Ruth 1:1).[8] In certain translations, the Pentateuch featured divisions of *parashot/sedarim*, aligning with the Jewish tradition, and overall, verse divisions followed the Hebrew tradition. However, distinct features indicate that these medieval translations were not exclusively based on the traditional Hebrew Bible. The purpose of their creation, whether for Jewish or Christian use, remains uncertain despite claims by some researchers.

According to Littlefield, certain manuscripts, such as Escorial Bible E5 and E19, were crafted for Jewish use, while E7 and E4 were intended for Christian use, and E3 and the Alba Bible were designed for both Jewish and Christian audiences.[9] Berger and others suggest that manuscript E3, and possibly E19, lean more towards a Jewish context and influence the tradition for Jewish translations published in the sixteenth century.[10] From my perspective, it seems more plausible that *Anusim*, the converted Jews to Christianity, might have utilized these medieval translations, as evidenced by the translation of *Megillat Esther* in *Sefer Teshuvah* ("Book of Repentance").[11] Jews were more accustomed to writing and reading Spanish texts in Hebrew script rather than in Latin script.

Ladino Translations

Numerous Judeo-Spanish texts in Hebrew script were composed in Spain by and for Jews before the expulsion, although the translation of the Bible itself did not occur.[12] Within these Judeo-Spanish texts, one discovers the Regulations of

---

8   All English translations are taken from the King James Version: *King James English Translation of the Bible*. https://www.biblegateway.com/versions/King-James-Version-KJV-Bible/. The order of the books in KJV is also different from the traditional Hebrew Bible regarding the book of Ruth, and other books, e.g., Chronicles appear immediately after Kings.
9   Littlefield, *Escorial Bible I.ii.19*, xxiii.
10 S. Berger, "Les bibles castellanes"; M. Lazar, "Targume hamiqra beladino," ["Ladino Bible Translations,"] *Sefunot* 8 (1964), 337–75; Lazar, *Biblia Ladinada I.j.3*, xix–xxi.
11 M. Lazar, ed., *Sēfer Tešuḇāh* (Culver City, CA: Labyrinthos, 1993), 83–94.
12 E. Gutwirth, "La cultura material hispano-judía: entre la norma y la práctica," ["Spanish-Jewish Material Culture: Between Norm and Practice,"] in *Una sefarad inventada? Los*

Valladolid, formal contracts, instructions for conducting the Passover Seder in old *Siddurim* and *Mahzorim*, and more.[13]

During the Middle Ages, there existed an oral Jewish tradition of translating the Bible in religious services, following the old practice of *shnayim miqra ve'eḥad targum* ("two portions of the Bible and one portion of [Aramaic] translation"). Bible translation was also integrated into the Jewish educational system, where children were taught to read the Bible in Hebrew, receiving word-for-word explanations in the local language.[14] Although these oral traditions were not documented in writing in Spain, they persisted after the expulsion in 1492 and were eventually printed.[15]

An ancient manuscript from the late-thirteenth century, presenting a Hebrew glossary explaining biblical words, includes special *le'azim* ("foreign words") elucidating biblical terms. These *le'azim* reflect the vernacular Spanish language of the Jews in the Iberian Peninsula and the Judeo-Spanish used in later centuries. For instance, the use of verbs with the suffix *-guar*, such as *aformosiguar* ("beatify, glorify"—Spanish *hermosear*), *fruchiguar* ("be fruitful"—Spanish *frutar*), the use of *afreición* ("poverty, misery"—Spanish *aflicción*), *arna(n)cio* ("generation"—Spanish *generación*), *barragán* ("brave, hero"), *doloriar* ("afflict, stress"), *ermollo* ("bud, sprout"—Spanish *armuello*), and more.[16] The presence of such explanations and subsequent glossaries suggests a tradition of explaining the Bible using the local language word-for-word.[17]

---

problemas de interpretación de los restos materiales de los judíos en España [*An Invented Sepharad? The Problems of Interpretation of the Material Remains of the Jews in Spain*], ed. J. Castaño (Córdoba: Ediciones El Almendro, 2014), 87–110.

13 Y. Baer, *A History of the Jews in Christian Spain*, vol. II, trans. L. Schoffman (Philadelphia, PA: Jewish Publication Society of America 1961); L. Minervini, *Testi giudeospagnoli medievali (Castiglia e Aragona)* [*Judeo-Spanish Medieval Texts (Castile and Aragon)*], I–II (Napoli: Liguori Editore, 1992); ibid., "Jewish Multilingual and Multigraphic Texts in Christian Spain," in *Multilingual and Multigraphic Documents and Manuscripts of East and West*, eds. G. Mandalà and I. Pérez Martín (Piscataway, NJ: Gorgias Press, 2018), 407–23.

14 E. Gutwirth, "Religión, historia y las biblias romanceadas," ["Religion, History, and the Romance Bibles,"] *Revista Catalana de Teologia* 13 (1988), 115–134; I.M. Hassán, "¿Es el ladino judeoespañol calco? (cfr. DRAE)," ["Is Ladino a Judeo-Spanish Calque?"] *Quaderns de Filologia. Estudis Lingüístics* IX (2004), 87–99.

15 D.M. Bunis, "Translating from the Head and from the Heart: The Essentially *Oral* Nature of the *Ladino* Bible-translation Tradition," in *Hommage á Haïm Vidal Sephiha*, eds. W. Busse and M-Ch. Varol-Bornes (Bern: Peter Lang, 1996), 337–57.

16 E. Alfonso, *Translating the Hebrew Bible in Medieval Iberia: Oxford, Bodleian Library, ms Hunt. 268* (Leiden: Brill, 2021), 341–42.

17 There were also Ladino glossaries to the Bible published in the sixteenth and seventeenth centuries: in 1588 – *Sefer Hesheq Shelomo* by Moshe Cordovero which reflect the

Researchers have assigned the term Ladino to refer to the distinctive rigid word-for-word translations of liturgical texts into Judeo-Spanish.[18] Within Ladino texts, one encounters translations of the Bible, prayer books (*Siddurim* and *Mahzorim*), *Pirkei Avot*, the Passover *Haggadah*, and *Ta'aniyot*.

A few years after the expulsion of the Jews from Spain, Ladino translations of the Bible emerged in the Sephardic Diaspora, notably in Constantinople, Thessaloniki, Ferrara, Amsterdam, and Venice. In the sixteenth century, various individual books such as Psalms, the Prophets, Esther, the Song of Songs, and others were published in Hebrew script alongside the Hebrew text.[19] Some editions of the Hebrew Bible included explanations of specific words in Ladino. However, the comprehensive translation of the entire Bible in Hebrew script was undertaken only between 1739 and 1745 by Abraham Asa. The *Anusim*, the converted Jews who returned to Judaism, also published translations of the Bible and other liturgical texts in Latin letters. A comprehensive list of Ladino translations in Hebrew script can be found in the *Thesaurus of the Ladino Book*.[20] Detailed lists of Ladino Bible translations in Latin script are available in Lazar and Pueyo Mena's publications.[21] These Bible translations adhere to the order of the books in the Hebrew Bible.

Two notable Ladino translations of the Bible were published in the mid-16th century, half a century after the expulsion from Spain: the Constantinople Pentateuch (CP) in 1547 and the Ferrara Bible (FB) in 1553.

Judeo-Spanish vernacular, and in 1639 – *Melo Kaf Nahat* by Jacob Lombroso whose explanations reflect the standard and literary style, see D.M. Bunis, "Tres formas de ladinar la biblia en Italia en los siglos XVI–XVII," ["Three Way of Ladinizing the Bible in Italy during the Sixteenth and Seventeenth Centuries,"] in *Introducción a la Biblia de Ferrara*, eds. I.M. Hassán and Á. Berenguer Amador (Madrid: Comisión Nacional Quinto Centenario, 1994), 315–45. And see a glossary intended for a student in A. Quintana, "From the Master's Voice to the Disciple's Script: Genizah Fragments of a Bible Glossary in Ladino," *Hispania Judaica Bulletin* 6 (2008): 187–235.

18   H.V. Sephiha, *Le Ladino: Deutéronome* (Paris: Centre de Recherches Hispaniques, 1973), 42–87. In many texts and circumstances the word Ladino has been referred to as Judeo-Spanish.

19   See D. Cohen, *Otsar hasfarim beladino 1490–1960* [*Thesaurus of the Ladino Books 1490–1960*], (Jerusalem: The Ben-Zvi Institute and Misgav Yerushalayim, 2021), 38–39. Cohen lists these translations along with their bibliographical details, asserting in many instances that they are derived from the Ferrara Bible of 1553. However, in reality, they resemble the Ferrara Bible due to the translation methods employed by the Jews, as elaborated upon below.

20   Ibid., 37–58.

21   Lazar, "Targume"; Pueyo Mena, "Biblias romanceadas"; ibid., "Ladino Bible Translations," in *Manual of Judaeo-Romance Linguistics and Philology*, eds. G. Mensching and F. Savelsberg (Berlin: De Gruyter, 2023), 209–31.

The front page of the Constantinople Pentateuch (CP) provides the following information: *Ḥamisha Ḥumshey Tora ketubim biktab Ashuri, 'im Haftarot vehamesh Megillot ... Targum hamiqra belashon Yevani ulshon La'az ... Kostandina, Defus Eliezer ben Gershom Sonsino, Š"Z* ("The five Chumashim of the Torah, with Haftarot and the five scrolls ... the translation of the Bible in the Greek language and Ladino, Constantinople, Sonsino Print House, [year] 307 [1547]").

The CP edition includes the Hebrew text at the center of the page, with Ladino and Judeo-Greek translations in Hebrew vocalized letters on either side of the Hebrew text. On top of the page, Onkelos' Aramaic translation is printed in Hebrew vocalized letters, and at the bottom, Rashi's explanations are presented in smaller non-vocalized square letters.[22] It is worth noting that the *Haftarot* and the five scrolls are absent in the text, presumably not printed despite the intentions of the printers.

The Ferrara Bible (FB) was exclusively published in Latin letters, aligning with the medieval tradition of Bible translation. Many discussions on the translations mentioned earlier regarded the Ferrara Bible as a direct continuation of this medieval tradition. The text is presented in two columns, and notably, the Hebrew text is not included.

The title page of the Ferrara Bible reads: *BIBLIA En lengua Española traduzida palabra por palabra de la verdad Hebrayca por muy excelente letrados, vista y examinada por el oficio de la Inquisición Con priuillegio del Yllustrissimo Señor Duque de Ferrara* ("The Bible in the Spanish language translated word-for-word from the true Hebrew by excellent translators, shown and examined by the Inquisition's office. With the right of the highly authored Duke of Ferrara").[23] The names of the publishers, Yom Tov Atias and Abraham Usque, are printed on the back of the title page.

---

22   See image 3.1. J. Hacker, "Defuse Kushta bame'a hashesh 'esre," ["The Printing Houses of Constantinople in the Sixteenth Century,"] *Areshet* 5 (1972): 482–83, no. 144; L. Amigo Espada, *El Pentateuco de Constantinopla y la Biblia medieval romaneceada judeo-española* [*The Pentateuch of Constantinople and the Medieval Romance Judeo-Spanish Bible*] (Salamanca: Universidad Pontificia, 1983); Cohen, *Thesaurus*, 37–8.

23   See image 3.2. L. Wiener, "The Ferrara Bible," *Modern Language Notes* 10 (1896): 81–85; ibid., "The Ferrara Bible," *Modern Language Notes* 11 (1896): 24–42, 84–105; M. Morreale, "La Biblia de Ferrara y el Pentateuco de Constantinopla," ["The Ferrara Bible and the Pentateuch of Constantinople,"] *Tesoro de los judíos sefaradíes* 5 (1962): 85–91; I.M. Hassán and Á. Berenguer Amador, eds., *Introducción a la Biblia de Ferrara* [*Introduction to the Ferrara Bible*] (Madrid: Comisión Nacional Quinto Centenario, 1994); F.J. del Barco, "Las formas verbales en las biblias de Alba y Ferrara: ¿fidelidad al texto hebreo?," ["Verb forms in the Alba and Ferrara Bibles: Fidelity to the Hebrew Text?,"] *Sefarad* 64 (2004): 243–67.

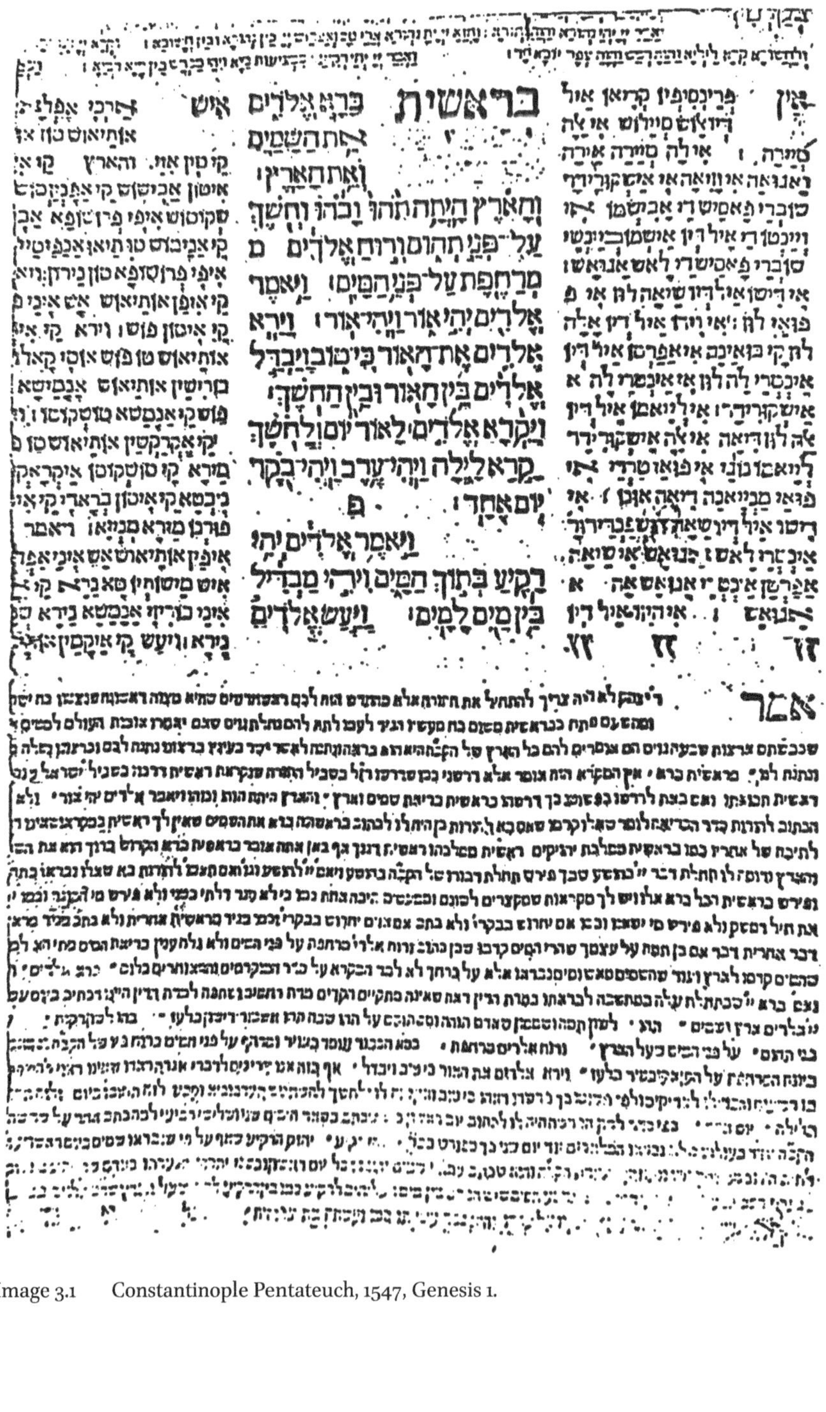

בראשית ברא אלהים את השמים ואת הארץ. והארץ היתה תהו ובהו וחשך על פני תהום ורוח אלהים מרחפת על פני המים. ויאמר אלהים יהי אור ויהי אור. וירא אלהים את האור כי טוב ויבדל אלהים בין האור ובין החשך. ויקרא אלהים לאור יום ולחשך קרא לילה ויהי ערב ויהי בקר יום אחד. ויאמר אלהים יהי רקיע בתוך המים ויהי מבדיל בין מים למים. ויעש אלהים

Image 3.1 Constantinople Pentateuch, 1547, Genesis 1.

GENESIS 17

Dio sobre las çiudades q̃ en sus derredores y no persiguieron empos hijos de Yahacob. Y vino Yahacob a Luz q̃ en tierra de Kenahã ella Bethel el y todo el pueblo q̃ con el. Y fragua alli ara y llamo al lugar el Bethel q̃ alli se descubrieron a el los angeles ẽ su huyr delãte su hermano. Y murio Deborah a lechadera de Ribkah y fue ẽterrada de baxo a Bethel debaxo de la ẽzina y llamo su nõbre Enzina del llãto. Y apareciosse el Dio a Yahacob mas ẽ su venir de Padã arã y bẽdixo a el y dixo a el el Dio: tu nombre Yahacob no sera llamado tu nõbre mas Yahacob q̃ salvo Ysrael sera tu nombre y llamo a su nõbre Ysrael. Y dixo a el el Dio yo Dio abastado fruchiguate y muchiguate: gẽte y congregacion de gẽtes sera de ti y reyes de tus lomos saldrã. Y a la tierra q̃ di a Abrahã y a Ysbac a ti la dare y a tu simiẽ empos ti dare a la tierra. Y alçosse de sobre el el Dio en el lugar q̃ fablo cõ el. Y paro Yahacob estãçia en el lugar q̃ fablo con el estãçia de piedra y tẽplo sobre ella tẽplãça y vazio sobre ella azeite. Y llamo Yahacob nombre del lugar q̃ fablo con el alli el Dio Bethel. Y movieronse de Bethel y fue aun como trecho de tierra por venir a Ephrath y pario Rahel y endurescoisse en su parir. Y fue en su ẽdurescerse en su parir y dixo a ella la partera no temas q̃ tambien este a ti hijo. Y fue en salir su alma q̃ murio y llamo su nombre Benoni y su padre llamo a el Binyamin. Y murio Rahel y fue enterrada en carrera de Ephrath ella Bethlahem. Y paro Yahacob estãçia sobre su fuessa ella estãçia de fuessa de Rahel fasta oy. Y moviosse Ysrael y tendio su tienda de allẽ de a torre de Heder. Y fue en morar Ysrael en la tierra essa y anduvo Reuben y yazio con Bilha mançeba de su padre y oyo Ysrael. Y fueron hijos de Yahacob doze. Hijos de Leah primogenito de Yahacob Reuben y Simhon y Levi y Yehudah y Ysahar y Zebulun. Hijos de Rahel Yoseph y Binyamin. Y hijos de Bilha sierva de Rahel Dan y Naphtali. Y hijos de Zilpa sierva de Leah Gad y Asser: estos hijos de Yahacob q̃ fueron nascidos a el ẽ Padã aram. Y vino Yahacob a Ysbac su padre a Mamre ciudad de Arbah ella Hebron q̃ moro alli Abrahã y Ysbac. Y fueron dias de Ysbac ciento y ochẽta años. Y trãsiosse Ysbac y murio y fue apañado a sus pueblos viejo y harto de dias y enterraron a el Hesau y Yahacob sus hijos.

Cap. 36.

Y estos generançios de Hesau el Edom. Hesau tomo a sus mugeres de hijas de Kenahan: a Hadah hija de Elõ el hitheo y a Aholibamah hija de Hanah hija de Zibhon el heveo. Y a Basmath hija de Ysmahel hermana de Nebayoth. Y pario Hadah a Hesau a Eliphaz y Basmath pario a Rehuel. Y Aholibamah pario a Yehus y a Yahlã y a Korah: estos hijos de Hesau q̃ fueron nascidos a el en tierra de Kenahã. Y tomo Hesau a sus mugeres y a sus hijos y a sus hijas y a todas almas de su casa y a su ganado y a toda su quatropea y a toda su cõpra q̃ gano en tierra de Kenahã: y anduvo a tierra (otra) de delãte Yahacob su hermano. Que fue su facultad mucha de estar ayuna y no podia tierra de sus moradas por soportar a ellos de delante sus ganados. Y estuvo Hesau en monte de Sehir: Hesau el Edom. Y estos generançios de Hesau padre de Edom: en monte de Sehir. Estos nombres de hijos de Hesau: Eliphaz hijo de Hadah muger de Hesau: Rehuel hijo de Basmath muger de Hesau. Y fueron hijos de Eliphaz Theman Omar Zepho y Gahatham y Kenaz. Y Thimnah fue mançeba a Eliphaz hijo de Hesau y pario a Eliphaz a

C

Image 3.2 Ferrara Bible, 1553, Genesis, 35–36.

The Ferrara Bible was published in both Jewish and Christian versions. The Jewish version was dedicated to Doña Gracia and signed by Yom Tov Atias and Abraham Usque, as mentioned earlier. The Christian version was dedicated to Don Hércole da Este al duque and signed by Jerónimo de Vargas y Duarte Pinel (the Christian names of the formers). Both versions are believed to have been written by *Anusim* who returned to Judaism, with some minor variations between them.[24] The discussion below pertains to the Jewish version.

Comparison of the Translations

I have selected two examples from Genesis 49:8 and Deuteronomy 33:7 to compare medieval and Ladino Bible translations. However, other verses could have been chosen to demonstrate the differences as well. Both verses pertain to the blessing bestowed upon Judah, first by Jacob and then by Moses. In these verses, Judah is appointed as a leader to his brothers, symbolizing the Jewish people. Judah emerges as the hero who leads them against their enemies. The formulation of the verses differs, offering an opportunity to highlight distinctions between medieval and Ladino translations.

The medieval translations are sourced from the *Corpus Biblia Medieval*,[25] with a focus on manuscripts considered the most Jewish in nature based on previous studies, namely E3, E19, and Arragel. Ladino translations are extracted from Lazar's transliteration of CP and the copy of FB.[26]

During this period, orthography was inconsistent. For example, in FB, the letters *v—u*, *i—j*, and sometimes *y* alternated freely, indicating either consonants or vowels (e.g., *Jvda—juda—Iuda* ("Judah"), *serviz—çerujz—ceruiz* ("neck, nape"), *aty—a ti* ("to you"). In CP, the Hebrew letter *bet* is occasionally marked with a diacritic, suggesting its pronunciation as [v], although the spelling with *b* in the Latin script versions likely indicated [v] or [β] pronunciation, as in *serviz* (שיר'בֿי). In FB, the letter *x* represents the sound [š] (like *sh* in "show"). The symbol "&" alternates with *e/E*, both indicating "and." Particles

---

24   One notable difference arises from the interpretation of the Hebrew word *'almā*, translated as *moça* [mosa] meaning "young woman" in the Jewish FB and as *virgen* meaning "virgin" in Isaiah 7:14. See M. Orfali, "Contexto teologico y social de la *Biblia de Ferrara*," ["Theological and Social Context of the Ferrara Bible,"] in Hassán and Berenguer Amador, *Introducción*, 229–49, esp. 232.

25   Consulted September 27, 2023.

26   M. Lazar, ed., *The Ladino Scriptures: Constantinople—Salonica* [*1540–1572*], I (Lancaster, CA: Labyrinthos, 2000), 106, 560; ibid., *The Ladino Bible of Ferrara* [*1553*] (Culver City, CA: Labyrinthos, 1992), 62, 181.

are attached to words or other particles (e.g., *del—de el* ["of the"], *ati—a ti* ["to you"]).

The translated versions will be presented first for each verse followed by their analysis. Tables 3.1 and 3.2 in the Appendix show the variations in the translations of each word.

Genesis 49:8

יְהוּדָה אַתָּה יוֹדוּךָ אַחֶיךָ יָדְךָ בְּעֹרֶף אֹיְבֶיךָ יִשְׁתַּחֲווּ לְךָ בְּנֵי אָבִיךָ

[yəhūdā 'attā yōdūkā 'aḥeykā yādəkā be'oref 'oyḇeykā yištaḥăwū ləkā bəneʸ 'āḇīkā]

"Judah, thou art he whom thy brethren shall praise: thy hand shall be in the neck of thine enemies; thy father's children shall bow down before thee."

Medieval Translations

E3: juda aty loar te han tus hermanos la tu mano sera enlas çerujzes de tus enemjgos omjllar te han los fijos de tu padre

E19: juda aty bendiran tus hermanos tu mano sera enel pescueço de tus enemjgos obedesçeran & omjllaran aty tus hermanos fijos de tu padre

Arragel: Juda tu loar te han los tus hermanos la tu mano sera en la çeruiz de tus enemigos adoraran ati los fiios del tu padre

Ladino translations

CP: Yehudah tu loartean tus ermanos, tu mano en cerviz de tus enemigos encorvarsean a ti hijos de tu padre

FB: Yehudah tu loartean tus hermanos tu mano en çeruiz de tus enemigos encoruarsean a ti hijos de tu padre

Deuteronomy 33:7

וְזֹאת לִיהוּדָה וַיֹּאמַר שְׁמַע יהוה קוֹל יְהוּדָה וְאֶל־עַמּוֹ תְּבִיאֶנּוּ יָדָיו רָב לוֹ וְעֵזֶר מִצָּרָיו תִּהְיֶה׃

[wəzot līhūdā wayyomar šəma' YHWH qōl yəhūdā və'ɛl 'ammō təḇī'ɛnnū yādāw rāḇ lō və'ezɛr miṣṣārāw tihyɛ]

"And this is the blessing of Judah: and he said, Hear, Lord, the voice of Judah, and bring him unto his people: let his hands be sufficient for him; and be thou and help to him from his enemies."

Medieval Translations

> E3: E a juda dixo oya el señor la boz de juda & al su pueblo metera sus manos abasten ael & ayuda de sus angustiadores sera
>
> E19: esto dixo a juda señor dios oye la boz de juda & traelo asu pueblo & sus manos le abasten para sus enemjgos sea ayudado
>
> Arragel: & esta oraçion fizo por juda & dixo asy oye señor la boz de juda & aduzelo asu pueblo [pelearan por el] abonden le sus manos & sey le ayudador de sus enemjgos

Ladino translations

> CP: Y esta a Yehuda, y dišo: oye YY en bozde Yehudah y asu pueblo lo traeras, sus manos abasto a el y ayuda de sus angustiadores seras
>
> FB: Y esta a Yehudah, y dixo: oye A. boz de Yehudah y a su pueblo lo traeras, sus manos abasto a el y ayuda de sus angustiadores seras

The comparison of the translations of these verses leads to the following generalizations (ignoring orthographic variations and using standard Spanish spelling in the discussion when applied):

(i) All the translations share the renderings of *'oyḇeyḵā* ("your enemies") as *tus enemigos*, and *yāḏāw* ("his hands") as *sus manos*.

(ii) Despite the different orthographies (Hebrew vs. Latin), the Ladino translations exhibit more resemblance to each other in both verses than they do to the medieval translations. The only disparity among them is revealed in the translation of the word *qōl* ("voice [of]"), where CP translates it as *en boz de* ("in voice of"), whereas FB translates it as *boz de* ("'voice of") in Deuteronomy, both without the definite article. All the medieval texts translate it similarly as *la boz de* ("the voice of").

(iii) Two words show fundamental differences between the medieval and Ladino translations: the translation of proper names and God's name:

   a. Hebrew proper names and place names are transcribed in the Ladino translations, while they are rendered into their Spanish equivalents in the medieval translations. In both verses, Judah's name appears in its Hebrew pronunciation, יהודה—Yehudah, in the Ladino translations, and in its Spanish form, *Juda*, in the medieval translations.

   b. God's name, spelled in Hebrew texts as *yhwh*, appears in the abbreviated spelling in the translations: יי (*yy*) in Hebrew script and *A.* in the Latin script, both referring to the pronunciation of [Adonay]. The medieval translations vary in their renderings: *el señor* ("the Lord") (E3), *señor dios* ("Lord God") (E19), and *señor* ("Lord") (Arragel).

The first feature extends to other proper names and toponyms in the Ladino translations. For example, the name Moses appears as משה [Moshe] in Hebrew script Ladino and as *Moseh* in the Latin script Ladino translations, whereas the medieval translations opt for the Spanish equivalent *Moisen* or *Moises*. The same applies to words like ירדן—*Yarden* vs. *Jordan*; יעקב—*Yahacob* vs. *Jacob*; ירושלים—*Yerusalaim* vs. *Jerusalén*, etc.[27]

The second feature pertains to the naming of God. In all the Ladino texts, YHWH is translated by יי or *A*. When the word אלהים appears in the Hebrew text,[28] it is consistently translated in the Ladino translations as *el Dio*, rather than *Dios*, *el Dios*, or *el señor* in the medieval translations.

(iv) Some translations are shared by most, but not all: *'aḥeykā* ("your brothers" is translated as *tus (h)ermanos* by most translations, except by Arragel, which uses *los tus hermanos* with the addition of the definite article; *'ābīkā* ("your father") is rendered as *tu padre*, except for Arragel, which uses *el tu padre*, again with the addition of the definite article; *šəmaʿ* ("listen") is translated as *oye*, except for E3, which employs the subjunctive form *oya*; *vəʾɛl-ʿammō* ("and unto his people") is rendered as *a su pueblo* (E19) without the connective particle, *& al su pueblo* ("and unto his people") with the addition of a definite article (E3), and *y/& a su pueblo* by all others.

The examples in (i) and (iv) involve commonly used words such as *enemigo, mano, hermano, padre, pueblo*. Hence, the variations are not very significant, typically involving the occasional addition of a definite article or the deletion of a connective particle.

(v) The medieval translations reveal some lexical variations among themselves in the translation of the Hebrew words, for instance:
   a. *yōdūkā* ("[they] will praise you"): *bendiran* ("[they] will bless you") (E19), *loar te han* ("[they] will praise you") (E3, Arragel + CP, FB *loartean*).
   b. *ʿorɛf* ("[back] neck"): *pescuezo* (E19), *cerviz* (all others).

---

27 O. (Rodrigue) Schwarzwald, "Personal Names, Toponyms, and Gentilic Nouns in Ladino and Spanish Translations of the Bible," *El Presente* 8–9 (2015): 209–28.
28 In CP and other texts, the word is spelled as אלדים ['ldym] to prevent the consecutive occurrence of the letters *h* and *y* of YHWH.

c. *yištaḥăwū ləḵā* ("[they] will bow down before you"): *omillar*[29] *te han* ("they will bow to you") (E3), *obedesçeran & omjllaran a ti* ("they will obey and bow to you") (E19), *adoraran a ti* ("they will admire you") (Arragel) vs. *encorvarsean a ti* ("they will bow down to you") (CP, FB).

d. *təḇīʾennū* ("you will bring him"): *meterá* ("he will put") (E3), *& traelo* ("and [you] bring him") (E19), *& aduzelo [pelearan por el]* ("and [you] adduce him [i.e., will fight for him]") (Arragel) vs. *lo traeras* ("you will bring him") (CP, FB).

e. *rāḇ lo* ("be sufficient for him"): *abasten a el* (E3), *le abasten* ("will be sufficient for him") (E19), *abonden* ("will suffice") (Arragel) vs. *abasto a el* ("was enough for him") (CP, FB)

f. *ʿezɛr* ("help"): *sea ayudado* ("will be helped") (E19), *ayudador* ("helper") (Arragel), *ayuda* ("help") (all others)

g. *ṣārāw* ("his enemies"): *sus enemigos* ("his enemies") (E19), *sus angustiadores* ("his distressings") (E3 + CP, FB)

The Ladino translations exhibit striking similarities with E3 in cases a, b, f, and g, and with Arragel in cases a and b. They also share a resemblance with E19, using the same verb in a different conjugation—*traer* ("to bring") in d and *abastar* ("be enough") in e, which is also employed in E3.

From a lexical standpoint as presented in (v), E3 appears to be the closest to the Ladino translations. It shares an identical choice of words in four cases and shows a close resemblance in two other instances. On the other hand, Arragel has identical translations for words in only two cases, and E19 has a resemblance in the choice of verbs in two instances, albeit with different forms.

(vi) There is a syntactic difference between the medieval and Ladino translations. While Ladino translations faithfully adhere to the Hebrew syntax word-for-word, the medieval translations exhibit variation:

a. Hebrew grammar does not necessitate a copulative verb between the subject and the predicate in nominal sentences. Consequently, Ladino translations omit a copulative verb, unlike the medieval

---

29 The verb *omillar*, an Old Spanish word, mainly found in religious texts, is documented in the Passover Ladino Haggadot after 1800 as a translation of the verb *qād* ("bow"). This stands in contrast to Hebrew *hištaḥăwā*, which translates to "bow down" or "prostrate oneself" and is generally rendered as *encorvar*. The linguistic evolution and contextual shifts in religious texts provide valuable insights into language usage and cultural expressions. See O. (Rodrigue) Schwarzwald, *Milon hahagadot shel Pesaḥ beladino [A Dictionary of the Ladino Passover Haggadot]* (Jerusalem: Magnes, 2008), 194–95.

translations. For instance, in the clause *yādəkā be'oref 'oybeykā* ("thy hand shall be in the neck of thine enemies") in Genesis, where the literal translation is "your hand in neck (of) your enemies," the verb *ser* ("be") is added in the medieval translations: *sera* (E3, E19, Arragel).

b. Three of the medieval translations interpret the word *'attā* ("you") as *a ti* ("to you") changing it from the head of a *casus pendens* structure to a simple complementizer of a verb. The Ladino translations and Arragel render it literally as *tu* ("you").

c. The connective &/E ("and") is either added or deleted in some verses, not in accordance with the Hebrew text. For example, it is absent in the translation of Deuteronomy for the phrase *wəzot* ("and this") in E19. Additionally, while *yādāw* ("his hands") is translated as *sus manos*, E19 adds & ("and") in front of the expression.

d. There is a change in word order and meaning in these instances: (a) *E a Juda dixo* ("and to Judah [he] said") in E3; *esto dixo a Juda* ("this [he] said to Judah") in E19; (b) *señor dios oye la boz de juda* ("Lord God, hear the voice of Judah") in E19, as opposed to "Hear, Lord, the voice of Judah"; (c) *& traelo a su pueblo* ("and bring him to his people") instead of "to his people, bring him" in E19; (d) *& sus manos le abasten para sus enemigos sea ayudado* ("and his hands are enough for his enemies to be helped") in E19, rather than "let his hands be sufficient for him, and be thou and help to him from his enemies"; (e) *& sey le ayudador de sus enemigos* ("and be the helper from his enemies") in Arragel, as opposed to "and be the help to him from his enemies" in Deuteronomy.

e. Some medieval translations include additional explanations, such as *obedesçeran & omjllaran* ("they will [obey and] bow") in Genesis and *tus hermanos fijos de* ("your [brethren] sons of") in E19 in Genesis. Arragel provides explanations for the initial words of the verse from Deuteronomy: *& esta oraçion fizo por juda"* ("and [this oration (he) made] for Judah"), adding *& dixo asy* ("and (he) said [so]"). Subsequently, he further explains: *& aduzelo asu pueblo [pelearan por el] abonden le"* ("and bring forward his people [they will fight for him] will suffice him").

The syntactic variations underscore that while medieval translations convey the content of the Hebrew verses, they do not strictly adhere to the structure of the Hebrew text, unlike the Ladino translations.

Conclusion

The Spanish language used by Jews immediately after the expulsion from Spain closely resembled Iberian varieties of Spanish, with some specific features developed in their speech during their time in Spain.[30] Their language was influenced by their Jewish education in Hebrew, and they customarily used the Hebrew script for writing. The use of Hebrew proper names was common among Jews, and they preferred the term *Dio* ("God") over the Spanish *Dios*. The Jews retained many Jewish words related to the Jewish calendar and life cycle. Sunday was referred to as *alḥad* ("the one, the first") instead of Spanish *domingo*. Additionally, they coined words like *desmazalado* ("poor, unlucky") from the Hebrew word *mazal*, which became part of the Spanish dictionary.[31]

The formation of Judeo-Spanish began in the Middle Ages and continued to develop independently after the expulsion from Spain in 1492.[32] Despite their dispersion, particularly in the Ottoman Empire, various communities maintained their distinct Iberian dialects and old Spanish traditions during the sixteenth century. Over time, Judeo-Spanish evolved from the seventeenth century into a *Koiné* with various dialects, incorporating influences from local languages and natural language evolution.[33]

The Bible held sacred value for the Jews, preventing them from making changes in the scriptures. This reverence extended to Ladino translations, maintaining a strict adherence to the original Hebrew text. The analyzed examples from Genesis and Deuteronomy illustrate the fidelity of Ladino translations compared to medieval ones, whether written in Hebrew or Latin script. Despite spelling differences, the translation of the Ferrara Bible in Latin letters closely aligns with the Constantinople Pentateuch in Hebrew letters, highlighting the enduring impact of oral tradition.

---

30 D.M. Bunis, "The Language of the Sephardim: A Historical Overview," in *Moreshet Sepharad: The Sephardi Legacy*, ed. H. Beinart (Jerusalem: Magnes Press, 1992), 399–422; O. (Rodrigue) Schwarzwald, "Judeo-Spanish Studies," in *Oxford Handbook of Jewish Studies*, ed. M. Goodman (Oxford: Oxford University Press, 2002), 572–600.

31 It is noteworthy that this Judeo-Spanish word was documented in non-Jewish texts until the seventeenth century, as per CORDE. See J. Corominas and J.A. Pascual, *Diccionario crítico etimológico castellano e hispánico* (Madrid: Gredos, 1981–1991), 2: 469–70.

32 See the discussion above about the glossary from the thirteenth century.

33 L. Minervini, "La formación de la *Koiné* Judeo-española en el siglo XVI," ["The Formation of a *Koiné* Judeo-Spanish in the Sixteenth Century,"] *Revue de Linguistique Romane* 263–64 (2002): 497–512; A. Quintana, "Judeo-Spanish: From Linguistic Segregation outside the Common Framework of Hispanic Languages to a *de facto standard*," in *Studies in Modern Hebrew and Jewish Languages Presented to Ora (Rodrigue) Schwarzwald*, ed. M. Muchnik and T. Sadan (Jerusalem: Carmel, 2012), 697–714.

The analysis of the use of common words in both medieval and Ladino translations, as well as the shared basic vocabulary and grammatical features with Spanish, emphasizes the strong connection between Judeo-Spanish and its Iberian roots.

The observations about the differences in spelling between the Ferrara Bible in Latin letters and the Constantinople Pentateuch in Hebrew letters, despite their textual similarities, highlight the resilience of oral traditions and the influence they had on written language. This underscores the significance of community practices and the preservation of language through religious texts.

In addition to the calque word-for-word translations, Ladino texts used the traditional proper names and God's name as shown in (iii) above. They preserved some old words in the translations such as *omillar* and refrained from changing word order or adding any explanations.[34]

In contrast, medieval translations, whether made by Jews or based on the Hebrew Bible, did not adhere to the same principles. Syntactic and lexical variations abound, as demonstrated in the previous sections (v) and (vi). While E3 shows some resemblance to Ladino translations, it did not serve as their direct basis. The use of some common words in both medieval and Ladino translations as shown in (i), (ii) and (iv) above is expected given their shared Iberian roots, with Judeo-Spanish maintaining a fundamental connection to Spanish despite its unique features.

The comparison between the Ladino translations and the medieval ones, including the Ferrara Bible, sheds light on the persistence of certain linguistic traditions and the distinctiveness of Judeo-Spanish. This historical and linguistic exploration offers insights into the intricate journey of Judeo-Spanish, reflecting its resilience, evolution, and the diverse influences that have contributed to its distinct character of the Ladino translations over the centuries. This linguistic continuity, despite variations and unique developments, provides valuable insights into the historical and cultural dimensions of the language.

---

34   Cf. A. Quintana, "Relexificación romance de la Biblia hebrea y sus consecuencias en los ladinamientos y las traducciones en ladino y romance," ["Romance Relexification of the Hebrew Bible and its Consequences in Ladinations and Translations in Ladino and Romance,"] *Anuario de Estudios Medievales* 53, no. 1 (2023): 351–79. One can find more on the Jewish nature of the Ladino translations in O. (Rodrigue) Schwarzwald, "On the Jewish Nature of Medieval Spanish Biblical Translations: Linguistic Differences between Medieval and Post Exilic Spanish Translations," *Sefarad* 70 (2010): 117–40.

Bibliography

Alfonso, Esperanza. *Translating the Hebrew Bible in Medieval Iberia: Oxford, Bodleian Library, Ms Hunt. 268, with a Linguistic Study and Glossary of the Le'azim by Javier del Barco*. Leiden: Brill, 2021.

Amigo Espada, Lorenzo. *El Pentateuco de Constantinopla y la Biblia medieval romaneceada judeo-española*. [*The Pentateuch of Constantinople and the Medieval Romance Judeo-Spanish Bible*.] Salamanca: Universidad Pontificia, 1983.

--------. "El influjo del latín en el vocabulario de la Biblia de Alba. Algunas voces raras." ["The Latin Influence on the Vocabulary of the Alba Bible: Some Rare Words."] *Helmantica* 46 (1995): 183–200.

Baer, Yitzhak. *A History of the Jews in Christian Spain*, vol. II, trans. L. Schoffman. Philadelphia, PA: Jewish Publication Society of America, 1961.

Berger, Samuel. "Les bibles castellanes." ["The Spanish Bibles."] *Romania* 28 (1899): 360–408, 508–567.

--------. *La Bible romane au Moyen Age (Bibles provençales, vaudoises, catalanes, italiennes, castillanes et portugaises)* [*The Romance Bible in the Medieval Period*.] Genève: Slatkine, 1977.

Bunis, David M. "The Language of the Sephardim: A Historical Overview." In *Moreshet Sepharad: The Sephardi Legacy*, edited by Haim Beinart, 399–422. Jerusalem: Magnes Press, 1992.

--------. "Tres formas de ladinar la biblia en Italia en los siglos XVI–XVII." ["Three Way of Ladinizing the Bible in Italy during the Sixteenth and Seventeenth Centuries."] In *Introducción a la Biblia de Ferrara*, edited by Iacob M. Hassán and Ángel Berenguer Amador, 315–45. Madrid: Comisión Nacional Quinto Centenario, 1994

--------. "Translating from the Head and from the Heart: The Essentially *Oral* Nature of the *Ladino* Bible-translation Tradition." In *Hommage á Haïm Vidal Sephiha*, edited by Winfried Busse and Marie-Christine Varol-Bornes, 337–57. Bern: Peter Lang, 1996.

Cohen, Dov. *Otsar hasfarim beladino 1490–1960*. [*Thesaurus of the Ladino Book 1490–1960: An Annotated Bibliography*.] Jerusalem: The Ben-Zvi Institute and Misgav Yerushalayim, 2021. [In Hebrew.]

CORDE: Corpus diacrónico del español. Real Academia Española: Banco de datos. http://corpus.rae.es/cordenet.html.

Corominas, Joan, and José Antonio Pascual. *Diccionario crítico etimológico castellano e hispánico*. [*Critical Etymological Dictionary of Castilian and Hispanic*] Madrid: Gredos, 1981–1991.

Del Barco, Francisco Javier. "Las formas verbales en las biblias de Alba y Ferrara: ¿fidelidad al texto hebreo?" ["Verb forms in the Alba and Ferrara Bibles: Fidelity to the Hebrew Text?"] *Sefarad* 64 (2004): 243–267.

Enrique-Arias, Andrés. "Texto subyacente hebreo e influencia latinizante en la traducción de la Biblia de Alba de Moisés Arragel." ["Underlying Hebrew Text and Latinizing Influence in Moisés Arragel's Translation of the Biblia de Alba."] In *Traducción y estandarización. La incidencia de la traducción en la historia de los lenguajes especializados* [*Translation and Standardization: The Impact of Translation in the History of Specialized Languages*], edited by Victoria Alsina Keith, 99–112. Madrid: Iberoamericana, 2004.

———. "Sobre el parentesco entre la Biblia de Alba y la Biblia de la Real Academia de la Historia MS 87." ["On the Relationship between the Alba Bible and the Bible of the Royal Academy of History MS 87."] *Romance Philology* 59 (2006): 241–64.

———. "Dos problemas en el uso de corpus diacrónicos del español: perspectiva y comparabilidad." ["Two Problems in the Use of Diachronic Corpora of Spanish: Perspective and Comparability."] *Scriptum* Digital 1 (2012): 85–106.

———., ed. *Traducción bíblica e historia de las lenguas iberorománicas*. [*Biblical Translation and the History of the Ibero-Romance Languages*.] Berlin: De Gruyter, 2022.

Enrique-Arias, Andrés, and Cristina Matute. "El estudio morfosintáctico de la lengua de la 'Biblia de Alba': Un acercamiento a la variación discursiva y dialectal del español en el siglo XV." ["The Morphosyntactic Study of the Language of the 'Bible of Alba': An Approach to the Discursive and Dialectal Variation of Spanish in the Fifteenth Century."] In *Actes du XXVe congres international de linguistique et de philologie romanes (Innsbruck, 3–8 septiembre 2007)* 4, edited by Maria Iliescu, Heidi Siller-Runggaldier and Paul Danler, 115–123. Berlin: De Gruyter, 2010.

Enrique-Arias, Andrés, and Francisco Javier Pueyo Mena. *Corpus Biblia Medieval*. Since 2010. http://www.bibliamedieval.es, last accessed November 2023.

Girón Negrón Luis Manuel, and Andrés Enrique-Arias. "La 'Biblia' de Arragel y la edición de traducciones bíblicas del siglo XV." ["Arragel's 'Biblia' and the Edition of Biblical Translations in the Fifteenth Century."] *Helmántica* 190 (2012): 291–310.

Gutwirth, Eleazar. "Religión, historia y las biblias romanceadas." ["Religion, History, and the Romance Bibles."] *Revista Catalana de Teologia* 13 (1988): 115–134.

———. "La cultura material hispano-judía: entre la norma y la práctica." ["Spanish-Jewish Material Culture: Between Norm and Practice."] In *Una sefarad inventada? Los problemas de interpretación de los restos materiales de los judíos en España* [*An Invented Sepharad? The Problems of Interpretation of the Remained Materials of the Jews in Spain*], edited by Javier Castaño, 87–110. Córdoba: Ediciones El Almendro, 2014.

Hacker, Joseph. "Defuse Kushta bame'a hashesh 'esre." ["The Printing Houses of Constantinople in the Sixteenth Century."] *Areshet* 5 (1972): 457–93.

Hassán, Iacob M. "¿Es el ladino judeoespañol calco? (cfr. DRAE)." ["Is Ladino a Judeo-Spanish Calque?"] *Quaderons de Filologia. Estudis Lingüístics* IX (2004): 87–99.

Hassán Iacob M., and Ángel Berenguer Amador, eds., *Introducción a la Biblia de Ferrara*. [*Introduction to the Ferrara Bible*.] Madrid: Comisión Nacional Quinto Centenario, 1994.

Hauptmann, Oliver H. *Escorial Bible* I.j.4: *The Pentateuch*, 1. Philadelphia, PA: University of Pennsylvania Press, 1953.

Hauptmann, Oliver H., and Mark Gibson Littlefield. *Escorial Bible* I.j.4. Madison, WI: Hispanic Seminary of Medieval Studies, 1987.

Keller, Adrian. "The Making of the 'Biblia de Alba'." In *La Biblia de Alba in the Collection of the Palacio de Liria*, edited by Jeremy Schonfield, 147–56. Madrid and London: Fundacion Amigos de Sefarad, 1992.

Lazar, Moshe. "Targume hamiqra beladino." ["Bible translations in Ladino."] *Sefunot* 8 (1964): 337–375.

--------., ed. *Sēfer Tešuḇāh: A Ladino Compendium of Jewish Law and Ethics*. Culver City, CA: Labyrinthos, 1993.

--------., ed. *The Ladino Bible of Ferrara [1553]*. Culver City, CA: Labyrinthos, 1992.

--------., ed. *Biblia Ladinada: Escorial* I.j.3. Madison, WI: The Hispanic Seminary of Medieval Studies 1995.

--------., ed. *The Ladino Scriptures: Constantinople—Salonica [1540–1572]*, I–II. Lancaster, CA: Labyrinthos, 2000.

Minervini, Laura. *Testi giudeospagnoli medievali (Castiglia e Aragona)*, I–II. [*Judeo-Spanish Medieval Texts (Castile and Aragon)*.]. Napoli: Liguori Editore, 1992.

--------. "La formación de la Koiné Judeo-española en el siglo XVI." ["The Formation of a Koiné Judeo-Spanish in the Sixteenth Century."] *Revue de Linguistique Romane* 263–64 (2002): 497–512.

--------. "Jewish Multilingual and Multigraphic Texts in Christian Spain." In *Multilingual and Multigraphic Documents and Manuscripts of East and West*, edited by Giuseppe Mandalà and Inmaculada Pérez Martín, 407–23. Piscataway, NJ: Gorgias Press, 2018.

Morreale, Margherita. "Apuntes bibliográficos para la iniciación al estudio de las traducciones bíblicas medievales en castellano." ["Bibliographic Notes for the Introduction to the Study of Medieval Biblical Translations in Spanish."] *Sefarad* 20, no. 1 (1960): 66–109.

--------. "El glosario de Rabí Mosé Arragel en la 'Biblia de Alba'." ["Rabbi Moses Arragel's Glossary on the 'Biblia de Alba'."] *Bulletin of Hispanic Studies* 38 (1961): 145–52.

--------. "La Biblia de Ferrara y el Pentateuco de Constantinopla." ["The Ferrara Bible and the Pentateuch of Constantinople."] *Tesoro de los judíos sefaradíes* 5 (1962): 85–91.

Littlefield, Mark Gibson. *Escorial Bible* I.ii.19. Madison, WI: The Hispanic Seminary of Medieval Studies, 1992.

Llamas, José. *Biblia medieval romanceada judío-cristiana*. [*The Jewish-Christian Medieval Romance Bible*.] Madrid: CSIC, 1950.

Orfali, Moises. "Contexto teologico y social de la Biblia de Ferrara." ["Theological and Social Context of the Ferrara Bible."] In *Introducción a la Biblia de Ferrara*, edited by Iacob M. Hassán and Ángel Berenguer Amador, 229–49. Madrid: Comisión Nacional Quinto Centenario, 1994.

Pueyo Mena, Francisco Javier. "Biblias romanceadas y en ladino." ["Romance and Ladino Bibles."] In *Sefardíes: literatura y lengua de una nación dispersa. Actas del XV curso de verano «Cultura hispano-judía y sefardí», organizado por la Univ. de Castilla-La Mancha y la Asociación de Amigos del Museo Sefardí (Toledo, 5–8 sep. 2005)* [*Sephardis: Literature and Language of a Dispersed People.*], edited by Elena Romero Castelló, 193–263, Ciudad Real et al: Universidad de Castilla-La Mancha, 2008.

--------. "Ladino Bible Translations." In *Manual of Judaeo-Romance Linguistics and Philology*, edited by Guido Mensching, and Frank Savelsberg, 209–31. Berlin: De Gruyter, 2023.

Pueyo Mena, Francisco Javier, and Andrés Enrique Arias. "Los romanceamientos castellanos de la biblia hebrea compuestos en la Edad Media: manuscritos y traducciones." ["The Spanish-Romance Translations of the Hebrew Bible Composed in the Middle Ages: Manuscripts and Translations."] *Sefarad* 73 (2013): 165–224.

Quintana, Aldina. "From the Master's Voice to the Disciple's Script: Genizah Fragments of a Bible Glossary in Ladino." *Hispania Judaica Bulletin* 6 (2008): 187–235.

--------. "Judeo-Spanish: From Linguistic Segregation outside the Common Framework of Hispanic Languages to a de facto standard." In *Studies in Modern Hebrew and Jewish Languages Presented to Ora (Rodrigue) Schwarzwald*, edited by Malka Muchnik and Tsvi Sadan, 697–714. Jerusalem: Carmel, 2012.

--------. "Relexificación romance de la biblia hebrea y sus consecuencias en los ladinamientos y las traducciones en ladino y romance." ["Romance Relexification of the Hebrew Bible and its Consequences in Ladinations and Translations in Ladino and Romance."] *Anuario de Estudios Medievales* 53, no. 1 (2023): 351–79.

Schwarzwald (Rodrigue), Ora. "Judeo-Spanish Studies." In *Oxford Handbook of Jewish Studies*, edited by Martin Goodman, 572–600. Oxford: Oxford University Press, 2002.

--------. *Milon hahagadot shel Pesah beladino*. [*A Dictionary of the Ladino Passover Haggadot.*] Jerusalem: Magnes, 2008.

--------. "On the Jewish Nature of Medieval Spanish Biblical Translations: Linguistic Differences between Medieval and Post Exilic Spanish Translations." *Sefarad* 70 (2010): 117–40.

--------. "Personal Names, Toponyms, and Gentilic Nouns in Ladino and Spanish Translations of the Bible." *El Presente* 8–9 (2015): 209–28.

Sephiha, Haïm Vidal. *Le Ladino: Deutéronome*. Paris: Centre de Recherches Hispaniques, 1973.

Wiener, Leo. "The Ferrara Bible." *Modern Language Notes* 10 (1896): 81–85.

--------. "The Ferrara Bible." *Modern Language Notes* 11 (1896): 24–42, 84–105.

Appendix: Lexical Variations

Table 3.1   The Lexical Variations in Genesis 49: 8

	yəhūḏā	'attā	yōḏūḵā	'aḥɛyḵā	yāḏəḵā
E3	juda	aty	loar te han	tus hermanos	la tu mano sera
E19	juda	aty	bendiran	tus hermanos	tu mano sera
Arragel	Juda	tu	loar te han	los tus hermanos	la tu mano será
CP	Yehudah	tu	loartean	tus ermanos	tu mano
FB	Yehudah	tu	loartean	tus hermanos	tu mano

	be'orɛf	'oyḇɛyḵā	yištaḥǎwū	ləḵā	bəney	'āḇīḵā
E3	enlas çerujzes de	tus enemjgos	omjllar	te han	los fijos de	tu padre
E19	enel pescueço de	tus enemjgos	obedesçeran & omjllaran	aty	tus hermanos fijos de	tu padre
Arragel	en la çeruiz de	tus enemigos	adoraran	ati	los fiios d	el tu padre
CP	en serviz de	tus enemigos	encorvarsean	a ti	hijos de	tu padre
FB	en çeruiz de	tus enemigos	encoruarsean	a ti	hijos de	tu padre

Table 3.2   The Lexical Variations in Deuteronomy 33:7

	wəzot	līhūḏā	wayyomar	šəma'	YY
E3		E a juda	dixo	oya	el señor
E19	esto	a juda	dixo[35]	oye	señor dios
Arragel	& esta oraçion	fizo por juda	& dixo asy	oye	señor
CP	Y esta	a Yehuda	y dišo	oye	YY
FB	Y esta	a Yehudah	y dixo	oye	A.

---

35   The word order changed here: *esto dixo a Juda* ("this said to Judah"). It also changed in the next words: *señor dios oye la boz de juda* ("God, hear the voice of Judah").

Table 3.2   The Lexical Variations in Deuteronomy 33:7 (cont.)

	qōl	yəhūdā	və'ɛl-'ammō	təbī'ɛnnū	yādāw
E3	la boz de	juda	& al su pueblo	metera	sus manos
E19	la boz de	juda	asu pueblo	& traelo[36]	& sus manos
Arragel	la boz de	juda	asu pueblo	& aduzelo [pelearan por el]	sus manos
CP	en boz.de	Yehudah	y a.su pueblo	lo traeras	sus manos
FB	boz de	Yehudah	y a su pueblo	lo traeras	sus manos

	rāb	lō	və'ezɛr	miṣṣārāw	tihyɛ
E3	abasten	ael	& ayuda	de sus angustiadores	sera
E19	le abasten		sea ayudado sus enemjgos	para sus enemjgos[37]	
Arragel	abonden	le	ayudador	de sus enemigos	& sey[38]
CP	abasto	a el	y ayuda	de sus angustiadores	seras
FB	abasto	a el	y ayuda	de sus angustiadores	seras

---

36   The word order is: *and traelo asu pueblo* ("and bring him to his people").
37   Change of word order.
38   Change of word order.

Textual History as Reception History: Rabbi Meir's Text of Isa 21:11

Armin Lange

I have previously engaged with Rabbi Meir and his master copies in more detail elsewhere.[1] In this article, I would like to come back to one particular variant reading attributed to Rabbi Meir that illuminates how closely related the textual and interpretative histories of the Hebrew Bible can be. In the first part of my article, I will describe different types of variant readings that occur in the textual transmission of the Hebrew Bible and explain why they are important for the interpretative history of it. In the second part, I will explain who Rabbi Meir was and why he is of importance of the textual history of the Hebrew Bible. In the third part, I will discuss one variant reading in Isa 21:11, which is attributed to a manuscript of Rabbi Meir in more detail. At the end of my article, I will draw some conclusions about how a seemingly insignificant variant reading can strongly affect the history of interpretation of a particular biblical text.

1. Textual Variants and Their Impact on the Interpretative History of the Hebrew Bible

I distinguish several categories of variant readings in the textual history of the Jewish scriptures.[2] The most basic distinctions are between orthographic and textual variants, and between secondary and original readings. To identify original readings is subjective, especially if multiple different variant readings exist. Orthographic readings are of little importance for the interpretative history of the Hebrew Bible. However, alterations to the scriptural text by copyists

---

[1] Cf. A. Lange, "Rabbi Meir and the Severus Scroll," in *"Let the Wise Listen and Add to Their Learning" (Prov 1:5): Festschrift for Günter Stemberger on the Occasion of His 75th Birthday*, ed. C. Cordoni and G. Langer (Berlin: De Gruyter, 2016), 53–76; ibid. "An Interpretative Reading in the Isaiah Scroll of Rabbi Meir," in *Hā-ʾîsh Mōshe: Studies in Scriptural Interpretation in the Dead Sea Scrolls and Related Literature in Honor of Moshe J. Bernstein*, ed. B. Y. Goldstein, M. Segal, and G. J. Brooke (Leiden: Brill, 2018), 210–22.

[2] Cf. A. Lange, "1.2.2 Ancient Hebrew-Aramaic Texts: Ancient and Late Ancient Hebrew and Aramaic Jewish Texts," in *Textual History of the Bible*, vol. 1, *The Hebrew Bible*, part 1a: *Overview Articles*, ed. A. Lange and E. Tov (Leiden: Brill, 2016), 127–31.

© ARMIN LANGE, 2025 | DOI:10.30965/9783657796946_005
This is an open access chapter distributed under the terms of the CC BY-NC-ND 4.0 license.

or translators had a significant impact on how the biblical text was read and understood. Secondary variants can go back to

scribal errors,
editorial activities,
linguistic adjustment and actualization,
harmonization,
abbreviation (especially in the case of scribal excerpts),
expansion,
rewriting/redaction,
compilation,
recension,
exegesis/interpretation.

How much these types of secondary variants in the transmission of the biblical text participate in the overall modes of text production in the Ancient Near East becomes evident when the above list is compared to the modes of text production described by Karel van der Toorn: transcription, invention, compilation, expansion, adaption, and integration.[3]

If the majority of the readings of a textual witness are harmonizing, erroneous, or expansive, this textual witness should be characterized as being harmonizing, erroneous, or expansive, or a combination of any of the above characterizations as a whole.

(1) An erroneous text is thus a text the majority of whose secondary readings go back to scribal error. An example is the Masoretic Text of the book of Hosea.

(2) A harmonizing text is intertextual in nature and is characterized by harmonizations of one passage to another one. An example is the Qumran manuscript 4QDeut^n (4Q41). Among the fifty-one variant readings of 4QDeut^n towards the Masoretic Text (MT), the Samaritan Pentateuch (SP), and the Septuagint (LXX), Eshel[4] identified seventeen harmonizing readings. These harmonizing readings are especially common in Deut 5:6–21 and adjust the deuteronomic Decalogue, or Ten Commandments, to the one in Exod 20:2–17. The largest of these harmonizations can be found in the Sabbath command at the end of Deut 5:15, which is taken from Exod 20:11a.[5] The two versions of the

---

[3] Cf. K. van der Toorn, *Scribal Culture and the Making of the Hebrew Bible* (Cambridge, MA: Harvard University Press, 2007), 109–41.

[4] The below description of the harmonizing variants of 4QDeut^n is guided by E. Eshel, "4QDeut^n–A Text That Has Undergone Harmonistic Editing," *Hebrew Union College Annual* 62 (1991): 117–54.

[5] Cf., e.g., J. H. Tigay, "Conflation as a Redactional Technique," in *Empirical Models for Biblical Criticism* (Philadelphia, PA: University of Pennsylvania Press, 1985), 55–7; S. A. White, "The All

Decalogue give different reasons for the Sabbath command: In MT-Deut 5:15, the Sabbath commemorates that the Lord brought Israel out of Egypt. In MT Exod 20:11, the Sabbath commemorates that the Lord rested on the seventh day after six days of creating the world. Given these differences, the scribe of 4QDeutⁿ, or the scribe of his *Vorlage*, have combined the two reasons given in MT-Deut und MT-Exod by inserting a part of the Exodus Decalogue into the Deuteronomy Decalogue, resulting in a text that gives both reasons for the Sabbath command.

(3) An editorial text is characterized by small textual changes of usually a single word or less. These achieve linguistic, stylistic, and orthographic alterations as well as changes, which may correct inconsistencies.[6]

(4) Linguistic actualizations are adjustments in the language of a given text either in grammar, syntax, or vocabulary. An example can be found in 1 Sam 20:34 where MT reads וַיָּקָם יְהוֹנָתָן מֵעִם הַשֻּׁלְחָן (*vayakam yehonatan me'im hashulchan*), "Jonathan got up from the table," instead of ויפחז יהונתן מעל השלחן (*vayiphoz yehonatan me'im hashulchan*), "and Jonathan shot up from the table," in 4QSam^a. The MT reading replaces the rare and archaic word ויפחז (*vayiphoz*) with the common וַיָּקָם (*vayakam*) to make 1 Sam 20:34 comprehensible to the reader.[7] A biblical text the majority of whose secondary readings are characterized by such linguistic updating is a linguistically actualizing text. It is often also editorial in nature.

(5) Whether a text should be described as expansive, redactional, or a rewriting is often difficult to decide. Depending on how many expansions a text includes, and depending on the coherence of these expansions, I would characterize it either as expansive or as a redaction, that is, as a variant literary edition. If a biblical text includes many expansions which are disconnected from each other and accumulated to it in a long time, it should be characterized as expansive. Examples are the pre-Samaritan manuscripts from the Qumran library and the Samaritan Pentateuch (SP) which includes various expansions without argumentative coherence.[8]

Souls Deuteronomy and the Decalogue," *JBL* 109 (1990): 200–1; ibid., "Reading Deuteronomy in the Second Temple Period," in *Reading the Present in the Qumran Library: The Conception of the Contemporary by Means of Scriptural Interpretations*, ed. K. de Troyer and A. Lange (Atlanta, GA: SBL, 2005), 129–30; ibid., *Rewriting Scripture in Second Temple Times* (Grand Rapids, MI: Eerdmans, 2008), 31–2; Eshel, "4QDeutⁿ," 145–46; J. A. Duncan, "Excerpted Texts of *Deuteronomy* at Qumran," *RevQ* 18 (1997–98): 55–56.

6 For the category of editorial texts, see A. Lange, "4QXII^g (4Q82) as an Editorial Text," *Textus* 26 (2016): 87–119.
7 Cf. A. Lange, "Die Wurzel *phz* und ihre Konnotationen," *VT* 51 (2001): 500–1.
8 For the Samaritan Pentateuch and the pre-Samaritan manuscripts of the Qumran library, see S. White Crawford, "Samaritan Pentateuch," in *Textual History of the Bible*, vol. 1, *The Hebrew Bible*, part 1a: *Overview Articles*, ed. A. Lange and E. Tov (Leiden: Brill, 2016), 166–75.

(6) If the expansions of a text and other secondary readings form a coherent layer of text for which one author or group of authors is responsible, it should be described as a variant literary edition or redaction. The distinction between such a variant literary edition or redaction from a rewriting, also characterized as "rewritten Bible"[9], is a matter of degree. From a certain point onwards, the expansions and alterations to a base text become so significant that a new literary work is born. An example for a redaction or variant literary edition is the Masoretic text of the book of Jeremiah. Examples for rewritings include the book of *Jubilees* and the *Temple Scroll*, whose textual changes to the Torah are even more extensive than the ones applied to the book of Jeremiah by MT-Jeremiah. The grey area between rewriting on the one hand and redaction or variant literary edition on the other hand is enormous.

(7) An abbreviated text deletes individual passages out of a biblical book. The Canticles manuscript 4QCantª, for example, erases Canticles 4:8–6:10. An excerpted text, on the other hand, reduces a biblical book to a collection of several select passages for liturgical or other purposes. An example is 4QDeutⁿ which includes now only Deut 8:5–10 and 5:1–6:1.

(8) Examples for compilational texts are various Psalms manuscripts from Qumran which include a different repertoire and sequence of Psalms as indicated in this list:

a. MT-Ps (for MT-Ps the reader is referred to its critical editions)
b. 11QPsª (... Ps 101–103→... →109→... →118→104→147→105→146→148→... →121–132→119→135→136+118:1, 15, 16, 8, 9, X, 29?→145→154→Plea for Deliverance→Ps 139→137–138→Sir 51:13–30→Apostrophe to Zion→Ps 93→141→133→144→155→142–143→149–150→Hymn to the Creator→2 Sam 23,[1–]7→David's Compositions→Ps 140→134→151A→151B ...)

---

9 For variant literary editions, see the articles collected in K. Finsterbusch, R. E. Fuller, and A. Lange, eds., *Between Textual Criticism and Literary Criticism* (Tübingen: Mohr Siebeck, 2020); and, especially, E. Ulrich, *The Biblical Qumran Scrolls: Transcriptions and Textual Variants* (Leiden: Brill, 2010); and ibid., *The Dead Sea Scrolls and the Developmental Composition of the Bible* (Leiden: Brill, 2015). I have engaged in detail with the terminological debate about the term rewritten Bible in "In the Second Degree: Ancient Jewish Paratextual Literature in the Context of Graeco-Roman and Ancient Near Eastern Literature," in *In the Second Degree: Paratextual Literature in Ancient Near Eastern and Ancient Mediterranean Cultures and Its Reflections in Medieval Literature*, ed. P. S. Alexander, A. Lange, and R. Pillinger (Leiden: Brill, 2010), 3–40, and would like to direct the attention of the reader to this article and the other contributions to this volume regarding the debate about the term "rewritten Bible."

11QPsᵇ (Ps 77→78; 119; 118;1, 15–16; Plea for Deliverance; Apostrophe to Zion; Ps 141→133→144)

4QPsᵉ (Ps 76→77; 78; 81; 86; 88; 89; 103→109; 114; 115→116; 118→104; 105→146; 120; 125→126; 129→130)

c. 4QPsᵃ (Ps 5→6; 25; 31→33; 34→35→36; 38→71; 47; 53→54; 56; 62→63; 66→67; 69)

4QPsᵍ (Ps 31→33[→34→]35)

d. 4QPsᵇ (Ps 91[→]92[→]93[→]94; 96; 98; 99[→]100; 102→103[→]112; 113; 115; 116; [117→]118)

e. 4QPsᵈ (Ps 106→147→104)

f. 4QPsᶠ (Ps 22; 107; 109→Apostrophe to Zion; Eschatological Hymn[→] Apostrophe to Judah)

g. 4QPsᵏ (Ps 135[→]99)

(9) A recensional text, or recension, adjusts one biblical text to another one. An example among the Hebrew biblical Dead Sea Scrolls is 5QDeut: in this manuscript a later hand added four corrections toward the text of LXX-Deut. As these later adjustments seem to be systematic, they can be described as creating a recension toward to the Hebrew *Vorlage* of LXX-Deut.

(10) Exegetical readings occur often in the Qumran *Pesharim* and other interpretative texts, as well as biblical quotations in Second Temple and rabbinic literature, which alter the text quoted in their *lemmata* guided by their interpretations. But exegetical readings are not restricted to quotations of the Jewish scriptures in commentary literature and elsewhere. They occur in biblical manuscripts as well.[10] An example can be found in Qoh 5:5: Because MT-Qoh wants to avoid the impression of saying something negative about God, it changes the πρὸ προσώπου τοῦ θεοῦ (*pro prosopou tou Theou*), "before God," (לִפְנֵי הָאֱלֹהִים, *lifnei ha'elohim*) of the Hebrew-Vorlage of LXX-Qoh to לִפְנֵי הַמַּלְאָךְ (*lifnei hamal'akh*), "before the angel." The range of possible interpretations inserted by exegetical readings into the biblical text is almost infinite.

My list of examples shows that, next to exegetical readings, other forms of textual variation are important for the interpretative history of the Hebrew Bible. Even variant readings that developed by way of scribal error facilitated new interpretations of biblical verses. Often, even the difference of one character was enough to evoke new meaning. An example for this phenomenon is a reading that tractate *Taanit* 1.1 (64a) of the Palestinian Talmud (*Talmud yerushalmi*) attributes to an Isaiah Scroll of Rabbi Meir. To be able to understand this

---

10 For interpretative readings in the Torah, see esp. D. A. Teeter, *Scribal Laws: Exegetical Variation in the Textual Transmission of Biblical Law in the Late Second Temple Period* (Tübingen: Mohr Siebeck, 2014).

passage, it is necessary to explain who Rabbi Meir was and how the readings attributed to him in rabbinic literature need to be understood.

2. Rabbi Meir and the Readings Attributed to Him

Rabbi Meir[11] belonged to the third generation of Tannaim (second century CE). He is recognized as one of the most important rabbis of his time and is known both for his halakhic and haggadic achievements. Rabbi Meir was a scribe by profession[12] and various rabbinic texts mention highly respected copies of the Torah, Isaiah, and Psalms in his possession. BerR 9.5; 20:20; 94.9, *Midrash Bereshit Rabbati* on Gen 45:8, and y. Taan. 1.1 (64a) attest to particular variant readings which are attributed to a Torah Scroll of Rabbi Meir and his copy of Isaiah.

These readings of Rabbi Meir have been subject to surprisingly little scholarly attention.[13] Among the few existing studies, which address Meir's readings,

---

11   For Rabbi Meir and his life, see N. Goldstein Cohen, "Rabbi Meir, a Descendant of Anatolian Proselytes," *JJS* 23 (1972): 51–9; A. Oppenheimer and S. G. Wald, "Meir," in *Encyclopaedia Judaica*, ed. M. Berenbaum and F. Skolnik, (2nd ed., Detroit, MI: Macmillan Reference, 2007), 13: 776–77; G. Hasan-Rokem, "Rabbi Meir: The Illuminated and the Illuminating," in *Current Trends in the Study of Midrash*, ed. C. Bakhos; (Leiden: Brill, 2006), 227–44.

12   Cf. b. Er. 13a; b. Git. 67a; QohR 13a.

13   See N. Brüll, "R. Meir," *Jahrbücher für Jüdische Geschichte und Literatur* 1 (1874): 235–36; A. Epstein, "Ein von Titus nach Rom gebrachter Pentateuch-Codex und seine Varianten," *MGWJ* 34 (1885): 337–51; ibid., "Biblische Textkritik bei den Rabbinen," in *Recueil des travaux rédigés en mémoire du Jubilé scientifique de Daniel Chwolson*, ed. D. Günzburg (Berlin: Calvary, 1899), 42–56; M. H. Segal, "The Promulgation of the Authoritative Text of the Hebrew Bible," *JBL* 72 (1953): 45–46; E. Y. Kutscher, *The Language and Linguistic Background of the Isaiah Scroll (1Q Isaᵃ)* (Leiden: Brill, 1974), 87; S. Lieberman, *Hellenism in Jewish Palestine: Studies in the Literary Transmission, Beliefs and Manners of Palestine in the I Century B.C.E–IV Century C.E.* (2nd ed.; New York, NY: Jewish Theological Seminary of New York, 1962), 24–25; S. Loewinger, "ספר תורה שהיה גנוז בבית כנסת סוירוס ברומא: יחסו אל מגילות ישעיהו במדבר יהודה ואל 'תורתו של רבי מאיר'," ("A Torah scroll that was stored in the Soveros synagogue in Rome: Its relation to the Isaiah scrolls from the Judean Desert and to 'The Torah of Rabbi Meir',") *Beth Mikra* 15 (1970): 257–63 [in Hebrew]; ibid., "Prolegomenon," in *Viktor Apotwitzer, Das Schriftwort in der rabbinischen Literatur*. ed. S. Loewinger (New York, NY: Ktav, 1970; reprint of the edition of Vienna 1906), xxxii–xxxviii; J. P. Siegel, *The Severus Scroll and 1QIsaᵃ* (Missoula, MT: Scholars Press, 1975), 43–8; T. Arndt, "Zur Tora des Rabbi Me'ir: Bemerkungen zu Uwe Glessmer," *Mitteilungen und Beiträge der Forschungsstelle Judentum* 12–13 (1997): 87–91; J. van Seters, *The Edited Bible: The Curious History of the "Editor" in Biblical Criticism* (Winona Lake, IN: Eisenbrauns, 2010), 73–6; N. Jastram, "The Severus Scroll and Rabbi Meir's Torah," in *The Text of the Hebrew Bible: From the Rabbis to Masoretes*, ed. L. Miralles-Maciá and E. Martín-Contreras

only a limited number draw some overall conclusions. Nevertheless, scholarly opinion differs widely regarding the character of Rabbi Meir's variants and of his biblical text.

Nehemias Brüll viewed the variants as a result of textual alterations made by Rabbi Meir for interpretative reasons.[14] Other scholars think that either all five variants[15], or at least a part of them[16], were marginal notes in proto-Masoretic master copies in the manner of Alexandrian scholia[17] and/or of homiletical character[18] by which Rabbi Meir collected divergent readings from different scrolls.

Shortly after the discovery of the Dead Sea Scrolls, Saul Lieberman introduced the idea that Rabbi Meir might have owned proto-Masoretic scrolls, but that to satisfy the demand of his customers he "copied the vulgate, the text to which the public was accustomed."[19] Rabbi Meir's scrolls were "copies of the average *vulgata* of the Jerusalem type."[20] Several scholars variegated Lieberman's theory. Based on a comparison with 1QIsaᵃ, Edward Y. Kutscher thinks that Rabbi Meir possessed copies of the Bible influenced by the popular orthography vernacular texts.[21] Jonathan P. Siegel argues that the Torah scroll of Rabbi Meir reflects "some ancient Palestinian manuscript tradition" not "entirely in conformity with other texts of his day."[22] Similarly, van Seters describes the Biblical scrolls of Rabbi Meir as texts that "correspond not entirely with the MT," but rejects Lieberman's theory of vulgar texts.[23]

A general problem with all the models described above is that their conclusions are based on very limited evidence. With only five preserved variant readings of Rabbi Meir, of which four are from Genesis and one from Isaiah, not much can be said about the textual character of Meir's biblical manuscripts. Even the Minor Prophets scroll from Wadi Muraba'at (MurXII), which common scholarly opinion regards as a classic example for an early

---

      (Göttingen: Vandenhoeck & Ruprecht, 2014), 144–5; and Lange, "Rabbi Meir and the Severus Scroll," 53–76.

14 Cf. Brüll, "R. Meir," 235–36.

15 Cf. Epstein, "Titus," 343; ibid., "Biblische Textkritik," 48–9; Loewinger, "Prolegomenon", xxxiii–xxxviii; ibid., "ספר תורה," 259–63.

16 Cf. Liebermann, *Hellenism*, 24; Segal, "Promulgation," 45 (Gen 46:23 is a real variant); Siegel, *Severus Scroll*, 43 (the readings of Gen 1:31 and Isa 21:11 are such marginal annotations).

17 Cf. Loewinger, "Prolegomenon," xxxiii–xxxviii; ibid., "ספר תורה," 259–63.

18 Cf. Segal, "Promulgation," 45.

19 Liebermann, *Hellenism*, 25.

20 Ibid., 26.

21 Cf. Kutscher, *Language*, 87.

22 Siegel, *Severus Scroll*, 43, and 48.

23 Van Seters, *Edited Bible*, 110.

proto-Masoretic text,[24] includes 23 orthographic and 28 textual variants toward the text of MT[L] in 3,803 preserved (partial) words. Nevertheless no one would characterize MurXII as a vulgar copy or as orthographically different from MT. The Hebrew text of MT-Genesis includes 32,046 words, the Hebrew text of MT-Isaiah comes up to 25,608 words. With only four variants for Genesis and one for Isaiah, lack of evidence precludes almost any conclusion about the textual and orthographic character of Rabbi Meir's biblical master copies for these two books.

A special focus of the discussion about Rabbi Meir's Torah scroll was its relation to the Severus Scroll. The first one to see a parallel between the two texts was Moshe Ha-Darshan (*Midrash Bereshit Rabbati* on Gen 45:8) in the eleventh century. David Kimchi (1160–1265) pointed to such a connection in his commentary to the book of Genesis as well (on Gen 1:31).[25] In modern times, several authors have emphasized the close relationship of the Severus Scroll with Rabbi Meir's Torah,[26] or have claimed the two to be identical.[27] Most publications though argue for a somewhat more vague relationship between the Severus Scroll and Rabbi Meir's Torah.[28] Joshua E. Burns regards their connection as a part of "Masoretic legend."[29] I myself have concluded that a single agreement between Rabbi Meir's Torah manuscript and the Severus Scroll is not enough evidence to construct any textual relation between these lost

---

24   For this scroll and its textual character, see A. Lange, *Die Handschriften biblischer Bücher von Qumran und den anderen Fundorten* vol. 1 of *Handbuch der Textfunde vom Toten Meer* (Tübingen: Mohr Siebeck, 2009), 346.

25   Cf. *The Commentary of R. David Qimhi to the Pentateuch, Perushe Radak li-Bereshit*, ed. A. Ginzburg (Pressburg: Schmid, 1842), 9b [in Hebrew].

26   Cf., e.g., Epstein, "Titus," 346; Lieberman, "Hellenism," 25; E. Tov, *Textual Criticism of the Hebrew Bible* (3rd ed. Minneapolis, MN: Fortress, 2012), 113; Arndt, "Zur Tora des Rabbi Me'ir," 87.

27   Cf., e.g., Sh. Talmon, "The Three Scrolls of the Law Found in the Temple Court," in *Text and Canon of the Hebrew Bible: Collected Studies* (Winona Lake, IN: Eisenbrauns, 2010), 330; E. Tov, "The Text of the Old Testament," in *The World of the Bible*, ed. A. S. van der Woude (Grand Rapids, MI: Eerdmans, 1986), 159; P. D. Wegner, *A Student's Guide to Textual Criticism of the Bible: Its History, Methods and Results* (Downers Grove, IL: InterVarsity, 2006), 124; R. Price, *Searching for the Original Bible* (Eugene, OR: Harvest House, 2007), 56; J. D. H. Norton, *Contours in the Text: Textual Variation in the Writings of Paul, Josephus, and the Yaḥad* (London: Clark, 2011), 113; A. Lehnardt, *Ta'aniyot Fasten: Übersetzt* (Tübingen: Mohr Siebeck, 2008), 94, n. 11.

28   Cf., e.g. Segal, "Promulgation," 45; Loewinger, "Prolegomenon", xxxi; ibid., "ספר תורה," 257; Siegel, *Severus Scroll*, 43.

29   Cf. J. E. Burns, "The Synagogue of Severus: Commemorating the God of the Jews in Classical Rome," *Henoch* 37 (2015): 102–7.

manuscripts. This is especially the case as the agreement in question regards a spelling convention and is thus orthographic in nature.[30]

In the following, I will summarize some of the results of my study on Rabbi Meir's variant readings. As part of his work as a scribe, Meir made notes in his master copies about alternate readings that he encountered during his career as a scribe. Some of these notifications are quoted in various rabbinic texts. It is unlikely though that the various rabbis who refer to readings of Rabbi Meir in rabbinic literature had access to his personal scrolls. R. Samuel b. Nahman (third to fourth century) claims, for example, that when he was a child, R. Simeon b. R. Eleazar had taught him a reading of Rabbi Meir (BerR 9.5). While the possibility of such an oral transmission should never be neglected in rabbinic circles, the tiny and precise textual details that the variants in question concern relate to a written transmission of Rabbi Meir's variant readings. It is thus more probable that a variant list of Rabbi Meir's readings existed in several copies in rabbinic times. Various rabbis had access to these copies at different times and in different locations. Two readings attributed to Rabbi Meir provide more information about how this variant list worked. In both cases, the rabbinic texts in question attribute two different readings for the same biblical reference to Rabbi Meir. The quotations of these readings are reminiscent of the structure of the Severus Scroll variant list as well as of other variant lists quoted in rabbinic literature.[31] In a *protasis*, the reading of MT is quoted and in an *apodosis* the variant reading noted by Rabbi Meir is given.[32]

	Apodosis with variant reading	*Protasis* with MT reading
BerR 9.5 regarding Gen 1:31	והנה טוב מות	והנה טוב מאד
y. Taan 1.1 (64a) regarding Isa 21:11	משא רומי	משא דומה

It seems likely that various rabbis and rabbinic texts perused a variant list which collected various variant readings of Rabbi Meir. This variant list most likely included more variant readings than quoted in rabbinic literature. It was probably not restricted to the Torah because a variant reading in Isa 21:11 is

---

30   Cf. Lange, "Rabbi Meir and the Severus Scroll."
31   For further variant lists in Rabbinic literature, see C. McCarthy, *The Tiqqune Sopherim and Other Theological Corrections in the Masoretic Text of the Old Testament* (Göttingen: Vandenhoeck & Ruprecht, 1981); G. Veltri, *Eine Tora für den König Talmai: Untersuchungen zum Übersetzungsverständnis in der jüdisch-hellenistischen und rabbinische Literatur* (Tübingen: Mohr Siebeck, 1994).
32   In grammar, particularly in the study of conditional sentences, the terms *protasis* and *apodosis* refer to the two parts of a conditional statement. While the *protasis* sets up a condition, the *apodosis* describes the result of that condition being true.

attributed to Rabbi Meir as well. The rabbis must have selected those readings out of the Rabbi Meir variant list for quotation that were of interpretative interest to them, but ignored the rest.

3. The Text of Isa 21:11 according to Rabbi Meir's Isaiah Scroll (y. Taan 1.1 [64a])

Tractate *Taanit* (1.1 [64a]) in the Palestinian Talmud (*Talmud yerushalmi*) includes an exegetical discussion about the meaning of Isa 21:11:

> Said R. Haninah son of R. Abbahu, "In the book of R. Meir they found that it was written, 'The oracle concerning Dumah, [that is,] the oracle concerning Rome (משא דומה משא רומי, *massʾa dumah, massʾa romi*). One is calling to me from Seir [Watchman, what of the night? Watchman, what of the night?]'" (Is. 21:11) ... Said R. Yohanan, "One is calling to me because of Seir." ... Said R. Simeon b. Laqish, "'To me.' From whence will there a match for me? 'From Seir.'" ... Said R. Joshua b. Levi, "If someone should say to you, 'Where 148 is your God,' say to him, 'He is in a(the) great city in Edom [in Rome],' What is the scriptural basis for this view? 'One is calling to me from Seir'." (Is. 21:11)[33]

As already detailed above, y. Taan. 1.1 (64a) attributes two different readings to Rabbi Meir's scroll: the MT of Isa 21:11 and a variant reading. To quote both readings was necessary in y. Taan. 1.1 (64a) because the immediate context of the Rabbi Meir reference did not provide the MT text of Isa 21:11. Y. Taan. 1.1 thus included both the MT reading and the alternate reading that Rabbi Meir had noted in his master copy. The list below shows how Rabbi Meir's reading relates to the most important textual witnesses of the Book of Isaiah. Manuscript MT[L] represents in my below list the Masoretic text.[34]

Rabbi Meir's reading according to y. Taan. 1.1 (64a): משא רומי (*massʾa romi*)

---

[33] Translation according to J. Neusner, *The Talmud of the Land of Israel: A Preliminary Translation* (Chicago, IL: University of Chicago Press, 1987), 18: 147–48.

[34] 1QIsa[a] refers to the first Isaiah scroll from Qumran cave 1. 4QIsa[b] refers to the second Isaiah scroll from Qumran cave 4. MT[L] refers to Codex Leningradensis, Codex EPB I B of the National Library of Russia in St. Petersburg. Manuscripts abbreviated as MT*Kenn* and MT*DeRossi* refer to B. Kennicott, *Vetus Testamentum hebraicum, cum variislectionibus* (2 vols.; Oxford: Clarendon Press, 1776–1780) and G. B. de Rossi, *Variae lectiones Veteris Testamenti* (5 vols.; Parma: Regio, 1784–1788; repr. Amsterdam: Philo, 1969), respectively. LXX refers to the Old Greek translation of Isaiah. Aquila refers to the Greek translation of the Jewish Scriptures by Aquila. Tg Neb refers to Targum Jonathan. V refers to Jerome's Vulgate translation of the Jewish Bible. P refers to the Old Syriac translation called *Peshitta*.

1QIsaᵃ: משא דומה (*massʾa dumah*)
4QIsaᵇ: משא דו[מֹ]ה (*massʾa du]mah*)
MT^L: מַשָּׂא דּוּמָה (*massʾa dumah*)
MT^Kenn187: משא גיא (*massʾa giʾa*)
MT^DeRossi20, 380marg: משא אדום (*massʾa ʾdom*)
MT^DeRossi319: רומה (*rumah*)
LXX: Τὸ ὅραμα τῆς Ιδουμαίας (*To horama tēs Idoumaias*, "the vision of Iudmea")
Aquila: *Duma* (according to Jerome's Commentary on Isaiah ad loc.)
Tg Neb: מטל כס דלוט לאשקאה ית דומה (*mital kas dᵉlut leʾashkʾa yat dumah*, "from the burden of the desolate, to drink the cup of Edom")
V: *onus Duma*
P: ܡܫܩܠܐ ܕܕܘܡܐ (*mešqālā d-dūmā*, "the burden/oracle of Edom")

The readings of LXX and MT^DeRossi20, 380marg as well as MT^Kenn187 show that the word דּוּמָה ("dumah") was difficult to understand even in antiquity. Since then, the meaning of the word דּוּמָה ("dumah") has been under debate. Because of the mention of Seir in Isa 21:11, until today, commentaries and dictionaries suggest that דּוּמָה is another designation for Edom,[35] or goes back to scribal error and should be emended to אֱדוֹם ("Edom").[36] Others want to identify דּוּמָה ("dumah") as the Dūmat el-Ǧandal in the oasis of el-Ǧōf in North Arabia.[37] Whatever the original reading of Isa 21:11 might have been and to whichever place דּוּמָה might have referred, Aquila, *Peshitta*, Targum Jonathan, and Vulgate leave little doubt that the proto-Masoretic text of Isa 21:11 read דומה (*dumah*) in late Antiquity. The Qumran evidence (1QIsaᵃ) argues the same for the Second Temple period. The readings of LXX (τῆς Ιδουμαίας; *tēs Idoumaias*, "of Idumea") and MT^DeRossi20, 380marg, 1004 (אדום; *ʾdom*) are linguistic actualizations which rightly or wrongly identify דומה (*dumah*) as Idumea or Edom. A similar linguistic actualization can be found in MT^Kenn187 (גיא, *giʾa*, "valley").

Although the reading of Rabbi Meir's Isaiah scroll is repeatedly quoted in scholarly discussions about the Rabbinic identification of Edom as Rome,[38]

---

35 See, e.g., W. Gesenius, *Hebräisches und Aramäisches Handwörterbuch über das Alte Testament* (18th ed., Heidelberg: Springer, 2013), 245.
36 See, e.g., O. Kaiser, *Der Prophet Jesaja: Kapitel 13–39* (Göttingen: Vandenhoeck & Ruprecht, 1976), 106.
37 See, e.g., H. Wildberger, *Jesaja*, vol. 2, *Kapitel 13–27* (3rd ed., Neukirchen-Vluyn: Neukirchener Verlag, 2003), 787; B. S. Childs, *Isaiah: A Commentary* (Louisville, KY: Westminster John Knox Press, 2001). 153.
38 See, e.g., F. Avemarie, "Esaus Hände, Jakobs Stimme: Edom als Sinnbild Roms in der frühen rabbinischen Literatur," in *Die Heiden: Juden, Christen und das Problem des Fremden*, ed. R. Feldmeier and U. Heckel (Tübingen: Mohr Siebeck, 1994), 182; M. Himmelfarb, "The

Jerome's remarks about Jewish readings of Isa 21:11 are mostly discussed in early treatments of Rabbi Meir's Torah but enjoy less attention today:[39]

> Besides what is said according to history: because of the word-similarity and the fact that *resh* and *daleth* are not much different from one another, some among the Hebrews read Rome instead of Duma because they want the prophecy to be directed against the Roman rule, out of their wrongful conviction by which they always consider the name of Idumea to indicate the Romans. Duma, however, is to be translated as "silence." (Jerome, *Commentary on Isaiah*, on Isa 21:11–12)[40]

> The Jews vainly dream that this prophecy is against the city of Rome and the Roman sovereignty; and they hold that in 'the burden of Dumah' in Isaiah [21:11], by a tiny alteration in the crown of a letter, *Resh* can be read for *Dalet*, so that the word becomes "Roma"; for in their language the letter *Waw* is used for both *u* and *o*.[41] (Jerome, *Commentary on Obadiah*, on Ob 1:1)

Mother of the Messiah in the Talmud Yerushalmi and Sefer Zerubbabel," in *The Talmud Yerushalmi and Graeco-Roman Culture*, ed. P Schäfer (Tübingen: Mohr Siebeck, 2002), 3: 381; J. Maier, "Israel und 'Edom' in den Ausdeutungen zu Dt 2,1–8," in *Studien zur jüdischen Bibel und ihrer Geschichte* (Berlin: Walter de Gruyter, 2004), 292.

39   But see G. B. de Rossi, *Scholia critica in V. T. libros seu supplementa ad varias sacri textus lectiones* (Parma: Ex regio typographeo, 1793), 50: "Ad hunc eundem Meirii codicem eaque vetustiorum rabbinorum verba alludere videtur Hieronymus, qui lib. V in Isaiam refert quosdam Hebraeorum pro Dumà legisse Roma, hancque prophetiam ad regnum Romanum applicasse." See further Brüll, "R. Meir," 236; Epstein, "Titus," 343; Epstein, "Biblische Textkritik," 48; A. Neubauer, "The Introduction of the Square Characters in Biblical MSS., and an Account of the Earliest MSS. of the Old Testament," in *Studia Biblica et Ecclesiastica: Essays Chiefly in Biblical and Patristic Criticism*, ed. S. R. Driver, T. K. Cheyne, and W. Sanday (Oxford: Clarendon Press, 1891), 3: 22; L. Ginzberg, *Die Haggada bei den Kirchenvätern und in der apokryphischen Litteratur* (Berlin: Calvary, 1900), 299.

40   "Hoc juxta historiam dictum sit: caeterum propter similitudinem litterae, et ex eo quod RES et DALETH, non multum inter se discrepent, quidam Hebraeorum pro Duma, Romam legunt, volentes prophetiam contra regnum Romanum dirigi, frivola persuasione, qua semper in Idumaeae nomine Romanos existimant demonstrari: Duma autem interpretatur silentium." For stylizing my rather literal translation into proper English, I am obliged to my good friend and colleague Zlatko Pleše.

41   "Judaei frustra somniant contra urbem Romam, regnumque Romanum hanc fieri prophetiam; et illud quod in Isaia scriptum est, Onus Duma, paululum litterae apice commutato pro DELETH legi posse RES, et sonare Romam: VAU quippe littera et pro u, et pro o, eorum lingua accipitur." Translation according to W. Horbury, "Old Testament Interpretation in the Writings of the Church Fathers," in *Mikra: Text, Translation, Reading and Interpretation of the Hebrew Bible in Ancient Judaism and Early Christianity*, ed. M. J. Mulder and H. Sysling (Assen: Van Gorcum, 1988), 774.

In the *Commentary on Obadiah*, Jerome does not refer to actual manuscripts but talks about a Jewish text-critical emendation of his time which allowed to identify *Duma* in Isa 21:11 as *Roma*, or Rome. But in his *Commentary on Isaiah*, Jerome argues slightly different. He accuses "some Hebrews" of reading *Roma* instead of *Duma*, because of their zeal against Rome, thereby confusing the letters *dalet* and *resh* that bear significant similarity. That Jerome uses the word *legunt* seems to imply the reading of a written text.[42] Jerome attests thus to a manuscript tradition which is very close to Rabbi Meir's variant reading רומי (*romi*).

Further evidence for the variant reading רומי/רומה (*romi/dumah*) might be found in a fifteenth century Bible codex (MT[DeRossi319])[43] which reads רומה (*romah*) instead of דומה (*dumah*). While it is not impossible that this reading goes back to a manuscript tradition whose ancestor is to be found in the manuscript tradition on which Rabbi Meir depends[44] and to which Jerome referred, a late codex such as manuscript de Rossi 319 could also be influenced by more recent factors in its variant readings. De Rossi[45] himself mentions that רומה (*romah*) is attested in a fifteenth century copy of David Kimchi's Isaiah commentary (manuscript de Rossi 1004)[46] and in an edition of the Latter Prophets from 1515 that includes Kimchi's Isaiah commentary, too.[47] It is therefore also possible that the reading of manuscript de Rossi 319 reflects the impact of Kimchi's commentary.

Given the cumulative evidence of Jerome's testimony, y. Taan. 1.1 (64a), and MT[DeRossi319], it is likely that Rabbi Meir's reading רומי (*romi*) preserves an ancient variant[48] that was attested by a significant number of Isaiah scrolls

---

42 Cf. Wildberger, *Jesaja*, 787.
43 For a brief description of the codex, see de Rossi, *Variae lectiones*, 1.cvii.
44 Thus seems to be the implication of R. Govett, *Isaiah Unfulfilled: Being an Exposition of the Prophet with New Version and Critical Notes* (London: James Nisbet and Co., 1841), 211.
45 De Rossi, *Scholia critica*, 50.
46 See de Rossi, *Variae lectiones*, 4.xxxii. I have not been able to verify this reading in Finkelstein's edition of Kimchi's commentary (E. U. Finkelstein, ed., *The Commentary of David Kimchi on Isaiah* [New York, NY: Columbia University, 1926], 1:121). It is possible that the רומה (*romah*) reading in Kimchi's commentary quoted by De Rossi goes back to a scribal error in the manuscript tradition of the commentary.
47 The edition was published in Pesaro by a member of the Soncino family and publishing house. See de Rossi, *Variae lectiones*, 1.cxlviii; C. D. Ginsburg, *Introduction to the Massoretico-Critical Edition of the Hebrew Bible* (London: Trinitarian Bible Society, 1897), 886–9.
48 Contra Kutscher, *Language*, 87, n. 3 (midrashic exegesis); Siegel, *Severus Scroll*, 45–46; G. D. Cohen who regards it as a "piquant play on words" by Rabbi Meir ("Esau as Symbol in Early

in (late) antiquity. That Rabbi Meir has רומי (*romi*) instead of רומה (*romah*) is due to the influence of Koiné-Greek as the dominant language in the eastern part of the Roman Empire The Greek word for Rome is Ῥώμη (*Rhomē*) which becomes *Rōmi* when pronounced with an *itacism*, a replacement of various vowel sounds with the "i" sound. The reading רומה (*romah*), on the other hand, reflects the city's Latin name *Roma*.

Originally, Rabbi Meir's variant might have gone back to a scribal error, a confusion of the Hebrew character *dalet* and *resh*: דומה→רומה (*dumah→romah*).[49] In the case of Josh 15:52, the same character confusion is attested in many manuscripts and version. Many important Masoretic manuscripts mention in this verse a town called רומה (*romah*, e.g. MT[A, L, C], LXX, Pesh., V)[50] while other witnesses call the same town דומה (*dumah*, MT[mss], T).[51] An idea how similar these two characters looked at the time of Rabbi Meir is provided in a paleographic chart compiled by Ada Yardeni, one of the best paleographic scholars:

Medieval Jewish Thought," in *Studies in the Variety of Rabbinic Cultures* [Philadelphia, PA: Jewish Publication Society, 1991], 245); and H. W. Guggenheimer who understands it as an interpretative variant (*The Jerusalem Talmud: Second Order Mo'ed; Tractates Ta'aniot, Megillah, Hagigah and Mo'ed Qatan (Mašqin)* [Berlin: De Gruyter, 2015], 16, n. 84).

49 Thus Loewinger, "Prolegomenon," xxxii; ibid., "ספר תורה," 259; Jastram, "The Severus Scroll and Rabbi Meir's Torah," 144, n. 84, who regard the reading of Rabbi Meir as a whole as the result of a scribal error. They ignore though the different orthographies of רומי (*romi*, interpretative reading, Rabbi Meir) and רומה (*romah*, scribal confusion, Jerome) which point to the different character of the two secondary readings. Siegel, *Severus Scroll*, 47 proposes an emendation by Rabbi Meir inspired by the similarity of *dalet* and *resh*. But in this case Rabbi Meir should have read רומה (*romah*) instead of his רומי (*romi*). Ginzberg, *Haggada*, 299, understands both Rabbi Meir's reading and the reading quoted by Jerome as haggadic interpretations based on the graphic similarity of *resh* and *dalet*. Segal, "Promulgation," 45, regards either a scribal corruption from דומה→רומה→רומי (*dumah→romah→romi*) or an interpretative reading inspired by משעיר (*mese'ir*, from Seir) as likely.

50 The *BHS* transcribes MT[L] here erroneously as דומה (*dumah*).

51 See the discussion in Y. Elitsur, "Duma-Ruma: The Original Version of a Biblical Toponym and its Effect on Historical and Geographical Problems," in *Rabbi Mordechai Breuer Festschrift: Collected Papers in Jewish Studies*, ed. M. Bar-Asher (Jerusalem: Academon Press, 1992), 2: 615–620 [in Hebrew]; cf. ibid., "Rumah in Juda," *Israel Exploration Journal* 44 (1994): 123–6.

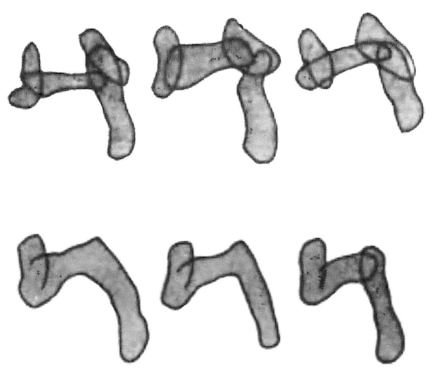

Image 4.1 A post-Herodian book-hand, reconstructed by Ada Yardeni from the Wadi Murabba'at Genesis fragments, demonstrating the similarities between *dalet* (above) and *resh* (below).[52]

By the time of Rabbi Meir, what began as scribal corruption gained an alternate meaning though. This is particularly evident in the reading attributed to Rabbi Meir. While the manuscripts to which Jerome referred apparently read רומה (*romah*), only changing *dalet* to *resh*, Rabbi Meir, instead of adhering to variant spellings of רומה (*romah*) or רומא (*rom'a*), used the widespread rabbinic spelling רומי (*romi*) thus identifying the *Dumah* as Rome. In Isa 21:11, Rabbi Meir's variant רומי (*romi*) for דומה (*dumah*) is interpretative in nature and needs to be read in the context of the rabbinic reception history of Isa 21:11. It identifies the *Dumah* of Isa 21:11 with the Roman Empire based on the graphic similarity of *resh* and *dalet*.

52 A. Yardeni, *The Book of Hebrew Script: History, Palaeography, Script Styles, Calligraphy & Design* (London: British Library, 2002), 183.

4. Conclusions

The example of Rabbi Meir's variant reading in Isa 21:11 shows that a seemingly minor variant reading that goes back to a scribal error can impact the interpretative history of a given biblical text significantly. It can create a new signification for a given biblical text that was not intended in the biblical text itself. In the case of Isa 21:11, Rabbi Meir's reading reflects a popular understanding of the prophetic oracle in Isa 21:11–12.

I have consciously chosen the example of Rabbi Meir's reading in Isa 21:11 instead of engaging with a variant literary edition of a biblical text or exegetical variant readings in the biblical text cited by an ancient Jewish commentary. While these types of variants are of obvious importance for the Hebrew Bible's interpretative history, they are only one part of the much more extensive interpretative process that is documented in the textual transmission of the Jewish Scriptures. As this more extensive interpretative process is mostly ignored in studies of the Jewish Scriptures' interpretative history, the article has drawn attention to this important part of the reception history of the Hebrew Bible. The textual history of the Jewish Scriptures is an important part of its interpretative history and should not be neglected by scholars who are interested in it.

Another often neglected area of the Hebrew Bible's reception history are its ancient translations. As each translation is necessarily also an interpretation, all biblical translations preserve evidence of how a given biblical text was understood by its translator(s). The study of these translations, however, would require a separate study that goes beyond what is possible in this brief article.

Bibliography

Arndt, Timotheus. "Zur Tora des Rabbi Me'ir: Bemerkungen zu Uwe Glessmer." *Mitteilungen und Beiträge der Forschungsstelle Judentum* 12–13 (1997): 87–91.

Avemarie, Friederich. "Esaus Hände, Jakobs Stimme: Edom als Sinnbild Roms in der frühen rabbinischen Literatur." In *Die Heiden: Juden, Christen und das Problem des Fremden*, edited by Reinhard Feldmeier and Ulrich Heckel, 177–210. Tübingen: Mohr Siebeck, 1994.

Brüll, Nehemias. "R. Meir." *Jahrbücher für Jüdische Geschichte und Literatur* 1 (1874): 235–36.

Burns, Joshua Ezra. "The Synagogue of Severus: Commemorating the God of the Jews in Classical Rome." *Henoch* 37 (2015): 101–18.

Childs, Brevard S. *Isaiah: A Commentary*. Louisville, KY: Westminster John Knox Press, 2001.

Cohen, Gerson D. "Esau as Symbol in Early Medieval Jewish Thought." In *Studies in the Variety of Rabbinic Cultures*, 243–69. Philadelphia, PA: Jewish Publication Society, 1991.

Cohen, Naomi Goldstein. "Rabbi Meir, a Descendant of Anatolian Proselytes." *Journal of Jewish Studies* 23 (1972): 51–9.

de Rossi, Giovanni B. *Scholia critica in V. T. libros seu supplementa ad varias sacri textus lectiones*. Parma: Ex regio typographeo, 1793.

--------.*Variae lectiones Veteris Testamenti*. 5 volumes. Parma: Regio, 1784–1788.

Duncan, Julie A. "Excerpted Texts of Deuteronomy at Qumran." *Revue de Qumrân* 18 (1997–98): 43–62.

Elitsur, Yoel. "Duma-Ruma: The Original Version of a Biblical Toponym and its Effect on Historical and Geographical Problems." In *Rabbi Mordechai Breuer Festschrift: Collected Papers in Jewish Studies*, edited by Moshe Bar-Asher, 2:615–20. Jerusalem: Academon Press, 1992. [In Hebrew.]

--------. "Rumah in Juda." *Israel Exploration Journal* 44 (1994): 123–8.

Epstein, Abraham. "Biblische Textkritik bei den Rabbinen." In *Recueil des travaux rédigés en mémoire du Jubilé scientifique de Daniel Chwolson*, edited by David Günzburg, 42–56. Berlin: Calvary, 1899.

--------. "Ein von Titus nach Rom gebrachter Pentateuch-Codex und seine Varianten." *Monatsschrift für Geschichte und Wissenschaft des Judenthums* 34 (1885): 337–51.

Eshel, Esther "4QDeut^n—A Text That Has Undergone Harmonistic Editing." *Hebrew Union College Annual* 62 (1991): 117–54.

Finkelstein, Eliezer U., ed. *The Commentary of David Kimchi on Isaiah*. New York, NY: Columbia University, 1926.

Finsterbusch, Karin, Russell E. Fuller, and Armin Lange, eds. *Between Textual Criticism and Literary Criticism*. Tübingen: Mohr Siebeck, 2020.

Gesenius, Wilhelm. *Hebräisches und Aramäisches Handwörterbuch über das Alte Testament*. 18th edition. Heidelberg: Springer, 2013.

Ginzberg, Louis. *Die Haggada bei den Kirchenvätern und in der apokryphischen Litteratur*. Berlin: Calvary, 1900.

Ginsburg, Christian D. *Introduction to the Massoretico-Critical Edition of the Hebrew Bible*. London: Trinitarian Bible Society, 1897.

Ginzburg, Abraham, ed. *The Commentary of R. David Qimhi to the Pentateuch, Perushe Radak li-Bereshit*. Pressburg: Schmid, 1842. [In Hebrew.]

Govett, Robert. *Isaiah Unfulfilled: Being an Exposition of the Prophet with New Version and Critical Notes*. London: James Nisbet and Co., 1841.

Guggenheimer, Heinrich W. *The Jerusalem Talmud: Second Order Mo'ed; Tractates Ta'aniot, Megillah, Hagigah and Mo'ed Qatan (Mašqin)*. Berlin: De Gruyter, 2015.

Hasan-Rokem, Galit. "Rabbi Meir: The Illuminated and the Illuminating." In *Current Trends in the Study of Midrash*, edited by Carol Bakhos, 227–44. Leiden: Brill, 2006.

Himmelfarb, Martha. "The Mother of the Messiah in the Talmud Yerushalmi and Sefer Zerubbabel." In *The Talmud Yerushalmi and Graeco-Roman Culture*, edited by Peter Schäfer, 3: 369–90. Tübingen: Mohr Siebeck, 2002.

Horbury, William. "Old Testament Interpretation in the Writings of the Church Fathers." In *Mikra: Text, Translation, Reading and Interpretation of the Hebrew Bible in Ancient Judaism and Early Christianity*, edited by Martin J. Mulder and Harry Sysling, 727–87. Assen: Van Gorcum, 1988.

Jastram, Nathan. "The Severus Scroll and Rabbi Meir's Torah." In *The Text of the Hebrew Bible: From the Rabbis to Masoretes*, edited by Lorena Miralles-Maciá and Elvira Martín-Contreras, 137–45. Göttingen: Vandenhoeck & Ruprecht, 2014.

Kaiser, Otto. *Der Prophet Jesaja: Kapitel 13–39*. Göttingen: Vandenhoeck & Ruprecht, 1976.

Kennicott, Benjamin. *Vetus Testamentum hebraicum, cum variislectionibus*. 2 volumes. Oxford: Clarendon, 1776–1780.

Kutscher, Edward Y. *The Language and Linguistic Background of the Isaiah Scroll (1 Q Isaa)*. Leiden: Brill, 1974.

Lange, Armin. "1.2.2 Ancient Hebrew-Aramaic Texts: Ancient and Late Ancient Hebrew and Aramaic Jewish Texts." In *The Hebrew Bible, part 1a: Overview Articles*, vol. 1 of *Textual History of the Bible*, edited by Armin Lange and Emanuel Tov, 112–66. Leiden: Brill, 2016.

--------. "4QXII^g (4Q82) as an Editorial Text." *Textus* 26 (2016): 87–119.

--------. "An Interpretative Reading in the Isaiah Scroll of Rabbi Meir." In *Hā-'îsh Mōshe: Studies in Scriptural Interpretation in the Dead Sea Scrolls and Related Literature in Honor of Moshe J. Bernstein*, edited by Binyamin Y. Goldstein, Michael Segal, and George J. Brooke, 210–22. Leiden: Brill, 2018.

--------. *Handbuch der Textfunde vom Toten Meer*, vol. 1: *Die Handschriften biblischer Bücher von Qumran und den anderen Fundorten*. Tübingen: Mohr Siebeck, 2009.

--------. "In the Second Degree: Ancient Jewish Paratextual Literature in the Context of Graeco-Roman and Ancient Near Eastern Literature." In *In the Second Degree: Paratextual Literature in Ancient Near Eastern and Ancient Mediterranean Cultures and its Reflections in Medieval Literature*, edited by Philip S. Alexander, Armin Lange, and Renate Pillinger, 3–40. Leiden: Brill, 2010.

--------. "Rabbi Meir and the Severus Scroll." In *"Let the Wise Listen and Add to Their Learning" (Prov 1:5): Festschrift for Günter Stemberger on the Occasion of His 75th Birthday*, edited by Constanza Cordoni and Gerhard Langer, 53–76. Berlin: De Gruyter, 2016.

--------. "Die Wurzel *phz* und ihre Konnotationen." *Vetus Testamentum* 51 (2001): 497–510.

Lehnardt, Andreas. *Ta'aniyot Fasten: Übersetzt*. Tübingen: Mohr Siebeck, 2008.

Lieberman, Saul. *Hellenism in Jewish Palestine: Studies in the Literary Transmission, Beliefs and Manners of Palestine in the I Century B.C.E–IV Century C.E.* 2nd edition. New York, NY: Jewish Theological Seminary of New York, 1962.

Loewinger, Samuel. "ספר תורה שהיה גנוז בבית כנסת סוירוס ברומא: יחסו אל מגילות ישעיהו' שבמדבר יהודה ואל 'תורתו של רבי מאיר'," ("A Torah scroll that was stored in the Soveros synagogue in Rome: Its relation to the Isaiah scrolls from the Judean Desert and to 'The Torah of Rabbi Meir'.") *Beth Mikra* 15 (1970): 237–62. [In Hebrew.]

--------. "Prolegomenon." In *Viktor Apotwitzer, Das Schriftwort in der rabbinischen Literatur*, edited by Samuel Loewinger, vii–xlv. New York, NY: Ktav, 1970 (reprint of the edition of Vienna 1906).

Maier, Johann. "Israel und 'Edom' in den Ausdeutungen zu Dt 2,1–8." In *Studien zur jüdischen Bibel und ihrer Geschichte*, 285–325. Berlin: Walter de Gruyter, 2004.

McCarthy, Carmel. *The Tiqqune Sopherim and Other Theological Corrections in the Masoretic Text of the Old Testament*. Göttingen: Vandenhoeck & Ruprecht, 1981.

Neubauer, Adolph. "The Introduction of the Square Characters in Biblical MSS., and an Account of the Earliest MSS. of the Old Testament." In *Studia Biblica et Ecclesiastica: Essays Chiefly in Biblical and Patristic Criticism*, edited by Samuel R. Driver, Thomas K. Cheyne, and William Sanday, 3: 1–36. Oxford: Clarendon, 1891.

Neusner, Jacob. *The Talmud of the Land of Israel: A Preliminary Translation*. Volume 18: *Besah and Taanit*. Chicago, IL: University of Chicago Press, 1987.

Norton, Jonathan D. H. *Contours in the Text: Textual Variation in the Writings of Paul, Josephus, and the Yaḥad*. London: Clark, 2011.

Oppenheimer, A'hron, and Stephen G. Wald. "Meir." In volume 13 of *Encyclopaedia Judaica*, ed. Michael Berenbaum and Fred Skolnik, 2nd edition, 776–77. Detroit, MI: Macmillan Reference, 2007.

Price, Randall. *Searching for the Original Bible*. Eugene, OR: Harvest House, 2007.

Segal, Moses H. "The Promulgation of the Authoritative Text of the Hebrew Bible." *Journal of Biblical Literature* 72 (1953): 35–47.

Siegel, Jonathan P. *The Severus Scroll and 1QIsaᵃ*. Missoula, MT: Scholars Press, 1975.

Talmon, Shemaryahu. "The Three Scrolls of the Law Found in the Temple Court." In *Text and Canon of the Hebrew Bible: Collected Studies*, 329–46. Winona Lake, IN: Eisenbrauns, 2010.

Teeter, David A. *Scribal Laws: Exegetical Variation in the Textual Transmission of Biblical Law in the Late Second Temple Period*. Tübingen: Mohr Siebeck, 2014.

Tigay, Jeffrey H. "Conflation as a Redactional Technique." In *Empirical Models for Biblical Criticism*, 53–95. Philadelphia, PA: University of Pennsylvania Press, 1985.

Tov, Emanuel. "The Text of the Old Testament." In *The World of the Bible*, ed. Adam S. van der Woude, 156–90. Grand Rapids, MI: Eerdmans, 1986.

———. *Textual Criticism of the Hebrew Bible*, 3rd edition. Minneapolis, MN: Fortress, 2012.

Ulrich, Eugene. *The Biblical Qumran Scrolls: Transcriptions and Textual Variants*. Leiden: Brill, 2010.

———. *The Dead Sea Scrolls and the Developmental Composition of the Bible*. Leiden: Brill, 2015.

van der Toorn, Karel. *Scribal Culture and the Making of the Hebrew Bible*. Cambridge, MA: Harvard University Press, 2007.

van Seters, John. *The Edited Bible: The Curious History of the "Editor" in Biblical Criticism*. Winona Lake, IN: Eisenbrauns, 2010.

Veltri, Giuseppe. *Eine Tora für den König Talmai: Untersuchungen zum Übersetzungsverständnis in der jüdisch-hellenistischen und rabbinische Literatur*. Tübingen: Mohr Siebeck, 1994.

Wegner, Paul D. *A Student's Guide to Textual Criticism of the Bible: Its History, Methods and Results*. Downers Grove, IL: InterVarsity, 2006.

White, Sidnie A. "The All Souls Deuteronomy and the Decalogue." *Journal of Biblical Literature* 109 (1990): 193–206.

White Crawford, Sidnie A. "Reading Deuteronomy in the Second Temple Period." In *Reading the Present in the Qumran Library: The Conception of the Contemporary by Means of Scriptural Interpretations*, edited by Kristin de Troyer and Armin Lange, 127–40. Atlanta, GA: Society of Biblical Literature, 2005.

———. *Rewriting Scripture in Second Temple Times*. Grand Rapids, MI: Eerdmans, 2008.

———. "Samaritan Pentateuch." In *Textual History of the Bible, vol. 1, The Hebrew Bible, part 1a: Overview Articles*, edited by Armin Lange and Emanuel Tov, 166–75. Leiden: Brill, 2016.

Wildberger, Hans. *Jesaja*. Volume 2: *Kapitel 13–27*. 3rd edition. Neukirchen-Vluyn: Neukirchener Verlag, 2003.

Yardeni, Ada. *The Book of Hebrew Script: History, Palaeography, Script Styles, Calligraphy & Design*. New edition, revised and expanded from the original Hebrew edition. London: British Library, 2002.

PART II

Reception

Memory, Orality and Textuality in the Reception of the Biblical Text in Rabbinic Literature

Lawrence H. Schiffman

One of the underlying principles of rabbinic Judaism is the centrality of the biblical corpus. The Bible is seen as providing fundamental beliefs, principles and rituals that serve as the basis for later Jewish life. The role of the Bible is itself predicated on the belief that it represents divine revelation, most directly in the Torah, somewhat less directly in the Prophets, and even more indirectly in the Writings. Complex issues surround the reception of the Bible in rabbinic Judaism, and we will deal here with only one of them, namely, the reception of the text and issues surrounding its transmission through oral and written channels.

This paper will begin with (1) a survey of the state of the canon and text of the Hebrew Bible as quoted and interpreted in rabbinic literature, establishing clearly that the text under discussion is uniformly the one that modern scholars term proto-Masoretic. We will then (2) explain the effects of the rabbinic requirement that the biblical text be transmitted in writing, discuss the regulations regarding its transmission, and explain the rabbis' view of the Oral Law and the oral nature of its transmission. (3) This study will then show how textuality and orality intersect in the public reading of the Torah (and other Scriptures) and how specific halakhic requirements guarantee this. We will (4) trace the types of textual variation in rabbinic quotations of Scripture and propose a general classification system for them. We will then (5) investigate rabbinic references to textual variants and their understanding of textual accuracy. Finally (6), a summary of the intersection of orality and textuality in rabbinic literature will be presented, explaining how both contribute to the perpetuation of cultural and religious memory.

1. Canon and Text of the Hebrew Bible in Rabbinic Literature

Any discussion dealing with the reception of the Bible in rabbinic literature is, of course, based on the assumption that there exists something that would have been identifiable as the Bible to Jews in Antiquity.[1] Indeed, one term for

---

[1] L. H. Schiffman, "What is a Jewish Biblical Text?" *HBAI* 9 (2020): 296–305.

authoritative scriptures already appears in the book of Daniel, *ha-sefarim*, "the books."[2] Two other terms for the Bible appear in rabbinic texts, already from the tannaitic period. *Kitve ha-Qodesh*, literally "writings of holiness,"[3] is best translated as "Holy Scriptures." This term assumes that the Bible is a collection of writings (*ketavim*), each of which is considered to be holy. A second term, often translated "Scripture" as well, is *Miqra*,[4] however this term really means "that which is read." It is used, for example, in distinction to the oral teachings of the Mishnah (m. Qid. 1:10). This term serves as a collective noun but, in contrast to *Kitve ha-Qodesh*, emphasizes not the aspect of writing, that is, composition or copying, but rather that of reading. In reality, for the rabbis as well as the later Jewish tradition, the transmission of the Jewish Bible involved both steps, copying the holy texts and then reading them liturgically and studying them. While reading in Antiquity represents an oral activity, it is extremely tightly bound to the written text from which it is read. The biblical term *sefer*, meaning "document" or "book," is used extensively by the rabbis.[5] When used for an extensive written text, this term emphasizes the form in which it was preserved, namely, in a scroll, which was the usual form in which books were written in ancient Israel.[6] We should call attention here to the fact that the

---

2 Dan 9:2, referring to the book of Jeremiah. Old Greek and Theodotion both have ἐν ταῖς βίβλοι.
3 This term occurs four times in the Mishnah: m. Shab. 16:1, m. Eruv. 10:3, m. B. Bat. 1:6 and m. Yad. 4:6. The examples in the rest of the rabbinic corpus are too numerous to list.
4 This term with this meaning occurs six times in the Mishnah, m. Shek. 1:4, m. Ḥag. 1:8, m. Ned. 4:3 (2x), m. Qidd. 1:10, m. Avot 5:21 (and the baraita in Avot 6:5). It can also refer to a verse or passage, as in m. Soṭ. 5:2, 5:3, Mak. 3:14 (2x). The examples in the rest of the rabbinic corpus for both usages are too numerous to list.
5 Often in the phrase *sefer Torah*, referring to a Torah scroll, e.g., m. Yoma 7:1, m. Beṣ. 1:5, m. Soṭ. 7:8, for a total of nine occurrences in the Mishnah alone.
6 On the formal characteristics of scrolls see E. Tov, *Scribal Practices and Approaches Reflected in the Texts Found in the Judean Desert* (Leiden: Brill, 2004), 39–43; idem, "Scribal Practices Reflected in the Documents from the Judean Desert and in the Rabbinic Literature: A Comparative Study," in *Texts, Temples, and Traditions: A Tribute to Menahem Haran*, ed. M. V. Fox et al. (Winona Lake, IN: Eisenbrauns, 1996), 383–403; idem, "The Scribal and Textual Transmission of the Torah Analyzed in Light of Its Sanctity," in *Pentateuchal Traditions in the Late Second Temple Period. Proceedings of the International Workshop in Tokyo, August 28–31, 2007*, eds. A. Moriya and G. Hata (Leiden: Brill, 2012), 57–72; M. Haran, "Melekhet ha-Sofer bi-Tequfat ha-Miqra': Megillot ha-Sefarim ve-'Avizare ha-Ketivah," *Tarbiz* 50 (1981): 65–87; idem, "Book-Scrolls in Israel in Pre-Exilic Times," *JJS* 33 (1982): 161–73. An outdated work on this topic is L. Blau, *Studien zum althebräischen Buchwesen und zur biblischen Litteratur- und Textgeschichte* (Strassburg: J. Trübner, 1902).

codex was not adopted by the Jewish people until after the core compositions of the rabbinic corpus were complete.[7]

A further term indicating canonicity is *ṭum'at yadayim*, "impurity of the hands." It is necessary here to make a brief digression into how to understand canonicity in relation to Jewish texts. Here, scholars have adopted the term, "canon," borrowed from discussions of the collection of texts included in the New Testament.[8] While it is perfectly appropriate to use such borrowed terms, it needs to be recognized that both the term "canon" and the concept are quite different from the Jewish approach. The closest thing to a term for canonical Scriptures used by the rabbis would be the very difficult expression *meṭame' 'et ha-yadayim*, "renders the hands impure."[9] Ironically, while the real reason why holy texts should render the hands of those who handle them impure is not understood,[10] it is known that this is an effective test of whether books are considered to be "canonical." However, besides connoting inclusion in the collection of "biblical" books, canonical status implies two additional characteristics in Jewish terms: first, that the book in question is considered to be the result of divine inspiration at some level; second, that it is one of those texts that may serve as the building blocks for later texts that will derive expressions, terminology, or ideas from them. Indeed, in the entire history of Judaism, the only books that have served this type of role are those that were later considered to be those of the Tanakh, the three-part collection of Torah, Prophets, and Writings. Further, it is these books that are subjected in Late Antiquity and the Middle Ages to systemic biblical exegesis.

Despite the difficulties of applying the term "canon" to the Hebrew Scriptures, because it assumes a formal process of "canonization," we shall use it here to describe the corpus of texts that are actually included in the Bible, designated by the rabbis by the terminology we have just discussed. Two approaches could be used to determine what books were viewed as authoritative in rabbinic

---

7   D. Stern, *The Jewish Bible: A Material History* (Seattle, WA: University of Washington Press, 2017), 66–8 and 226 n. 15. Cf. I. M. Resnick, "The Codex in Early Jewish and Christian Communities," *Journal of Religious History* 17 (1992): 1–17, and J. del Barco, "From Scroll to Codex: Dynamics of Text Layout Transformation in the Hebrew Bible," in *From Scrolls to Scrolling: Sacred Texts, Materiality, and Dynamic Media Cultures*, ed. B. A. Anderson (Berlin: de Gruyter, 2020), 91–4. For early Jewish avoidance of the codex format, see S. Lieberman, *Hellenism in Jewish Palestine* (New York, NY: Jewish Theological Seminary, 1962), 203–8.
8   J. Trebolle, "Canon of the Old Testament," *NIDB* 1:548–49.
9   For rabbinic passages using this terminology, see S. Z. Leiman, *The Canonization of Hebrew Scripture: The Talmudic and Midrashic Evidence* (Hamden, CT: Archon Books, 1976), 102–10.
10 See the survey of explanations in Leiman, *Canonization*, 110–20.

literature. The first, and easiest, is simply to investigate the tannaitic source that lists the biblical books of the Prophets and Writings,[11] including all those in a Hebrew Bible that one would buy today. These books are already divided by the rabbis into the three descending classes of authority/sanctity, namely the Torah, Prophets, and Writings.[12] However, another approach to very same question would be to investigate what texts are actually cited or quoted by the rabbis as authoritative for their teachings. Such an examination would add one book to the mix, namely Ben Sira, since it is quoted several times with the very same quotation formulae used to indicate scriptural quotations.[13] Yet any argument to the effect that this additional book, part of the Septuagint canon of the Apocrypha, was actually considered to be canonical by the Talmudic rabbis would run up against the specific designation of this text as part of the *sefarim ḥiṣoniyyim*, the "external books," clearly referring to its not being part of the biblical collection.[14]

2. Written and Oral Law

At the core of rabbinic Judaism there lies a fundamental concept that God revealed two Torahs to Israel at Sinai, the written Torah and the oral.[15] According to rabbinic teachings, the written Torah, indeed the entirety of Scripture, must be transmitted in written format. Oral transmission is reserved—indeed permitted—only for those traditions believed to be part of the Oral Law.[16] Essentially, the Oral Law was understood to take in a great body of exegetical and legal traditions that had been passed down, in the understanding of the Talmudic rabbis, from the time of the Mosaic revelation, or that had somehow stemmed from and been built upon those early revelations. While modern scholars look differently at the history of the rabbinic tradition,[17] it was the

---

11   B. B.B. 14b.
12   Leiman, *Canonization*, 57, 60–66.
13   M. Z. Segal, *Sefer Ben Sira ha-Shalem* (Jerusalem: Bialik Institute, ²1971), 12–13.
14   M. Sanh. 10:1 as interpreted in y. Sanh. 10:1 (28a), attributed to Rabbi Akiva as is the Mishnaic statement; Leiman, *Canonization*, 99–102.
15   For sources, see L. H. Schiffman, *Texts and Traditions: A Source Reader for the Study of Second Temple and Rabbinic Judaism* (Hoboken, NJ: Ktav, 1998), 517–22.
16   For the pre-history of this concept see J. M. Baumgarten, *Studies in Qumran Law* (Leiden: E. J. Brill, 1977), 13–35.
17   M. Strack and G. Stemberger, *Introduction to the Talmud and Midrash* (Edinburgh: T & T Clark, 1991), 35–49; J. Neusner, *Uniting the Dual Torah: Sifra and the Problem of the Mishnah* (Cambridge: Cambridge University Press, 1990), 11–30; E. E. Urbach, *The Sages: Their Concepts and Beliefs*. 2 vols., trans. I. Abrahams (Jerusalem: Magnes Press, The Hebrew

understanding just explained that molded the rabbinic views of textuality and orality. These views, in turn, impacted numerous practices as we will see.

When in the aftermath of the Great Revolt of 66 to 73 CE and the destruction of the Temple in 70, the tannaim (teachers of the Mishnaic period) began to collect their post-Hebrew biblical traditions into collections, they sought to maintain the distinction between what they saw as the divinely inspired teachings of the Bible, the Written Law, and their own teachings, the Oral Law. Because they wanted to accent this distinction, they insisted on presenting their own teachings as oral and in fact initially prohibited the writing of these teachings.[18] Only later on, according to most views after the completion of the Talmuds soon before the Muslim conquest, were rabbinic traditions in the Mishnah, Midrashim and Talmuds committed to writing.[19] Another view maintains that the Mishnah may have been written down already at its completion, ca. 200 CE.[20]

Numerous rabbinic texts make clear that the rabbis insisted that what they saw as the two parts of the revelation, the written and oral, were required to be transmitted in accordance with the manner in which they had been revealed. Accordingly, biblical manuscripts were required to be copied from other manuscripts.[21] Rabbinic law included numerous regulations to make sure that texts were copied exactly, preserving also a variety of textual peculiarities like large or small letters, dots placed over some letters, and the poetic form of certain passages.[22] Clearly, such an approach would not have been appropriate in a system such as that of the Dead Sea Scrolls biblical manuscripts in which large textual variations and expansions seem to have been able to coexist within one

---

University, 1987), 1:286–314; M. S. Jaffee, *Torah in the Mouth: Writing and Oral Tradition in Palestinian Judaism 200 BCE–400 CE* (Oxford: Oxford University Press, 2001), 65–156.

18   Strack and Stemberger, *Introduction*, 48–49; Lieberman, *Hellenism*, 84, 204–5.

19   On the oral publication of the Mishnah, see Lieberman, *Hellenism*, 83–99; Strack and Stemberger, *Introduction*, 155.

20   Lieberman, *Hellenism*, 84.

21   B. Meg. 18b (attributed to the Palestinian amora Rabbi Yohanan), cf. b. Men. 32b.

22   E. Tov, *Textual Criticism of the Hebrew Bible* (Minneapolis, MN: Fortress Press, [4]2022), 47–62. It is probable that the *Tiqqune Soferim* ("corrections of the scribes") and *'Itture Soferim*, ("omissions of the Scribes") described in Rabbinic literature were exegetical expressions rather than descriptions of actual changes made in the biblical text. See Tov, *Textual Criticism*, 4th ed., 314–5 and the more detailed discussion in Tov, *Textual Criticism of the Hebrew Bible*, 3rd ed. (Minneapolis, MN: Fortress Press, 2012), 59–61. On this usage of the term *'ittur*, see the entry "*'tr* II," meaning "omit, remove," in M. Jastrow, *Dictionary of the Targumim, Talmud Bavli, Talmud Yerushalmi and Midrashic Literature* (New York, NY: Pardes Publishing, 1959), 2:1064–5.

community.[23] This is despite the fact that comparison of the scribal techniques and practices in evidence in the Qumran Scrolls conforms almost entirely to the regulations found already in tannaitic sources that govern the preparation and writing of scrolls.[24]

Those traditions believed to have been revealed orally, as well as the ongoing development of the oral tradition that took place during Late Antiquity, were understood by the rabbis to require oral transmission. That is the reason most rabbinic materials were written down only later. In fact, traditions were passed on orally within the context of the tannaitic and amoraic academies in the Land of Israel and in the less formal study circles that prevailed among the Babylonian amoraim. In other words, oral performance was required for the oral traditions. This is true even though some scholars maintained personal notebooks in which they recorded substantial amounts of oral tradition.[25]

Indeed, the word *tannaim*, in one of its uses, designated the memorizers whose job it was to recite those texts to be studied and, at the same time, to record orally the additional traditions and explanations that were attached to those earlier texts.[26] The various parallel versions of rabbinic traditions found in different rabbinic texts seem to reflect, in their textual differences, the result of the passing on of these traditions orally. Often, they show evidence of expansion and explanation, or, on the other hand, they may be shortened and/or reshaped in order to be presented as part of a dispute form. In any case, the presentation of various versions of the same or similar traditions is best described with the term "intertextuality," and indicates that in certain ways the various redacted texts derive their source material from a kind of large oral collection of data that they, to a great extent, sorted and reshaped.

---

23 Tov, *Textual Criticism*, 4th ed., 109–38; E. Ulrich, *The Dead Sea Scrolls and the Origins of the Bible* (Grand Rapids, MI: W.B. Eerdmans, 1999), 17–50, 79–120.
24 L. H. Schiffman, "Jerusalem Talmud Megillah 1 (71b-72a)—'Of the Making of Books': Rabbinic Scribal Arts in Light of the Dead Sea Scrolls," in *Talmuda de-Eretz Israel: Archaeology and the Rabbis in Late Antique Palestine*; eds. S. Fine and A. J. Koller (Berlin: de Gruyter, 2014), 97–109.
25 Lieberman, *Hellenism*, 84, 204–5; Strack and Stemberger, *Introduction*, 41–2, 49.
26 Strack and Stemberger, *Introduction*, 13–14.

3. Public Reading of Scripture

Another area where written and oral performance intersected was in the public reading of Scripture.[27] Public reading of the Bible is already referred to in the Dead Sea Scrolls. The reading of the Pentateuch was a central part of the synagogue service in tannaitic times. Some scholars even think that the synagogue originally developed as a place for study and reading of Scripture, and that its function as a place of prayer was only acquired later on.[28] Despite the prominence of the Torah, both in terms of Jewish law and symbolism, tannaitic texts testify also to the reading of the haftarah, a prophetic portion that went along with the lectionary drawn from the Torah.[29] This practice seems to have already existed by the turn of the era, as it is in evidence in the Gospels. The prophetic portions were read each week, originally out of scrolls, but later virtually everywhere out of codices. The Torah was read over three and a fraction years in the Land of Israel (scholars call this the triennial cycle) and yet was completed each year in Babylonia (the annual cycle). Prophetic portions gradually became standardized both for each Sabbath of the year as well as for the festivals and other special occasions. Originally, the use of prophetic scrolls encouraged a greater aura of sanctity, but replacement with codices in most communities removed that aura.[30] We should note as well evidence that some Palestinian synagogues may have also read a Psalm each Sabbath.[31] The Scroll of Esther was read publicly as well. Here we are essentially dealing with oral performance of a written text.

From the Mishnah and later sources, we learn of the practice of providing Aramaic translations (Targum) of the biblical reading, between the verses for the Torah and between every three verses for the prophets. In rabbinic times

---

27 Cf. L. H. Schiffman, "The Early History of the Public Reading of the Torah," in *Jews, Christians, and Polytheists in the Ancient Synagogue: Cultural Interaction during the Greco-Roman Period*, ed. S. Fine (London: Routledge, 1999), 44–56.

28 L. I. Levine, *The Ancient Synagogue: The First Thousand Years* (New Haven, CT: Yale University Press, 2000), 134–59.

29 L. H. Schiffman, "The Haftarah: An Historical Introduction," in *From Within the Tent: The Haftarot, Essays on the Weekly Haftarah Reading from the Rabbis & Professors of Yeshiva University*, eds. D. Z. Feldman and S. W. Halpern (Jerusalem: Maggid Books, 2011), xix–xxvii.

30 Some synagogues are now returning to the use of scrolls, and so the Jewish community is again having the opportunity to see the Prophets as they would have been seen by Jews in the rabbinic period.

31 L. Rabinowitz, "Does Midrash Tillim Reflect the Triennial Cycle of Psalms?" *JQR* 26 (1936): 349–68.

it was required that these translations, considered to be part of the Oral Law, be recited from memory. Ultimately, toward the end of the rabbinic period or shortly afterwards, these translations ended up standardized in the form of several written texts. However, the normal practice seems to have been that the translators, passing on an oral tradition, recited, but at the same time adapted, and often expanded what was essentially a common substratum. We should note in passing that these written translations, especially that of Onkelos, sometimes evidence either textual variants in the consonantal text or variations in the pronunciation and parsing of words that differ from those of the Tiberian Masoretes. This same phenomenon can be observed in a few passages in the Job Targum from Qumran.[32]

The synagogue in the Land of Israel was the venue for another kind of oral performance, that of aggadic midrash.[33] Here rabbis strung together homilies based on Midrashic exegesis that constituted a passing on of oral tradition to the common worshipers in synagogues. The pattern in Babylonia seems to have been to hold afternoon study sessions, but it appears that these were more concerned with Jewish law than with homiletical interpretations. In any case, in both the Palestinian and Babylonia Jewish communities it is apparent that there were oral presentations of traditions that eventually ended up compiled in rabbinic literature. These originally ad-libbed translations developed extensively in their tellings and retellings, and the written texts of the so-called "Palestinian Targumim," namely, Pseudo-Jonathan,[34] the Fragment Targum[35] and the Neofiti Targum,[36] all show evidence of multiple halakhic and aggadic expansions.

---

32   M. Sokoloff, *The Targum to Job from Qumran Cave XI* (Ramat-Gan: Bar-Ilan University, 1974), 6–8.
33   L. H. Schiffman, *From Text to Tradition: A History of Second Temple and Rabbinic Judaism* (Hoboken, NJ: Ktav, 1991), 234–6; cf. J. Heinemann, "The Nature of the Aggadah," in *Midrash and Literature*, eds. G. H. Hartman and S. Budick, trans. M. Bregman (New Haven, CT: Yale, 1986), 41–55; Levine, *Ancient Synagogue*, 545–51.
34   M. Ginsburger, ed., *Pseudo-Jonathan: Thargum Jonathan ben Usiël zum Pentateuch* (Berlin: S. Calvary, 1903); M. L. Klein, ed. and trans., *Genizah Manuscripts of Palestinian Targum to the Pentateuch*, 2 vols. (Cincinnati, OH: Hebrew Union College Press, 1986).
35   M. Ginsburger, ed., *Das Fragmententhargum: Thargum jeruschalmi zum Pemtateuch* (Berlin: S. Calvary, 1899); M. L. Klein, ed. and trans., *The Fragment-Targums of the Pentateuch: According to their Extant Sources*, 2 vols. (Rome: Biblical Institute Press, 1980).
36   A. Díez Macho, *Neophyti 1: Targum Palestinense MS de la Biblioteca Vaticana*, 5 vols. (Madrid: Consejo Superior de Investigaciones Científicas, 1968–2000).

4. Quotations of the Bible in Rabbinic Literature

Another form of the intersection between the written and the oral comes when we examine quotations of biblical passages in the redacted rabbinic texts available to us.[37] Needless to say, such work must be based only on manuscripts and critical editions. Furthermore, we need to keep in mind that a small number of consonantal variants remained in the MT manuscripts that circulated in Late Antiquity and the Middle Ages. Both in the rabbinic period Itself and in the later stages of manuscript transmission of rabbinic literature, biblical texts were quoted both by memory and by reference to written texts. Both of these modes of transmission shaped the textual character of quotations of Scripture in rabbinic texts.

Examination of the innumerable quotations of Scripture in rabbinic literature (and these are very prominent in Midrashic texts) indicates the following kinds of correspondences: (1) quotations corresponding exactly to MT; (2) actual textual variants that can be confirmed due to their serving as the basis for exegetical derivations; (3) errors due to quotation from memory at the rabbinic oral, compositional stage or in oral transmission; (4) errors of copyists when rabbinic texts were transmitted in writing.[38]

In this context we need to indicate that especially prominent in these variations are the differences between plene and defective spelling. On the one hand, the Babylonian Talmud reminds us that the Babylonia sages were not expert as regards the presence or absence of the multiple vowel letters *vav* and *yod*.[39] On the other hand, the attempt to preserve an exact writing tradition for the MT was a major part of the efforts of the Masoretes in the last years of Late Antiquity and the early medieval period. However, an examination of rabbinic texts reveals several examples in which halakhic derivations are made depending on the presence or absence of these *matres lectionis* and in which cases the readings preserved in the Talmud do not match those of our Masoretic Bibles.[40] These anomalies have been discussed already by medieval Jewish

---

37   V. Aptowitzer, *Das Schriftwort in der rabbinischen Literatur*, with Prolegomenon by D. S. Loewinger (repr. Library of Biblical Studies; New York: Ktav, 1970), esp. 1–36. See also D. S. Loewinger's "Prolegomenon," VII–XLIV. (For some reason the title page refers to Samuel Loewinger, but the "Prolegomenon" is signed by D. S. Loewinger.).

38   Y. Maori, "Rabbinic Midrash as Evidence for Textual Variants in the Hebrew Bible: History and Practice," in *Modern Scholarship in the Study of Torah: Contributions and Limitations*, ed. S. Carmy (Northvale, NJ: Jason Aronson, 1996), 101–29.

39   B. Qidd. 30a.

40   Cf. the list of significant variants assembled by Akiva Eiger in "Gilyon ha-Shas," in the Vilna edition of the Babylonian Talmud to b. Shab. 55b and the discussion in B. B. Levy,

commentaries on the Talmud[41] and for our purposes are excellent examples of actual textual variation, rather than simply sloppy copying of verses in Talmudic manuscripts.

A related area regarding textuality is in a group of passages listed in the Babylonian Talmud where words are to be read that are absent from the text or where words in the text are to be omitted.[42] Although this list does not conform exactly to what one finds in our Masoretic Text, it shows that such instructions already existed before the work of the Masoretes. Furthermore, rabbinic texts contain references several times to the difference between how the text appears in their manuscripts and how it was read publicly.[43] This Qere/Ketiv function is indeed preserved in our Masoretic Bibles and continues in Jewish public reading as well.[44]

5. Concerns for Textual Accuracy

Rabbinic traditions allude to important activity that must relate to a major step in the standardization of the proto-Masoretic Text, the consonantal text that provided the raw material for the efforts of the Masoretes. (While it is beyond the scope of this study, we cannot avoid calling attention to the virtual revolution that the Masoretes brought to the biblical text by the development of signs to indicate vocalization/parsing, cantillation/phrasing, and punctuation of the biblical text.[45]) We know from comparison of the situation at Qumran, Masada, and the Bar Kokhba caves that the biblical text developed from the state of various text forms in the late Second Temple period into a relatively standardized text available in the years after the destruction of the Temple.

Fixing God's Torah: Accuracy of the Hebrew Bible Text in Jewish Law (Oxford: Oxford University Press, 2001), 164–6. This volume contains an enormous amount of information about medieval and early modern manifestations of the issues raised in the present study.

41 Tosafot b. Sanh. 4b and b. Zevaḥ. 37b.
42 B. Ned. 37b–38a, Sof. 6:9; *Sefer 'Okhlah ve-'Okhlah*, ed. S. Frendsdorff, *Das Buch Ochlah W'ochlah* (Hannover: Hahn, 1864), 96, list 97 (Tov, *Textual Criticism of the Hebrew Bible* [³2012], 56).
43 B. Eruv. 26a, b. Yoma 21b, b. Ned. 37b, Gen. Rab. 34:8 (ed. J. Theodor, C. Albeck, *Bereshit Rabbah* [Jerusalem: Wahrmann, 1965] 1.316), Sof. 7 (ed. M. Higger [repr. Jerusalem: Makor, 1970], 176–87), cf. Tov, *Textual Criticism* (³2012), 55.
44 Shulḥan 'Arukh, 'Oraḥ Ḥayyim 141:8; cf. Solomon ben Adret (Rashba, Responsa, 7:361) quoted in Bet Yosef to Ṭur 'Oraḥ Ḥayyim 141:8.
45 On the role of Masoretes, see Stern, *Jewish Bible*, 68–78.

It seems from the rabbinic account, the historicity of which can in no way be proven, that Temple officials were involved in this process. The rabbis describe text correctors, called *magihe sefarim* ("correctors of books") as employed by the Temple and paid out of the annual half-Shekel Temple tax.[46] Furthermore, the rabbis refer to three authoritative texts of the Torah kept in the Temple that themselves at some point were found to have a few textual variants that had to be corrected and regularized according to the majority reading.[47] If one extrapolates from this account, one can imagine a period in which texts were being corrected according to others that were assumed to be more authoritative and that this was part of the standardization process.[48]

There is one set of rabbinic traditions in which questions regarding textual accuracy of biblical tradition are addressed directly. There are a number of traditions, scattered in a variety of rabbinic collections, especially Midrashic texts, which deal with the establishment of the correct version or call attention to a variant based on a manuscript reported to have been copied by the famed Tanna Rabbi Meir (mid-second century) who was known to be an expert scribe. Some passages refer to the Torah (Scroll) of Rabbi Meir[49] but in other places the "book" (*sefer*).[50] It seems that the term "book" is applied in some of these passages either to the Pentateuch or to the latter two sections of the Bible, whereas the term "Torah" only refers to the Pentateuch. Here we have rabbinic traditions in which people are consulting a specific text regarding

---

46 B. Ket. 106a (Babylonian amoraic) referring to *sefarim*. Y. Shek. 4:3 (48a) and Num. Rab. 11:3 referring to *sefer ha-ʿazarah* (Palestinian amoraic).

47 Sifre Deut. 356 (*Sifre on Deuteronomy*, ed. L. Finkelstein [New York, NY: Jewish Theological Seminary of America, 1969], 423); Midrash Tannaim to Deut. 33:27 (ed. D. Hoffmann [vol. II, Berlin: I. Itzkowski, 1909]; y. Taʾan. 4:2 (68a); Sof. 6:4 (*Massekhet Soferim*, ed. Higger, 169–70); Avot de-Rabbi Nathan Version B, chap. 46 (ed. S. Z. Schechter [repr. New York, NY: Feldheim, 1967], 129). Cf. J. Z. Lauterbach, "The Three Books Found in the Temple at Jerusalem," in *The Canon and Masorah of the Hebrew Bible*, ed. S. Z. Leiman (New York, NY: Ktav, 1974), 416–54, and S. Talmon, "The Three Scrolls of the Law that Were Founds in the Temple Court," *The Canon and Masorah of the Hebrew Bible*, ed. S. Z. Leiman (New York, NY: Ktav, 1974), 455–68.

48 With the rise of printing, a similar process took place in many Jewish communities where Torah scrolls were corrected to accord with the printed texts that were now assumed to be authoritative.

49 Cf. A. Lange, "An Interpretative Reading in the Isaiah Scroll of Rabbi Meir," in *HĀ-ʾĪSH MŌSHE: Studies in Scriptural Interpretation in the Dead Sea Scrolls and Related Literature in Honor of Moshe J. Bernstein*, eds. B. Y. Goldstein, M. Segal, and G. J. Brooke (Leiden: Brill, 2017), 110–22.

50 Gen. Rab. 9.5 (eds. Theodor and Albeck, 1.70, *torato*), 94:9 (3.1181–2, *torato*), 20:12 (1.196, *torato*), Midrash Bereshit Rabbati 45 line 12 (ed. C. Albeck [Jerusalem: Mekize Nirdamim, 1940], 209, *sifro*), y. Taʾan. 1:1 (64a, *sifro*).

various passages. While this is not a common feature in rabbinic literature, no doubt because of the paucity of significant textual variants in the proto-MT manuscripts available to the sages, we can see that on rare occasions they made such comparisons.

Although there seem not to be outright discussions of textual variation in biblical texts, numerous techniques are used in the Talmudic texts, Babylonian and Palestinian, to correct earlier rabbinic oral traditions. Such passages include numerous corrections of, or debates about, the text of quotations from the Mishnah, as well as presentation of alternate versions of some passages, and attempts to establish the correct attribution of statements of various tannaim or amoraim.[51] Despite this interest in textual accuracy, we must again observe the way in which rabbinic collections contain numerous different versions of parallel or similar material as well as even different redactions of groups of traditions. One might have expected, in view of the stringencies that surrounded the transmission of Scripture, that similar concerns might have militated against such variations in the transmission of oral materials. Here we need to emphasize that for the rabbis, the medium of oral tradition brought with it the revision and expansion that produced these varying versions. While they remained concerned about the accurate transmission of such traditions, they seemingly were not bothered by the growth and development of parallel, extended, or recast versions of the same material. Somehow this was supposed to happen in the world of the Oral Law. Considering certain traditions pertaining to the publication of the Mishnah, however, it may be that here the rabbis sought to maintain an exactitude that for them stemmed from the authority of this document.[52]

6. Conclusions: Orality, Textuality and Memory

In general terms, one can say about the ancient rabbis that "the medium is the message."[53] On the one hand, they held to a considerable effort to maintain relatively exact transmission of the written traditions of ancient Israel as found in what was for them the canonized Bible. Not only could nothing

---

51 L. H. Schiffman, "Textual Criticism and the Evolution of Rabbinic Texts: Will There Ever Be a Final Text?" in *Comparative Textual Criticism of Religious Scriptures*, eds. K. Finsterbusch, R. Fuller, A. Lange, and J. K. Driesbach (Leiden: Brill, 2024), 133–51.
52 Cf. Y. Brandes, "The Canonization of the Mishnah," *JAJ* 10 (2019), 145–80.
53 The title of the first chapter of M. McLuhan, *Understanding Media: The Extensions of Man* (New York, NY: Mentor, 1969).

additional from later periods be admitted to this collection,[54] but the text had to be maintained carefully and as exactly as possible. They seem to have been aware that this corpus had a textual history, yet they saw the proto-Masoretic version in their hands as a reflection of divine revelation, and throughout their corpus they had no hesitation about interpreting its smallest details and peculiarities of spelling in developing both aggadic and halakhic principles.[55]

On the other hand, while adhering to certain standards of exactitude in the transmission of what they regarded as the Oral Law, they allowed numerous expansions and developments and parallel redactions of traditions. In this respect, they seem to have seen the Oral Law as a dynamic and developing entity that supplemented and explained the Written Law. Nowhere is this more evident than in the regulations regarding the exactitude of the reading of the Torah and the need to correct the reader in cases of mispronunciation, when contrasted with the loose structure of the on-the-spot translation into Aramaic, seen as part of the Oral Law.[56] Clearly, what we have here is the rabbinic concept of the interplay of the static and fixed written law providing the basis for the developing and growing Oral Law. Later Jewish interpretations understood this combination as what guaranteed the continuity of Judaism after the destruction of the Temple.

At the same time, the rabbis made room for a kind of combination of the oral and the written in the reading of Scripture. Here we have oral performance of a written text. In some ways we might say that the reverse happened when rabbinic literature was written down and what were originally oral "documents" became written texts.[57]

If what we have presented here demonstrates anything, it is the way orality and textuality work hand-in-hand in preserving the collective religious memory of Judaism in rabbinic times. This interplay of the oral and written, of the fixed and the organically developing, typifies rabbinic theology and practice. In many ways, therefore, the crowning achievement of the Masoretes, coming on the heels of the Talmudic period, may be seen as reducing to written symbols the oral component of the performance of the written text. This is

---

54 B. B.B. 12b.
55 Strack and Stemberger, *Introduction*, 17–34.
56 Y. Meg. 4:1 (74d).
57 On the transition from oral to written Talmud, see R. Brody, *The Geonim of Babylonia and the Shaping of Medieval Jewish Culture* (New Haven, CT: Yale University Press, 1998), 156–61; idem, "The Talmud in the Geonic Period," in *Printing the Talmud: from Bomberg to Schottenstein*, eds. S. Liberman Mintz and G. M. Goldstein (New York, NY: Yeshiva University Museum, 2005), 31–32.

probably the greatest example of the interrelationship of oral and written that lies at the basis of rabbinic Judaism.

Bibliography

Albeck, Theodor C., ed. *Bereshit Rabbah*. Jerusalem: Wahrmann, 1965.

Aptowitzer, Avigdor. *Das Schriftwort in der rabbinischen Literatur*, with Prolegomenon by D. Samuel Loewinger. Repr. Library of Biblical Studies. New York, NY: Ktav, 1970.

del Barco, Javier. "From Scroll to Codex: Dynamics of Text Layout Transformation in the Hebrew Bible." In *From Scrolls to Scrolling: Sacred Texts, Materiality, and Dynamic Media Cultures*, edited by Bradford A. Anderson, 91–118. Berlin: de Gruyter, 2020.

Baumgarten, Joseph M. *Studies in Qumran Law*. Leiden: Brill, 1977.

Blau, Ludwig. *Studien zum althebräischen Buchwesen und zur biblischen Litteratur- und Textgeschichte*. Strassburg: J. Trübner, 1902.

Brandes, Yehuda. "The Canonization of the Mishnah." *Journal of Ancient Judaism* 10 (2019): 145–80.

Brody, Robert. *The Geonim of Babylonia and the Shaping of Medieval Jewish Culture*. New Haven, CT: Yale University Press, 1998.

--------. "The Talmud in the Geonic Period." In *Printing the Talmud: from Bomberg to Schottenstein*, edited by Sharon Liberman Mintz and Gabriel M. Goldstein, 31–32. New York, NY: Yeshiva University Museum, 2005.

Díez Macho, Alejandro. *Neophyti 1: Targum Palestinense MS de la Biblioteca Vaticana*. 5 volumes. Madrid: Consejo Superior de Investigaciones Científicas, 1968–2000.

Finkelstein, Eliezer A., ed. *Sifre on Deuteronomy*. New York, NY: Jewish Theological Seminary of America, 1969.

Frendsdorff, Salomon. *Das Buch Ochlah W'ochlah*. Hannover: Hahn, 1864.

Ginsburger, Moses, ed. *Das Fragmententhargum: Thargum jeruschalmi zum Pentateuch*. Berlin: S. Calvary, 1899.

--------. *Pseudo-Jonathan: Thargum Jonathan ben Usiël zum Pentateuch*. Berlin: S. Calvary, 1903.

Haran, Menahem. "Book-Scrolls in Israel in Pre-Exilic Times." *Journal of Jewish Studies* 33 (1982): 161–73.

--------. "Melekhet ha-Sofer bi-Tequfat ha-Miqra': Megillot ha-Sefarim ve-'Avizare ha-Ketivah." *Tarbiz* 50 (1981): 65–87. [In Hebrew.]

Heinemann, Joseph. "The Nature of the Aggadah." In *Midrash and Literature*, edited by Geoffry H. Hartman and Sanford Budick, 41–55. New Haven, CT: Yale, 1986.

Higger, Michael, ed. *Massekhet Soferim*. New York, NY: Debe Rabanan, 1937.

Jaffee, Martin S. *Torah in the Mouth: Writing and Oral Tradition in Palestinian Judaism 200 BCE–400 CE*. Oxford: Oxford University Press, 2001.

Jastrow, Marcus. *Dictionary of the Targumim, Talmud Bavli, Talmud Yerushalmi and Midrashic Literature*. 2 volumes. New York, NY: Pardes Publishing, 1959.

Klein, Michael L., ed. and trans. *The Fragment-Targums of the Pentateuch: According to their Extant Sources*. 2 volumes. Rome: Biblical Institute Press, 1980.

--------. *Genizah Manuscripts of Palestinian Targum to the Pentateuch*. 2 volumes. Cincinnati, OH: Hebrew Union College Press, 1986.

Lange, Armin. "An Interpretative Reading in the Isaiah Scroll of Rabbi Meir." *HĀ-'ÎSH MŌSHE: Studies in Scriptural Interpretation in the Dead Sea Scrolls and Related Literature in Honor of Moshe J. Bernstein*, edited by Binyamin Y. Goldstein, Michael Segal, and George J. Brooke, 110–22. Leiden: Brill, 2017.

Lauterbach, Jacob Z. "The Three Books Found in the Temple at Jerusalem." In *The Canon and Masorah of the Hebrew Bible*, edited by Sid Z. Leiman, 416–54. New York, NY: Ktav, 1974.

Leiman, Sid Z. *The Canonization of Hebrew Scripture: The Talmudic and Midrashic Evidence*. Hamden, CT: Archon Books, 1976.

Levine, Lee I. *The Ancient Synagogue: The First Thousand Years*. New Haven, CT: Yale University Press, 2000.

Levy, B. Barry. *Fixing God's Torah: Accuracy of the Hebrew Bible Text in Jewish Law*. Oxford: Oxford University Press, 2001.

Lieberman, Saul. *Hellenism in Jewish Palestine*. New York, NY: Jewish Theological Seminary, 1962.

Maori, Yeshayahu. "Rabbinic Midrash as Evidence for Textual Variants in the Hebrew Bible: History and Practice." In *Modern Scholarship in the Study of Torah: Contributions and Limitations*, edited by Shalom Carmy, 101–29. Northvale, NJ: Jason Aronson, 1996.

McLuhan, Marshall. *Understanding Media: The Extensions of Man*. New York, NY: Mentor, 1969.

Neusner, Jacob. *Uniting the Dual Torah: Sifra and the Problem of the Mishnah*. Cambridge: Cambridge University Press, 1990.

Rabinowitz, L. "Does Midrash Tillim Reflect the Triennial Cycle of Psalms?" *The Jewish Quarterly Review* 26 (1936): 349–68.

Resnick, Irven M. "The Codex in Early Jewish and Christian Communities." *Journal of Religious History* 17 (1992): 1–17.

Schechter, Salomon Z., ed. *Avot de-Rabbi Nathan*. Reprinted New York, NY: Feldheim, 1967.

Schiffman, Lawrence H. "The Early History of the Public Reading of the Torah." In *Jews, Christians, and Polytheists in the Ancient Synagogue: Cultural Interaction during the Greco-Roman Period*, edited by Steven Fine, 44–56. London: Routledge, 1999.

--------. *From Text to Tradition: A History of Second Temple and Rabbinic Judaism*. Hoboken, NJ: Ktav, 1991.

--------. "The Haftarah: An Historical Introduction." In *From Within the Tent: The Haftarot, Essays on the Weekly Haftarah Reading from the Rabbis & Professors of Yeshiva University*, edited by Daniel Z. Feldman and Stuart W. Halpern, xix–xxvii. Jerusalem: Maggid Books, 2011.

--------. "Jerusalem Talmud Megillah 1 (71b–72a)—'Of the Making of Books': Rabbinic Scribal Arts in Light of the Dead Sea Scrolls." In *Talmuda de-Eretz Israel: Archaeology and the Rabbis in Late Antique Palestine*, edited by Steven Fine and Aaron J. Koller, 97–109. Berlin: de Gruyter, 2014.

--------. *Texts and Traditions: A Source Reader for the Study of Second Temple and Rabbinic Judaism*. Hoboken, NJ: Ktav, 1998.

--------. "Textual Criticism and the Evolution of Rabbinic Texts: Will There Ever Be a Final Text?" In *Comparative Textual Criticism of Religious Scriptures*, edited by Karin Finsterbusch, Russell Fuller, Armin Lange, and Jason K. Driesbach, 133–51. Leiden: Brill, 2024.

--------. "What is a Jewish Biblical Text?" *Hebrew Bible and Ancient Israel* 9 (2020): 296–305.

Segal, Moshe Z. *Sefer Ben Sira ha-Shalem*. Jerusalem: Bialik Institute, ²1971.

Sokoloff, Michael. *The Targum to Job from Qumran Cave XI*. Ramat-Gan: Bar-Ilan University, 1974.

Stern, David. *The Jewish Bible: A Material History*. Seattle, WA: University of Washington Press, 2017.

Strack, Hermann L. and Günter Stemberger. *Introduction to the Talmud and Midrash*. Edinburgh: T & T Clark, 1991.

Talmon, Shemaryahu. "The Three Scrolls of the Law that Were Founds in the Temple Court." In *The Canon and Masorah of the Hebrew Bible*, edited by Sid Z. Leiman, 455–68. New York, NY: Ktav, 1974.

Tov, Emanuel. *Scribal Practices and Approaches Reflected in the Texts Found in the Judean Desert*. Leiden: Brill, 2004.

--------. "Scribal Practices Reflected in the Documents from the Judean Desert and in the Rabbinic Literature: A Comparative Study." In *Texts, Temples, and Traditions: A Tribute to Menahem Haran*, edited by Michael V. Fox and Menahem Haran. Winona Lake, IN: Eisenbrauns, 1996.

--------. "The Scribal and Textual Transmission of the Torah Analyzed in Light of Its Sanctity." In *Pentateuchal Traditions in the Late Second Temple Period. Proceedings of the International Workshop in Tokyo, August 28–31, 2007*, edited by Akio Moriya and Gohei Hata. Leiden: Brill, 2012.

--------. *Textual Criticism of the Hebrew Bible*. Minneapolis, MN: Fortress Press, ³2012, ⁴2022.

Trebolle, Julio. "Canon of the Old Testament." *New Interpreter's Dictionary of the Bible* 1:548–49.

Ulrich, Eugene. *The Dead Sea Scrolls and the Origins of the Bible.* Grand Rapids, MI: W.B. Eerdmans, 1999.

Urbach, Ephraim E. *The Sages: Their Concepts and Beliefs.* 2 volumes. Translated from the Hebrew by Israel Abrahams. Jerusalem: Magnes Press, The Hebrew University, 1987.

Converts' Souls in the *Zohar*: A Reception History

Yuval Katz-Wilfing

1. Introduction

Soul transmigration was already understood by the great Kabbalah researcher Gershom Shalom (1897–1982) as one of the central elements of Kabbalah literature.[1] One of the principles of Kabbalistic soul mechanics is that the more righteous the soul, the further up in the sefirot it can climb and the less righteous, the further down it will move.[2] This Kabbalistic interest in the soul and its mechanics led to new discussions regarding not only the Jewish soul, but also the gentile soul. As the Kabbalistic quandary in these topics could not receive any answers from the canonized text as they were read up until then, a new way of reading and understanding the texts developed. This innovative reception of the biblical texts is evident in the *Zohar*, which is mostly made up of Midrashim about the biblical texts which explore new, more esoteric, topics.

In the *Zohar* we find several developments in the ideas regarding converts and their souls. These are a part of a longer tradition dealing with biblical texts and their reception. This article will follow these developments and the way they use the older texts to support existing ideas and create new ideas about converts and their souls. In the center of the Zoharic discourse are those texts from the Torah which deal with the genesis of Jewish identity, such as narratives about Abraham (the first monotheist) the giving of the Torah on Mount Sinai, and the encounter of the emerging People of Israel with their new homeland. The *Zohar* also uses other texts from the Hebrew Bible which deal with joining the Jewish nation, such as the story of Ruth and verses from the Book of Proverbs. The reception of these texts is sometimes very innovative and goes in quite different directions than the reception tradition before it.

One must remember that the concepts of conversion to Judaism, the Jewish soul, and soul transmigration in general cannot be explicitly found in the Hebrew Bible's text. As these ideas emerged and developed, they interacted

---

1 See G. Scholem, *Pirqei Yesod Behavanat Hakabbalah Vesimleiha* [*Foundations in Understanding Kabbalah and its Symbols*] (Jerusalem, 1991), 257–308.
2 See Y. Weiss, "Dehiyah, Halifah, Ve'ibur, Tefisot Sefirotiot Bedavar Gilgul Neshamot Bein Gufim Besifrut Hakabbalah Hamukdamah Veyediheihen," ["Delay, Exchange, and Transition: Sefiratic Perceptions Regarding the Transmigration of Souls between Bodies in Early Kabbalistic Literature and Their Consequences,"] *Jewish Studies* 57 (2022): 65–105.

with the canonized texts and changed the way these texts were read, understood and received. Indeed, these concepts had emerged before the *Zohar* itself, creating a potential conflict between the accepted practice of conversion to Judaism (*giur*) and the idea that the Jewish soul is somehow distinct from the non-Jewish soul. In other words, how is it possible to become a Jew, if being a Jew is dependent on having such a seemingly unchangeable character as having a unique type of soul? The *Zohar* deals with this issue in a few places and gives several answers to this possible paradox.

The drastic change in the development of ideas dealing with souls and converts can be exemplified by the reception of Genesis 12:5. The non-esoteric tradition of commentary to Genesis 12:5, which started in the first centuries BCE, was predicated upon the assumption that humans cannot create life and living creatures:

והלא אם מתכנסין כל באי העולם לברות יתוש אחד ולהכניס בו נשמה - אינן יכולין

> And even if all the people of the world convened to create one mosquito and put a soul in him, they cannot. (GenR 39:14).

This basic assumption has been central to all the moral, legal and theological commentary before the Kabbalistic tradition emerged. The esoteric tradition which will be surveyed in this paper sometimes continues the trends of the commentary before it, but it also breaks with this tradition and contradicts its basic assumption. They may use some of the same expressions and ideas as the non-esoteric tradition but view them in a very different context and through a world view which is sometimes in complete contradiction to the non-esoteric one. Since this contextual shift is very deep, I feel that I must elaborate on the background to these new ideas.

2. Kabbalah and the *Zohar*

Kabbalah can be defined as a worldview encompassing all life and existence, which seeks to use a religious, esoteric approach to find solutions to the world's mysteries and life's upheavals. At its heart lies the secret of knowing the divine reality, or the system in which the divine manages our human reality. Kabbalah deals with the hidden areas of the divine life, with humans as individuals and with the relationship between them.[3] Some of the most important ideas in the

---

3 See M. Halamish, *Mavoh le Qabbalah* [*An Introduction to the Kabbalah*] (Jerusalem: Elinor Vehakibuts Hame'uchad Press, 1991). 13.

hermeneutics of Kabbalah are emanations, soul transmigration, and divine sparks as links to the upper worlds, their symbols, letters and names.[4]

The Kabbalah tradition can be seen as an answer to the philosophical quandaries that occupied Jewish thought at the end of the first millennium and the beginning of the second.[5] These quandaries caused a new genre of rabbinic literature to emerge, thus creating the last of the four major forms of reading in the *pardes* (פרדס). *Pardes* is an acronym for *peshat, remez, drash* and *sod* (פשט, רמז, דרש, סוד).[6] *Sod*, secret, is the esoteric understanding of biblical texts, the one that was received via Kabbalah, literally reception. The Kabbalah tradition grew to be very influential, and some of the most prominent figures in Jewish thought and law are kabbalists who are at least well versed if not immersed in Kabbalah thought and practice.[7] The main Kabbalistic work or volume is the *Zohar*. According to the Jewish tradition, The *Zohar* (זוהר), also known as the *Holy Zohar* (הזוהר הקדוש, *Hazohar Haqodesh*), was attributed to the Tannah Rabbi Shimon bar Yochai, who lived in the second century CE.

The scientific-critical research consensus however, does not consider late antiquity as the origin of the *Zohar*. Zoharic texts first appear at the end of the thirteenth century in Castile[8] and major researchers, such as Heinrich Graetz and Gershom Scholem, have reasoned that Rabbi Moses de Leon in Spain[9] was its sole creator. Later scholars have argued that the *Zohar* is a collaborative work of about three generations around Moses de Leon, and it may reflect a much larger circle rather than merely one person. Even though the book emerged at a specific time in the Middle Ages, it is possible that it is only a compilation of older traditions that have not reached us. This may be because of their esoteric nature and oral tradition in which they were preserved. Others claim that "the Zohar is not woven from fragments found here and there, but that it preserves the ancient warp and woof of a tradition more antique than Sifre and Midrash Tannaim."[10] Even if we accept that the *Zohar* has much older sources, we can still identify trends unique to the *Zohar* and its time, which manifest developments unique to the Middle Ages.

The Zohar is subdivided into three main parts: the *Zohar* on the Torah, *Tikkunei Hazohar* (lit. *Repairs of the Zohar*) and *Zohar Hadash* (*New Zohar*).

---

4 See G. Langer, *Midrasch* (Tübingen: Mohr Siebeck, 2016), 260.
5 See Halamish, *Mavoh le Qabbalah*, 11.
6 *Peshat* is the literal, accepted reading, *remez* is allegorical, *drash* is the midrashic reading and *sod* is the mystic reading.
7 See Halamish *Mavoh le Qabbalah*, 13.
8 See A. Green, *A Guide to the Zohar* (Stanford, CA: Stanford University Press, 2004), 162.
9 See ibid., 164–165.
10 H. Basser, "Midrash Tannaim," in *Encyclopaedia of Midrash*, ed. J. Neusner and A. Avery-Peck (Leiden: Brill, 2005), 1:516.

The *Zohar* does not suppress the *peshat* (simple) meaning of the text, it simply gives it a different but still important role in understanding the scriptures.[11] The content of the *Zohar*'s first three books is arranged after the order of the weekly reading portion of the Pentateuch. The first two books are dedicated to Genesis and Exodus, and the third deals with the other three books of the Pentateuch. The *Zohar* also has a part called *New Zohar, Zohar Hadash* (זוהר חדש). Even though it is named new, it may include some of the earliest Zoharic material.[12] This part has more texts on the Pentateuch and also on Ruth,[13] Lamentations and the Song of Songs.[14]

3. Afterlife and Soul Concepts before the *Zohar*

In order to appreciate its revolutionary role in the way souls are viewed in Kabbalistic tradition, we must first discuss the way souls were viewed before the Kabbalah. In the Hebrew Bible, one hardly finds the concept of a soul or an afterlife.[15] The word *nefesh* (נפש) has many meanings, mostly to do with life force and the attributes of living people and beings. The notion of soul and *nefesh* as we now understand it, as an incorporeal part of the human being, has much to do with the notion of afterlife in that the human being continues to exist after the body perishes. That necessitates a concept of non-physical existence of human beings: therefore necessitating the idea of the soul.

In most of the Hebrew Bible when one dies, it is stated that he "gathers with his people/ancestors" as in Genesis 25:8.[16] It is not clear what that means. Maybe it hints at the practice of family burial. The body or bones of the deceased is literally gathered with their ancestors. It is also possible that it hints at a different metaphysical reality.

In other places in the Hebrew Bible we find that people who die descend to *she'ol* (שאול) a mysterious place not really described: somewhere below where the dead go indiscriminately, independent of how they lived their lives—as

---

11   Langer, *Midrasch*, 262.
12   See *The Zohar: Pritzker Edition*, vol. 11, ed. J. Hecker (Stanford, CA: Stanford University Press, 2016), xi.
13   For more information, see the preface for *The Zohar: Pritzker Edition*, vol. 11.
14   Green, *A Guide to the Zohar*, 63.
15   See J. Pedersen, *Israel, Its Life and Culture* (London: Oxford University Press, 1953), 460ff.
16   The full verse reads: "Then Abraham breathed his last and died at a good old age, an old man and full of years; and he was gathered to his people/ancestors" (ויגוע וימת אברהם בשיבה טובה זקן ושבע ויאסף אל עמיו). A more critical view may be found in G. von Rad, *Old Testament Theology* (Edinburgh: Oliver & Boyd, 1962).

king or slave, just or evil (Job 3: 11–19) whether Jew or gentile (Isaiah 14:9)—and they stay there for eternity (Job 7:9). They can still be summoned by the living (Samuel I 28:13–15). This shadowy *she'ol* is similar to the Greek Hades and the Mesopotamian world of the dead. It is dark (Psalms 88:7) and lies in the depths of the earth (Deuteronomy 32:22). At this point it is not clear if their existence in *she'ol* is totally incorporeal or if they retain their personality.

The conceptual differentiation of destinies in the afterlife (eternal life or eternal death) necessitates the connection between the personality and this destination in a way which implies the personality being tied up in the incorporeal side of the human being. That incorporeal element of the human is the soul. The belief that there are different destinies for different people in the afterlife can be found at the beginning of the First Book of Enoch (chapters 1, 2–9) dated to the third century BCE, and in the last chapter of the Book of Daniel,[17] possibly written during or shortly before the Maccabean revolt. Josephus Flavius writes in the *Jewish War* that it was the belief of the Pharisees.[18]

Another belief not found in the Hebrew Bible holds that in the afterlife, good people go to a place which is all good (paradise-like) and evil people to a place which is all bad (hell-like). This position is found in the last parts of the Second Book of Enoch (44:1–6) which probably stems from the first century BCE. Josephus Flavius attributes these beliefs to the Essenes.[19] This can still be understood as happening to the entire person without the clear differentiation between soul and body.

In the Mishnah (redacted around the beginning of the third century CE), we also find an uncompromising belief in the revival of the dead:

> All of Israel have a part in the world to come … And those who do not have a part in the world to come are the ones who say that the revival of the dead is not mentioned in the Torah and that the Torah does not come from heaven … (m. San. 10:1)

---

17 See, e.g., Dan. 12:2: "Many of them that sleep in the dust of the earth shall awake, some to everlasting life, and some to reproaches and everlasting abhorrence." See also Isa. 26:19; Ezek. 37:1ff.

18 See Josephus, *J.W.* 2.163: "Every soul, they maintain, is imperishable, but the soul of the good alone passes into another body, a while the souls of the wicked suffer eternal punishment." Trans. Thackeray, LCL 203, 385–87.

19 See Josephus, *J.W.* 2.155: "Sharing the belief of the sons of Greece, they maintain that for virtuous souls there is reserved an abode beyond the ocean, a place which is not oppressed by rain or snow or heat, but is refreshed by the ever gentle breath of the west wind coming in from ocean; while they relegate base souls to a murky and tempestuous dungeon, big with never-ending punishments." Trans. Thackeray, LCL 203, 383.

Alongside a belief in heaven and hell. Another view from the Mishna is that the arrogant one is headed for Gehinnom and the blushing one for the Garden of Eden.[20] This fate can still be understood as happening to the entire person, without the differentiation between soul and body. In the Gemara (detailing Jewish Babylonian rabbinical discourse from the third to the fifth century) we find a more complex idea of the soul as accompanying the body[21] and focusing more on the concept of resurrection.[22] Although the soul is different from the body, again in this description the soul and the body make up one unit and cannot be judged separately. Rather, they have the same destiny. Rabbi Saadya Gaon (882–942) developed a neo-platonic philosophy which led him to conceptualize the soul as a divine emanation stowed away at death until the Messiah comes, at which point the dead rise, the good ones to paradise and the evil ones to *she'ol*. Rabbi Saadya Gaon, however, strongly opposed the idea of the soul transmigration, calling it illusions and confusions.[23]

In the work which is considered the first Kabbalah book, *Sefer Habahir* (*The Book of Brightness*, first mentioned in late twelfth century), we find a further developed idea of the soul, its origin and destiny. There seems to be an idea of soul transmigration, independent of the body altogether. In *Sefer Habahir*, the delay in the coming of the anticipated messianic age is also explained through the transmigration of souls, a concept which is linked to the sins of Israel.[24] In this view, souls come from the divine and all of them must emanate before the Messiah comes; however, new souls are released into the world only when the old ones finish their transmigration cycles. This is explained by a parable of a king sending bread to feed his army; he will not send any new bread until the old bread is consumed.[25] As long as the people of Israel are sinful, their souls

---

20   M. Avot 5:20: "The impudent are destined for Gehinnom, and the shamefaced for the Garden of Eden."
21   B. San. 91b: "Even the Creator brings a soul and places it in the body and judges them together."
22   See A. Marmorstein, "The Doctrine of the Resurrection of the Dead in Rabbinic Theology," *The American Journal of Theology* 19, no. 4 (1915): 577–91.
23   *Sefer Ha'emunot Vehade'ot*, art. iv, part viii: "I hereby state that among those who are called Jews, I have found believers in reincarnation, who regard it as the transmigration of souls. Their belief is that the spirit of Reuben will be in Simeon, and afterwards in Levi, and then in Judah. Some of them, or most of them, believe that there are cases where the spirit of a human will be in an animal, and the spirit of an animal will be in a human, and many such absurdities and confusions." In *Saadia Ben Yosef Gaon According to the Translation of Judah Ben Tibbon* (Constantinople, 1562). Translation by the author of this article.
24   *Sefer Habahir*, 155 (קנה).
25   *Sefer Habahir*, 184 (קפד).

keep being reused. It is thus the sins of the people that prevent new souls from appearing and, therefore, also delay the coming of the Messiah. Only when all souls are new will the Messiah come.[26] The role of the individual is central here: one must study the Torah and keep away from sin not only to ensure one's individual destiny in the afterlife, but also to play a major role in history and the future of the people. If people are good, their actions are actually bringing the Messiah. *Sefer Habahir* offers not only responsibility, but also hope. Even if we do know that the people are and will be sinful, the top limit seems to be a thousand transmigration cycles. This is explained by the parable of the vineyards.[27] The number of cycles of planting and ripping out of the vineyards is limited to one thousand. So, the infinite nature of the cycle (*gilgul*) is boxed by linear history, which ends with the coming of the Messiah. The details of soul transmigration in Bahir are used mainly as an explanation for other problems. *Sefer Habahir* is more occupied with the explaining power of the transmigration of souls, rather than the mechanics of the process —the why, not the how, of soul transmigration. Further details are added in later Kabbalah literature, eventually gaining a life of their own.

An example of the influence of *Sefer Habahir* can be found in the writings of Rabbi Moshe ben Nachman (1194–1270). In his influential book *Sha'ar Hagemul* (*Gate of Reward*),[28] he wrote that when one dies, he is judged by God. The righteous head to heaven, a place in this world where souls train for the world to come. Sinners head to hell, also a place in this world, where souls undergo suffering by fire. The duration of the stay depends on their sinfulness, where the worst sinners stay in hell for eternity.

The process of soul mechanics as presented by the *Zohar* is made possible by two previous developments: one is the idea expressed in *Sefer Habahir* that the soul (of the *tsadik*, the righteous person) originates in a divine reality. The other is the idea that gentiles possess a deep otherness from Jews, a different character. We find that this comes from a kind of "soul filth"[29] which was common to all humans. We find this idea in the Talmud:

---

26 See G. Scholem, *Reshit Haqabbalah Vesefer Habahir, Hartzau'tav shel Prof. G. Scholem, Shanat Tashkav* [*Beginning of Kabbalah and the Book of Bahir, Lectures by Prof. G. Scholem*], ed. R. Shatz (Jerusalem, 1962), 168.

27 *Sefer Habahir*, 195 (קצה).

28 Part of his larger work *Sha'ar Ha'emuna* (שער האמונה, *The Gate of Faith*).

29 See also A. Kosman, *Masechet Shalom: Hasichsuch Ha'israeli-aravi Le'or Mekorot Midrashiyim Verabaniyim* [*Tractate Peace: The Arab-Israeli Conflict in Light of Midrashic and Rabbinic Sources*] (Jerusalem: Miskal, 2014).

"Rav Yosef taught" … why are idolaters lustful? "Because they did not stand at Mount Sinai. For when the serpent copulated with Eve, he injected her with *zohama*, slime. Israel, who stood at Mount Sinai their *zohama* ceased. Star-worshipers who did not stand at Mount Sinai- their *zohama* did not cease." Rav Aha son of Aava asked Rav Ashi "what about proselytes?" … Rabbi Abba son of Kahana said, "until three generations the *zohama* did not disappear from our forefathers: Abraham begat Ishmael, Isaac begat Esau, (but) Jacob begat the twelve tribes in whom there was no taint whatsoever." (b. Shab. 145b–146a)

We find that not only do gentiles differ from Israelites, but that also gerim are not fully Jewish, since it takes a few generations for them to discard their *zohama*, or slime. This *zohama* and the difficulty of its removal in converts is also dealt with in the *Zohar*.[30]

Yehudah Halevi (1075–1141) also sees the Jew as another type of creature, essentially different from his gentile counterpart. Yehudah Halevi finds it difficult to accept that a convert becomes fully Jewish, and claims that they only come closer to God but do not receive the uniquely Jewish ability to prophesize.[31] The essential problem, as J. Katz expresses it, is that "the divinely revealed Torah seemed to be inconsistent in that it permitted a non-Jew to become a Jew, while at the same time regarding the Jewish people as being different from all the others."[32]

While some, like Maimonides, recognize the convert as a full Jew and reject the Kabbalistic ideas about the convert's soul, the Zohar offers models and theories which make it possible to hold that full conversion to Judaism is possible while still holding that Jews are beings apart from Gentiles.

4. Creating Souls for Converts in the *Zohar*

The Zohar has several texts which give some details about how souls are created. One of these texts can be found in the part dealing with Parashat Terumah. Parashat Terumah is the seventh Torah reading portion in the Book of Exodus (25:1–27:19) and it deals with instructions on how to build the tabernacle. The *Zohar* reads this *parasha* as hinting at the structure of reality and this part of the Zohar it deals with the positive and negative sides of creation,

---

30 See *Zohar* 2:87b; 3:14b.
31 This idea is expressed by the Rabbi Character (haCHaver) in the *Kuzari* by Yehudah ha-Levi (Warsaw, 1880), part 1, 115. See also J. Guttmann, *Die Philosophie des Judentums* (Munich: Ernst Reinhardt, 1933), 146.
32 See J. Katz, *Exclusiveness and Tolerance: Studies in Jewish-gentile Relations in Medieval and Modern Times* (Oxford: Oxford University Press, 1961), 146.

called up or down,[33] or holy side (*tsad haqedusha*) and the other side. Within this reality, God shines a light:

> Once that primordial light became sweetly steady, the blessed Holy One treasured it away. For whom did He hide it? For the righteous. And who are they? Righteous one and Righteousness, so as to generate through that primordial light fruit for the world, fruit destined to come into the world.[34] For Abraham and Sarah formed souls and fruit, as is written, and the souls they had made in Haran. Just as they made souls on the side of Holiness, so too they made souls on the Other Side. For without that arousal aroused by Abraham on the Other Side, there would be no converts in the world at all. (*Zohar*, Terumah 2:147b)[35]

This text, by using Genesis 12:5, explains the existence of converts in the world and how they came to be. According to this text, converts are fruit made by the righteous using the divinely originated primordial light. Here, we see that the righteous are actually creating souls, and it is clear that this is not just an expression meaning teaching, educating or converting. The actions of Abraham and Sarah have multiple products in two separate sides of creation, the side of Holiness and the Other Side, and the products on the other side are necessary for the creation of converts.

Do we understand, therefore, that converts on the holiness side and the products on the other side are necessary balancing products? Or are the converts themselves actually the products on the other side, which eventually join the side of holiness when they convert?[36] In any case, the righteous are given extensive creative powers.

Another place in the Zohar which considers souls and their creation is the chapter dealing with Parashat Shelah Lekha from the Book of Numbers, which deals with the first mission in the land of Israel from the children of Israel after they left Egypt. In the Zoharic text we find a narrative surrounding the figure of Rav Metivta. Rav Metivta, head of the Academy/Yeshivah, is a narrative

---

[33] "Pillars above amidst the seven pillars below" (הָעַמּוּדִים שֶׁלְמַעְלָה תּוֹךְ שִׁבְעַת הָעַמּוּדִים שֶׁלְמַטָּה, פרשת תרומה).

[34] The light that is hidden and saved only for the righteous can already be seen in b. Hag.12a.

[35] See *The Zohar: Pritzker Edition*, ed. D. C. Matt (Stanford, CA: Stanford University Press, 2009), 5: 341.

[36] In the Pritzker edition of the Zohar, 5: 342 n 427, we find the opinion that Rabbi Elazar focuses not on the conversion of residents of Haran but rather on Abraham and Sarah forming actual souls for future converts (who derive from the other side). This creative act is usually reserved for the righteous in the Garden of Eden. Abraham himself was the prototypical convert. And in b. Sukk. 49b he is described as the first convert. On the Midrashic interpretation of the verse in Genesis, see note 43. On the formation of souls see note 21. On Abraham making souls for future converts, see *Zohar* 3:168a.

dealing with Rabbi Shimon bar Yochai and his students' travels in the Garden of Eden and what they learn from the head of the heavenly academy, mainly about the world to come. The text is incorporated into the text dealing with the weekly reading portion of Shelach Lecha which mainly deals with the sin of the Israelite spies who were reluctant to fight and settle the land of Canaan after they explored it.[37]

While dealing with the various details from Genesis chapters 11 and 12, the *Zohar* compares soul creation and giving birth. This allows for the usage of Genesis 12:5 to further explain the scripture and develop the idea that converts gain Jewish souls:

> The head of the Yeshiva said and it is written: "and Sarai is barren, she has no born child" (Gen 11) from that which is said "Sarai is barren," don't I know that "she has no born child." What does "she has no born child" mean? But that is what the head of the Yeshiva said, she did not give birth to children, but she did give birth to souls. In the *devequt* (passion) of these two *tsadiqim* (righteous people) they gave birth to the souls of converts all the time they were in Haran, like the Zaddikim do in Heaven, as it is said "and the souls which they had made in Haran" so they must have made souls. (*Zohar*, Rav Metivta 3:168a)[38]

In this text we find a verse intended to prove the distinction between "spiritual" soul making and "biological" people making. Sarah is then seen as bringing forth souls into the world and not bearing biological children. This power to make souls is given to all righteous people in heaven. Sarah and Abraham are unique in that they have this creative ability also while on earth.

This reading possibly follows ideas similar to the human ability to create souls as expressed in the Book of Creation, where Abraham's unique knowledge allowed him to create life. This text goes further to directly oppose the older Sifre assertion relating directly to Genesis 12:5 that no human is able to create souls. Here, it is not only Abraham with his unique abilities but also Sarah with her righteousness, and then it is all righteous people. We see a turn from the "workshop" creating of soul to a more "bedroom" method, that is souls are not created via the application of a craft but by the joining of the right males and females. Another striking change here is the move away from a Midrashic-metaphoric reading of the text to an attempt at a more literal reading. Making souls no longer means just a formative spiritual influence of one

---

37   See I. Tishby, "General Introduction," in *Wisdom of the Zohar: An Anthology of Texts*, vol. 1, ed. I. Tishby and F. Lachower (Oxford: Oxford University Press, 1989), 3.

38   Translation from *The Zohar: Pritzker Edition*, ed. D. C. Matt (Stanford, CA: Stanford University Press, 2016), 9: 106.

person on another, but the actual making of souls expressed in the text by adding the בוודאי (*bevvaday*, certainly, for sure) Now we are to understand that "they must have (actually) made souls."

5. Dispensing the Converts' Souls in the *Zohar*

Above, we explored texts about the souls of converts and their creation in heaven. The *Zohar* also contains text about how the souls are actually delivered to the converts. What is the process which takes place, whether on the soul's side or that of the convert? These descriptions vary as to the time the soul is dispensed, what kind of soul is dispensed, and what kind of body receives the soul. Another difference concerns the main character in the narrative. That is, who has the agency during the conversion process? Who is seen as the responsible agent, the one with the authority and the power to perform the conversion process?

A New Jewish Soul in an Old Gentile Body

In the narrative surrounding the figure of Rav Metivta we find another text regarding the conversion process. Here we see how the soul gets to its new body, its new abode:

> When a proselyte converts, a soul flies from that palace and enters beneath the wings of the Shekhinah. She kisses the soul, since she is the fruit of the righteous, and she sends it into that convert, within whom it dwells. From that time on, a convert is called *ger tsedeq*, convert of rightness.[39] This accords with the mystery that is written: the fruit of the righteous is a tree of life (Proverbs 11:30). Just as the tree of life yields souls, so, too, does the fruit of the righteous person yield souls. (*Zohar*, Rav Metivta 3:168a)[40]

From this passage, we understand that the righteous actually procure souls for converts in heaven, souls that the converts need access to in order to complete the conversion process and become fully Jewish. The convert gets the Jewish soul at the time of conversion, and the soul itself is dispatched by the divine presents—the *shekhinah*.

---

39   The rabbinic tradition differentiates between a *ger tsedeq*, a righteous convert accepting all Jewish law and fully joining the Jewish people, and *ger toshav*, a resident convert who accepts a small part of Jewish law and only lives among Jews in the land of Israel without becoming a full member of the Jewish people.
40   Translation from *The Zohar: Pritzker Edition*, 9: 106.

Midrash Ruth sees Ruth's second husband, Boaz, as the main agent in her conversion process. Even though, in the biblical narrative, Boaz has a more passive role at the start of the relationship and was more reacting to Ruth's actions, which were managed by Naomi, Boaz's role becomes crucial as the one that makes her appropriateness for conversion apparent:

> "Parcel of land" (Genesis 33:19)—a parcel of land of the righteous. She (Ruth) had gone there, entering a particular section, learning its way, becoming an expert in it from these reapers. who are they? Scholars, called "reapers of the field." "Meanwhile, presently, Boaz arrived (Ruth 2:4). Look, the righteous one has arrived, laden with blessings and bountiful sanctification. And he created the reapers—who were the reapers? Heavenly court, great Sanhedrin above, the Lord be with you! Now he bestows blessings from holy ones. and they responded, the Lord blesses you, granting him power to draw from the source of life, from the midst of the world that is coming. (*Zohar Hadash*, Midrash Hane'lam 85c)[41]

This text describes the conversion process with its earthly and otherworldly parts—a convert should come to where the sages are and learn from them. Then the righteous person, probably a great rabbinical figure, can come before the court and ask for the conversion to be completed. The conversion is completed with the drawing of life force, maybe a new soul from the otherworldly dimension. The text describes the process as a mystical yet legalistic ritual, resembling the halachic process of conversion whereby a Rabbi in charge of the conversion process brings the case in front of a rabbinical court. Only with the approval of all these men can the conversion process, of the woman, be completed.

The text about Ruth and Boaz may demonstrate how these souls, this divine life force, are accessed via the power of the *tsadiq*, the great righteous man.

This process gives the Torah-studying male elite and the rabbis all the authority in the conversion process. Where the text of the book of Ruth assigned a major role to Naomi and to Ruth herself, this text places all the power in the hands of the male authorities. Boaz the righteous may be likened to the rabbis, who should only passively accept converts and not be active in pursuing them. It is their duty to examine the candidates and to accept the worthy.

---

41 Translation from *The Zohar: Pritzker Edition*, 11: 204. According to the footnotes on page 105, this is about the divine tree of *sefirot*, here it is analyzed as if this text can be read on a more *peshat* level, just looking at the characters taking part.

An Old Jewish Soul Born in a New Gentile Body

Another possibility to solve the *giur* paradox, allowing conversion to Judaism while claiming the essential otherness of gentile souls from those of Jews, is to claim that a Jewish soul can end up in a gentile embryo. The soul of the potential convert was already given to them at birth. That is, the convert's soul is already Jewish, they do not need a new one, nor is their soul one of a gentile with all the impurity with which it comes. A text which seems to describe such a position is to be found in *Sitrei Torah* (*Secrets of the Torah*). *Sitrei Torah* comments on the book of Genesis. It is interested in the soul, the Godhead and "the other side."[42]

Let us look at a Zoharic commentary from *Sitrei Torah* about Parashat Lekh Lekha:

> All the good they had gotten—good works that a person performs in this world through the arousal of the soul. And the soul (*nefesh*) they had made in Haran— that *nefesh* originally cleaving and joining the foreskin in the body, refined afterwards. But from thirteen and on, *nishmeta* is aroused to rectify the body, and the two of them repair the *nefesh* that had partnered with the serpent's severity and with its wicked desire. This is as is written: and the soul they had made in Haran. Nonetheless, *nishmeta* overcomes that serpent, smashing it with the subjugation of *teshuvah*, with the subjugation of Torah—dragging him to synagogues and study halls, to prevent him from prevailing over *ruha* as before. (*Zohar*, Sitrei Torah 1:79a)[43]

This text explains how the soul is purified with the growth of the person. The soul is refined through circumcision at the place of the foreskin, then it is refined at the age of thirteen when it accepts the *mitsvot* (commandments) and then at adulthood, by regularly visiting the synagogue and *beit midrash*. The text recalls the *zohama* (slime) from the serpent contaminating the soul as mentioned in b. Shab. and how this slime can be dealt with. The text also employs Genesis 12:5 to show that this purification, remodeling or creation of the soul is possible. From the context, it would seem possible that the text is referring to a convert, such as Abraham himself—the subject of the scriptural text being commented on. In the paragraph before, the subject seems to be a person, *bar nash* (בר נש, lit. son of a soul). This could mean anybody, perhaps a Jewish born person too. In this case, the following citation of Genesis 12:5 would relate to the education of a Jewish boy and the creation of soul as a pedagogical act as seen by Resh Lakish.[44]

---

42 Tishby, "General Introduction," 2–3.
43 Translation *The Zohar: Pritzker Edition*, 11: 639–60.
44 B. San. 99b.

However, in our paragraph we also find a reference to the filth originating in the serpent, which ceased to exist in the Israelites after Mount Sinai. Therefore, we can understand the body dealt with is not of a born Israelite. This text could relate to the convert who comes forth from gentile parents; therefore, the foreskin. One possibility is that the special (Jewish) soul enters the body after *giur*, but then the process which intensifies at the age of thirteen seems unclear. The more likely possibility seems to me that we are dealing with a gentile born with a special (Jewish) soul. This potential convert has already received his special soul, but he still needs to purify himself from the slime linked to his gentile biological body. This process can be seen as intensifying at the age of thirteen when two parts of his soul, *nefesh* and *nishmata*, start the cleansing process, fighting the poison of the serpent, the *zohama*.

This process culminates with the smashing of the serpent when the person converts—here the citation of Genesis 12:5 about the souls they made in Haran. The conversion process is, thus, actually a return (*teshuvah*) of the soul to its original, Jewish, purpose. A "subjugation to Torah" and a life of prayer and learning, "synagogues and study halls" is needed to keep his gentile, non-Jewish, nature in check even more than for a born Israelite.

In this text we see a clear path allowing people who were not born as Jews to gain their Jewish status through a process of purification, which is made possible only by their possessing a unique nature, a unique *nefesh*. Without this special soul component, the whole process would not be possible, and the effect of the serpent would last, making conversion impossible since the person remains a different kind of being from a Jew.

6. The End of a Converts Soul's Cycle in the *Zohar*

Another option to reconcile the possibility of conversion with the uniqueness of the Jewish soul is to hold that the potential convert already had a Jewish soul (or a special soul) to begin with, thus making the conversion process and the eventual full Jewish status possible.

Sava Demishpatim, a text intricately connected to the weekly Torah portion of Mishpatim,[45] delves into profound mystical interpretations far beyond the practical laws outlined in Exodus. Its significance, emphasized by generations of Kabbalists, lies not only in its length and diverse themes but also in its unique style. Recent scholarly discourse has centered on gender-related

---

45 See Tishby, "General Introduction," 3.

motifs,[46] particularly the portrayal of the maiden,[47] symbolizing various aspects including the human soul, divine presence, and the Torah itself. The titular character, the enigmatic *Sava*, initially dismissed as eccentric, unfolds as a profound sage whose wisdom gradually emerges amidst hesitance and secrecy, akin to the hidden depths of the Torah. Encountering him, Rabbi Chai and Rabbi Yossi, disciples of Rabbi Shimon bar Yochai, are initially perplexed but ultimately recognize his profound insights, dubbing him the "superior lion." The text oscillates between depicting him as a hesitant elder and a courageous navigator of divine knowledge, employing metaphors of a lost mariner navigating the vast seas of wisdom.

In *Sava Demishpatim* we find a strong link between "soul mechanics" (*gerim*), and the image of Abraham. The starting point for this link is Abraham.[48] That is established rather early when Abraham is mentioned as the first or primary of all converts:[49]

> If the daughter of a priest, supernal soul, daughter of our father Abraham, first of all converts, who draws the soul from a supernal place. (*Zohar*, Sava Demishpatim 95a)[50]

This is a clear reference to Genesis 12:5 "the soul they have made." This creation is further explained by the ability of Abraham, as a righteous man, to extract souls from where they reside. Here we see that the daughter of a priest is likened to the higher soul which Abraham pulls from a high place. The Ashlag interpretation does not give any importance to calling Abraham the first among *gerim* but, to me, it seems unique within the Jewish tradition to use this

---

46 See, e.g. R. Kara-Ivanov Kaniel, "'She Uncovered His Feet': Redemption Journey of the Shekhinah: Ruth the Moabite as a Messianic Mother in Zoharic Literature," *Da'at* 72 (2012): 99–141; D. Abrams, *Haguf Ha'elohi Hanashi Bakabbalah – Iyun betsurot Shel Ahavah Gufnit Uminyut Nashit Shel Ha'elohot* [*The Feminine Divine Body in Kabbalah – Examination of Forms of Physical Love and Feminine Sexuality of the Deity*] (Jerusalem: Magnes, 2005).
47 See T. Weiss, "Who Is a Beautiful Maiden without Eyes? The Metamorphosis of a Zohar Midrashic Image from a Christian Allegory to a Kabbalistic Metaphor," *The Journal of Religion* 93, no. 1 (2013): 60–76.
48 On conversion in Europe see Katz, *Exclusiveness and Tolerance*, 77–81; 143–48. On the custom to adopt the name Abraham or son of Abraham see *Zohar* 1: 96a, trans. *Pritzker Edition*, ed. D. C. Matt (Stanford, CA: Stanford University Press, 2003), 2: 109 n 835.
49 On Abraham as first of converts see b. Sukk. 49b.
50 Translation from *The Zohar: Pritzker Edition*, ed. D. C. Matt (Stanford, CA: Stanford University Press, 2009), 5: 5.

title, and it stresses the focus on the figure of the convert.[51] Abraham is mentioned again when relating the story of Hagar and Ishmael.[52]

The Zoharic exploration of the *Sava* gives us a few hints about converts and their souls. The connection between the *ger* and the soul is made with this verse:

> Wretched is this holy soul, if she is married to an alien man, drawn upon the converted proselyte (*ger*), flying to him from the Garden of Eden by a concealed path, to a structure built from impure foreskin! This one belongs to an alien man. (*Zohar*, Sava de-Mishpatim 95b)[53]

These verses may relate to the daughter as well as to the soul. Just as the maiden is unfortunate that she is given to a stranger, the (Jewish) soul is unfortunate if it ends up with a convert whose body and biological father is not circumcised and, thus, stems from impurity. Here we see the idea that a convert must accept a soul from paradise in the conversion process, even though we are not told how this process occurs. Alternatively, this idea relates to the pre-birth situation in which the embryo gains a Jewish soul.

A more detailed description regarding the convert's "soul mechanics" follows in these verses:[54]

> Souls of *gerim* (converts) all fly from the Garden of Eden by a concealed path. Departing from this world—their souls that they gained from the Garden of Eden, where do they return? We have learned: "whoever first seizes the possessions of a *ger* (*convert*), is entitled to them." Those sacred, supernal souls that the blessed Holy One designated below, as we have said, all emerge at certain times in order to delight in the Garden of Eden. Encountering those souls of the *gerim* (converts), whichever one of these souls (ascending) grasps them is entitled to them, and they clothe themselves in them and ascend. (*Zohar*, Sava Demishpatim 98b)[55]

In this text, we see the conclusion to the cycle of the soul of the *ger* (convert). The soul of the *ger* should finally return to the place where it originated, the Garden of Eden. The proof of that is taken from the scriptural writings and the

---

51   See *Zohar 'im pirush Hasulam* [*Zohar with the Commentary of the Ladder*], ed. Y. Ashlag (Jerusalem, 1953), 10.
52   Ibid., 14.
53   Translation from *The Zohar: Pritzker Edition*, ed. D. C. Matt (Stanford, CA: Stanford University Press, 2009), 2: 7 n. 21: The souls intended to *gerim* from heaven.
54   *Zohar 'im pirush Hasulam*, 27.
55   Translation from *The Zohar: Pritzker Edition*, 2: 30.

halachic law regarding inheritance from a *ger*. The law[56] determines that in the absence of relatives, not counting his still not-Jewish biological relatives, the *ger*'s assets are taken by the first person who claims them. The law of inheritance here is applied beyond the grave to his very soul. The higher souls that have held onto the *ger*'s soul are now responsible for it—they "own" it, and when they ascend into heaven, they take it with them.

7. Conclusion

The change we see in the Kabbalistic tradition turns the entire previous hermeneutic tradition on its head. The driving force behind the reading of souls as converts in Sifre, the first Midrashic source about Genesis 12:5, is that humans cannot—under any circumstances and regardless of their prowess and wisdom—create life in the literal sense. As *Sifre* puts it: "even if all the men of the world gather, they cannot create even a *gnat* (mosquito)." However, in the *Sefer Yetsirah* we find the opposite view, that men like Abraham, with his keen wit and understanding of the underlying forces that control the universe, such as God, actually *can* create life, have power over the life force and can fabricate souls. The contradiction between the two views is stark and undeniable. The ability of the Jewish tradition to hold both views simultaneously is a testimony to the power of the multilayered mode of Jewish hermeneutics.

What we see in the Zoher is that these souls created by Abraham are then used for converts, we are witnessing an integration of the *Sifre* reading of Genesis 12:5, which relies on the impossibility of human life creation, with the Kabbalistic notion that allows for this creation. This synthesis has far-reaching implications for the understanding of conversion. Now, in parallel with the older explanations about Genesis 12:5 relating to education and *giur*, we find an esoteric tradition with a holistic story about the converts and their soul.

Sefer Habahir clearly shows us that souls can inhabit various bodies, meaning that it is conceivable for "Jewish souls" to enter non-Jewish bodies. *Sefer Habahir* also tells us that the souls of the righteous stem from a special place in spiritual space.

In the *Zohar* we find many accounts of soul making and converts. Midrash Ruth tells about the conversion of Ruth where Boaz the righteous man must go before the heavenly court and extract a soul for her. In Sava Demishpatim, we find Abraham also extracting souls from heaven to be used by *gerim*

---

56 This is since they are *hefker*, property that no one can claim.

(proselytes). He is also said to create the souls. In Rav Metivta, we find Abraham and Sarah as examples for other righteous in heaven who are creating souls for *gerim*. We find two possibilities for a non-Jewish body to gain a Jewish soul. One is at the moment of conversion with the help of the righteous person who "makes" the soul. The other is in the womb, making the process of conversion a return to the "true" identity of the soul. A victory of the Jewish soul over the other elements of a person's being. The official moment of conversion is recognition by the rabbinical authority and by society of the person's real identity given in the womb.

Now the process of conversion gains a whole new dimension, beyond the halachic. A layer is added, one with clear soul mechanics. A soul is created in the heavens by the righteous, to be then extracted by righteous people to be "implanted" into *gerim*. Only then, can a person finally be considered a *ger tsedeq*, a full and righteous convert into Judaism. It is not the person's affiliation to Jews or Judaism. It is not the person's adherence to rules and regulations which govern Jewish life. Furthermore, it is not a person's knowledge and studious learning of Jewish texts. All those may still be required, especially as proof of his already Jewish soul or his readiness to accept one, but the real component of a person's legitimate Jewish identity lies in the person's soul.

The change in the understanding of the converts' soul in the Kabbalistic tradition may be said to be a "Copernican" shift of the Jewish soul. The Copernican shift replaced the earth with the sun at the center of the universe. Previously, the sun was thought to revolve around the earth but subsequently, the earth was thought to revolve around the sun. Similarly, before the interpretational shift, Jewishness was seen to be about the power of society (via special people like Abraham) to mold the personality of an individual. After the shift, the verse is about the individual's soul and its origin in a world beyond. In many ways, this is the modern shift of identity: if before, Jewish identity was in the group outside the individual—between the individual and society—afterward, it is between the individual and the divine. It is something inherently individual, something linking the individual to the transcendental. This era's reading centers the actual creation of souls, putting an emphasis on the individual's soul and its link to the Almighty and the transcendental.

Bibliography

Primary Sources

זוהר עם פירוש הסולם
(*Zohar 'im pirush Hasulam, Zohar with the Commentary of the Ladder*). Edited by Rabbi Yehuda Leib Halevi Ashlag. Jerusalem, 1953. [In Hebrew.]

ספר האמונות והדעות סעדיה בן יוסף גאון לפי תירגום של יהודה אבן תיבון
(*Sefer Ha'emunot Vehade'ot*, in *Saadia Ben Yosef Gaon Lefi Targum Shel Yehuda Ben Tibbon; Book of Beliefs and Opinions*, in *Saadia Ben Yosef Gaon According to the Translation of Judah Ben Tibbon*.) Constantinople, 1562. [In Hebrew.]

ספר הבהיר הנקרא מדרש רבי נחוניא בן הקנה, מוסד הרב קוק
(*Sefer Habahir Hanikra Midrash Rabbi Nechunya Ben Hakana, Book of Brightness Called Midrash of Rabbi Nechunya Ben Hakana*). Edited by Reuven Margaliot. Jerusalem: Kook Institute, 1951. [In Hebrew.]

ספר הבהיר על פי כתבי היד הקדומים, עם דברי מבוא מאת משה אידל, הוצאת כרוב
(*Sefer Habahir Al Pi Ktavai Hayad Hakedumim, Im Divrei Mavo Me'et Moshe Idel, Book of Brightness According to Ancient Manuscripts, with Introductory Words by Moshe Idel*). Edited by Daniel Abrams. Los Angeles, CA: Karov, 1994. [In Hebrew.]

Yehuda HaLevi. ספר הכוזרי (*Sefer Hakuzari, The Book of the Kuzari*). Warsaw, 1880. [In Hebrew.]

The Zohar: Pritzker Edition. Translation and commentary by Daniel Matt. Stanford, CA: Stanford University Press, 2003–2018.

Secondary Sources

Abrams, Daniel. *Haguf Ha'elohi Hanashi Bakabbalah—Iyun betsurot Shel Ahavah Gufnit Uminyut Nashit Shel Ha'elohot* (*The Feminine Divine Body in Kabbalah—Examination of Forms of Physical Love and Feminine Sexuality of the Deity*). Jerusalem: Magnes, 2005. [In Hebrew.]

Basser, Herbert. "Midrash Tannaim." In Volume 1 of *Encyclopaedia of Midrash*, edited by Jacob Neusner and Alan Avery-Peck, 510–20. Leiden: Brill, 2005.

Green, Arthur. *A Guide to the Zohar*. Stanford, CA: Stanford University Press, 2004.

Guttmann, Julius. *Die Philosophie des Judentums*. Munich: Ernst Reinhardt, 1933.

Halamish, Moshe. *Mavoh le Qabbalah* (*An Introduction to the Kabbalah*). Jerusalem: Elinor Vehakibuts Hame'uchad Press, 1991. [In Hebrew.]

Kaniel, Ruth Kara-Ivanov. "'She Uncovered His Feet': Redemption Journey of the Shekhinah: Ruth the Moabite as a Messianic Mother in Zoharic Literature." *Da'at* 72 (2012): 99–141.

Katz, Jacob. *Exclusiveness and Tolerance: Studies in Jewish-gentile Relations in Medieval and Modern Times*. Oxford: Oxford University Press, 1961.

Kosman Admiel. *Masechet Shalom: Hasichsuch Ha'israeli-aravi Le'or Mekorot Midrashiyim Verabaniyim* (*Tractate Peace: The Arab-Israeli Conflict in Light of Midrashic and Rabbinic Sources*). Jerusalem: Miskal, 2014. [In Hebrew.]

Langer, Gerhard. *Midrasch*. Tübingen: Mohr Siebeck, 2016.

Marmorstein, Arthur. "The Doctrine of the Resurrection of the Dead in Rabbinic Theology." *The American Journal of Theology* 19, no. 4 (1915): 577–91.

Pedersen, Johannes. *Israel, Its Life and Culture*. London: Oxford University Press, 1953.

Scholem, Gershom. *Pirqei Yesod Behavanat Hakabbalah Vesimleiha* (*Foundations in Understanding Kabbalah and its Symbols*). Jerusalem, 1991.

--------. *Reshit Haqabbalah Vesefer Habahir, Hartzau'tav shel Prof. G. Scholem, Shanat Tashkav* (*Beginning of Kabbalah and the Book of Bahir, Lectures by Prof. G. Scholem*). Edited by Rivka Shatz. Jerusalem, 1962. [In Hebrew.]

Tishby, Isaiah. "General Introduction." In *Wisdom of the Zohar: An Anthology of Texts*, volume 1. Edited by Isaiah Tishby and Fischel Lachower. Oxford: Oxford University Press, 1989.

Weiss, Tzahi. "Who Is a Beautiful Maiden without Eyes? The Metamorphosis of a Zohar Midrashic Image from a Christian Allegory to a Kabbalistic Metaphor." *The Journal of Religion* 93, no. 1 (2013): 60–76.

Weiss, Yehudit. "Dehiyah, Halifah, Ve'ibur, Tefisot Sefirotiot Bedavar Gilgul Neshamot Bein Gufim Besifrut Hakabbalah Hamukdamah Veyediheihen" ("Delay, Exchange, and Transition: Sefiratic Perceptions Regarding the Transmigration of Souls between Bodies in Early Kabbalistic Literature and Their Consequences"). *Jewish Studies* 57 (2022): 65–105.

Von Rad, Gerhard. *Old Testament Theology*. Edinburgh: Oliver & Boyd, 1962.

Examples of Medieval Judith Midrashim: The Reception of the Pre-Modern Niddah

Rosalie Gabay Bernheim

The reception of the Book of Judith in medieval Judaism is an interesting matter as it is excluded from the Jewish canon. Indeed, between the earliest surviving version of the Book of Judith, dating from the second century BCE and written in Greek, and the tenth century, discussions surrounding the eponymous heroine were limited to Christian circles. This omission is likely due to the tale's non-canonical status in Judaism, in contrast to its deuterocanonical inclusion in Christian scripture.[1] The oldest surviving version is from the Greek Septuagint; the Book of Judith was translated by Jerome into Latin in the fourth century CE, becoming part of the crucial Latin Vulgate.[2] Thus, Judith became a focal point for patristic and medieval Christian authors, portraying her as an exemplary Christian woman.[3] Conversely, there was a notable absence of discourse about the Judith narrative within Jewish tradition, with no mention until approximately the tenth century CE.[4] As the first millennium turned, the story of Judith suddenly resurfaced in Jewish literature.[5]

---

1 See. M. S. Enslin, *The Book of Judith: Greek Text* (Leiden: Brill, 1972), 37.
2 On the Latin translation of Judith, see E. L. Gallagher, "Why Did Jerome Translate Tobit and Judith?" *HTR* 108, n. 3 (2015): 356–75; G. K. Hasselhoff, "Revising the Vulgate: Jerome and His Jewish Interlocutors," *Zeitschrift für Religions- und Geistesgeschichte* 64, n. 3 (2012): 209–21.
3 See more on Judith as an exemplary Christian woman in E. Ciletti and H. Lähnemann, "Judith in the Christian Tradition," in *The Sword of Judith: Judith Studies Across the Disciplines*, eds. K. Brine et al. (Cambridge: Cambridge Open Book Publishers, 2010), 41–66; F. Stella, "The Women of the Old Testament in Early Medieval Poetry: Judith and the Others," in *The Early Middle Ages*, eds. F. E. Consolino and J. Herrin (Atlanta, GA: SBL, 2020), 231–58.
4 The earliest Hebrew version of this tale, hereby referred to as the Midrash de Gaster or Midrash n. 1, was found in a manuscript dating inconclusively to either the tenth or eleventh century. For the sake of clarity, I will be assuming that Midrash n. 1 dates from the tenth century. See: A.-M. Dubarle, *Judith: Formes et Sens des Diverses Traditions* (Rome: Institut Biblique Pontifical, 1966), 80.
5 D. Levine Gera, "The Jewish Textual Traditions," in *The Sword of Judith: Judith Studies Across the Disciplines*, eds. K. Brine et al. (Cambridge: Cambridge Open Book Publishers, 2010), 23–40.

Medieval Jewish authors not only (re)translated[6] it into Hebrew,[7] but engaged in a comprehensive rewriting of the narrative. Although still excluded from the Jewish canon, the story seems to gain new importance and interest within specific literary Jewish circles. This resulted in thirteen known pre-modern Jewish versions of the Judith stories, spanning from the tenth to the sixteenth centuries. Intriguingly, the majority of these versions share a distinctive plot device absent in earlier renditions: Judith is transformed into a menstruant, her menstrual cycle becoming the pivotal tool for securing victory over Holofernes.

During the latter half of the Middle Ages, the practices surrounding niddah[8] transcended the confines of patriarchal control over the female Jewish body. In medieval Jewish devotional literature, including biblical commentaries, apologetic texts, and the emergence of Kabbalah,[9] the figure of the niddah evolved into a symbol embodying the ideals of contemporary Jewish culture and practices. These depictions aimed to religiously appropriate or distinguish female bodies, portraying meticulous adherence to regulations and traditions as a means for women to forge a closer communion with their community and establish a covenant with God. This adherence signified both sacred and societal worth, asserting superiority over the Christian counterpart; the niddah became a representation of everything the Christian woman was not. Thus, the niddah functioned as a tool for Judaism to underscore its distinctive values, perspectives, and culture. Indeed, Ilana Cohen's study on developing a critical menstrual studies approach stated that menstrual practices "contribute to better understanding the ways a religious community defines and (re)produces

---

6   It is unclear whether the original Book of Judith was written in Hebrew or Greek, and many academics have worked on this. See: Gallagher, "Why did Jerome Translate Tobit and Judith;" Hasselhoff, "Revisiting the Vulgate;" C. A. Moore, *The Anchor Bible – Judith: A New Translation with Introduction and Commentary* (New Haven, CT: Yale University Press, 1985); D. Börner-Klein, "Judith in the Hebrew Literature of the Middle Ages," in *The Jewish Middle Ages*, eds. C. Bakhos and G. Langer (Atlanta, GA: SBL, 2023), 55–70.

7   The first known translation of the Latin Vulgate into Hebrew is from the twelfth century. See Dubarle, *Judith*, 25.

8   The concept of niddah is not exactly translatable to menstruation. "Niddah" is a term to describe the state of a menstruating woman, it encompasses her very being; her identity changes and does not change back until she immerses herself into the mikvah, even if she has stopped bleeding; a menstruant is any person at any point who menstruates; menstruation is the act of bleeding. It becomes the site of an intersection between the menstruating reality and the imagined cultural and religious mores surrounding it.

9   See more on menstruation in Kabbalah in S. F. Koren, *Forsaken: The Menstruant in Medieval Jewish Mysticism*, (Brandeis University Press, 2011); ibid., "Kabbalistic Physiology: Isaac the Blind, Nahmanides, and Moses de Leon on Menstruation," *AJS Review* 28, no. 2 (2004): 317–39; ibid. "The Menstruant as "Other" in Medieval Judaism and Christianity," *Nashim* 17 (2009): 33–59.

itself."¹⁰ Specifically in medieval biblical commentaries, there was a consistent emphasis on adhering to halakhah and mitzvot related to niddah, including practices such as mikvah immersion and abstaining from sexual intercourse during the days of bleeding. The menstrual cycle was not viewed as inherently negative but rather as an opportunity for Jewish women to manifest their faith and unwavering commitment to Jewish regulations.¹¹ This chapter will examine the medieval Jewish reception of the Book of Judith, with a special focus on the *Megillat Yehudit*, as these texts transformed the eponymous heroine into a niddah. Jewish midrashim (re)appropriate the heroine to illustrate Jewish tradition. These texts depict Judith strategically using her menstrual cycle as a triumphant tool for the Jewish people against non-Jewish adversaries. I argue that the niddah practices and traditions provided the midrashic authors with a means to re-appropriate their text and heroine from Christianity, firmly anchoring Judith as the "Jewess." From the tenth-century onwards, the story of Judith as niddah is received and transmitted for Jews to differentiate themselves from Christians, but also to strengthen their own identity and self-perception.

Receiving Niddah in the Middle Ages

The Book of Judith revolves around a courageous Jewish widow named Judith, who lives in the city of Bethulia whilst it is under siege by the Assyrian army led by Holofernes. Facing defeat and starvation, the people of Bethulia decide to surrender if no help arrives within five days. Judith, inspired by her faith in God, devises a plan to save her city and her people. She dresses in her finest attire and goes to the Assyrian camp, where her beauty captivates Holofernes. Over time, she gains his trust, and her plan is set into motion. On the third night, she is allowed to leave the confines of the camp to wash and pray by a spring of water.

> And sent this message to Holofernes, "Let my lord now give orders to allow your servant to go out and pray." So Holofernes commanded his guards not to hinder her. She remained in the camp three days. She went out each night to the valley of Bethulia and bathed at the spring in the camp. After bathing, she prayed the Lord God of Israel to direct her way for the triumph of his people. Then she

---

10   I. Cohen, "Menstruation and Religion: Developing a Critical Menstrual Studies Approach," in *The Palgrave Handbook of Critical Menstruation Studies*, ed. C. Bobel et al. (Singapore: Palgrave Macmillan, 2020), 125.

11   See more on menstruation as covenantal in D. Biale, *Blood and Belief, The Circulation of a Symbol between Jews and Christians* (Berkeley, CA: University of California Press, 2007); and S. Cohen, *Why Aren't Jewish Women Circumcised? Gender and Covenant in Judaism* (Berkeley, CA: University of California Press, 2005).

returned purified and stayed in the tent until she ate her food toward evening. (Judith 12: 6–9, NRSVue)

By the fourth night, Holofernes invites her to a feast, in which he becomes intoxicated in her company. Judith seizes this opportunity and beheads him. She then returns to Bethulia with his head, inspiring the Israelites to launch a surprise attack on the Assyrian army, leading to a Jewish victory.

The thirteen known examples of pre-modern Jewish interpretations of the Judith narrative were compiled in André-Marie Dubarle's 1966 work, *Judith: Formes et Sens des Diverses Traditions*.[12] These narratives exhibit a remarkable consistency despite being copied across diverse regions (for example, Tunisia, Persia, Provence, Italy, Carcasonnne, and Catalonia) and historical periods (from the tenth to the sixteenth centuries), establishing a cohesive representation of menstruation. Deborah Levine Gera categorises these midrashim into five main groups: Vulgate-based versions, Hanukkah-Judith renditions, combinations of Vulgate and Hanukkah versions, unrelated Hanukkah Judith tales, and liturgical poems for Hanukkah.[13] Variations include commonly relocating the setting from Bethulia to Jerusalem, merging Nebuchadnezzar and Holofernes into a single character beheaded by Judith, and fluctuating aspects of Judith's character, such as her virginity, widowhood, and familial ties to prophets, which differ across narratives. Among these, ten midrashim undergo a transformative process, recasting Judith as a niddah, and thus, her menstrual cycle emerges as the decisive instrument for securing victory for her people. Seven of the ten explicitly use the term "ndh,"[14] with the remaining three, midrash n.8 (or the *Megillat Yehudit*), the midrash n.10 (*Ioser of Hanoukah*), and midrash n.12 using varying terms describing (flows of) impurity. This interpretation holds particular significance as Judaism had neglected this narrative in preceding centuries.

Megillat Yehudit

The *Megillat Yehudit*[15] elaborates, in particularly rich detail, on the role of Judith's adherence to niddah traditions and in defining Jewish identity in late medieval Jewish writing. By portraying the heroine in such a positive light, the

---

12   A.-M. Dubarle, *Judith: Formes et Sens des Diverses Traditions* (Rome: Institut Biblique Pontifical, 1966).
13   See D. Levine Gera, *Judith* (Boston, MA: De Gruyter, 2014), 21.
14   Midrash n.1; midrash n.2; midrash n.4; midrash n.5; midrash n.7a; midrash n.7b; midrash n.9 use "ndh."
15   Known as the midrash n.8 in Dubarle's compilation of medieval Jewish versions of Judith.

author showcases the elevation of importance of the menstruant that is found within certain circles of medieval Judaism. The *Megillat Yehudit* is the longest of the ten midrashim that Dubarle collected, and is found in a single manuscript copied by Moses Shmeil Dascola in 1402.[16] Neubauer describes the script as "Provencal rabbinic,"[17] giving us some clue to the otherwise unknown scribe. However, the original author and date of composition is unknown, but ultimately it is thought to have been originally composed before this manuscript. This particular midrash illustrates the medieval Jewish reception of the Book of Judith, and how and why the transmission of this non-canonical narrative found its place within a Jewish literary tradition.

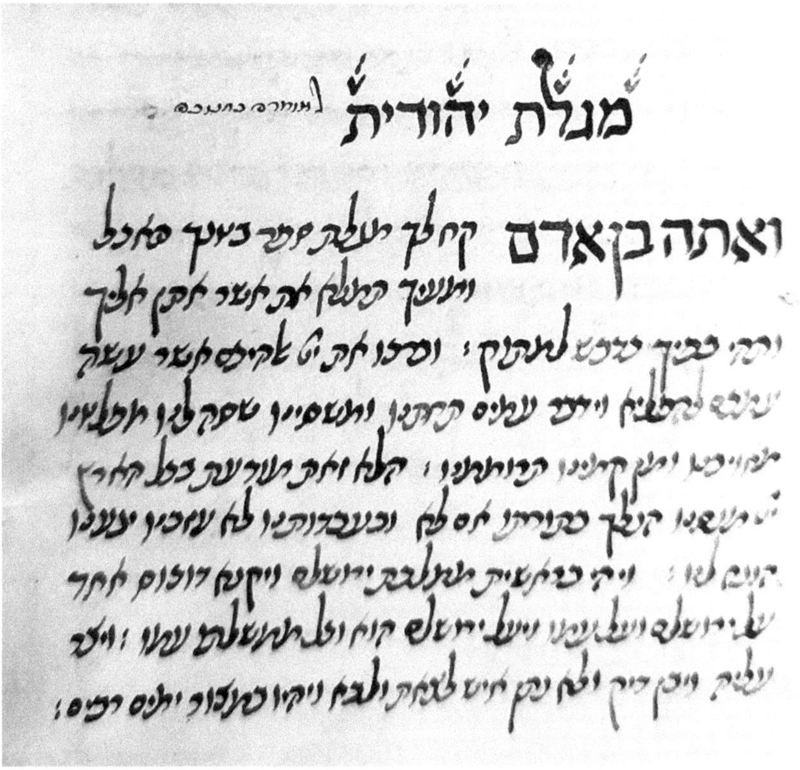

Image 7.1   Oxford, Bodleian Library Ms. Neubauer n. 2746, heb e. 10, fol 66v ("Megillat Yehudit").

---

16   It is found in only one manuscript, housed in the Bodleian Library in Oxford, A. Neubauer Catalogue no. 2746 = Heb. e. 10, fol. 66v-72v.
17   A. Neubauer, *Catalogue of the Hebrew Manuscripts in the Bodleian Library and in the College Libraries of Oxford : Including MSS. in Other Languages, Which Are Written with Hebrew Characters, or Relating to the Hebrew Language or Literature; and a Few Samaritan MSS* (Oxford: Clarendon, 1994), 2: x, and 170.

Judith's Menstrual State

Receiving the niddah regulations from more ancient Jewish prescriptions allows the authors of the Judith corpus to anchor her into a Jewish framework through her menstrual status and her purification rituals. However, unlike the other six midrashim that explicitly use the term "niddah," the *Megillat Yehudit* instead opts for a more ambiguous phrase to explain the reason behind her purification. As with the other menstruant-midrashim, Judith arrives at Holofernes' camp, who is seduced by her beauty and demands that she sleep with him, to which Judith responds:

> אך בליל אטהר מזובי וארחץ בנקיון כפי עד העירו תנח ידיך: ויאמר כדברך אחותי אך אל תאכרי אותי הלילה רחצי הזכי

> But tonight I shall cleanse myself from my discharge and I shall wash my hands in innocence. Until tonight, withhold your hand. Then he said: "As you say my sister. But do not approach me tonight, wash and be pure."[18]

The phrase parallels two acts of purification: Judith "cleans[ing]" her body and then "wash[ing]" her hands. This puts emphasis not only on the act, but also on the terminology and phrasing used, as we shall see below. Within Leviticus the term זוב (*zov*, flow)—used in this midrash with the preposition *min* מ (from) "מזובי" (*mezuvi*, from my flow/issue/discharge)—describes a flow of blood that can either be connected to the menstruation or abnormal, non-menstrual bleeding. It is connected to *zavah* (זבה; one who[se body] flows) was, originally, distinct from the niddah, described a woman who bled vaginally not on the days of menstruation (whether before her time, or after the "normal" amount of bleeding days).[19] However, the Talmudic text Niddah conflates these two, stating that "[t]he 'daughters of Israel' imposed a stringency upon themselves that they would wait out seven clean (days) even if they saw a drop of blood the size of a mustard seed only."[20] Thus, by the Middle Ages, the differentiation between *niddah* and *zavah* had dissipated, and a Jewish woman with vaginal bleeding, no matter when or for how long, was considered ritually impure. This clarifies that even if the *Megillat Yehudit* opts to describe Judith as cleansing her "flow" rather than her "menstrual blood," the consequences and rituals

---

18 Dubarle, *Judith*, 149. All translations of the midrashim from Hebrew into English are based off Dubarle's translation into French and my own.
19 Lev 15:25: "When a woman has had a discharge of blood for many days, not at the time of her menstruation, or when she has a discharge beyond the period of menstruation, she shall be impure, as though at the time of her menstruation, as long as her discharge lasts."
20 B. Nid. 66:a.

remain the same: she must cleanse in the mikvah before resuming marital—or extramarital in Judith's case—intercourse.

Judith's execution of menstrual purification in these midrashim defines her identity as a Jewish woman. The performance of the niddah commandments belong to the three mitzvot that are reserved for Jewish women. Performing these mitzvoth—lighting the candles, breaking the bread, and niddah—enable the female Jew to access a higher sacrality. They allow her to illustrate her faith and inclusion in her community, strengthening her self-perception. Elisheva Baumgarten concludes succinctly that "over time, within the broad context of religious praxis, these three commandments became elevated as paradigmatic observances of Jewish women, especially in the writing of men."[21] This specific menstrual state of Jewish women is of extreme importance to Judaism, providing the woman space not only to perform religious rituals, and giving her an identity within her community, but also to differentiate her from Christians. Judith, here, is set apart from Holofernes and her non-Jewish adversaries by prioritising her religious rituals.

Indeed, Judith sets herself even further apart by drawing a firm physical and religious line between her and the non-Jewish soldiers. After having stated to Holofernes her need for purification due to her—menstrual—flow, Judith explains that:

גם אם־יראו אותנו בעיינות ובנחלים אל־יגעו בנו ודברנה דבר

> Even if the soldiers see us [Judith and her serving woman] in the springs and streams, let them not touch us or talk.[22]

Thus Judith's emphasis on the "springs and streams," alongside her desire to "cleanse" herself imply that she is immersing herself in some kind of natural mikvah, as mikvot have to be sources of running, natural water. Judith clarifies that Holofernes must wait "עד־הערב" (*'ad ha'erev*, until evening), and he accepts, stating "הלילה בדם הזכי" (*halaylah bedam hazakhi*, tonight, wash and make yourself clean). According to the prescriptions in Leviticus, anything or anyone that touches a *niddah* or *zavah* is "unclean until the evening," and when they have counted the set amount of "clean" days before the purification, the last day ends at nightfall. The tractate Niddah imposes the custom that it is the very evening after the purification in the mikvah that the couple may now

---

21 E. Baumgarten, *Biblical Women and Jewish Daily Life in the Middles Ages* (Philadelphia, PA: University of Pennsylvania Press, 2022), 28.
22 Dubarle, *Judith*, 148.

resume—and indeed, must resume—sexual intercourse.²³ Whether or not Holofernes knows these customs, or even whether Judith is actually ritually impure, or whether it is simply a tactic on her part, does not change the narrative: she is using her Jewish traditions, and her Jewish body, to reach victory over a non-Jew. However, it is important to acknowledge that the immersion in the mikvah is reserved for married Jewish women—as is sexual intercourse—a status Judith does not hold.²⁴ The authors of this narrative, including those of the other midrashim, were clearly well-versed in the laws pertaining to niddah, making it improbable that the inclusion of this detail was a mere oversight—especially considering its consistent presence in multiple retellings. This prompts the consideration that the inclusion of Judith's mikvah immersion could be a deliberate choice. Exploiting Holofernes' unfamiliarity with Jewish halakhah, Judith capitalised on his lack of understanding regarding the intricacies of niddah commandments. This could be interpreted as a critique on their Christian contemporaries, akin to Holofernes, who, being non-believers, might be similarly unaware of the proper protocols associated with menstruation.

The other midrashim, written prior to the *Megillah*, follow similar menstrual narratives. Midrash n.1, as identified by Dubarle, originates from a Persian manuscript dating back to the tenth or eleventh century, housing over three hundred Talmudic tales.²⁵ This manuscript presents the earliest known version of a menstruating Judith, potentially serving as the foundational narrative for subsequent tales. Departing from the original Book of Judith, where the eponymous heroine is a widow from Bethulia, this midrash revolves around a beautiful "young girl" or "maiden" (הנערה, *hana'arah*) from Jerusalem, who rescues her people by infiltrating Holofernes' camp. Upon her arrival, Holofernes propositions her for sexual intercourse. However, she firmly rejects him, citing her impurity:

אבל בשעה זו אי אפשר. שאני בנדותי. ולילה זו טבילתי

But at this hour, it is impossible, as I am in my impurity. And tonight, it is my purification.²⁶

---

23 See R. Wasserfall, *Women and Water: Menstruation in Jewish Life and Law* (Waltham, MA: Brandeis University Press, 1999), 6.
24 See ibid., 5.
25 From a Persian manuscript dating from the fifteenth century, though Gaster dates ms. Heb. 82 as being from the tenth or eleventh century. See M. Gaster, *An Unknown Hebrew Version of the History of Judith* (London: Harrison and Sons, n.d.), 3.
26 Dubarle, *Judith*, 102.

Whereas the *Megillah* simply refers to Judith's "flow," the midrash n.1 opts for a more explicit term, with Judith stating "אני בנדותי" (*ani beniddoti*, I am in my impurity/I am niddah), unambiguously referring to her menstrual state. As Moses Gaster notes, "as to the bathing in the fountain, it is only here we have a perfectly clear explanation, in conformity with the Law."[27] In his opinion, this midrash provides justification for the original Judith's need to purify, though, it should be noted that Christians had interpreted it as a moral purification, perhaps even mirroring some kind of baptism.

Following this, midrash n. 2, traced to Nissim ben Jacob in Tunisia during the late tenth-to-eleventh centuries, features Judith as an anonymous young girl.[28] She willingly presents herself to the unnamed king as one of "your maidservants"[29] (שפחותיך, *shfahotekha*) but discloses her impurity:

אבל אודיעך אדוני המלך שאנכי נדה ובערב אנכי ראויה לטבילה

> But I will have you know, my Lord, that I am impure and tonight I will be ready to bathe.[30]

Subsequent midrashim follow this same narrative, where, after infiltrating the enemy's camp and encountering a lustful Holofernes, Judith invokes menstrual impurity and emphasises the imminent need for purification. Each version shares, on the whole, a common structure, presenting the menstrual justification and concluding with Judith's commitment to bathing in the evening. Seven of the ten explicitly use the term niddah,[31] with the remaining three, midrash n.8 (*Megillat Yehudit*), the midrash n.10 (*Ioser of Hanoukah*), and midrash n.12 using varying terms describing (flows of) impurity. These narratives exhibit a remarkable consistency across diverse regions, historical periods, and communities of origin, establishing a cohesive representation of menstruation.

Judith's Sexual (Un)Availability

However, Judith's desire to properly follow the niddah commandments, to purify and only after this being able resume having sexual intercourse, becomes a risk as she is rejecting the sexual advances of Holofernes. This risk

---

27 Gaster, *An Unknown Hebrew Version*, 2.
28 See Dubarle, *Judith*, 107; Börner Klein, "Judith in the Hebrew Literature," 59.
29 Dubarle, *Judith*, 107.
30 Ibid., 106.
31 Midrash n.1; midrash n.2; midrash n.4; midrash n.5; midrash n.7a; midrash n.7b; midrash n.9 use "ndh."

emphasises the worth that the author of the *Megillah* puts upon the correct performance of mitzvot. The *Megillat Yehudit* presents throughout the entire narrative non-Jewish men who desire Jewish women: the king from the beginning of the narrative "desires" (חפץ, *hefets*)[32] the daughters of Israel and does not shy away from taking them by force; thus, when the reader is faced with Holofernes who "desires" Judith, there is a foreshadowing of a potential sexual assault. The author of the *Megillah* adds emphasis to the dangers that Judith may face by claiming sexual sanctuary with Holofernes' demand that Judith must:

אי נא שכבי עמי אחותי כי גדולה אהבה אשר אהבתיך אהבת תענוגים

> Come now, lie with me, my sister, for it is a great love that I have for you, a love full of delights.[33]

The identical phrase is found in Samuel II 13:11, uttered by Amnon to his sister, Tamar. Tamar rejects him, claiming that it is vile and shameful, but she is ignored, and results in her rape. The inclusion of this reference is a kind of narrative threat, suggesting a potential violation of not only Judith's body, but also of her adherence to the Jewish niddah commandments. By borrowing Amnon's phrase, the author strongly associates Holofernes with a biblical sexual predator and criminal, one who is unwilling to consider either religious or moral laws.

Holofernes' threat is not simply of sexual violence but also threatening to break Jewish commandments. Jewish law forbids physical relations—any kind of physical touch, let alone intercourse—with a woman who is niddah. Sexual intercourse with a woman who is niddah incurs *karet* for the couple (כרת, *karet*, death or excision from the people of Israel [Lev 20:18]). However, the tractate Niddah also provides a positive turn to this interdiction. The text intertwines the notions of desire and menstruation, by claiming that the forced separation and prohibition from sexual intercourse is to make sure that the wife "will be dear to her husband as at the time when she entered the wedding canopy with him." Ultimately, the tractate argues that regular, constant intercourse would result in the husband becoming bored of the wife, and eventually be "repulsed by her."[34] This explanation defines the wife as a sexual object for the husband, and is intent on ensuring that the married couple have sex at ideal time for conception. It is indeed the tactic that Judith uses against

---

32 Dubarle, *Judith*, 148.
33 Ibid., 148.
34 B. Nid. 31b:12.

Holofernes: she manipulates his desire through restricting access to her body. By making him wait due to menstrual impurity, and planning a ritual bath to cleanse herself, Judith implicitly promises sexual intercourse. It is this very tantalising possibility that leads Holofernes to initiate a "feast of Judith" (את משתה יהודית, *'et mishteh Yehudit*),[35] drinking himself to unconsciousness for "his heart was merry" (וייטב לבו, *vayitav libo*).[36] Tamber-Rosenau, whilst examining the Septuagint, claims that Judith

> may plan for word of her baths to reach and excite him ... He would be even more interested if he knew or deduced that Judith's baths were not merely for cleanliness, but might serve to purify her and put her in a state where she would be receptive to sexual intercourse.[37]

Tamber-Rosenau's observation is also helpful for understanding the *Megillah*. Indeed, Judith's bathing can be understood to have two aims: to purify herself from her menstrual impurity, and to sexually arouse Holofernes in order to lure him into a position of vulnerability. Tamber-Roseneau points out that the narrative of a woman bathing and attracting male (sexual) attention is not reserved to Judith, but extends also to Bathseba and Susannah.[38] The narrative of menstrual separation and repressed sexual desire does indeed end in a climax, though not a sexual one as Holofernes desired, but rather a strategic climax for a Jewish victory.

The Association Between Menstruation and Leadership

The authority and leadership that Judith's menstrual bleeding bestows on her in the *Megillat Yehudit* echoes that of another famous biblical female leader who also associates her power to menstruation: Esther. the heroine of the *Megillat Esther*, one of the five megillot in the Hebrew Bible.[39] She is a Jewish woman who marries the non-Jewish king of Persia, Ahasuerus, while concealing her religious identity. After Esther uncovers a plot by Haman, the king's advisor, to annihilate the Jews, however, she uses her influence as queen to thwart him. She reveals her Jewish identity to her husband and persuades him

---

35   Dubarle, *Judith*, 148.
36   Ibid.
37   C. Tamber-Rosenau, "Biblical Bathing Beauties and the Manipulation of the Male Gaze: What Judith Can Tell Us about Bathsheba and Susanna," *Journal of Feminist Studies in Religion* 33, no. 2. (2017): 69.
38   Ibid.
39   The five megillot include Song of Songs, Ruth, Lamentations and Ecclesiates. They are also included in the Christian Old Testament.

to spare her people. Following this Jewish victory, Esther becomes a celebrated Jewish heroine, and the festival of Purim is established to remember the story. More importantly, the Septuagint version of the narrative compares Esther's crown to a menstrual cloth. Judith may not be portrayed in the *Megillat Yehudit* as the military leader that she is in the Greek Septuagint or the Latin Vulgate, she instead attains an even higher form of power, similarly to that of Esther. The *Megillah* concludes the narrative with Judith ascending to new heights:

ותהי יהודית מולכת על־הארץ ושפטה את־ישראל

then Judith became queen over the land and judged Israel[40]

This is foreshadowed precisely in the episode when she is leaving to go see Holofernes, where Judith is described as having a noble disposition and royal appearance:

ותשם כתר מלשות בראשה

she had a royal crown on her head[41]

יְהוּדִית נֹשֵׂאת חֵן בְּעֵינֵי כָּל־רֹאֶיהָ

[she] won the admiration of all who saw her[42]

This suggests that it is her actions against Holofernes that lend her the authority to lead her people. Her interior and moral worth is reflected in the royal aspect of her external appearance. However, the meaning behind these descriptions of Judith heading to the enemy's camp goes deeper than simply to laud the virtues of the heroine. Indeed, both quotations find a direct parallel in the Book of Esther, respectively in 2:17 and 2:15:

וישם כתר־מלכות בראשה וימליכה תחת ושתי (2:17)
So he set a royal crown on her head and made her queen instead of Vashti

אסתר נשאת חן בעיני כל־ראיה (2:15)
Yet Esther won the admiration of all who saw her.

The Book of Judith was—and still is—already popularly compared to that of Esther, but the author of the *Megillat Yehudit* furthered this parallel between both heroines: both Judith and Esther are women who are in a relationship

---

40   Dubarle, *Judith*, 150.
41   Ibid. 144.
42   Ibid.

with a non-Jew (in Judith's case, this is a pretence); both are women whom are crowned (metaphorically in Judith's case) before their victory over the non-Jewish enemy; and both are women who save the Jewish people and become their queen. Through this association, Judith is elevated above other women, comparable only to the most famous of Jewish queens. This nobility—both physical through the royal diadem, and moral through her bravery – is specifically interesting when considered alongside the impurity of a menstruant. A niddah is a figure who carries ritual impurity, and can impart it to whatever or whomever she has contact with. One would assume that the figure of the niddah is one who has power, perhaps, but a power of defilement and impurity. And yet, in the narratives of both Judith and Esther, menstruation is linked to positive power, one that saves the Jewish people.

In the Septuagint and in Jerome's translation of Esther, texts surely known by the author of the *Megillah*, Esther surprisingly links her royal power to menstruation:

> You know my duty: that I loathe that symbol of my exalted position which is upon my head. When I appear [at court] I loathe it like a menstruous rag. I do not wear it when I am not at court. (VII, Book of Esther, Add. C: 27; RSV, 10:16)

> You know not my necessity, that I abominate the sign of my pride and glory, which is upon my head in the days of my public appearance, and I detest it as a menstruous rag, and I do not bear in the days of my silence [...]. (Jerome's *Vulgate*, 14:16)

Queen Esther loathes the crown that was given to her by her non-Jewish husband as it is symbolic of her necessary concealment of her faith and culture: she must hide who she truly is so as to wear the crown that will ultimately save her people's lives. By comparing her crown to a menstrual cloth, Esther illustrates that it—symbolically—defiles her as much as her menstrual cycle does. However, it is the crown that is symbolic of Esther's relationship to the king, as it is her royal status that allows her to foil Haman's plans to destroy her people. In Judith's case, it is not a symbolic crown that renders her impure, but her menstrual cycle. However, this menstrual impurity is indeed what allows Judith to be crowned queen: without the necessary menstrual purification in the waters of the mikvah, and the forced sexual separation between Judith and Holofernes, she would not have achieved victory. Thus, the menstrual cloth, and the defilement that come with it—whether symbolic in Esther's case, or physical in Judith's—is what permits both Jewish heroines to attain victory. Clearly, the author of the *Megillah* is tying together both queens, emulating each other's noble countenance and bearing, and showing that a "defiling" menstrual crown can and should be used against non-Jewish enemies.

Yet, it is not only through the parallel to Queen Esther[43] that Judith's menstrual worth is emphasised, but also through that to King David. When Judith states that she "shall wash [her] hands in innocence," the author of the *Megillah* is establishing a comparison to David in Psalms 26:6. He speaks the exact same words when he confesses his sins and expresses atonement: he is declaring his commitment to a righteous and blameless life. David's "washing of hands" is a symbolic purification, contrasting with Judith's physical immersion of her entire body into the mikvah, ritually washing away her defilement. However, the author is not simply drawing a connection between two kinds of "washing"—whether metaphorical or physical, both symbolise a loyalty to God and Jewish traditions—but also, as with Esther, linking Judith to the most renowned Hebrew kings, the ancestor of the future Messiah. By doing so, he not only emphasises Judith's general worth and valour, but also puts a menstruating woman on the same level as King David. Thus, he not only emphasises Judith's general worth and valour, but also puts a menstruating woman on the same level as King David. Weingarten views this parallel particularly positivity:

> the identification of Judith, the victorious Jewish savior, with David, can be seen as part of the Jewish polemic of *Megillat Yehudit*, which presents the true Davidic redeemer against Christian claims.[44]

Indeed, the reception of these more ancient Jewish biblical figures within the *Megillat Yehudit* illustrate the importance of the transmission of Jewish tradition. Indeed, this ties Judith to these Jewish kings and queens of old, not only appropriating her from Christian parallels with the Virgin Mary or Ecclesia, for example, but also highlights the rich history of Judaism. In fact, contrary to Levine's argument, in which she suggests that the midrashim's addition of Judith's menstrual cycle is a way to weaken her and diminish her worth and importance, the *Megillah* actually makes menstrual cycle the very thing that elevates her to the ranks of David and Esther.

---

43 For a comparison between the Book of Esther and the Book of Judith see S. White Crawford, "Esther and Judith: Contrasts in Character," in *The Book of Esther in Modern Research*, eds. L. Greenspoon and S. White Crawford (London: T& T Clark International, 2003), 61–77.

44 S. Weingarten, "Food, Sex, and Redemption in Megillat Yehudit (the "Scroll of Judith")," in *The Sword of Judith: Judith Studies Across the Disciplines*, eds. K. Brine, et al. (Cambridge: Cambridge Open Book Publishers, 2010), 109.

Judith, the "Jewess"

This collection of menstruant-midrashim all illustrate the Jewish re-appropriation of Judith. The fact that in the *Megillat Yehudit*—as well as the other menstruant-midrashim—the heroine, literally named the "Jewess," uses Jewish niddah practices to attain victory over the non-Jewish enemies is a striking addition to the original Book of Judith, especially as it only appears in the later Middle Ages. From the eleventh century, the significance of menstruation underwent a transformative evolution within Judaism.[45] It ceased to be merely a physiological occurrence but attained a profound symbolic dimension. Menstruation became not only emblematic of female Jewish identity, but also served as a contrasting symbol, highlighting distinctions between Jewish and Christian women. Jewish women by following the niddah regulations demonstrated their commitment to halakha, thereby affirming their allegiance to both community and God. In contrast, Christians neglected these prescribed practices, leading to their perception by Jewish thinkers as in a constant state of ritual impurity and disobedience of true religious practices. Thus, beyond its traditional associations with physical or ritual purity, the menstrual cycle emerged as a potent political and religious marker, delineating the boundaries of community and signalling inclusion—or exclusion. The *Megillat Yehudit* constitutes a deliberate effort by a Jewish writer to distinguish a Jewish woman from her Christian counterparts, with the menstrual cycle emerging as a pivotal element in this endeavour. It is not necessarily Judith's menstrual cycle, but the Jewish practices surrounding niddah that become a strategic tool, even a weapon wielded in the struggle against Holofernes. Though Christian texts had appropriated the heroine—literally the "Jewess"—the authors of the menstruant-midrashim, specifically of the *Megillah*, succeed in re-appropriating Judith, transforming her from a pure Christian widow into an impure Jewish queen.

The author of *Megillat Yehudit* consistently incorporates biblical references and allusions, some of which were mentioned above. Indeed, she considers it to have:

> confused phraseology made up of strings of biblical quotations. *But* it is precisely this sort of work which can perhaps shed light on the thoughts and feelings of medieval Jews, a beleaguered minority in triumphantly Christian Europe, striving to preserve their own customs and way of life, and doing it here by reclaiming Judith, the Jewess, as their own.[46]

---

45   See Biale, *Blood and Belief*.
46   Weingarten, "Food, Sex, and Redemption," 109. Italics mine.

This deliberate integration, though not unusual, serves as a powerful means of reclaiming the narrative from potential Christian interpretations, instead preserving and transmitting the traditions and cultures of a minority within a dominant societal context. Notably, the author intertwines references to significant biblical figures with the character of Judith, drawing parallels with esteemed individuals such as King David and Queen Esther. This not only aligns Judith with their regal legacy and revered status in Jewish circles but also firmly anchors her within the broader Jewish textual heritage. The midrashim transform Judith into the ideal Jewish woman.[47]

Building upon this notion of Judith as the ideal Jewish woman is the possibility of drawing parallels between Judith and Jerusalem which reveals a compelling allegorical relationship, with Judith symbolising the essence of Jewish womanhood akin to Jerusalem's representation of the Jewish people. The transformation of the city of Bethulia, as seen in the original Book of Judith, into the city of Jerusalem immediately discloses a further importance to the latter. When arriving to Holofernes' camp, her first words to the king are "I am one of the daughters of Israel" (מבנות ישראל, *mebanot Israel*).[48] This ties in with Holofernes' counsellor's promise:

עפל בת־ציון עדיך תאתה ובאה הממשלה הראשנה לבת ירושלם

> Hill of Zion's daughter, to you it shall come, and the former sovereignty shall come again to the daughter of Jerusalem[49]

Judith is the promised daughter of Jerusalem who brings an end to Holofernes' rule and the return of a Jewish reign. Thus, her identity with Jerusalem becomes almost inextricable. As mentioned in a previous chapter, Lamentations introduces a menstruating Jerusalem, who takes on the sins of her people. This allows us to draw a parallel with the impure Judith who also assumes responsibility for her people, and only succeeds in saving them through her use of the menstrual cycle. Notably, the narrative underscores Judith's role as she "became queen over the land and judged Israel," linking her not just to her people, but to the actual country and land. This linkage draws a parallel between Judith and the city-woman archetype embodied by Jerusalem: she, in turn, becomes some kind of allegorical figure, beyond a simple individual. Both figures bear a representative significance: Jerusalem as the emblematic city of the Jews, and Judith as the archetypal "Jewess." Judith's name, after all, transcends a specific

---

47 Weingarten, "Food, Sex, and Redemption," 107–109.
48 Dubarle, *Judith*, 146.
49 Ibid., 142.

individual, instead serving as a generalised and all-encompassing title for all Jewish women. It is not Judith who saves her people, but rather all Jewish women who follow the correct niddah practices.

Covenant of Blood

The latest of the compiled midrashim, midrash n.12, originating from Venice in the latter half of the sixteenth century, offers a compelling perspective on the evolution and comprehension of Judith's menstrual cycle throughout the pre-modern period. In this midrash, Judith is not described as a widow, or related to prophets, but is rather the beautiful daughter of Matathias, who offers herself to the heavens and pledges to confront the uncircumcised enemy, vowing to slay him:

> כיון שראתה צער ישראל מסרה עצמה לשמים ואמרה אלך אני בעצמי לערל הזה שאני
> בטוחה במקום שיעשו לי נס ואהרוג את הערל הזה ויושיע את ישראל אל ידי ותעש לה חרב

> Once she saw the distress of Israel, she dedicated herself to heaven and said, "I will go myself to this uncircumcised man, as I am confident in God that he'll make me into a prodigy and I will kill this uncircumcised one, and Israel, and Israel will be saved by hand." She took a sword, and acted accordingly.[50]

This starkly distinguishes her Jewish identity from the non-Jewish adversary, emphasising the significance of circumcision rituals integral to Judaism—paralleling the niddah practises to which she herself adheres. The juxtaposition of her speech with the sword illustrates Judith's dynamism, portraying her female body not as passive but as an active force in this Jewish victory – one that bleeds and causes bleeding. Arriving at the enemy king's camp, Judith tells him

> אבל אודיע לך כי אני טמיאה והיום נשלמו ימי לבוני וכתוב בתורתינו לטבול במים וכדי
> שאטהר אני צריכה לעשות טבילה קודם שאשבה עדך ואחר אעשה כדור המלך

> But I will have you know that I am impure, and today end my days of my purification. It is written in our law to bathe in water. So that I may be pure, I am obligated to take a bath before coming towards you. After this I shall do whatever the king wishes.[51]

---

50   Dubarle, *Judith*, 171.
51   Ibid., 172.

This declaration represents the most explicit justification of Judith's purification baths in the midrashim. It goes beyond mere restoration of menstrual purity, emphasising adherence to Jewish law and traditions. The stark contrast between Judith's menstruating body and Holofernes' uncircumcised one specifically highlights the distinction between Jewish and gentile bodies. A female Jewish body defines her covenant with God not through circumcision, as her male counterpart does, but through her adherence to the niddah regulations. This is evident in polemical texts, such as the following *Nizzahon Vetus* from the late thirteenth or early fourteenth centuries.

> The heretics ask: We baptize both males and females and in that way we accept our faith, but in your case only men and not women can be circumcised. One can respond: Women are accepted because they watch themselves and carefully observe the prohibitions connected with menstrual blood.[52]

The unnamed author of the *Nizzahon Vetus* addresses the Christian challenge asserting that Jewish women were not fully integrated into their community due to the absence of circumcision. He counters by emphasising that despite lacking circumcision, Jewish women, who diligently adhere to the restrictions and commandments regarding niddah, are considered equal to circumcised Jewish men. Importantly, this places Jewish women not only above Christian women, who do not observe these prohibitions and remain "uncircumcised," but also on par with Jewish men in their commitment to forming a covenant with God. Thus, drawing a direct juxtaposition between the menstrual status of Judith and the uncircumcised one of Holofernes illustrates the contrasting statuses of moral, physical, and spiritual superiority. Despite the ritual impurity of Judith's body, she remains superior to Holofernes, as she follows the practices required in Judaism to purify herself. The combination of references to menstrual purification, circumcision and Jewish practices within the midrash n.12 underscores the paramount importance of Jewish customs, setting this rendition of the Judith narrative in stark and explicit contrast to Christian interpretations. It serves as a resolute re-appropriation of the Jewish heroine, and the inclusion of the menstrual cycle becomes pivotal in achieving this reinterpretation.

---

52 D. Berger, ed. *The Jewish-Christian Debate in the High Middle Ages: A Critical Edition of the Nizzahon Vetus with an Introd., Translation, and Commentary* (Boston, MA: Jewish Publication Society of America, 1979), 224.

Conclusion

During the Middle Ages, Jewish communities grappled with their minority status, particularly in the face of a prevailing Christian majority that often propagated anti-Jewish rhetoric and outright persecution. To counteract this marginalisation, Jews found it necessary to reinforce their distinct religious and cultural identity. Emphasising the importance of the Torah and their adherence to Jewish laws, Jews sought to distinguish themselves from Christians: both spiritually and physically. Jewish scholars actively engaged in theological discourse, defending their beliefs and practices, often underscoring the centrality of the covenant between Jew and God. The preservation of dietary laws as well as the physical circumcision and ritual bathing served as distinctive markers, visibly setting Jews apart from Christians. Circumcision and ritual (im)purity were integral for the covenantal aspect of their faith, and were practices that Christians no longer followed. Thus, these rituals became symbolic expressions of difference and, for the Jewish community, evidence of the superiority of their faith.

In religious discourse, the concept of niddah emerged as a means to differentiate Jewish women from their Christian counterparts, elevating them to a status akin to circumcised men. This shift gave female figures in biblical and religious texts newfound importance, providing a platform for Jewish authors to accentuate the status of *niddah* as well as the adherence to this Jewish mitzvah. Indeed, Moshe Idel calls Judaism a "halokhocentric religion,"[53] in which the following of the religious commandment or law lies at the very heart of the religion in question. Jewish female figures also gained heightened importance due to the surge in popularity of the Virgin Mary in the twelfth century. Ephraim Shoham-Steiner argues that "the empowerment [of Jewish female figures] appears to be a response to the rise of the Christian cult of Mary and its perceived threat to Jews."[54] In this context, Judith emerged as a pivotal figure for medieval Jews, serving as a counterbalance to the idealised portrayal of Mary. Christian texts had previously appropriated Judith, transforming her into a Marian prototype and symbolising virtues such as Chastity, Humility,

---

53 M. Idel, *Kabbalah and Eros* (New Haven, CT: Yale University Press, 2005), 23.
54 E. Shoham-Steiner, "The Virgin Mary, Miriam, and Jewish Reactions to Marian Devotion in the High Middle Ages," *AJS Review* 37, no. 1 (2013), 77. See more on Jewish female figures in response to Christianity in A. Green, "Shekhinah, the Virgin Mary, and the Song of Songs: Reflections on a Kabbalistic Symbol in Its Historical Context," *AJS Review* 26, no. 1 (2002): 1–52; S. F. Koren, "Immaculate Sarah: Echoes of Eve/Mary Dichotomy in the Zohar," *Viator* 41, no. 2 (2010): 183–97.

and Ecclesia.⁵⁵ However, in the later Middle Ages, a number of Jewish authors took the opportunity to reclaim Judith, reshaping her narrative to counterbalance the Christian depiction of the ideal woman: she became the ultimate Jew, one who adhered to Halakhah and prioritised the meticulous observation of mitzvot. By firmly reintegrating Judith into Judaism, the Jewish community aimed to assert its identity and respond to the prevailing cultural influences.⁵⁶

The reintroduction of the story of Judith within Jewish texts in the Middle Ages not only highlights the importance of niddah within the Jewish religion, but also participates in medieval Jewish self-definition. Despite Christianity idealising Judith as Marian prototype, the midrashim re-appropriate her through her adherence to Jewish practices connected to the menstrual cycle, such as her purification at the mikvah and restricting herself from sexual intercourse, no matter the risk. Judith becomes the embodiment of her name, "the Jewess," whose Jewish female body and bodily functions become the heart of the tale, the very elements pushing the narrative and climax forwards. The pre-modern mishrashic authors of the Judith tale receive the figure of the niddah not purely as a woman in a status of ritual impurity, but instead a figure that they could inscribe and idealise their faith and identity upon. By rewriting Judith as niddah, they inscribe themselves into this medieval tradition of using the rituals and traditions of circumcision and niddah as a way to differentiate themselves from their Christian neighbours. It serves simultaneously as a critique of Christians and as a way to strengthen their own self-perception. Whilst following the niddah rules, Judith highlights her own Jewish identity. Thus, by transforming Judith into a menstruating leader, the authors of the midrashim elevate her status and underscore the significance of Jewish practices in the face of Christian appropriation. Menstruation, in this context, serves as a symbolic tool. Just as circumcision was used to differentiate Jewish men from their Christian counterparts, menstruation became the defining factor that separated Jewish from Christian women. It is both a marker of differentiation from non-Jews, as well as a symbolic marker of Jewish community and faith.

---

55   See L. Abend Callahan, "Ambiguity and Appropriation: The Story of Judith in Medieval Narrative and Iconographic," in *Telling Tales: Medieval Narratives and the Folk Tradition*, eds. F. Canadé Sautman, et al. (Basingstoke: Macmillan, 1998), 79–99; Weingarten "Food, Sex, and Redemption."

56   See A. J. Levine, "Sacrifice and Salvation: Otherness and Domestication in the Book of Judith," in *A Feminist Companion to Esther, Judith and Susanna*, ed. A. Brenner (Sheffield: Sheffield Academic Press, 1995), 208–23.

Bibliography

Baumgarten, Elisheva. *Biblical Women and Jewish Daily Life in the Middles Ages*. Philadelphia, PA: University of Pennsylvania Press, 2022.

Berger, David, ed. *The Jewish-Christian Debate in the High Middle Ages: A Critical Edition of the Nizzahon Vetus with an Introduction, Translation, and Commentary*. Boston, MA: Jewish Publication Society of America, 1979.

Biale, David. *Blood and Belief: The Circulation of a Symbol between Jews and Christians*. Berkeley, CA: University of California Press, 2007.

Börner-Klein, Dagmar. "Judith in the Hebrew Literature of the Middle Ages." In *The Jewish Middle Ages*, edited by Carol Bakhos and Gerhard Langer, 55–70. Atlanta, GA: The Society of Biblical Literature, 2023.

Callahan, Leslie Abend. "Ambiguity and Appropriation: The Story of Judith in Medieval Narrative and Iconographic." In *Telling Tales: Medieval Narratives and the Folk Tradition*, edited by Francesca Canadé Sautman, Diana Conchado, and Guiseppe Carlo Di Scipio, 79–99. Basingstoke: Macmillan, 1998.

Ciletti, Elena, and Henrike Lähnemann. "Judith in the Christian Tradition." In *The Sword of Judith: Judith Studies Across the Disciplines*, edited by Kevin Brine, Elena Ciletti, and Henrike Lähnemann, 41–66. Cambridge: Cambridge Open Book Publishers, 2010.

Cohen, Ilana. "Menstruation and Religion: Developing a Critical Menstrual Studies Approach." In *The Palgrave Handbook of Critical Menstruation Studies*, edited by Chris Bobel, Inga T. Winkler, Breanne Fahs, Katie Ann Hasson, Elizabeth Arveda Kissling, and Tomi-Ann Roberts, 115–29. Singapore: Palgrave Macmillan, 2020.

Cohen, Shaye. *Why Aren't Jewish Women Circumcised? Gender and Covenant in Judaism*. Berkeley, CA: University of California Press, 2005.

Crawford, Sidnie White. "Esther and Judith: Contrasts in Character." In *The Book of Esther in Modern Research*, edited by Leonard Greenspoon and Sidnie White Crawford, 61–77. London: T & T Clark International, 2003.

Dubarle, André-Marie. *Judith: Formes et Sens des Diverses Traditions*. Rome: Institut Biblique Pontifical, 1966.

Enslin, Morton S. *The Book of Judith: Greek Text*. Leiden: Brill, 1972.

Gallagher, Edmon L. "Why Did Jerome Translate Tobit and Judith?" *Harvard Theological Review* 108, n. 3 (2015): 356–75.

Gaster, Moses. *An Unknown Hebrew Version of the History of Judith*. London: Harrison and Sons, date unknown.

Gera, Deborah Levine. "The Jewish Textual Traditions." In *The Sword of Judith: Judith Studies Across the Disciplines*, edited by Kevin Brine, Elena Ciletti, and Henrike Lähnemann, 23–40. Cambridge: Cambridge Open Book Publishers, 2010.

--------. *Judith*. Boston, MA: De Gruyter, 2014.
Green, Arthur. "Shekhinah, the Virgin Mary, and the Song of Songs: Reflections on a Kabbalistic Symbol in Its Historical Context." *AJS Review* 26, no. 1 (2002): 1–52.
Hasselhoff, Görge K. "Revising the Vulgate: Jerome and His Jewish Interlocutors." *Zeitschrift für Religions- und Geistesgeschichte* 64, n. 3 (2012): 209–21.
Idel, Moshe. *Kabbalah and Eros*. New Haven, CT: Yale University Press, 2005.
Koren, Sharon Faye. *Forsaken: The Menstruant in Medieval Jewish Mysticism*. Waltham, MA: Brandeis University Press, 2011.
--------. "Immaculate Sarah: Echoes of Eve/Mary Dichotomy in the Zohar." *Viator* 41, no. 2 (2010): 183–97.
--------. "Kabbalistic Physiology: Isaac the Blind, Nahmanides, and Moses de Leon on Menstruation." *AJS Review* 28, no. 2 (2004): 317–39.
--------. "The Menstruant as "Other" in Medieval Judaism and Christianity." *Nashim* 17 (2009): 33–59.
Levine, Amy Jill. "Sacrifice and Salvation: Otherness and Domestication in the Book of Judith." In *A Feminist Companion to Esther, Judith and Susanna*, edited by Athalya Brenner, 208–23. Sheffield: Sheffield Academic Press, 1995.
Moore, Carey A. *The Anchor Bible—Judith: A New Translation with Introduction and Commentary*. New Haven, CT: Yale University Press, 1985.
Neubauer, Adolf. *Catalogue of the Hebrew Manuscripts in the Bodleian Library and in the College Libraries of Oxford : Including MSS. in Other Languages, Which Are Written with Hebrew Characters, or Relating to the Hebrew Language or Literature; and a Few Samaritan MSS*. Volume II. Oxford: Clarendon, 1994.
Shoham-Steiner, Ephraim. "The Virgin Mary, Miriam, and Jewish Reactions to Marian Devotion in the High Middle Ages." *AJS Review* 37, no. 1 (2013): 75–91.
Stella, Francesco. "The Women of the Old Testament in Early Medieval Poetry: Judith and the Others." In *The Early Middle Ages*, edited by Franca Ela Consolino and Judith Herrin, 231–58. Atlanta, GA: The Society of Biblical Literature, 2020.
Tamber-Rosenau, Caryn. "Biblical Bathing Beauties and the Manipulation of the Male Gaze: What Judith Can Tell Us about Bathsheba and Susanna." *Journal of Feminist Studies in Religion* 33, no. 2. (2017): 55–72.
Wasserfall, Rachel. *Women and Water: Menstruation in Jewish Life and Law*. Waltham, MA: Brandeis University Press, 1999.
Weingarten, Susan. "Food, Sex, and Redemption in Megillat Yehudit (the "Scroll of Judith")." In *The Sword of Judith: Judith Studies Across the Disciplines*, edited by Kevin Brine, Elena Ciletti, and Henrike Lähnemann, 97–126. Cambridge: Cambridge Open Book Publishers, 2010.

PART III

History

Strengthening the Faith of the Ex-Conversos: Karaites, Translation, and Biblical Exegesis in Northwest Europe

Benjamin Fisher

Karaites—a scripturalist Jewish movement that emerged in eighth and ninth-century Palestine, before spreading to centers in the Ottoman Empire, and ultimately into Crimea, Lithuania, and Poland—had few friends and admirers among the rabbinic Jews living in northwest Europe during the seventeenth century. Rabbi Menasseh ben Israel, one of Amsterdam's leading rabbis, made this abundantly clear in his *Conciliador*, a massive four volume compilation reconciling hundreds upon hundreds of seemingly contradictory biblical verses, published in Amsterdam between 1632–1651. As part of his monumental effort to resolve all apparent biblical discrepancies and inconsistencies, Menasseh considered Exodus 34:27, "Then the Lord said to Moses, 'Write down these words, for in accordance with these words I have made a covenant with you and with Israel',"[1] and the obvious reality that a substantial corpus of law and teachings in Judaism were oral and thus were excluded, apparently, from this concord. Ruminating on this subject brought Menasseh's attention to a group in the Jewish past that had responded to this challenge by eschewing any relationship with the Oral Law—the Karaites. Regarding this Jewish movement, Menasseh wrote that "Saadia [Gaon] defeated them [the Karaites] and as a result very few are left who advocate their repugnant view."[2] Speaking disparagingly of the quality and strength of Karaite religious knowledge and doctrines, Menasseh continued, adding that "They who still remain are unable

---

1 Biblical citations, unless quoted directly from medieval manuscripts explored in this study, rely upon the *The Contemporary Torah*, JPS, 2006 edition. New Testament quotations rely upon the New Revised Standard Version, unless otherwise noted.
2 For the relationship between Jews in the Sephardi Diaspora in general, Karaites, and the idea of Karaism, see Y. Kaplan, "'Karaites' in Early Eighteenth-Century Amsterdam," in *Sceptics, Millenarians, and Jews*, ed. D. Katz and R. Popkin (Leiden: Brill, 1990), 196–236. The original text of Menasseh's thoughts about the Karaites is located in Menasseh ben Israel, *Conciliador, o de la conveniencia de los lugares de la S.Escriptura, que repugnantes entre si parecen* Vol. 1 (1632), 262. For a wider study of the *Conciliador*, see B. Fisher, "God's Word Defended: Menasseh ben Israel, Biblical Chronology, and the Erosion of Biblical Authority," in *Scriptural Authority and Biblical Criticism in the Dutch Golden Age: God's Word Questioned*, ed. D. van Miert et al. (Oxford: Oxford University Press, 2017), 155–74.

to compose any kind of book, and they are ignorant and outcast by all Jewish communities."[3]

Menasseh's coreligionists in the ex-converso community of seventeenth-century Amsterdam, both before his time and afterward, held equally negative views of the Karaite movement—and often went well beyond the level of Menasseh rejectionism. The Spanish and Portuguese Jewish community of seventeenth-century northwest Europe was significantly comprised of ex-conversos, descendants of individuals who forcibly, reluctantly, or in some cases enthusiastically converted to Christianity in the fourteenth and fifteenth centuries, some of whom later joined Jewish communities in different locations around the European world and the Mediterranean. Within these communities, some skeptical members were uncomfortable with, questioned, or rejected rabbinic authority and literature outright. This led many communal leaders to show an acute sensitivity regarding any antinomian or skeptical sign, and a tendency to see "Karaite" tendencies lurking around the corner and underneath the bed. Isaac Uziel—an early leader of the Amsterdam Jewish community—encountered a New Christian named Hector Mendes Bravo whom he rebuked for advancing the "views of the Karaites," and condemning those who hold such views as "heretics." The Venetian rabbi Leon Modena was also concerned by the specter of Karaism. Modena was consulted by the Sephardi communal boards of Hamburg and Amsterdam between 1615–1617 over a dispute about Uriel da Costa's heterodox ideas and printed works. Modena's attention was drawn to Karaite associations by da Costa himself, who rejected the rabbinic requirement to wear phylacteries and summoned the precedent set by the Karaites as a crucial element of support.[4] Many of these examples attest to the antipathy felt toward Karaites and Karaite scholarship in the Amsterdam ex-converso community, as well as authorities in Venice. As Yosef Kaplan concluded, "In Sephardi Jewish polemical literature of the 17th century, the concept of 'Karaism' had become synonymous with schismatics and sectarians."[5]

The attitude and tenor of Amsterdam's leading authorities toward Karaite thought, culture, and society was undeniably negative. It is therefore more than surprising that Isaac Athias, a young rabbi trained in Venice who also served in Hamburg, decided to translate a Karaite anti-Christian polemical treatise—*Hizzuk Emunah* (*Strengthening of the Faith*), written by Isaac ben Abraham of

---

3   Kaplan, "Karaites in Early Eighteenth Century Amsterdam," 212.
4   Ibid., 204–7.
5   Ibid., 207.

Troki in 1593. Why did Athias see the Karaite text as essential literature to be translated into Spanish for the edification of new members of the Spanish and Portuguese Jewish community? Why highlight the importance of a Karaite work in an environment so inimical toward the movement and its ideas?

The inclusion of Karaite texts in the literature intended for the education of ex-conversos joining Jewish communities has not traditionally been noted or emphasized. Yosef Hayim Yerushalmi once remarked that "the returning Marrano remained essentially an autodidact and, like all autodidacts, he needed books to read."[6] The scope of the literature that Yerushalmi surveys, which was translated into Spanish and Portuguese and made available to the ex-conversos who joined Jewish communities at this time was indeed remarkable and cut across literary genres. This Spanish literature for ex-conversos included editions of the Bible, such as numerous editions of the 1553 Ferrara Bible, and liturgical works such as the *Libro de oraciones de todo el anno*—also printed in Ferrara.[7] Books on the performance of Judaism's commandments such as Rabbi Isaac Athias' (more traditional) *Tesoro de preceptos*, and halakhic works like Ladino abridgements of Joseph Karo's classic halakhic manual the *Shulhan Arukh* were printed in 1568 and 1602. Across the sixteenth and seventeenth centuries, Spanish editions of the Mishnah were printed in Venice and Amsterdam in 1606 and 1663 respectively, historical works such as Samuel Usque's *Consolacam as tribulacoens de Israel* and Solomon Ibn Verga's *Shebet Yehudah* printed in Ferrara, in 1553 and Amsterdam in 1640.

This list of Jewish classics makes unusual company for the Karaite scholar Isaac ben Abraham of Troki's *Hizzuk Emunah*, which was reprinted widely in the seventeenth and eighteenth centuries, and translated into Yiddish, Latin, Dutch, Spanish, and Portuguese, among other languages during this period. The many editions of *Hizzuk Emunah* include Isaac Athias' manuscript copy produced at Hamburg in 1621 under the title *Fortificaçion de la Fee* (*Strengthening of the Faith*), which was also copied at Amsterdam in 1624 under the title

---

6   Y. H. Yerushalmi, *The Re-education of Marranos in the Seventeenth Century* (Cincinnati, OH: University of Cincinnati, 1980), 7.

7   Regarding the printing of biblical translations and Spanish-language liturgical works in the western Sephardi diaspora, see H. den Boer, *La Literatura Sefardi de Amsterdam* (Alcala: Instituto Internacional de Estudios Sefardiés y Andalucíes, Universidad de Alcalá, 1995). The Ferrara Bible and its adaptations were among the most ubiquitously reprinted biblical texts among Spanish and Portuguese Jews in northwest Europe from the sixteenth century into the eighteenth century, although there were also frustrations with what was seen as a heavily literal style of translation, which led to further translation efforts and even a turn to Christian version of the Bible that were seen as more linguistically appealing.

Fortificaçion de la Ley de Moseh (*Strengthening of the Law of Moses*).[8] Unlike the books cited by Yerushalmi above, Troki's writings were not classics of the Sephardi world. Their author was not a figure of significance in the Sephardi world, or a member of the Spanish and Portuguese community with whom the ex-conversos could identify. The author was not even a rabbinic Jewish figure in the first instance—a fact that was seen as significantly problematic by Isaac Athias, and which is discussed below. Given all of this, why would a respected rabbi of the Jewish world during this period, such as Athias, turn to a Karaite work in order to help bridge the gap between Christianity and Judaism that the conversos sought to traverse? Why was it necessary to focus ex-conversos' attention on the thought and writings of a Karaite scholar so early in the history of the northwest European Sephardi diaspora in Amsterdam and Hamburg? Might this decision even be counterproductive, risky, or even dangerous—in light of the incomplete understanding of rabbinic Judaism that many conversos possessed on their arrival in Amsterdam? Could exposure to the scholarship of Karaite authors undermine the effort to integrate members of the converso world into Jewish communities?

After introducing the original author of *Hizzuk Emunah*—Isaac ben Abraham of Troki, and its translator Isaac Athias, this essay will trace how a multi-tiered translation effort both presented the text of a Karaite anti-Christian polemic to an audience of ex-conversos, and simultaneously expanded upon the original work, intervening in the language of Troki's *Hizzuk Emunah* to calibrate the text at an even higher level for Spanish and Portuguese Jews, who were either ex-conversos themselves or descendants of ex-conversos. This translation effort goes beyond the linguistic and most frequent meaning of the term—and enabled Athias to craft a version of *Hizzuk Emunah* that was a useful tool in the process of educating conversos joining the Jewish communities of Hamburg and Amsterdam in the early seventeenth century. The work that Athias produced—*Fortificaçion de la fee*—was similar in title to the exemplar that he worked from, *Hizzuk Emunah*. But it was a very different work overall. The expanded version of the *Fortificaçion* accentuated Christian teachings to an even higher degree, drew attention to the differences between rabbinic Judaism and Karaite traditions, and emphasized rabbinic teachings to make

---

8 I. Athias, *Fortificaçion de la fee*, Mss. EH 48 D 05 (Hamburg, 1621); *Fortificaçion de la Ley de Moseh*, EH 48 C 6 (Amsterdam, 1624). Most citations in this article utilize the Hamburg manuscript, but key differences evident in the Amsterdam copy are noted below.

Hizzuk Emunah more compatible with the norms of the Sephardi Jewish community in Amsterdam.

Troki and Athias, Writer and Translator

Isaac ben Abraham of Troki, and Isaac Athias of Venice, could not have been more seemingly different. Born in 1533 in Troki, near Vilna, Isaac ben Abraham was part of a Karaite community and tradition in the region that had been established earlier in the fourteenth century. During his lifetime, the region was one of the major centers of Karaism in Poland-Lithuania, and he was educated by one of the more prominent Karaite figures of the region, Zefania ben Mordechai in Troki. Living in a multicultural milieu that included rabbinic and Karaite Jews; Roman Catholic; Greek Orthodox Christians; Protestant; and Anti-Trinitarian Christians, Troki was well versed in the beliefs and doctrine of Christian and rabbinic Jewish communities, and he wrote polemical works against both: *Hizzuk Emunah* against his Christian opponents in 1593; and his (undated) manuscript *Polemic Against the Rabbanites*.[9] As Carsten Wilke has argued, Troki's anti-Christian polemic belongs to a style that confronts an imagined opponent and aims to strengthen the self-confidence of the Jewish reader, rather than providing a manual for conducting heated, face-to-face disputations.[10]

Hizzuk Emunah is divided into two parts, comprised of 50 and 100 chapters, focusing on Christian allegations against Jews and Judaism in the first section and on aspersions cast against the New Testament in the second. Troki provides answers in both sections informed by historical and philological interpretations and investigations to both Scriptures. Throughout, the text is heavily

---

9   See G. Akhiezer, "The Karaite Isaac ben Abraham of Troki and his *Polemic Against the Rabbanites*," in *Tradition, Heterodoxy, and Religious Culture: Judaism and Christianity in the Early Modern Period*, ed. Ch. Goodblatt and H. Kreisel (Be'er-Sheva: Ben Gurion University of the Negev Press, 2006), 437–68. See also Miriam Benfatto, "The Work of Isaac ben Abraham of Troki (16th Century): On the Place of Sefer Hizzuq Emunah in the Quest for the Historical Jesus," *Journal for the Study of the Historical Jesus* 17 (2019): 102–20; and ibid., "The Manuscript as a *medium*. A critical look at the circulation of the *Sefer Hizzuq Emunah* by Isaac ben Abraham Troki (c. 1533–1594), in *Studi e materiali di storia delle religioni* 85, no. 1 (2019): 235–43. As noted in Akhiezer, "Isaac ben Abraham of Troki," 449, no date is discernable for the composition of Troki's polemic against rabbinic Judaism.

10 See C. Wilke, "Clandestine Classics: Isaac Orobio and the Polemical Genre Among the Dutch Sephardim," in *Isaac Orobio: The Jewish Argument with Dogma and Doubt* (Boston, MA: De Gruyter, 2018) 66.

informed by intra-Christian polemics waged between Catholics, Protestants, and radical anti-Trinitarian Christians in the regions in which he lived. Isaac of Troki read and utilized the "Christian Dialogues" by Marcin Czechowicz along with the Italian skeptic Niccolo Paruta's *De Uno Vero Deo*. He utilized the Bible translated by the heterodox figure Szymon Budny (1530–1593) who rejected the divinity of Jesus and argued for the universal acceptance of the Seven Noachide Laws.[11]

Unexpectedly—at first glance—Troki also refers to an array of rabbinic writings on halakhah, Talmudic literature, and exegesis. However, by the late sixteenth century there was a significant degree of intermingling of Karaite scholars with rabbinic Jewish society. Many leading Karaite figures and their students cross-pollinated in educational settings with rabbinic teachers, in part due to the small size of their community, and in part due to the crescendo of printed material circulating at this time, which created a vast and accessible library of rabbinic texts.[12] In general though, at a theological level, Karaite scholars continued to reject rabbinic claims about the authority of Oral Torah and the chain of transmission of rabbinic Judaism's oral law—perspectives that, as we shall see, greatly disturbed Isaac Athias as he translated Troki's writings for an audience of ex-converso rabbinic Jews. While Isaac of Troki wrote the bulk of *Hizzuk Emunah*, the work was completed by a student—Yosef ben Mordecai Malinowski (~1569–1610) after the original author's death, also adding of his own accord a preface and index.[13]

Isaac Athias, who translated *Hizzuk Emunah* into Spanish, was born to a converso family in Lisbon in 1585, whose family moved to Castile, before settling in Venice—where Athias studied with Saul Levi Mortera. His mentor would soon relocate to Paris and then Amsterdam, where Mortera would spend the rest of his life. Athias, meanwhile, served as the inaugural rabbi of the Portuguese Jewish community in Hamburg before returning to Venice as rabbi of the Sephardi community in this center in 1622.[14] Athias certainly remembered his time in the Hamburg community fondly, dedicating his *Tesoro de preceptos* (*Treasury of Precepts*; Venice, 1627) to the city's ex-conversos, and "to the years that I spent in their pleasant company and domain."[15] The *Tesoro*, a description of Judaism's 613 commandments in the long and venerable

---

11   See Akhiezer, "Isaac ben Abraham of Troki," 442–44.
12   See ibid., 445ff.
13   See ibid., 437, n.1.
14   See Y. E. Demota, "Early Modern Portuguese Jewish Conceptions of *Dominium* and *Libertas* and Constructions of Community," *Studia Rosenthaliana* 49, no. 1 (2023): 29.
15   I. Athias, *Tesoro de Preceptos* (Venice, 1627) "Al venerado kahal kadosh Talmud Torah de Hamburgo" (unpaginated).

tradition of literature on this subject, was very much part of the body of literature Yerushalmi identified as being intended for the ex-converso arrivals in the Sephardi diaspora.

As Athias wrote, the treatise was intended for the most noble nation of Spain, with expulsions, calamities, deaths, and extreme troubles," and those who "emerged from such a bitter captivity" and returned to Judaism. Athias envisioned his treatise as providing ex-conversos who "until now ... have enjoyed only the Bible, with no commentary whatever, and the holy prayers, and some few other compilations" with "this great foundation of the commandments, making these known to [them] who, for lacking the language, cannot see them in their original source."[16] Athias' treatise indeed was a crucial work studied by Abraham Cardoso, the brother of Yerushalmi's famous ex-converso subject Isaac Cardoso, as he integrated into the Jewish world of sixteenth century Venice.[17] In translating *Hizzuk Emunah* for an audience of newly converted Sephardi ex-conversos, Athias has been seen as part of a group of rabbis whose anti-Christian writings perpetuated a more "medieval mode of polemical expression: they compiled inventories of exegetical arguments in the order of the biblical text."[18]

Traditional though the organization, purpose, and methodology may be, Athias' decision to translate *Hizzuk Emunah* into Spanish for an audience of ex-conversos, and to expand upon and elaborate its arguments is nevertheless unexpected. It is not intuitively obvious why a rabbinic author seeking to make edifying information about the Jewish tradition available to an audience of ethnic peers would select a polemical anti-Christian work written by an East European Karaite figure. Athias' deliberate choice is even more perplexing in light of the ambivalent attitude (at best) toward Karaite Jews in ex-converso Amsterdam, described above. Isaac Athias himself was likewise hardly enamored with Karaism and Karaite scholarship generally.

In Athias' detailed introduction to the *Fortificaçion de la fee*, he observes with some consternation the fact that the original author of *Hizzuk Emunah* "was a Karaite from those who deny the Oral Law received at Sinai by Moses, our master."[19] Athias acknowledged that there were "some matters in the book that were severely contradictory" to rabbinic Jewish interpretations—"as will

---

16   Ibid., 3–4. See Yerushalmi's quotation and translation in *From Spanish Court to Italian Ghetto: Isaac Cardoso: A Study in Seventeenth-Century Marranism and Jewish Apologetics* (New York, NY: Columbia University Press, 1971), 204.
17   Yerushalmi, *From Spanish Court*, 205.
18   Wilke, "Clandestine Classics," 72.
19   Athias, *Fortificaçion*, Introduction: "... fue Karrai de los que negan la ley de boca recibida en sinay por Mosseh nuestro maestro."

be seen."[20] Athias—seemingly unable to wait until encountering such claims in the main body of the book he is translating, felt the need to interrupt Isaac ben Abraham of Troki already in the prologue to *Hizzuk Emunah*, in order to inveigh against how there are numerous beliefs and assumptions in the book that "cannot be supported except through our blessed rabbis [*nuestros bienauenturados*] whom they deny, and their sublime expositions."[21]

Later, in an annotation located in Chapter 7 of the *Fortificaçion*, Athias expresses his disdain for Karaites again and at greater length. Here, in a prolonged discourse on the duration of the current "captivity" in which the Jews were held, Athias writes particularly disparagingly about Karaites and Karaism. In this section of the work, Troki confronted Christian adversaries who argued that all previous "captivities" had not only been dramatically shorter, and also that their duration was foretold to select, privileged individuals. Consequently, the duration of the current exile, and its unknown duration, are signs of irrevocable permanence. Troki's rebuttal is based on compelling biblical exegesis—but Athias remained dissatisfied: despite everything that Troki had deployed against his Christian readers, in defense of Judaism, Athias writes that "it is not sufficiently proven for the author who is not a Karaite (*no ser Carray*)," as Athias was most certainly not. He was dissatisfied because, as he writes, "the *caraim* ... do not even know who the talmudists are, and beyond this they are by their very nature insufficiently educated and learned ("*muy poco letrados y estudiosos*") in order to read these books." Without the additional interpretations, guidance, and expertise of rabbinic Jewish sages, the correct understanding of the duration of Israel's captivity was impossible—in Athias' estimation. Athias was at one with his contemporaries and their worldview in casting a skeptical eye at Karaites and Karaism.

Scripture and Salvation

Why, despite his evident contempt for Karaites, did Athias nevertheless choose to translate *Hizzuk Emunah* and craft it into the *Fortificaçion*? Athias justifies translating the book into Spanish for the ex-conversos, explaining that in spite of these reservations, "I did not refrain from accepting this book, since we have an obligation (as the sages have taught) to accept the truth from whoever

---

20 Ibid.: "... tiene algunas cosas en el libro que lo repugnan como severa."
21 Ibid.: "... no se pueden ajudar sino de nuestros bienauenturados aquien ellos negan y sus altas esposisiones ..."

speaks it."[22] Problematic though the text might be in some respects, the appeal must have outweighed the negative aspects. The appeal of *Hizzuk Emunah* in the context of northwest Europe's ex-converso communities of Hamburg and Amsterdam lay at least partly in the way that their communities accentuated direct engagement with the Bible—socially, educationally, and intellectually in ways that other Jewish communities of medieval and early modern Europe did not, where the study of Talmud was centered to a higher degree.

In Amsterdam for example, the community school system was structured to teach the Bible systematically to children, progressively moving through the Pentateuch, Prophets, and Writings, adding along the way instruction in the biblical cantillation marks, and sometimes the commentaries of Rashi—but completely leaving rabbinic literature to the side. Talmud and halakhic works were reserved for the highest levels of the school system that few students in fact reached. It was commonplace for adults as well to delve deeply into the Bible within confraternities such as the *Gemilut Hasadim* burial society, where members of the confraternity met every Sabbath to discuss passages from the Bible, systematically working their way through the entire text—over the course of a period of almost twenty-five years.[23] Children and adults alike in Amsterdam were often comfortable and fluent in the world of Scripture, in a way that they were not with the direct study of rabbinic literature and halakhah.

A polemical, anti-Christian work based on debates about biblical interpretation, such as *Hizzuk Emunah*, may have been seen as aligning with the sensibilities of the ex-converso community to a greater degree than literature more heavily dependent upon prior knowledge of rabbinic literature, or a deep education in rabbinic texts or traditions. The title page of the *Fortificaçion* itself may offer additional, insightful clues about the appeal of the text. The title emphasizes that the *Fortificaçion de la Fee* was "the pillar that fortifies the afflicted hearts of Israel in its captivity, showing them the eternally expected salvation, and demonstrating the obscurity and falsity of their adversaries' opinions, for which all of the passages of Scripture that they interpret in their favor against us are noted."[24] After attempting to thwart the Christian interpretations, the verses are "explained according to their true sense with an

---

22   Athias, *Fortificaçion*: "Tenemos obligacion como los sabios ensenan de recibir la verdad de quien la dixiere."

23   See B. Fisher, *Amsterdam's People of the Book: Jewish Society and the Turn to Scripture in the Seventeenth Century* (Cincinnati, OH: Hebrew Union College Press, 2020), 66–9.

24   Athias, *Fortificaçion*, Title Page: "Coluna que fortifica los aflictos coracones de la casa de Israel captiva anunciándoles la sempiterna salvación esperado ymostrando la escuridad delos adversarios y falsedad de sus opiniones."

amenable style and great erudition."[25] The *Fortificaçion* promised to lead its readers–and their community—on the path toward salvation by helping them shift from a Christian mode of reading and understanding the promises of the Bible, to a Jewish vantage point.

In emphasizing the role of reading and engaging with the Bible in leading the Jewish reader to salvation, Athias drew upon a concept linking the Bible and salvation that strongly resonated with the Jewish community of early seventeenth century Amsterdam and that in the future would form a bedrock of how the Bible was perceived among the ex-conversos. The assumed connection between salvation and engagement with Scripture is evident pervasively in this world. Menasseh ben Israel's *Humas de Parasioth y Aftharoth* (Amsterdam, 1627), a liturgical text for following the weekly Torah portions and *haftaroth* in synagogue, offers a very early parallel in the period just after Athias' translation of the *Fortificaçion*. In the Portuguese introduction to his work, Menasseh affirms to his readers why it is important to regularly read Scripture: "'During the day and the night you shall not have any other occupation than divine meditation': because in this ... the path to salvation is found," and insists that the "advantage I wished to show you [the reader], of this book, of assiduously reading Scriptures each week, was eternal salvation."[26]

Menasseh's *Conciliador* is replete with similar arguments emphasizing the connection between the Bible and salvation. In the preface to the initial 1632 volume, Menasseh's pitch to the prospective buyer of his enormous tome is that the investment of their money will pay off beneficially for them in their "enjoyment and salvation."[27] In Question 125 of the *Conciliador*, in the main body of the text, Menasseh discusses what he views as the perfect manner of the giving of the law from a number of perspectives, and emphasizes that the conditions under which the law was given in the desert had to be perfect, because it is through the Bible and its doctrines upon which the Israelites' salvation depended. The desert, Menasseh emphasizes, is a geographic location "common to all," and so too the Bible is a text shared by "all those who desire to be saved by it, even though at first it was given only to Israel."[28] The connection made in the *Fortificaçion* between scripture and salvation was shared deeply by Menasseh, and other members of his community, helping us to understand

---

25   Athias, *Fortificaçion*, title page [unpaginated].
26   M. ben Israel, *Humas de Parasioth y Aftharoth*, Prologo ao lector. See also Fisher, *Amsterdam's People of the Book*, 89–90.
27   M. ben Israel, *Conciliador*, vol. 1 "Al lector" [unpaginated]. See also Fisher, *Amsterdam's People of the Book*, 90.
28   M. ben Israel, *Conciliador*, vol. 1, 285.

the appeal of such a text to Spanish and Portuguese Jews—even if it came from the pen of a Karaite.

Other Spanish and Portuguese Jews in Amsterdam made this connection as well—not just Menasseh. The casual, idiomatic way in which they uses the terms suggests that they did not fear push back or objection, but rather that they were saying something that reflected broadly held sentiments in the community. In a *mahzor* printed compiled by David Pardo and Salom ben Yosseph in 1630, described Scripture as "the source and deliverer of life and salvation."[29] In 1640, Saul Levi Mortera—one of Amsterdam's leading rabbis—preached to the Spanish and Portuguese Jewish community in Amsterdam about the importance of active performance of the commandments in attaining salvation, in contrast to Christian teachings emphasizing that faith alone led an individual to eternal spiritual reward.[30] Later in the seventeenth century, Daniel Levi de Barrios would describe a the *Keter Sem Tob* (*Crown of the Good Name*) confraternity, where young boys and girls from the Portuguese Jewish community engaged in collective Bible study. He emphasizes that the young members of this charitable society "study the Holy Law one hour every Sabbath ... in order to attain eternal reward," and to leave the path of "ruin" for "the path of salvation."[31] A shared concern and identification with the link between Scripture and the individual's quest for salvation of their soul may have led Athias to select Troki's *Hizzuk Emunah* as an important text to make available to the ex-converso community in Amsterdam.

Reshaping *Hizzuk Emunah* into the *Fortificaçion*

While the text of *Hizzuk Emunah* had notable appeal to Athias and members of the Sephardi community in Hamburg and Amsterdam, the process of translation was not an act of mere mimicry, reproducing precisely the text of Troki's original in Spanish. Rather, the transformation from *Hizzuk Emunah* into the *Fortificaçion* involved authorial interventions, both large and small. The ways in which Isaac Athias manipulated, rearranged, and added substantially to its contents profoundly altered the way in which readers encountered *Hizzuk Emunah*, and these elements must also be addressed. One of these elements is the title ascribed to the Karaite author of *Hizzuk Emunah*, R. Isaac ben Abraham of Troki. Turning to the title page of Athias' translation, an

---

29　Fisher, *Amsterdam's People of the Book*, 91.
30　Ibid., 111.
31　Ibid., 50.

ex-converso reader would encounter the presentation of Troki as "the very learned Señor H:H: R. Yshac de Lithuania." The scholar who is promised to give readers the "true meaning [of Scripture] in a most accessible and erudite style"[32] is an East European Karaite Jew who has been restyled as a Sephardi *hakham*. Troki was thus introduced to readers of the *Fortificaçion* as an authority on a similar level to the most important religious leaders of Sephardi Jews in northwest Europe during this time, and that was used by the *Mahamad* (the lay board of governors) in Amsterdam in the drafting of contracts appointing the community's most senior rabbis.[33] Although the title page indicated that Troki was Lithuanian, he became—at least partly, at least a little bit—a Sephardi rabbinic authority, in the way that he was presented to the readers of the *Fortificaçion*. Crafting the title page in this fashion, and re-fashioning the identity of the Karaite author, primed Sephardi readers of the manuscript in Amsterdam and Hamburg to see Troki as a respected authority on par with the most venerated leaders of their own communities.

Athias' interventions in *Hizzuk Emunah* were not limited to the title page. The *anotaciones*—substantive interjections, comments, and discourses that Athias scatters throughout the text were a crucial device in the making of *Hizzuk Emunah* for Sephardi eyes. It is in the *anotaciones* where Athias could consider the type of edifying explanations that members of the ex-converso community most needed, but were lacking in Troki's original text of *Hizzuk Emunah*, and where Athias is able to recalibrate the text for ex-converso sensibilities. Later, in the introduction to the *Tesoro de preceptos* in 1627, Athias wrote with some alarm that the ex-conversos "emerged from such a bitter captivity, without having been instructed since childhood in the discipline of the Law," and that "they remained, *even up to now*, deprived of its treasures." Continuing, he stresses that "until now, they have enjoyed only the Bible, with no commentary whatever, and the holy prayers, and some few other compilations."[34] Athias was concerned about the Bible centered culture of the former conversos and sought to help members of the Sephardi diaspora understand the Bible better from a Jewish perspective. He does this by weaving rabbinic Jewish traditions into the *Fortificaçion*, and by fortifying *Hizzuk Emunah*'s rebuttal of Christian exegesis and beliefs—which the ex-conversos knew so well.

The effect of Athias' *anotaciones* is evident in his translation of *Hizzuk Emunah*'s sixteenth chapter, which focuses on a classic locus for Jewish-Christian

---

32   Athias, *Fortificaçion*, title page [unpaginated].
33   See A. O. Albert, *Jewish Politics in Spinoza's Amsterdam* (London: The Littman Library of Jewish Civilization and Liverpool University Press, 2022), 198–99.
34   Athias, *Tesoro de preceptos*, 3–4, and Yerushalmi, *From Spanish Court*, 204.

disputation, Deut. 27:26 "Cursed be whoever will not uphold the terms of this Teaching and observe them." The Christian position is presented first— "The adversaries say that since the Divine Law says 'shall be cursed,' anyone who does not uphold all of its precepts shall be cursed, we shall all be cursed because it is impossible for anyone to uphold and perform all of the commandments." The *Fortificaçion* responds, and builds a case that in no way is the biblical text implying that "all those who do not uphold the law in its entirety shall be cursed, the affirmative and negative precepts, which is impossible."[35] The *Fortificaçion* bases this case and argument on the long lineage of Israelites (biblical and otherwise) who have manifestly not observed each and every law and commandment, but nevertheless were either not cursed due to this shortcoming, or—conversely—unmistakably thrived and were blessed. On the contrary, biblical passages such as Deut. 28:15 "But if you do not obey your God to observe faithfully all the commandments and laws which I enjoin upon you this day, all these curses shall come upon you and take effect," should be understood to convey that those who do not follow the word of God will be cursed—"if they do not turn around and make complete repentance" for their misdeeds.[36]

Athias, acting simultaneously as translator and author, makes two *anotaciones* to Troki's original text at this juncture. First, he provides evidence that sinners from among the biblical Israelite community could be redeemed, despite their failure to fully adhere to the law flawlessly. Athias' first *anotacion* is utilized to show that King David transgressed grievously, in the case of Bathsheba—the wife of Uriah, with whom David had sexual relations before arranging for Uriah to be killed in battle as his compatriots abandoned him. Even in light of all of this, David performed "complete repentance" (*perfeta penitencia*) and was not cursed. Indeed, despite dynastic instability described in I Kings 15, in which Adonijah attempts to succeed as king, David's dynasty continues and is not annulled—something that we would not expect if complete and total fulfillment of every commandment were required to avoid the specter of the biblical curse.

A second *anotacion* in this chapter provided ex-converso readers of Athias' translation with assurance that this interpretation was deeply rooted in rabbinic Jewish traditions and had the support of highly respected Jewish authorities: "Thus as well R. Moses of Egypt (i.e. Maimonides) says in his commentary on the Mishnah, and it is a very well accepted and approved doctrine, and he says this in regard to the teaching of the celebrated [Talmudic sage]

---

35   Athias, *Fortificaçion*, fol. 82–83.
36   Ibid., fol. 84.

R. Hananiah."[37] The implication of these *anotaciones* together is that ex-converso readers of Athias' translation—individuals from families that had been unable to fulfill the commandments at any level close to their entirety—would be reassured that they were not condemned due to this failure, and that Athias' reassurance had the deep approbation and support of rabbinic tradition.

From their time spent living as Christians in the Iberian Peninsula, or as descendants of families that converted from Christianity to Judaism in the Sephardi Diaspora during the sixteenth and seventeenth-centuries, members of Athias' audience of readers were often thoroughly familiar with the texts of the New Testament—and it is to these narratives that the *Fortificaçion* turns next in its attempts to help reorient the mindset of ex-converso readers from Christian perspectives toward Jewish perspectives. Addressing the language of the New Testament head on, in a serious way was necessary in order to convince and persuade readers who knew these texts and traditions well. Flippant or casual denials would be insufficient.

As Chapter 16 continues, the *Fortificaçion* explains that "The Christians accuse us ... however, we shall accuse them according to the truth of the verse that we find in the Gospels."[38] The *Fortificaçion* quotes Revelation 22:18–19, "I warn everyone who hears the words of the prophecy of this book: if anyone adds to them, God will add to that person the plagues described in this book; if anyone takes away from the words of the book of this prophecy, God will take away that person's share in the tree of life and in the holy city, which are described in this book." Interpreting this passage, the *Fortificaçion* zeros in on the danger of adding to or diminishing from biblical precepts, and insists (with biting sarcasm) that

> It is obvious and public to all that the Christians are honored in the net of the curse, since they add to and diminish from the words of the Gospel, as in the observance of the next day of the week as the Sabbath, which is not commanded in the Gospels nor by Jesus nor did his Apostles command it.[39]

While there is no specific *anotacion* in this particular chapter elaborating on the polemical, anti-Christian material in Troki's *Hizzuk Emunah*, this is something that is a notable feature in other locations of the *Fortificaçion*. Athias was very much aware of the Christian background shared by many of his readers and was careful to add polemical *anotaciones* calibrated to address the knowledge that these members of the Western Sephardi Diaspora brought with them into

---

37   Athias, *Fortificaçion*, fol. 84.
38   Ibid., fol. 85.
39   Ibid., fol. 85–86.

their lives as ex-converso Jews. This is illustrated already in the second chapter of the *Fortificaçion*, where the text considers, "Regarding what they accuse us, saying: God has rejected the Nation of Israel because they did not follow Jesus and for having executed him, and elected the people of Christianity."

In this chapter, the *Fortificaçion* ranges widely regarding the persecution of early Christians by Roman emperors, and the execution of Apostles and early Christians by Roman authorities, as a way of showing that in no way was the privileging of Christianity causally tied to the degraded status of Jews. God, in other words, did not elect Christianity at the same time as Jews were allegedly abandoned, because the historical record contradicts this theological construct. In this context, Athias adds an *anotacion* amplifying the historical record of early Christianity in order to reassure ex-converso readers (who, after all, were just beginning to read the *Fortificaçion*) that Christianity was and continued to be divided and contradictory in doctrine and practice.

In this *anotacion*, Athias first offers a moderate correction to Troki—who in the main body of the translated text above the *anotacion* presents the archbishop Arius of Alexandria as a general opponent of Christianity "who wrote much against the Christians, but Constantine did not accept his ideas." In fact, Athias informs the reader, Arius "did not deny Jesus … however his opinion was to separate the substance of the son and the father," and to "ruin all of the basis" of the emerging new religion.[40] Likewise, the *anotacion* notes that the Christians initially observed the Saturday Sabbath but then arbitrarily altered its observance to Sunday in the year 500 CE, "which Jesus never commanded, nor his Apostles."[41] Athias observes dryly that the doctrinal divisions of the Christian world were not limited to the fourth century, but in fact persist to his own day. Likely drawing upon debates of the Protestant Reformation, Athias shines a spotlight on critiques of Catholic aesthetics and worship: "We see that even today … even in their churches the idols of wood and stone and silver and gold did not cease, and especially the Hosts that they worship … all of which is against the doctrine of Jesus."[42] By enriching the text of Troki's *Hizzuk Emunah* in the *anotaciones* with further information about divisions in the early Christian world and ongoing debates about Christian worship and doctrine, Troki plays to his readers sensibilities as ex-converso Jews. He addresses their thirst for confirmation of their choice to live as Jews in northwest Europe and provides ammunition for their anti-Christian polemical sensibilities.

---

40   Athias, *Fortificaçion*, fol. 23–24.
41   Ibid., fol. 24.
42   Ibid.

From Fortificaçion to the Questions Posed by the Priest from Rouen

The *Fortificaçion de la fée*, the Spanish translation of Isaac ben Abraham of Troki's *Hizzuk Emunah*, was an early and very popular manuscript in the Sephardi Diaspora communities of Hamburg and Amsterdam, where it circulated and was copied systematically multiple times early in the histories of these communities. Most of the remarks in this study have focused on the earliest edition of the translation available, the 1621 manuscript copied at Hamburg. A brief—but significant—reference in the manuscript copied at Amsterdam in 1624 is revealing, however, of the larger importance and impact of the *Fortificaçion* on the thought, identity, and polemics of the ex-converso diaspora in western Europe in the early seventeenth century. The Amsterdam manuscript, appearing under a slightly different title—*Fortificaçion de la Ley de Moseh* (*Strengthening of the Law of Moses*, as opposed to *faith*), accentuates the biblical centrality of Amsterdam Jewish community, whose systems of children's education, rabbinic scholarship, adult learning opportunities, and leisure activities were often centered on different ways of engaging with Scripture.[43]

Chapter 38 of the Hamburg and Amsterdam copies of the *Fortificaçion* concentrate on Malachi 1:11–12:

> For from where the sun rises to where it sets, My name is honored among the nations, and everywhere incense and pure oblation are offered to My name; for My name is honored among the nations—Said God of Hosts. But you profane it when you say, "The Table of the Sovereign is defiled and the meat, the food, can be treated with scorn."

In the Hamburg manuscript, the contentions of the Christian "adversaries" are presented followed by the Jewish response. "The adversaries contend" that this verse foretells the honoring of God by Christians throughout the world and is a "great proof of their faith."[44] The *Fortificaçion* denies this forcefully. In the first place, the *Fortificaçion* insists, Jesus had not yet been born and Christianity did not yet exist and thus Malachi's remarks cannot refer to Christian worship and belief.[45] Yet, perhaps self-conscious that this explanation would not survive a prophetic, futuristic reading of the passage in question—one that could see Malachi as prefiguring the future of Christianity, additional explanations are offered. Beyond this initial explanation, the *Fortificaçion* insists that the kinds

---

43 I. Athias, *Fortificaçion de la Ley de Moseh*, Mss. Ets Haim (Amsterdam) EH 48 C 6.
44 Isaac Athias, *Fortificaçion*, fol. 162–63.
45 Ibid., fol. 163.

of worship described in Malachi as being practiced by the Nations of the world were services, incense, gifts, and sacrifices offered "to the seven planets and the twelve signs [of the Zodiac], and to idols and images."[46] At best, according to the *Fortificaçion*, the worship practices of the Nations described by Malachi were inappropriate but well intentioned. When the verse states that "incense" is offered in the name of the Lord, what the text really means—according to the *Fortificaçion*—is that

> Even when the Nations practiced idolatry, it was with the intent to worship the Lord, because in the time that they were sacrificing to their idols, if they were to be asked to whom they were sacrificing ... they would respond we are sacrificing to God who created the heavens and the earth, and this incense is offered in my name.[47]

Chapter 38 in the Hamburg *Fortificaçion* of 1621 has no *anotaciones*, no editorial interruptions that color and reshape so many other chapters of the work. The *Fortificaçion* copied at Amsterdam in 1624, however, does have *anotaciones*—one of which offers an enticing clue into the impact of the manuscript and the future of Jewish-Christian polemics in Amsterdam and the Western Sephardi diaspora. Midway through the chapter, an *anotacion* appears and interjects the copyist's thoughts into the body of the original text: "For a more satisfactory understanding, I will give an interpretation of my *señor* and master, R. Saul Levi Mortera, which is very literal."[48] According to Mortera, Malachi's intent was simply to rebuke the practice of sacrificing blemished or stolen animals and to discourage this type of divine service, since it would render impure the House of the Lord.[49]

Rabbi Saul Levi Mortera, an Ashkenazi figure born in Venice, served as a spiritual companion to the ex-converso physician Elijah Montalto, with whom he traveled to Paris in 1612. After the death of his patron, Mortera traveled to Amsterdam, buried Montalto, and would remain in Amsterdam where he served as a leader of the Spanish and Portuguese Jewish community in Amsterdam from approximately 1616 until his death in 1659.[50] Mortera was appointed rabbi of the Beth Jacob congregation in 1618—one of the original three ex-converso congregations in the city. He was hired to teach Bible, Talmud, and grammar in

---

46 Athias, *Fortificaçion*.
47 Ibid.
48 Athias, *Fortificaçion* [Amsterdam, 1624] 316.
49 Ibid., 316–317.
50 See C. Wilke, "Questions d'un Prêtre de Rouen à un Rabbin d'Amsterdam," *La Lettre Clandestine* 27 (2019): 142.

the nascent school system that was being established in the community. The presence of an *anotacion* in the Amsterdam, 1624 manuscript relating Mortera's exegetical interpretation, which is absent in the Hamburg, 1621 edition of the manuscript, strongly suggests that the translator or copyist of the Amsterdam, 1624 manuscript had some kind of direct contact with Mortera. Did the translator or copyist ask for Mortera's views upon this particular verse? Did Mortera read the *Fortificaçion* directly, in either the Hamburg or the Amsterdam versions, and decide to share his interpretation with the editor?

The translator seems to have a high degree of respect for Mortera, presenting himself deferentially as Mortera's subordinate and disciple. Might they have been friends? Beyond the possibility of personal contact and exchange between Mortera and this translator, the presence of this *anotacion* in the Amsterdam, 1624 copy also suggests that the copyists of the Spanish and Portuguese ex-converso diaspora felt a certain flexibility in their copying and transmission of Jewish knowledge contained in manuscript. Malachi Beit Arié once observed that medieval Hebrew manuscripts in the hands of a "talmid *hakham*" stood a certain risk of being subject to critical intervention by the highly learned copyist who feels entitled to modify, add, and subtract material according to his own criteria.[51] As Beit-Arié illustrates through numerous twelfth and fourteenth-century examples, the authors of medieval Hebrew manuscripts had limited control over their works. These works were copied in part and in whole, amended, and expended according to the goals and desires of other copyists and scholars.[52] In this respect, the experience of *Hizzuk Emunah* in Athias' hands—not to mention those of later translators and copyists—embodies some of these "dangers," and offers a poignant reminder that the fluidity of medieval Hebrew manuscript culture was alive and well in the seventeenth century. The copyists of *Hizzuk Emunah* and the *Fortificaçion* were eminently comfortable interjecting in the text on which they worked, adding authorial interjections, and even expanding upon an existing translated exemplar already in their hands.

Mortera was a preacher and teacher in the Spanish and Portuguese Jewish community—and a prolific author. His first extensive treatise as a religious and intellectual leader was the "Questions Posed by a Priest from Rouen" (*Preguntas que hizo un clerigo de Ruan*), written in manuscript form in 1631. The *Preguntas*, written in response to a series of theological questions from a French priest (Diego de Cisneros) was copied and translated from its original

---

[51] See M. Beit-Arié, "Transmission of Texts by Scribes and Copyists: Unconscious and Critical Interferences," *Bulletin of the John Rylands Library* 75, no. 3 (1993): 33–51.

[52] Ibid., 34–35.

Portuguese into at least seventeen known additional versions in Latin and Spanish that today are found in archives across Europe.[53] The *Preguntas* in its original form of 1631 contained responses to the twenty-three questions posed by Cisneros, followed by twenty-three aggressive rejoinder questions focusing on the contents of the New Testament. However, Mortera later expanded the scope of the questions targeting the New Testament, bringing the total number of queries in the manuscript to 179.[54] Carsten Wilke's survey of manuscript copies of the *Preguntas* across Europe and North America reveals that different versions of the work containing diverse ranges of questions and counter-questions are preserved in copies produced by different authors, sometimes enclosed in miscellanies that join the *Preguntas* with other texts, and other times as a standalone work.[55] The *Preguntas* and the *Fortificaçion* alike were Jewish manuscripts whose contents and form were intimately shaped not only by their original authors, but by the translators, copyists, and scholars who engaged with the texts.

Was the *Fortificaçion de la Ley de Moseh*, copied in Amsterdam in 1624, an inspiration for Mortera's *Preguntas*? There are certainly structural similarities—both texts are anti-Christian polemical works divided into sections that juxtapose defenses of Judaism in Part I, with a subsequent Part II that advances specific attacks against the New Testament, and there is an overlap of some of the specific contentions and doctrines that both of the texts address—up to a point. H. P. Salomon, the pioneering scholar of ex-converso Jewish Amsterdam and its intellectual activity, affirmed that the connection between Isaac Troki's late sixteenth-century *Hizzuk Emunah*, the *Fortificaçion*, and Mortera's *Preguntas* was deep and consequential based on structural similarities shared by the two works, and some similarities in contents. However, as Carsten Wilke argues in his thoroughly comprehensive and revealing study of the recension history of the *Preguntas*, only around nineteen percent of the allegations found in the second part of the *Fortificaçion* are addressed also in the *Preguntas*, leading Wilke to infer that there was less of a connection between the polemical works than might at first have appeared to be the case: "Either Mortera had a supplementary source, or he was more original as an author than Salomon's review suggests."[56] It is also notable that the similarities of format, and the structuring of both polemical works according to numbered propositions, is traceable to conventional forms of scholastic disputation and

---

53   Wilke, "Questions," 143.
54   Ibid., 148–49.
55   Ibid., 152–64.
56   Ibid., 154.

composition in the medieval world, and is not especially unique to Troki, Athias, or Mortera.[57]

Between these two perspectives, that of Salomon and that of Wilke, what we can perhaps say here is that the intellectual and literary environment in which Saul Levi Mortera immersed himself in the early 1620s clearly promoted the model of this type of literature and writing in polemical contexts. The specific reference to Mortera found in the Amsterdam, 1624 version of the *Fortificaçion* allows us to suggest that Mortera was directly aware of this type of writing—and was perhaps inspired by it. Indeed, a few short years after the appearance of the Amsterdam *Fortificaçion* manuscript, Mortera would author his own illicit, anti-Christian manuscript—the *Preguntas*—which would become a classic of Amsterdam ex-converso culture in its own right.

Like the *Fortificaçion*, the *Preguntas* would go on to be copied, amended, reorganized, and expanded, producing numerous versions of the text in Latin, Spanish, Portuguese, and other languages. In the Spanish and Portuguese communities of northwest Europe, Jewish readers interested in Jewish-Christian debates over biblical interpretation could now turn to versions of the *Preguntas*—a polemical, anti-Christian work by a rabbinic scholar—Mortera—who was a spiritual leader in one of their own communities, alongside the Karaite book that may have inspired him—the *Fortificaçion*.

Bibliography

Primary Sources

Athias, Isaac. *Fortificaçion de la fee*. Mss. EH 48 D 05. Hamburg, 1621.

--------. *Fortificaçion de la Ley de Moseh*. EH 48 C 6. Amsterdam, 1624.

--------. *Tesoro de Preceptos*. Venice, 1627.

Israel, Menasseh ben. *Conciliador, o de la conveniencia de los lugares de la S.Escriptura, que repugnantes entre si parecen* Vol. 1. Frankfurt, 1632.

--------. *Humas de Parasioth y Aftharoth*. Amsterdam, 1627.

Secondary Sources

Albert, Anne O. *Jewish Politics in Spinoza's Amsterdam*. London: The Littman Library of Jewish Civilization and Liverpool University Press, 2022.

Akhiezer, Golda. "The Karaite Isaac ben Abraham of Troki and his *Polemic Against the Rabbanites*." In *Tradition, Heterodoxy, and Religious Culture: Judaism and Christianity*

---

57   Ibid., 168.

in the Early Modern Period, edited by Chanita Goodblatt and Howard Kreisel, 437–68. Be'er-Sheva: Ben Gurion University of the Negev Press, 2006.

Beit-Arié, Malachi. "Transmission of Texts by Scribes and Copyists: Unconscious and Critical Interferences." *Bulletin of the John Rylands Library* 75, no. 3 (1993): 33–51.

Benfatto, Miriam. "The Work of Isaac ben Abraham of Troki (16th Century): On the Place of Sefer Hizzuq Emunah in the Quest for the Historical Jesus." *Journal for the Study of the Historical Jesus* 17 (2019): 102–20.

--------. "The Manuscript as a *medium*. A critical look at the circulation of the *Sefer Hizzuq Emunah* by Isaac ben Abraham Troki (c. 1533–1594)." *Studi e materiali di storia delle religioni* 85, no. 1 (2019): 235–43.

Demota, Yehonatan Elazar. "Early Modern Portuguese Jewish Conceptions of *Dominium* and *Libertas* and Constructions of Community." *Studia Rosenthaliana* 49, no. 1 (2023): 23–39.

Den Boer, Harm. *La Literatura Sefardi de Amsterdam*. Alcala: Instituto Internacional de Estudios Sefardiés y Andalucíes, Universidad de Alcalá, 1995.

Fisher, Benjamin. *Amsterdam's People of the Book: Jewish Society and the Turn to Scripture in the Seventeenth Century*. Cincinnati, OH: Hebrew Union College Press, 2020.

--------. "God's Word Defended: Menasseh ben Israel, Biblical Chronology, and the Erosion of Biblical Authority." In *Scriptural Authority and Biblical Criticism in the Dutch Golden Age: God's Word Questioned*, edited by Dirk van Miert et al., 155–74. Oxford: Oxford University Press, 2017.

Kaplan, Yosef. "'Karaites' in Early Eighteenth-Century Amsterdam." In *Sceptics, Millenarians, and Jews*, edited by David Katz and Richard Popkin, 196–236. Leiden: Brill, 1990.

Wilke, Carsten. "Questions d'un Prêtre de Rouen à un Rabbin d'Amsterdam." *La Lettre Clandestine* 27 (2019): 141–69.

--------. "Clandestine Classics: Isaac Orobio and the Polemical Genre Among the Dutch Sephardim." In *Isaac Orobio: The Jewish Argument with Dogma and Doubt*. Boston, MA: De Gruyter, 2018.

Yerushalmi, Yosef Hayim. *From Spanish Court to Italian Ghetto: Isaac Cardoso: A Study in Seventeenth-Century Marranism and Jewish Apologetics*. New York, NY: Columbia University Press, 1971.

--------. *The Re-education of Marranos in the Seventeenth Century*. Cincinnati, OH: University of Cincinnati, 1980.

A Profoundly Religious Expression: The Role of Scripture and Ritual in the American Campaign for Soviet Jewish Emigration, 1964–1974

Amy Fedeski

Introduction

In October 1971, a visitor to the United States Mission to the United Nations in New York City would have seen an unusual sight: a group of smartly dressed young men, busy unfurling banners, putting up posters, and making a large booth out of bars and cloth. Megaphones in hand, the group soon informed passers-by of their intentions: "We are here to demand that the US government speak out clearly and specifically against the antisemitic persecutions now in the USSR, and that the UN show its support of Russian Jews."[1] These young men belonged to the Student Struggle for Soviet Jewry (the SSSJ), a national organisation formed in 1964 to advocate for the rights of Soviet Jews. By 1971, their cause had garnered international attention, and the SSSJ in particular was famous for its creative approach to advocacy. As historian Shaul Kelner puts it, "the SSSJ's rallies and vigils combined a penchant for high drama, a sensitivity to the power of religious symbolism, and, not unrelated, a delight in what [SSSJ leader Glenn] Richter called shtick;"[2] that is, drama and gimmick.

The group's protest at the US Mission to the UN that day in October 1971 might have seemed eccentric and even silly to onlookers, but the SSSJ was more than just another countercultural youth movement. Leaflets handed to passers-by explained that the protest was imbued with spiritual meaning:

> The booth we have here is a sukkah. Our sukkah is composed of prison bars symbolising the imprisonment of Soviet Jews who wish to go to Israel. Yet, the sukkah, this fragile structure, manages to stand during the week-long period of the holiday, and in doing so symbolises the Russian Jew who, despite difficulties, has and will survive.[3]

---

1 Soviet Jewry Sukkah flyer, October 1971, Student Struggle for Soviet Jewry Records, Box 8, Yeshiva University Archives, Mendel Gottesman Library, New York, NY.
2 S. Kelner, "Ritualized Protest and Redemptive Politics: Cultural Consequences of the American Mobilization to Free Soviet Jewry," *Jewish Social Studies* 14, no. 3 (2008): 15.
3 Soviet Jewry Sukkah flyer, October 1971, Student Struggle for Soviet Jewry Records, Box 8, Yeshiva University Archives, Mendel Gottesman Library, New York, NY.

This was a typical approach for the group, whose advocacy was informed by their religious observance and who strategically planned their protests to maximise their use of Jewish religious symbolism. For the SSSJ, protest was a religious act.

Focusing on the work of the SSSJ in the 1960s and 1970s, this paper will explore the place of the Hebrew bible and of Jewish religious ritual in the activism of the American movement for Soviet Jewish emigration. It will argue that religious symbolism lay at the heart of the SSSJ's work, with the organisation's entire approach to campaigning imbued with spiritual meaning. The SSSJ's emphasis on public observance of religion in its protests and advocacy aligned with the background of its members, some 65 percent of whom identified as observant Modern Orthodox Jews.[4] This distinguished the SSSJ from the broader Jewish American community, the majority of whom were Conservative or Reform Jews. The SSSJ also stands out among the Soviet Jewry Movement for the way it combined the visual culture of the counterculture with the language and ritual of Orthodox Judaism.

Yet as this paper will show, the SSSJ was not an Orthodox movement; that is, a movement designed exclusively for Orthodox Jews. Just as it welcomed non-Orthodox and indeed non-Jewish members, the SSSJ's rhetoric was designed to appeal to a broad audience with a range of religious backgrounds, education levels and approaches to observance. To do so, the SSSJ worked to translate the Hebrew Bible (sometimes literally, in its slogans' translations from Hebrew to English) and render Jewish ritual understandable and meaningful. This paper will focus on selected examples of this process, considering how the SSSJ used biblical stories, holiday observance, and religious ritual to advocate for the rights of Soviet Jews. It will begin by exploring the religious, social, and political currents that led to the development of the SSSJ's unique approach to advocacy, before considering the particular elements of religious engagement that the SSSJ used in its work.

Jewish Identity and the Development of the Soviet Jewry Movement

Although there had been a small Jewish population in America since the seventeenth century, the majority of Jewish Americans in the postwar era were descended from a more recent wave of immigration; the two million Jews

---

4 A. S. Ferziger, "'Outside the Shul': The American Soviet Jewry Movement and the Rise of Solidarity Orthodoxy, 1964–1986," *Religion and American Culture* 22, no. 1 (2012): 92.

who left the Russian Empire's Pale of Settlement between 1880 and 1924. As such, by the 1960s, the majority of young Jewish adults were third generation Americans; this group became the majority of the total Jewish American population in around 1975.[5] The political and religious effects of the rise of the third generation of Jewish Americans were compounded by its size: Jewish Americans, like other demographic groups, had seen a significant rise in the birth rate in the years following the Second World War. These third generation Americans did not feel the same "uncertainty surrounding ethnic identity"[6] which had plagued their parents. Young Jewish Americans in the postwar years were comfortably integrated into American life. Few spoke Yiddish, fewer still retained a dedication to the culture and values of the immigrant generation.

Yet this comfortable American-ness did not lead young Jewish Americans to abandon their Jewish identities for total assimilation. Indeed, quite the opposite effect occurred; now that Jewish Americans were an integral part of American society, young people could accentuate their Jewishness publicly and confidently.[7] The Jewishness these young people chose to explore was not usually the Orthodoxy of their grandparents' generation, though for a significant minority—including many in the SSSJ—returning to observance of religious ritual was a key part of maintaining Jewish identity in postwar America.[8] Rather, the new Jewishness meant belief in a civil religion, with the emphasis on the cultural and political aspects of Jewish life as much as, if not more than, on tradition and observance. The rise of Jewish-centred campaigns such as the Soviet Jewry Movement was thus symptomatic of a wider shift in Jewish American identity and values, as young people began to place Jewish interests at the heart of their political, social, and cultural lives.[9]

The changing nature of Jewish American identity was not merely the result of demographic factors. As part of the American mainstream, American Jews were at the centre of wider currents in the postwar years which helped to bring about this renewal and re-emphasis of the Jewish half of Jewish American identity. Two trends in particular shaped Jewish identity in transformative ways in the postwar years: the Cold War, and the rise of a new ethnic politics. The

---

5   S. M. Cohen, "From Integration to Survival: American Jewish Anxieties in Transition," *The Annals of the American Academy of Political and Social Science* 480 (1985): 80.
6   W. Herberg, Protestant – Catholic – Jew: An Essay in American Religious Sociology (Garden City, NY: Doubleday, 1960), 18.
7   J. Wertheimer, *A People Divided: Judaism in Contemporary America* (Hanover NH: Brandeis, 1997), 29.
8   H. M. Sachar, *A History of the Jews in America* (New York, NY: Knopf, 1993), 689.
9   S. Svonkin, Jews against Prejudice: American Jews and the Fight for Civil Liberties (New York, NY: Columbia University Press, 1997), 178.

latter became particularly important in the 1960s, as a variety of other minority groups—African Americans, Native Americans, Asian Americans—began to emphasise their ethnic identities in new ways. Jewish Americans were an important part of a wider movement in American life as many minority groups discovered or rediscovered their ancestral cultures and identities. As Barnett puts it, "identity politics had become fashionable. Jews were acting just like others."[10]

The impact of the Cold War was felt earlier than the impact of ethnic politics, as part of the wider shift in American society prompted by the changes in international alliances and the start of US-Soviet tensions in the late 1940s and early 1950s. This shift placed religion at the heart of American Cold War life, setting the theistic USA against the atheistic USSR. Judaism was thus "mobilised in the struggle against communism."[11] America in the 1950s was supposedly "One Nation Under God"—and it mattered little whether that God was Christian or Jewish. As Herberg argues, the emerging social structure of American society in the late 1950s consisted of "three great branches or divisions of American religion"[12] with Judaism taking its place alongside Protestantism and Catholicism as one of the "three big sub-communities"[13] at the heart of "the American's faith in faith."[14] Religion in the Cold War was "our greatest resource, and most powerful secret weapon;"[15] religious belief was seen as the duty of every patriotic American citizen in the early Cold War decades. To emphasise one's Jewishness now made one not just more Jewish, but more American as well.

Information about the "all pervasive discrimination"[16] faced by the roughly three million Jews of the USSR thus reached the West at a key moment for Jewish American identity and advocacy. The community responded with the creation of a variety of organisations, among them the SSSJ, collectively known as the Soviet Jewry Movement. In its early years, the movement focused on highlighting antisemitic policies in the USSR; advocating, for example, for

---

10 M. N. Barnett, *The Star and the Stripes: A History of the Foreign Policies of American Jews* (Princeton, NJ: Princeton University Press, 2016), 156.
11 E. S. Shapiro, *A Time for Healing: American Jewry since World War II*, vol. 5 of *The Jewish People in America*, ed. H. L. Feingold (Baltimore, MD: Johns Hopkins University Press, 1992), 53.
12 Herberg, Protestant – Catholic – Jew, 38.
13 Ibid., 38.
14 Ibid., 89.
15 Ibid., 60.
16 P. Buwalda, *They Did Not Dwell Alone: Jewish Emigration from the Soviet Union 1967–1990* (Baltimore, MD: Johns Hopkins University Press, 1997), 30.

the publication of books and newspapers in Yiddish, and speaking out against the closure of synagogues and Jewish schools.[17] But by the 1970s, the Soviet Jewry Movement had changed its focus—now, its campaigning pushed for the right of Soviet Jews to emigrate from the USSR to the West or Israel.[18]

Broadly speaking, the many organisations of the Soviet Jewry Movement can be split into two strands: establishment groups, and grassroots groups. Establishment groups had older members and preferred private lobbying over public protest, which the grassroots put at the centre of its approach. The SSSJ sits firmly within the grassroots end of the spectrum: indeed, Jacob (later Ya'akov) Birnbaum created the SSSJ in 1964 with the intention of focusing its work on direct nonviolent protest in the vein of that practised by the civil rights movement in the United States. He began his efforts to create the organisation by specifically targeting young, politically engaged Jewish students at the universities of New York City, tailoring his rhetoric to resonate with "idealistic students who hoped to change the world."[19] A significant portion of those who joined the SSSJ had experience in other grassroots movements—initially, usually the Civil Rights Movement of the late 1950s and early 1960s; later, the anti-Vietnam movement.[20] Their complementary experience of rising Jewish consciousness and civil rights activism would shape the choice of rhetoric used by the SSSJ's campaigns, with its unique blend of religious and countercultural symbolism.

Let My People Go: Ritualising Protest and Protest Ritual

The SSSJ presented the Jewish American community as having a duty towards the Soviet Jewish community on the basis of a collective, transnational Jewish identity—an identity which transcended the Cold War barriers of US and Soviet nationality. The group's very first press releases referred to Soviet Jews as "our brethren,"[21] with the early slogan "I am my brother's keeper" reflecting the notion of American responsibility towards their Jewish "family" in the Soviet Union. The strength of this bond is referenced over and over by the SSSJ, indicating that notions of brotherhood and solidarity towards the Soviet

---

17   Y. Ro'i, *The Struggle for Soviet Jewish emigration 1948–1967* (Cambridge: Cambridge University Press, 1991), 6.
18   Shapiro, *A Time for Healing*, 214.
19   Ferziger, "'Outside the Shul'," 89.
20   Ro'i, *The Struggle*, 209.
21   Prayer Service for Soviet Jewry, 25 August 1964, Student Struggle for Soviet Jewry Records, Box 1, Yeshiva University Archives, Mendel Gottesman Library, New York, NY.

Jewish community were deeply felt and seen as uncontroversial. This is potentially surprising given that the Jewish American community had for much of its history been subject to allegations of split loyalties due to its supposed links with Jewish communities abroad. Although the Cold War made expressing solidarity or brotherhood with those oppressed by the Cold War enemy relatively easier, the SSSJ's leaders and activists were clearly secure enough in their American identities to publicly identify themselves as being eternally and deeply connected to a group of people living in a state which was viewed as the greatest enemy of the American people.

Literature on the Soviet Jewry Movement has usually attributed this idea of transnational Jewish identity to the "grandparent factor,"[22] arguing that American Jews felt "a direct personal link with Jews in a country from which they themselves or their ancestors had come."[23] However, analysis of the SSSJ's rhetoric in the 1960s and 1970s reveals that the organisation focused not on the literal familial relationship between American and Soviet Jews, but rather on a more spiritual connection between the two groups. Rather than emphasising their shared recent ancestry, the Jewish American activists of SSSJ emphasised the notion of *Klal Yisroel*—a spiritual bond connecting Jewish people across the world.[24] It was this notion—grounded in Jewish learning and expressing a religious, rather than a familial, connection, on which the SSSJ's activism was based. The SSSJ campaigned not on behalf of the cousins left behind, but on behalf of their fellow Jews—wherever they may be.

The SSSJ's activism was publicly and proudly Orthodox, featuring activists dressed as if for a synagogue service, in formal suit, yarmulke and tallit; some went further and wore additional symbols of personal observance such as tzitzit and tefillin.[25] Protests frequently featured additional displays of Jewish ritual, including prayer, religious singing, and the presence of Orthodox rabbis leading the events.[26] SSSJ leaders felt that presenting their organisation as Jewish—and, even more emphatically, as *religiously* Jewish—would be neutrally if not positively received by such witnesses and by the media. This was not an assumption without basis in fact. While the Cold War and the rise of ethnic politics had made publicly expressing one's religious beliefs acceptable and

---

22 S. Altshuler, *From Exodus to Freedom: A History of the Soviet Jewry Movement* (Lanham, MD: Rowman & Littlefield, 2005) 12–13.
23 Ro'i, *The Struggle*, 202.
24 12E1974.
25 Exodus March photograph, 1970, Student Struggle for Soviet Jewry Records, Box 6, Yeshiva University Archives, Mendel Gottesman Library, New York, NY.
26 Jewish Chronicle Article, 8 May 1964 Student Struggle for Soviet Jewry Records, Box 1, Yeshiva University Archives, Mendel Gottesman Library, New York, NY.

even fashionable, it was the dramatic fall in antisemitism which really transformed Jewish Americans' attitude towards public expression of their religious beliefs. The drop in antisemitic attitudes in American life was astounding in its speed and completeness. In 1946, according to an American Jewish Committee Poll, some eighteen percent of non-Jewish Americans, when asked "which national, religious, or racial groups pose a threat to America, if any?" answered Jews. By 1964, fewer than one percent gave the same response.[27] Thus, the SSSJ's activists could be confident in identifying themselves as Jewish without fear of backlash or antisemitic incidents.

Given that the activists of the SSSJ were themselves religious, it is not surprising that the organisation made many attempts to engage with religious Jews in its campaigning. Indeed, on occasion it even tried to appeal to those who were strictly Orthodox, through references to Haredi rabbis' support for the Soviet Jewry Movement.[28] The SSSJ consistently sought to accommodate Orthodox Jews through ensuring that protests did not impede religious observance; all food offered at the SSSJ's protests was kosher, and regional groups of the SSSJ were instructed not to offer literature for individuals to take away on Shabbat, so as not to prevent observant audiences from accessing SSSJ materials.[29]

Repeatedly, the SSSJ presented activism on behalf of Soviet Jews as a religious imperative. In 1965, the SSSJ argued that "we must not allow ourselves to be in the position of Joseph's brothers," thereby comparing inaction in the Soviet Jewry Movement with the infamous Torah story of fraternal betrayal.[30] The SSSJ's later slogan, Let My People Go, placed religion at the heart of activism. In this slogan, SSSJ activists are in the position of Moses saving the Israelites from slavery—with God firmly on their side.[31] As a slogan, Let My People Go epitomises the Soviet Jewry Movement. It is a clear, short, and accessible phrase, a biblical reference familiar both to Jewish and non-Jewish

---

27 G. Beckerman, 'When They Come for Us, We'll Be Gone: The Epic Struggle to Save Soviet Jewry (Boston, MA: Houghton Mifflin Harcourt, 2011), 42.

28 Picket Sign Slogans List for Brooklyn March, 27 February 1966, Student Struggle for Soviet Jewry Records, Box 2, Yeshiva University Archives, Mendel Gottesman Library, New York, NY.

29 National Conference on Campus Action for Soviet Jewry information booklet, 23–25 January 1972, Student Struggle for Soviet Jewry Records, Box 9, Yeshiva University Archives, Mendel Gottesman Library, New York, NY.

30 Soviet Jewry handbook, June 1965, Student Struggle for Soviet Jewry Records, Box 220, Yeshiva University Archives, Mendel Gottesman Library, New York, NY.

31 World Day for Soviet Jewry suggested placard slogans, 20 September 1970, Student Struggle for Soviet Jewry Records, Box 7, Yeshiva University Archives, Mendel Gottesman Library, New York, NY.

Americans. In the postwar period, the Exodus narrative was associated with the struggle for African American civil rights and particularly with Paul Robeson's 1953 recording of the spiritual *Go Down Moses* (*Let My People Go*). The SSSJ made this connection between the Soviet Jewry Movement and the Civil Rights Movement in a 1967 flyer, stating "when Paul Robeson sang Let My People Go, his meaning was clear."[32] Thus, the slogan linked the SSSJ's work with wider civil rights advocacy, and offered a pithy summary of their aims which could be understood and engaged with by both Jews and non-Jews.

It is clear from the use of language such as this that the SSSJ sought to appeal not just to Orthodox or religious Jews, but also to secular Jews and non-Jewish people. The SSSJ took care to ensure that all its religious symbolism was accessible to these different groups. For example, the SSSJ used familiar Jewish holidays for symbolic purposes in its work. Holidays were an effective means of appealing to a wider audience for two reasons. Firstly, most Americans were aware of Jewish holidays such as Hanukkah and Passover. Most Jewish people—no matter their usual affiliation or level of observance—celebrated these holidays annually, while most non-Jewish Americans would be familiar with the holidays' basic narratives and meaning. Secondly, the holidays' stories of redemption, survival and escape easily lent themselves to the SSSJ's rhetoric. The Shofar of Rosh Hashanah was reframed as representing "the call to conscience and the hope for redemption and freedom;"[33] the booths of Sukkot designed to represent "the imprisonment of Soviet Jews who wish to go to Israel."[34]

While holidays such as Sukkot, Purim and Tisha B'Av were employed as part of the SSSJ's rhetoric, the majority of references to religious holidays by the organisation featured either Passover or Hanukkah. This was because both holidays were very well known and widely practised, and because they offered useful narratives for the Soviet Jewry struggle. Passover, as "the most widely practised Jewish holiday in the USA,"[35] was at the very heart of SSSJ activism. Each year huge events were organised to coincide with the holiday, and the Exodus narrative was "invoked as a rhetorical frame"[36] with the Soviet Jewish community cast as the enslaved Israelites and the Soviet government

---

32   New York Times Passover Advertisement, 28 April 1967, Student Struggle for Soviet Jewry Records, Box 3, Yeshiva University Archives, Mendel Gottesman Library, New York, NY.

33   Prayer Service for Soviet Jewry, 25 August 1964, Student Struggle for Soviet Jewry Records, Box 1, Yeshiva University Archives, Mendel Gottesman Library, New York, NY.

34   Soviet Jewry Sukkah flyer, October 1971, Student Struggle for Soviet Jewry Records, Box 8, Yeshiva University Archives, Mendel Gottesman Library, New York, NY.

35   Kelner, "Ritualized Protest," 10.

36   Ibid., 9.

as Pharaoh. The SSSJ's rhetoric described the holiday as "the festival of freedom"[37] and suggested that the restrictions on matzah baking by the Soviet government were a direct result of the food being symbolic of "deliverance from bondage."[38] The Passover story was brought into the present and the repression in the Soviet Union was stylized with the slavery of the Israelites in Egypt. This example shows how the SSSJ used Jewish and biblical narratives and transferred them to political reality.

A key element of the SSSJ's rhetoric on Passover was the assumption that its American Jewish audience would be celebrating, and attempts to link this celebration to Soviet Jewry activism through guilt trips and direct appeals. In 1970, the SSSJ asked "How can you celebrate Passover—the festival of the Exodus—in good conscience without bringing your family to the Exodus March?"[39]; the following year, the organisation argued "As we sit with our families and friends at the Seder table this year, we are obligated to remember the three million Soviet Jews for whom freedom is not yet a reality."[40] Hanukkah, with its natural symbolism of freedom from oppression, also lent itself to SSSJ activism; the holiday was described in a press release as "commemorating the Jewish fight for religious and national freedom."[41]

By using popular holidays which were understood by the wider population and celebrated by most Jewish Americans, the SSSJ was able to employ an effective rhetorical device to persuade its audience to support its activism. In doing so, it reflected its role as part of a community which was proud of its Jewishness. The SSSJ was a publicly religious organisation, neither ashamed nor embarrassed of its Jewish identity, but rather confidently expressing that identity on the national and international stage. In doing so, its rhetoric helped to construct a wider Jewish American identity which was proudly and unequivocally *Jewish*.

---

37 Passover Vigil Poster, April 1967, Student Struggle for Soviet Jewry Records, Box 2, Yeshiva University Archives, Mendel Gottesman Library, New York, NY.

38 New York Times Passover advertisement, 28 April 1967, Student Struggle for Soviet Jewry Records, Box 3, Yeshiva University Archives, Mendel Gottesman Library, New York, NY.

39 So You've Never Gone to a Rally Flyer, Spring 1970, Student Struggle for Soviet Jewry Records, Box 6, Yeshiva University Archives, Mendel Gottesman Library, New York, NY. The Exodus March was a large rally held in New York City by the SSSJ, its route representing the movement of the Israelites out of Egypt and the hoped-for migration of Soviet Jews out of the USSR.

40 We were slaves unto Pharaoh in Egypt leaflet, April 1971, Student Struggle for Soviet Jewry Records, Box 226, Yeshiva University Archives, Mendel Gottesman Library, New York, NY.

41 Why Freedom Lights newsletter/information sheet, December 1971, Student Struggle for Soviet Jewry Records, Box 8, Yeshiva University Archives, Mendel Gottesman Library, New York, NY.

Conclusions

This paper has used the work of the Student Struggle for Soviet Jewry as a lens through which to consider the place of Jewish ritual and religious observance in the American Soviet Jewry Movement. The SSSJ represented the grassroots end of a movement characterised by significant variation in approach and ideology. It also represented the youth wing of the Soviet Jewry Movement; the SSSJ's activists were rarely older than thirty, and many were teenagers. Their generational consciousness is reflected in their confident, public approach to protest; while their elders negotiated with diplomats and politicians, the SSSJ's activists could be found on the streets outside, handing out flyers and holding placards. The SSSJ was inspired by the approach of civil rights protestors; in the drama of its advocacy, one can see an irreverent approach it shared with groups like the Youth International Party.

If the activists of the SSSJ had read Martin Luther King and Jack Kerouac, they had also read Abraham Joshua Heschel—to say nothing of the Torah itself. The organisation, unusually among the sometimes-uneasy coalition which made up the Soviet Jewry Movement, consisted of activists with an Orthodox Jewish background and education. Led by rabbis and buoyed by students at Yeshiva University, the SSSJ imbued its activism with religious meaning. Viewing the Soviet Jewry Movement as a Jewish imperative—indeed, as a *mitzvah*—the activists of the SSSJ considered themselves to be working for a higher cause. Peppering their vocabulary with phrases like *Klal Yisroel* and *Pidyon Shvuyim*, SSSJ protestors revealed both a knowledge of Jewish law and a confidence in expressing religious devotion in the American political sphere.

Yet the SSSJ's members were conscious of their place within Jewish American life, aware that most Jewish Americans were less religiously observant and less knowledgeable about Jewish religious concepts. Adjusting these concepts for a broader audience was therefore a cornerstone of the SSSJ's work, exemplified in their use of pithy religious slogans like "Let My People Go." In using such terms, the SSSJ both literally translated the Hebrew bible into English and metaphorically translated Jewish tradition for a broader audience which was less familiar with the intricacies of Jewish ritual. Doing so allowed the SSSJ to reach a larger group of people with their activism, balancing their religious observance with the need for broad public appeal. The aim of the SSSJ's work was not to bring the non-observant to Orthodox Judaism. Instead, the SSSJ took a pragmatic approach, imbuing their protests with biblical symbolism and religious ritual in a way that was accessible and understandable for non-Orthodox Jews and indeed for Christians. This strategic approach to advocacy was highly effective, making the SSSJ the most visible and public reminder of the cause of Soviet Jewish emigration rights from 1964 to 1991.

Bibliography

Altshuler, Stuart. *From Exodus to Freedom: A History of the Soviet Jewry Movement.* Lanham, MD: Rowman & Littlefield, 2005.

Barnett, Michael N. *The Star and the Stripes: A History of the Foreign Policies of American Jews.* Princeton, NJ: Princeton University Press, 2016.

Beckerman, Gal, *'When They Come for Us, We'll Be Gone: The Epic Struggle to Save Soviet Jewry.* Boston, MA: Houghton Mifflin Harcourt, 2011.

Buwalda, Piet, *They Did Not Dwell Alone: Jewish Emigration from the Soviet Union 1967–1990.* Baltimore, MD: Johns Hopkins University Press, 1997.

Cohen, Steven M. "From Integration to Survival: American Jewish Anxieties in Transition," *The Annals of the American Academy of Political and Social Science* 480 (1985): 75–88.

Ferziger, Adam S. "'Outside the Shul': The American Soviet Jewry Movement and the Rise of Solidarity Orthodoxy, 1964–1986." *Religion and American Culture* 22, no. 1 (2012): 83–130.

Herberg, Will. *Protestant – Catholic – Jew: An Essay in American Religious Sociology.* New ed., completely revised. Garden City, NY: Doubleday, 1960.

Kelner, Shaul. "Ritualized Protest and Redemptive Politics: Cultural Consequences of the American Mobilization to Free Soviet Jewry." *Jewish Social Studies* 14, no. 3 (2008): 1–37.

Ro'i, Yaacov. *The Struggle for Soviet Jewish Emigration 1948–1967.* Cambridge: Cambridge University Press, 1991.

Sachar, Howard M. *A History of the Jews in America.* New York, NY: Knopf, 1993.

Shapiro, Edwars S. *A Time for Healing: American Jewry since World War II.* Volume 5 of *The Jewish People in America*, edited by Henry L. Feingold. Baltimore, MD: Johns Hopkins University Press, 1992.

Svonkin, Stuart. *Jews Against Prejudice: American Jews and the Fight for Civil Liberties.* New York, NY: Columbia University Press, 1997.

Wertheimer, Jack. *A People Divided: Judaism in Contemporary America.* Hanover, NH: Brandeis, 1997.

The Discipline of Textual Criticism as Experienced in 1970–2020

Emanuel Tov

Because of the many changes in scholarship, society, and data, it is worthwhile to ask ourselves whether the field of textual criticism has changed in the past half-century (approximately 1970–2020) and, if so, in which ways. I will do this under several headings.[1] This is not a topic I have reflected on much before, but I had passing thoughts about several aspects. We must first ask ourselves whether textual criticism is a separate field.

1. Is There a Separate Discipline of Textual Criticism?

The term "discipline" is more professional than "field." Yes, there exists a separate field, approach, or discipline that comprises one particular aspect of Scripture research and that is guided by rules of its own different from those that guide other approaches. The nature and scope of this discipline may be defined in different ways. I quote my own definition, while realizing that other definitions also exist:

> Textual criticism is a discipline applied to the textual traditions of all written sources. Textual critics focus on the various texts of a composition by conducting an analysis of its ancient and medieval manuscripts, as well as its modern printed editions. This analysis is complex in the case of the Hebrew Bible because of its labyrinthine written transmission over the course of at least 2,500 years, and possibly several centuries more. The analysis pertains to an investigation of the Hebrew texts (especially the ones from the Judean Desert, as well as their medieval masoretic sequels) and several ancient translations that were made from Hebrew texts that differed from those known to us: the Septuagint (LXX) in Greek, the Peshitta (S) in Syriac, the targumim (T) in Aramaic, and the Vulgate (V) in Latin. All these are branches of the Bible text … Textual scholars consider it their task to analyze all the known ancient and medieval texts because the exegesis of the Hebrew Bible should be based on the totality of the available texts.[2]

---

[1] An earlier version of this survey appears in my *Studies in Textual Criticism, Collected Essays, Volume 5* ((Leiden: Brill, 2024), 403–24.).

[2] E. Tov, *Textual Criticism of the Hebrew Bible* (4th ed., Minneapolis, MN: Fortress, 2022), 1–2.

There is a vast theoretical literature, especially in nineteenth-century Germany, about the different approaches to the Hebrew Bible. Leaving that discussion aside, we realize that there is a separate approach that may be named the "textual approach." From the earliest days of the theoretical preoccupation with these approaches, it was realized that the Scripture text needs to be established before exegetical activity can take place. That is why textual criticism used to be named "lower criticism," on which "higher criticism" or "literary criticism" is based. The term "lower criticism" has been abandoned in the meantime because it is unrealistic. Textual criticism is not the only area that needs to be tackled before exegesis can take place; linguistic exegesis is equally significant as a preparatory stage before exegesis. Further, both exegesis and literary criticism are based to some extent on textual criticism.

The terminological issue should not prevent us from designating textual criticism as a separate discipline bound by its own rules. In an ideal world, the same persons deal with the textual criticism, exegesis, and literary criticism of a text. In nineteenth-century Germany, that broad preoccupation was called "philology," since it is often hard to distinguish between the various layers of text treatment. However, text-critical analysis has become so specialized that often/usually scholars specialize in that area.

Since the text-critical approach deals with texts, one may think that it is regulated by more objective data than exegesis and literary criticism. This is only partially true. Exegesis is fully subjective, although commentators attempt to convince with what they consider to be objective arguments. Linguistic and textual analysis are seemingly objective, but when their methods are defined well, they, too, comprise many subjective elements. The notation of variation between Hebrew textual sources is roughly objective, though not always. The identification of differences between the Masoretic Texts (MT) and the ancient versions is more complex because translations may be understood in different ways. If one takes the task of textual criticism as being merely the indication of the differences between MT and the ancient witnesses, there are many objective aspects to textual criticism as opposed to exegesis.

However, if we expand the task of textual critics to include an evaluation of the variants between MT and the ancient sources, the evaluative part of textual criticism becomes as subjective as exegesis. In my view, textual critics ought to be involved in this process, and the arguments they use during this process render them full participants in biblical exegesis since they need to take the details of the context into consideration.

Ideally, a scholar should master both disciplines, but in practice, it is difficult to expect from a textual scholar dealing with the short text of the Septuagint (LXX) of Job to know all the intricacies of the exegesis of the Hebrew book.

By the same token, it is hard to expect from the commentator of the Hebrew book of Job to know the intricacies of the translation technique of the LXX translation of that book. Likewise, in order to use the diverse textual materials in Samuel-Kings, the exegete needs to be up-to-date regarding the theories on *kaige*-Th.

In short, I believe that textual criticism and exegesis represent two separate disciplines, but those who are involved in them by necessity interact much. In this essay, I deal especially with textual criticism in general.

2. Increased Interaction between Textual Criticism and Exegesis

Has the interaction between textual criticism and exegesis changed in the past half-century? To some extent, yes. Traditionally there has not been much interaction between these disciplines, but there are notable exceptions. Already in 1842, Otto Thenius realized that the exegetical procedure is possible only after serious engagement with text-critical data. Single readings in the LXX cannot be evaluated well without a thorough knowledge of that book's translation technique. He therefore preceded his commentary on Samuel with an analysis of the LXX.[3] Likewise, in 1868, Cornill set the correct example by providing a long introduction to the LXX before embarking on the reconstruction of the original text of that book based on textual evidence mixed with literary judgments.[4] Nevertheless, numerous commentaries have been written since that time that do not do justice to the textual evidence.[5]

A change in the approach to the textual data has been felt in the past half-century. That change was caused by the discovery of the Dead Sea Scrolls, which brought home the understanding that in the last centuries BCE many different Hebrew texts were extant in ancient Israel. In the minds of many scholars, the prominence of this textual variety undermined the dominance of MT, which otherwise would have overshadowed the commentaries. Furthermore, thanks to the Qumran scrolls that agree occasionally in detail with the LXX, confidence has grown in reconstructing the Hebrew source of that translation. As a result of these developments, if I am not mistaken, a trend is visible to involve

---

3   O. Thenius, *Die Bücher Samuels erklärt*, ed. M. Löhr (Leipzig: Hirzel, 1898), XXIV–XXIX.
4   C. H. Cornill, *Das Buch des Propheten Ezechiel* (Leipzig: Hinrichs, 1886), 13–109.
5   See the analysis of the textual treatment of commentaries in my earlier study "The Use of the Septuagint in Critical Commentaries," in *New Avenues in Biblical Exegesis in Light of the Septuagint*, ed. L. Pessoa da Silva Pinto and D. Scialabba (Turnhout: Brepols, 2022), 41–58.

more textual evidence in the most recent commentaries, even though no statistics are available. I see this development in the following series:

Kurzgefasstes exegetisches Handbuch zum Alten Testament (KeHAT).
International Critical Commentary (ICC), New Series.
Anchor Bible (AB), New Series.
Herders Theologischer Kommentar zum Alten Testament (HThKAT).

3. A New Wave of Interactions between Textual and Literary Criticism

In the past half-century, a major change has taken place in the interaction between textual and literary criticism. This new wave of activity was influenced directly by the Dead Sea Scrolls.

Literary criticism is an extensive field based on principles that differ from those of textual criticism. Textual criticism is based on manuscript evidence, while literary criticism "seeks to reconstruct the same processes without such empirical evidence."[6] Literary criticism deals with the structure, date, origin, authorship, authenticity, form, poetic structure, relationship to other compositions, development, literary layers, and unity of the composition. The two disciplines are thus remote from each other and do not overlap; they only converge when *coincidentally* textual sources preserve evidence from an earlier or later developmental stage of the Scripture book that differs from that of MT. In such a case, the data are initially analyzed with textual procedures because they are found in textual sources; subsequently they are evaluated with literary procedures. There is a very practical implication of the evaluation based on the principles of literary criticism, since within the latter discipline one literary layer is not preferred to another, just as the pre-deuteronomistic layer of Joshua is not preferred to the present (MT–LXX) text that had undergone a deuteronomistic revision. In this regard, there are major differences between the individual Scripture books. For example, we witness much literary development in Jeremiah in textual witnesses, and little in Isaiah.

Prior to the discovery of the scrolls, some scholars had recognized that textual and literary criticism occasionally converge when the textual sources coincidentally contain material that throws light on literary developments. Probably the most famous statement is that by Wellhausen in 1871 regarding

---

6   Cf. R. Müller, J. Pakkala, and B. ter Haar Romeny, *Evidence of Editing: Growth and Change of Texts in the Hebrew Bible* (Atlanta, GA: SBL, 2013), 225.

his findings in Samuel: "… it is difficult to find the border where literary criticism ends and textual criticism starts."[7] Wellhausen referred i.a. to the short version of the LXX in 1 Samuel 16–18. Similar findings were recognized before 1947 regarding the LXX of Jeremiah by Movers who, in 1837, posited two different text recensions in the MT and LXX.[8] Likewise, Abraham Kuenen emphasized the differences between the LXX and MT in Exodus 35–40.[9] Holmes considered the LXX of Joshua to be more original than MT, but he did not go as far as naming it a different literary edition.[10]

These voices were not numerous, but the recognition of literary phenomena in the textual witnesses was advanced significantly after the discovery of the scrolls. This new stream in scholarship took place not because such features were recognized in Hebrew Qumran scrolls, but because of the very recognition of deviating *Hebrew* sources that were not known previously. Scholars thus gained confidence that the Hebrew traditions behind the LXX, in which most of the literary variants were found, may indeed be reconstructed. A first collection of case studies was edited by Jeffrey Tigay, and additional ones were found in collections and studies edited and written by Schenker, Talshir and Amara, Müller, Pakkala and ter Haar Romeny, Müller and Pakkala, Tov, and Rofé.[11] This is a veritable new wave of interest.

---

7   J. Wellhausen, *Der Text der Bücher Samuelis* (Göttingen: Vandenhoeck & Ruprecht, 1871), xi: "… und es ist schwierig die Grenze zu finden, wo die Literarkritik aufhört und die Textkritik beginnt." For a summary of Wellhausen's views, see A. van der Kooij, "De tekst van Samuel en het tekstkritisch onderzoek," *NedTT* 36 (1982): 177–204.

8   F. Movers, *De utriusque recensionis vaticiniorum Ieremiae graecae alexandrinae et hebraicae masoreticae indole et origine commentatio critica* (Hamburg: Fredericus Partner, 1837).

9   A. Kuenen, *An Historico-Critical Inquiry into the Origin and Composition of the Hexateuch* (London: Macmillan, 1886), 76–80.

10 S. Holmes, *Joshua: The Hebrew and Greek Texts* (Cambridge: Cambridge University Press, 1914).

11 J. H. Tigay, ed., *Empirical Models for Biblical Criticism* (Philadelphia, PA: University of Philadelphia, 1985); A. Schenker, ed., *The Earliest Text of the Hebrew Bible: The Relationship between the Masoretic Text and the Hebrew Base of the Septuagint Reconsidered* (Atlanta, GA: Scholars, 2003); Z. Talshir and D. Amara, eds., *On the Border Line: Textual Meets Literary Criticism* (Beer Sheva: Ben-Gurion University of the Negev Press, 2005) [in Hebrew]; Müller, Pakkala, and ter Haar Romeny, *Evidence of Editing*; R. Müller and J. Pakkala, eds., *Insights into Editing in the Hebrew Bible and the Ancient Near East: What Does Documented Evidence Tell Us about the Transmission of Authoritative Texts?* (Leuven: Peeters, 2017); Tov, *Textual Criticism of the Hebrew Bible*, 323–34; A. Rofé, *The Religion of Israel and the Text of the Hebrew Bible: Corrections in the Biblical Texts in the Light of the History of the Religion of Israel* (Jerusalem: Carmel, 2018) [in Hebrew].

This line of research became known especially through the work of Eugene Ulrich, who named the deviating traditions "variant literary editions."[12] The number of such variant editions identified in recent research may be smaller than suggested,[13] but they were there, although the unit named "edition" is usually much smaller than that of a Scripture book.[14] At the same time, in Jeremiah, we are faced with a book-length shorter edition embodied in the LXX and 4QJer[b,d], discussed much in modern research.[15] Also the shorter edition of LXX-Ezek pertains to the complete book.[16] According to Ulrich, followed by several colleagues,[17] this phenomenon reflects a widespread phenomenon.[18]

12 E. Ulrich, *The Dead Sea Scrolls and the Developmental Composition of the Bible* (Leiden: Brill, 2015). Ulrich discusses text samples in the following units: the Torah (with examples from pre-Samaritan scrolls 4QpaleoExod[m], 4QExod-Lev[f], 4QNum[b]), Joshua (with examples from 4QJosh[a]), Judges (based on 4QJudg[a]), Samuel (with examples from 1QSam and 4QSam[a]), Jeremiah (with examples from 4QJer[a,b]), Isaiah (with examples from 1QIsa[a] and 1QIsa[b]), and Canticles (4QCant[a,b]).

13 For some criticisms regarding Isaiah, see D. Longacre, "Developmental Stage, Scribal Lapse, or Physical Defect? 1QIsa[a]'s Damaged Exemplar for Isaiah Chapters 34–66," *DSD* 20 (2013): 17–50, and H. G. M. Williamson, "Scribe and Scroll: Revisiting the Great Isaiah Scroll from Qumran," in *Making a Difference: Essays on the Bible and Judaism in Honor of Tamara Cohn Eskenazi*, ed. D. J. A. Clines et al. (Sheffield: Sheffield Phoenix Press, 2012), 329–42. The additions in 1QIsa[a] do not attest to content pluses in MT, but to scribal phenomena when in most cases scribe B left spaces that were filled in subsequently by other scribes, sometimes with petite letters: Isa 34:17b–35:2 (col. XXVIII 19, space left); 37:4 end–7 (col. XXX 11, space left); 38:19–22 (col. XXXII 12b, 13, 14, space left); 40:7b–8 (*parablepsis* = LXX); 40:14b–16 (col. XXXIII 14b, 15, 16, space left).

14 G. J. Brooke, "What is a Variant Edition? Perspectives from the Qumran Scrolls," in *In the Footsteps of Sherlock Holmes: Studies in the Biblical Text in Honour of Anneli Aejmelaeus*, ed. K. De Troyer et al. (Leuven: Peeters, 2014), 607–22.

15 For the latest studies, see *The Oxford Handbook of the Book of Jeremiah*, ed. E. Silver and L. Stulman (New York, NY: Oxford University Press, 2021), including my own study "The Last Stage of the Literary History of the Book of Jeremiah," 129–47.

16 E. Tov, "Recensional Differences between the MT and LXX of Ezekiel," in *The Greek and Hebrew Bible: Collected Essays on the Septuagint* (Leiden: Brill, 1999), 397–410.

17 H. Debel, "'Greek Variant Editions' to the Hebrew Bible?" *JSJ* 41 (2010): 161–90; I. E. Lilly, *Two Books of Ezekiel: Papyrus 967 and the Masoretic Text as Variant Literary Editions* (Leiden: Brill, 2012); M. B. Shepherd, *Textuality and the Bible* (Eugene, Or.: Wipf & Stock, 2016), 61–77; K. Finsterbusch, "Traditional Textual Criticism Reconsidered: MT (codex L)-Ezek 35, LXX (papyrus 967)-Ezek 35 and Its Hebrew Vorlage as Variant Editions and the Implications for the Search for the 'Original' Text," *HBAI* 9 (2020): 334–45; T. Elgvin, *The Literary Growth of the Song of Songs during the Hasmonean and Early-Herodian Periods* (Leuven: Peeters, 2018); K. Hauspie, "Ezekiel," in *Oxford Handbook of the Septuagint*, ed. A. G. Salvesen and T. M. Law (Oxford: Oxford University Press, 2021), 275–89.

18 In their case studies, Müller, Pakkala and ter Haar Romeny, provided valuable examples of editorial processes that created literary differences without implying that they represent a universal phenomenon, cf. Müller, Pakkala and ter Haar Romeny, *Evidence of Editing*. For a discussion of the variant literary editions, see H. Debel, "'Greek Variant Editions';"

The literary processes visible in several text units may have existed also in other sources now lost. Through these studies, modern textual criticism has elevated the textual inquiry to a higher level by involving literary evidence. By doing so, the modern branch of textual criticism differs much from the textual criticism of half a century ago.

In the writing of some, this wave of interest also has feasible implications. The practical results of the analysis of literary variants are a component of the evaluation process of all the variants, textual and literary. In the past, literary variants were analyzed as any other variant, that is, they were compared with the readings of MT and an opinion was expressed on them.[19]

However, there is a trend in modern research to acknowledge that literary and textual criticism work with different sets of rules. While textual critics often prefer certain readings to others in their search for the best (original) reading, literary critics analyze such differences without preferring one stage to another. This notion is most clearly visible in the systems used in the Biblia Hebraica Quinta (BHQ). The Biblia Hebraica Stuttgartensia (BHS) edition still expressed preference for literary variants,[20] while the later BHQ edition is open to a notation "lit," meaning that a literary variant so indicated will not be evaluated with textual tools.[21] In my own writings I expressed the same view as BHQ.[22]

---

and Lange, "The Textual Plurality of Jewish Scriptures in the Second Temple Period in Light of the Dead Sea Scrolls," in *Qumran and the Bible: Studying the Jewish and Christian Scriptures in Light of the Dead Sea Scrolls*, ed. N. Dávid and A. Lange (Leuven: Peeters, 2010), 43–96.

19   Thus, details in the short edition of LXX-Ezek were often preferred to their counterparts in the long edition of MT in that book. These and many similar minuses in the LXX (3:18, 5:14, 5:15, 6:6, 8:3, 16:13, 20:28, etc.) were often preferred to MT, while described as frequent glosses or interpolations in MT-Ezek. See P. Rost, "Miszellen, I. Ein Schreibgebrauch bei den Sopherim und seine Bedeutung für die alttestamentliche Textkritik," *OLZ* 6 (1903): 403–7, 443–46; 7 (1904): 390–93, 479–83; J. Herrmann, "Stichwortglossen im Buche Ezechiel," *OLZ* 11 (1908): 280–82; idem, "Stichwortglossen im Alten Testament," *OLZ* 14 (1911): 200–204; G. Fohrer, "Die Glossen im Buche Ezechiel," *ZAW* 63 (1951): 33–53 = *BZAW* 99 (1967): 204–21; M. Dijkstra, "The Glosses in Ezekiel Reconsidered: Aspects of Textual Transmission in Ezekiel 10," in *Ezekiel and His Book: Textual and Literary Criticism and Their Interrelation*, ed. J. Lust (Leuven: University Press, 1986), 55–77; L. C. Allen, "Some Types of Textual Adaptation in Ezekiel," *ETL* 71 (1995): 5–29.

20   For example, in the apparatus of Jer 27:19, 22; Ezek 1:27; 7:6–7.

21   The notation heralds much progress. However, the first eight volumes of BHQ published until 2021 do not use this term for the canonical books. See E. Tov, "A New Volume in the *Biblia Hebraica Quinta* Series: Genesis, by Abraham Tal," in *Like Nails Firmly Fixed (Qoh 12:11): Essays on the Text and Language of the Hebrew and Greek Scriptures Presented to Peter J. Gentry on the Occasion of His Retirement*, ed. Ph. S. Marshall, J. D. Meade, and J. Kiel (Leuven: Peeters, 2022), 15–35.

22   Tov, *Textual Criticism of the Hebrew Bible*, 331.

4. New Players in the Field

The principles of textual criticism have not changed in the period under review, but many new players have appeared in the field and have made an enormous difference. The largest corpus of such sources was found in the Judean Desert between 1947 and 1956. These texts were discovered more than half a century ago, but they were only made available later and their importance for scholarship was realized only within the period under review.

LXX scholars look with satisfaction at small fragments of the Greek Torah from Qumran that some regard as representatives of the Old Greek as opposed to the presumably revised text of the large uncials.[23] They also learned much from the Greek Minor Prophets Scroll from Naḥal Ḥever (8ḤevXII gr) that embodies an early revision of the LXX, which brought about a real revolution in LXX research.[24] Targum specialists were pleased to find at Qumran the earliest fragments of that literature.[25]

But the greatest revolution of all in conceptions was brought about by the discovery of a few hundred specimens of Hebrew Scripture at Qumran and other places in the Judean Desert. A place of honor was taken by individual texts and groups of texts, the likes of which were unknown in the research of earlier decades and centuries. Deserving of special mention are a group of nonsectarian Jewish texts that share all the characteristic features of the medieval text of SP (named pre-Samaritan texts in research), a group of texts written with an extremely full orthography and peculiar morphology, and several texts that include a great amount of content exegesis (4QRP). Even the proto-Masoretic texts from the Judean Desert that are almost identical to the medieval codices are remarkable. All these texts were added to the text-critical analysis, were integrated in the text editions of the Hebrew Bible and included in a changed perception of the text-critical *Weltanschauung*.

---

23 E. Tov, "The Greek Biblical Texts from the Judean Desert," in *Hebrew Bible, Greek Bible, and Qumran: Collected Essays* (Tübingen: Mohr Siebeck, 2008), 339–64.

24 P. J. Gentry, "Pre-Hexaplaric Translations, Hexapla, Post-Hexaplaric Translations," *Textual History of the Bible*, Vol. 1A, 211–35.

25 B. Ego, "1.3.3. Targumim," in *Overview Articles*, vol. 1A of *Textual History of the Bible, The Hebrew Bible*, ed. A. Lange and E. Tov (Leiden: Brill, 2016), 239–62.

5. Textual Variety

The discovery of new documents in the Judean Desert brought about a new understanding of the textual situation in the last two centuries BCE and the first century CE.[26] This situation may be described as textual plurality within the Qumran community and ancient Israel as a whole.

We have become so accustomed to the concept of textual variety that we sometimes forget that this concept was only born after the discovery of the Judean Desert scrolls. It could not have existed previously since insufficient texts were known at the time. Before 1947 the world of scholarship was limited to MT, SP, and the LXX in the Torah, and to the MT and the LXX in the other books.

These data almost necessarily led towards the dominance of MT in the perception of scholars because of the devastating judgment of SP by Wilhelm Gesenius in 1815,[27] and because the LXX often did not deviate much from MT in the Prophets and Writings or because some scholars did not hold that translation in high esteem. The earlier textual outlook was accompanied by wrong principles. If you have very little evidence, unconsciously you try to create an illusion of more evidence. In that way, the evidence of the Peshitta, the targumim, and the Vulgate was upgraded in the textual apparatuses and introductions, even though they do not have much to offer beyond MT. The medieval manuscripts of MT were also upgraded as *individual* witnesses in textual editions and commentaries even though their deviations from the Leningrad and Aleppo Codices are mainly products of the Middle Ages.[28] Likewise, the secondary translations made from the Septuagint and the Peshitta were upgraded as if they were independent sources, but except for some evidence from the Old Latin,[29] they have little to offer as independent witnesses beyond the primary translations. Therefore, most of the joint references to the Old Latin and the LXX in BH 1, 2, and BHS are irrelevant. In short, before 1947, there simply was no evidence for textual variety. Scholars knew three texts, not even "text types" since that term is a misnomer of scholarship.[30]

---

26 Tov, *Textual Criticism of the Hebrew Bible*, 119–21.
27 W. Gesenius, *De Pentateuchi Samaritani origine indole et auctoritate commentatio philologico-critica* (Halle: Bibliotheca Rengeriana, 1815).
28 See the verdict of M. H. Goshen-Gottstein, "Hebrew Biblical Manuscripts: Their History and Their Place in the HUBP Edition," *Biblica* 48 (1967): 243–90.
29 Mainly in Exodus, Kings, Jeremiah, and Esther.
30 It is unclear when the term was introduced into the scholarly jargon. H. M. Wiener, "The Recensional Criticism of the Pentateuch," *Biblical Studies* 70 (1913): 278–90, uses both the terms 'text types' and 'recensions.' In discussions of the ancient Scripture texts, it is often

The textual reality was changed fundamentally with the first finds of the scrolls in 1947, but it took a long time for scholars to realize that a change had taken place and to understand what kind of change it was. It started to dawn slowly that *textual variety* was the new name of the game. When the scrolls were published, at first scholars lived in denial regarding the new situation, assigning the scrolls to the so-called "text types" that were surmised before the discovery of the scrolls.[31] Later it was realized that Qumran displays a veritable multitude of texts beyond MT.

In my view, the textual variety of Qumran could not have been created at Qumran itself, but was formed in other places in ancient Israel, then imported into Qumran, where additional new texts were created. Admittedly, this view reflects my own interpretation,[32] but the multitude of text branches at Qumran is a fact.

What are the practical implications? Certain aspects of the textual *Weltanschauung* had been changed, but other aspects remained the same. We still need to decide whether to prefer a model of a single original text à la Paul de Lagarde or that of several parallel pristine texts à la Paul Kahle. For that

---

    assumed that within the textual variety some 'text types' may be recognized, but the recognition of a text type is problematic. In my view, except for the editorial changes of the SP group, it is difficult to identify typological features in the other texts known before and after 1948.

31   The assigning of individual Qumran texts to a specific 'text type' is reflected in the literature from the first volumes of the *DJD* series onwards, when most of the new scrolls were described as belonging to the 'type' of MT, while some scrolls were assigned to the 'type' of the LXX or SP. For example, 2QDeut^c was described as reflecting a textual tradition close to the LXX and V in *DJD* III, 61. According to J. T. Milik, 5QDeut was systematically revised according to the Hebrew *Vorlage* of the LXX (*DJD* III, 170). Milik similarly described 5QKings as reflecting a mediating position between the recension of MT and that of the LXX (*DJD* III, 172). While these three short texts did not display a convincing level of agreement with the LXX, other texts showed surprising proximity to the LXX. The first such scroll to be considered close to the LXX was the rather well-preserved 4QSam^a. The approach to this scroll, which was soon to be accepted in scholarship, was indicated by the name of an early study by F. M. Cross, "A New Qumran Fragment Related to the Original Hebrew Underlying the Septuagint," *BASOR* 132 (1953): 15–26. Similar claims were made afterwards by Cross regarding 4QSam^b in "The Oldest Manuscripts from Qumran," *JBL* 74 (1955): 147–72. In *ALQ^1*, 133–40, Cross had remarkably good insights into the scrolls that he considered to be close to the LXX and that were eventually accepted as such. The argumentation was completed when additional ('pre-Samaritan') texts that belonged to the SP 'type' were discovered at Qumran: 4QpaleoExod^m and 4QNum^b.

32   "The Background and Origin of the Qumran Corpus of Scripture Texts," in Sacred Texts and Disparate Interpretations: Qumran Manuscripts Seventy Years Later: Proceedings of the International Conference Held at the John Paul II Catholic University of Lublin, 24–26 October 2017, ed. H. Drawnel (Leiden: Brill, 2020), 50–65.

purpose, it does not matter whether we see in front of us two, three, or an endless number of texts. The *Editionstechnik* relating to the type of edition has not changed either. What has changed is that we no longer ought to think in terms of a straitjacket of three traditions or text types, but rather of a plethora of texts (and possibly readings) in any given verse, and an even greater number of texts that have been lost.

6. Changed Approach to the Textual Sources

The approach to the textual sources has changed in the past half-century, mainly resulting from the discovery of the Dead Sea Scrolls. The approach to the ensemble of the textual sources has changed, since scholars are now aware of the textual variety existing in the last two centuries BCE and the first century CE, and towards individual sources.

6.1 *Septuagint*

The reliability of the reconstruction of the Hebrew source of the ancient translations, especially the LXX, is supported much by the Qumran Scrolls since details in several Hebrew texts are identical to the text of the LXX, especially in Samuel and Jeremiah. This confidence supported the reconstruction of the Hebrew sources not only in these two Greek translations, but in all the Scripture translations, as long as the translation technique of these books may be regarded as relatively faithful to the translators' sources. The LXX thus received an upgrade in the eyes of many scholars. It is remarkable that in the period under review in which commentators lean heavily on MT in writing their commentaries, four scholars give equal chances to the LXX in their commentaries: John Collins in Daniel 4–6, Hermann-Josef Stipp and Michael B. Shepherd in Jeremiah, and Francis I. Andersen and David N. Freedman in Micah. These scholars systematically translate the text of the LXX alongside or within the translation from MT and also exegete both texts.[33] This is a remarkable sign of progress.

---

[33] For the full details, see Tov, "The Use of the Septuagint in Critical Commentaries." Note further several commentary series on the LXX mentioned there. These commentaries react to the text of the LXX, and only some of them (especially *Septuaginta Deutsch*) comment on the relation between the Hebrew and the Greek. None of them relate to the LXX and MT as equal partners as do the four commentaries mentioned here.

6.2 Samaritan Pentateuch

The evaluation of SP also underwent a change, this time in the wake of Qumran scrolls very close to the medieval text of SP (pre-Samaritan texts). The novel aspect of these scrolls is that the Qumran texts share all the major and minor features with SP, while not carrying a sectarian Samaritan character. These texts, confirming the ancient character of SP, are Jewish documents from which presumably SP was created in the second century BCE by accepting and very slightly rewriting one of them. The nonsectarian character of most elements in SP becomes increasingly clear,[34] and all these changes necessitated a major change in the evaluation of SP.

6.3 Masoretic Text

As in the case of SP, the ancient character of MT has been confirmed by the discoveries in the Judean Desert. Before 1947 it was known that the medieval codices of MT were based on ancient texts. All the targumim, *kaige*-Th, and Aquila, were translated around the turn of the era or in the first two centuries CE from sources almost identical to MT,[35] and this pertains also to the Vulgate that was translated in 400 CE.[36] At the same time, the antiquity of the Hebrew form of MT was a mere assumption until the consonantal base of that text was found in nineteen fragmentary manuscripts at sites in the Judean Desert,[37] but not at Qumran.[38] Early on in research, this was recognized by Dominique Barthélemy, who named them pre-Masoretic.[39] These texts, including two *tefillin*, now named proto-Masoretic, are virtually identical to the consonantal framework of the medieval MT.

---

34 See the summary of S. White Crawford, "The Jewish and Samaritan Pentateuchs: Reflections on the Difference (?) between Textual Criticism and Literary Criticism," *HBAI* 9 (2020): 320–33.

35 Ego, "1.3.3 Targumim," 239–62.

36 M. Graves, "1.3.5 Vulgate," in *Overview Articles*, vol. 1A of *Textual History of the Bible, The Hebrew Bible*, ed. A. Lange and E. Tov (Leiden: Brill, 2016), 278–89.

37 Initially there was some confusion regarding which ancient texts could be named the precursors of the medieval text. The confusion started with W. F. Albright, "New Light on Early Recensions of the Hebrew Bible," *BASOR* 140 (1955): 28–29, probably the first scholar to use the term 'proto-Masoretic,' as he applied that term even to 1QIsa^a describing it as a text "belonging to the proto-Massoretic type, though it has a much fuller vocalization." In the same year, O. Lofgren wrote his "Zur Charakteristik des 'vormasoretischen' Jesajatextes," in *Donum natalicium H.S. Nyberg oblatum* (Uppsala: Almqvist & Wiksells, 1955), 171–84.

38 Tov, *Textual Criticism of the Hebrew Bible*, 37–40.

39 *Critique textuelle 1992*, xcviii–cxvi; idem, *Studies*, 383–409 (389). See E. Tov, "'Proto-Masoretic,' 'Pre-Masoretic,' 'Semi-Masoretic,' and 'Masoretic': A Study in Terminology and Textual Theory," in *Textual Developments: Collected Essays* (Leiden: Brill, 2019), 4: 195–213.

One could say that these finds are insignificant, as they do not add new variants, but their agreement with the medieval text signifies their importance. They confirm the antiquity of the medieval MT. They also show us which groups possessed this text and quoted from it and, further, it can be shown that this text was not used by reworked Bible compositions that quoted mainly from the shared LXX-SP tradition.[40]

6.4 Evaluation of Textual Sources

The evaluation of the textual sources has shifted in the period under review and also beforehand. The best method of reviewing the changing opinions is by examining the systems used in the critical text editions since some of the best textual critics are involved in preparing them. Now, when examining these editions, I discovered some surprising facts regarding the changing views during the last century. All of them point in the same direction of an *increasing acceptance of MT*.

When studying the trend regarding recording deviations from MT starting with the edition of Cornill, *Ezechiel* (1868), one notes some remarkable phenomena. When the amount of deviation from MT is analyzed in sample chapters, it is recognized that what started as a hurricane-force breakaway from MT in 1886 (Cornill, *Ezechiel*) ended as a light breeze in the twenty-first century. From around 1900 onwards, we see a regression in risk-taking in textual judgment and in the reconstruction of the earliest texts. In other words, we witness a steady and conservative move towards MT.

Influenced by Hitzig's eclectic translation,[41] Cornill changed as much as 25 or 30 percent of the words in MT in certain segments in Ezekiel;[42] this percentage was reduced to between 5 and 15 percent in the samples from other books

---

40 E. Tov, "The Textual Base of the Biblical Quotations in Second Temple Compositions," in *Textual Developments: Collected Essays* (Leiden: Brill, 2019), 4: 3–20.

41 F. Hitzig, *Die Prophetischen Bücher des Alten Testaments* (Leipzig: Hirzel, 1854).

42 Cornill's far-reaching reconstructions follow the rules set up in his theoretical introduction. Thus, in the reconstruction of Ezek 1:1–13 (160 words; v. 1 was excluded by Cornill as an editorial addition), twenty-four words differ from MT based on the LXX (= 15%) and seventeen words were emended (= 11%), creating a text that differed from MT in 26 percent. In 7:1–14 (182 words), forty-eight words (26%) were corrected with the LXX, and thirteen words were emended (7%), together 33 percent. The changes in the latter case are more pervasive than indicated by the percentages since Cornill also followed the sequence of the verses of the LXX in vv. 2–9. Cornill's reconstructions reflect a very bold approach. For further details, see E. Tov, "The Search for an Original Text Form of the Hebrew Bible: Theory and Praxis," *Contributions to Biblical Exegesis and Theology* (Leuven: Peeters, forthcoming).

in Haupt's series.⁴³ A decade later, the percentage is similar in the BH 1 edition, 5–15 percent at the high end and 2–5 percent at the low end. The BHS edition presents a lower percentage, usually 2–5 percent at the low end and 3–10 percent at the high end. Emendations appear frequently in all these editions, sometimes more so than readings supported by the versions. The fewest deviations from MT are recorded in the editions produced most recently, BHQ and HBCE (The Hebrew Bible: A Critical Edition, previously known as the "Oxford Bible"). BHQ prefers variants in no more than 1 percent of the instances. The same pertains to the only published edition of HBCE (0–2 percent).⁴⁴ This trend is also visible in the projects of Dominique Barthélemy⁴⁵ and his textual commentaries.⁴⁶ While Barthélemy's volumes take the evidence of all textual sources into consideration, in practice they almost always decide in favor of MT.⁴⁷

In short, at the beginning of the twenty-first century, we may well be entering a new stage in textual criticism in which textual judgment is limited to errors and the recognition of scribal tendencies, such as theological variants. This new trend in textual criticism should be considered both cautious and conservative, and results in an increased adherence to MT. These results, clear

---

43   In Cornill's edition of Jeremiah in the Haupt series, the level of deviation from MT was not as massive as in his own Ezekiel edition, but the sequence changes need to be added to these small changes. In chapter 27 (419 words), Cornill changed (mainly omitted) fifty-two words with the LXX (12 percent) and emended fourteen words (3 percent) together 15 percent. However, the level of deviation is greater since the sequence of the chapters was changed as well. In 1 Samuel 1 (414 words), Budde changed MT in twenty-two words following the LXX (5 percent) and emended the text in twenty-eight words (7 percent), together 12 percent. I mention these percentages in order to contrast them with modern editions.

   In comparison with Cornill, Wellhausen's edition of Psalms in the Haupt series is characterized by modest intervention, mainly by way of emendation. For example, in Psalm 68, Wellhausen corrected sixteen details in MT, two words (0.5%) with the versions and fourteen emendations = 4.5 percent (together 5 percent of the text words). For further details, see Tov, "Search for an Original Text Form."

44   M. V. Fox, *Proverbs: An Eclectic Edition with Introduction and Textual Commentary* (Atlanta, GA: SBL, 2015).

45   D. Barthélemy et al., *Preliminary and Interim Report on the Hebrew Old Testament Text Project, 5 vols.* (New York, NY: United Bible Societies, 1974, 1979–1980).

46   Idem, *Critique textuelle de l'Ancien Testament, 3 vols.* (Fribourg: Éditions Universitaires; Göttingen: Vandenhoeck & Ruprecht, 1986, 1992, 2005).

47   No changes from MT are recorded in the volumes of the HUB, but they do witness the trend that is described here, since from the very first volume (M. H. Goshen-Gottstein, *The Hebrew University Bible: The Book of Isaiah: Sample Edition with Introduction* [Jerusalem: Magnes, 1965]) they have abstained from any judgment concerning differences between MT and the versions.

as they may be, cannot be representative for the field as a whole since we also reported an increased openness toward textual criticism among commentators including four commentaries that comment in an egalitarian way on the text of MT and the LXX (§§ 2, 6.1).

7. New Printed and Digital Editions of Hebrew Scripture

While some less successful critical editions were published in the nineteenth century, the twentieth century was *the* century of the critical editions, in particular in the second half.[48] The critical editions, differing in text base and concept and all accompanied by a critical apparatus, are used as the basis for further textual and exegetical analysis. Their precision, thoroughness, and the width of their scope determine the success of that enterprise. In 2024, the older edition, BHS, is the most frequently used among the editions since it is the only complete one. The more recent form of the Biblia Hebraica series, BHQ, is used for the eight Scripture books that have been published in the meantime.[49] A single volume has been published of the HBCE.[50] The volumes of the HUB (Hebrew University Bible) are used for the Latter Prophets; no further volumes have been published in 2023.[51]

---

48   E. Tov, "Modern Editions of the Hebrew Bible," in *Textual Developments: Collected Essays* (Leiden: Brill, 2019), 4: 77–96.

49   For a critical analysis of BHQ, see Tov, "The Philosophy of the Biblia Hebraica Quinta Edition," in *La Bible en face. Études textuelles et littéraires offertes en homage à Adrian Schenker, à l'occasion de ses quatre-vingts ans*, ed. I. Himbaza and C. Locher, *Cahiers de la Revue Biblique* 95 (2020): 19–39; and idem, "A New Volume in the Biblia Hebraica Quinta Series: Genesis, by Abraham Tal," in *Like Nails Firmly Fixed (Qoh 12:11): Essays on the Text and Language of the Hebrew and Greek Scriptures Presented to Peter J. Gentry on the Occasion of His Retirement*, ed. P. S. Marshall, J. D. Meade, and J. Kiel (Leuven: Peeters, 2022), 15–35.

50   Fox, *Proverbs*. The system is outlined by R. S. Hendel, "The Oxford Hebrew Bible: Prologue to a New Critical Edition," *VT* 58 (2008): 324–51; idem., *Steps to a New Edition of the Hebrew Bible* (Atlanta, GA: SBL, 2016). For an analysis, see E. Tov, "Eclectic Text Editions of Hebrew Scripture," in *Textual Criticism of the Hebrew Bible, Qumran, Septuagint: Collected Essays* (Leiden: Brill, 2015), 3: 121–31; H. G. M. Williamson, "Do We Need A New Bible? Reflections on the Proposed Oxford Hebrew Bible," *Biblica* 90 (2009): 153–75; E. J. C. Tigchelaar, "Editing the Hebrew Bible: An Overview of Some Problems," in *Editing the Bible: Assessing the Task Past and Present*, ed. J. S. Kloppenborg and J. H. Newman (Atlanta, GA: SBL, 2012), 41–65.

51   Goshen-Gottstein, *HUB: Isaiah*; C. Rabin, Sh. Talmon, and E. Tov, *The Hebrew University Bible: The Book of Jeremiah* (Jerusalem: Magnes, 1997); M. H. Goshen-Gottstein, and Sh. Talmon, *The Hebrew University Bible: The Book of Ezekiel* (Jerusalem: Magnes, 2004).

Digital text editions followed the publication of the printed text editions. These editions have great advantages over the printed editions due to the availability of versatile search programs and statistical packages,[52] but there are also drawbacks.[53] The digital editions copy the text of printed editions or manuscripts and do not introduce novel editorial concepts.

8. The Age of Specialization

Specialization is the hallmark of our times, and it has not skipped our area. Scholars know increasingly more about an increasingly smaller area. Literary critics no longer say that they study Scripture, but often describe their area as the Torah, the Prophets, or wisdom literature. Before the 1970s (this is not an exact date, but it is half a century ago), there were not so many scholars who would say that they spend most of their research time on textual criticism, but in the past half-century there definitely is a growing number of such creatures. I am one of them. Some of them would publish mainly on text-critical topics, while others would additionally write on other issues.

Within textual studies, there are natural specializations. Gone are the days of Johann Gottfried Eichhorn, *Einleitung in das Alte Testament*, who produced competent and thorough introductions to all the texts and versions of Scripture (in addition to the literary aspects)[54]; of Paul A. de Lagarde who produced a text edition of the Antiochian text of the LXX,[55] and further edited texts in Syriac, Aramaic, Arabic, Coptic, Armenian, and Persian; of Paul Kahle who showed the many aspects of his knowledge relating to the Aramaic targumim, Peshitta, Genizah fragments, Septuagint, Diatessaron, Samaritan Hebrew, masoretic Hebrew, and wrote a programmatic study on the text history of the Torah.[56] Scholars now know fewer languages, but they are often more knowledgeable in their area of specialization. As a result, textual scholars now cover smaller areas. For example, some scholars are interested in all areas of LXX studies,

---

52   Tov, Textual Criticism of the Hebrew Bible, 407–10.
53   E. Tov, "Textual Criticism of the Hebrew Bible in the Digital Age: Advantages and Disadvantages of the Use of Digital Tools," in *Biblicum Jassyense, Romanian Journal for Biblical Philology and Hermeneutics* 8 (2021): 5–14.
54   J. G. Eichhorn, *Einleitung in das Alte Testament*, 3 vols. (Leipzig: Weidmann, 1780–1783).
55   P. A. de Lagarde, *Librorum Veteris Testamenti Canonicorum, pars prior, graece* (Göttingen: Dieterich, 1883).
56   P. E. Kahle, "Untersuchungen zur Geschichte des Pentateuchtextes," *Theologische Studien und Kritiken* 88 (1915): 399–439. Reprinted in Paul E. Kahle, *Opera Minora* (Leiden: Brill, 1956), 3–37.

while others specialize in the LXX as a reflection of early Hebrew texts, LXX language, the Hellenistic background of the LXX, the translation technique of the LXX, or the Hexaplaric revisions of the LXX. Likewise, some scholars focus on the dating of the targumim, the differences between them, their vocabulary, their interactions, relations with rabbinic sources, etc., while other targumic specialists are interested in all these topics.

Other specializations are the Hebrew scrolls from the Judean Desert, medieval biblical manuscripts, the Masorah, Peshitta, Vulgate, and each of the secondary translations made from the LXX and Peshitta, and the computerized study of these texts.[57]

Specialization is beneficial for scholarship, as long as the results of that activity are shared with non-specialists.[58] Textual studies published in general journals such as *Zeitschrift für die Alttestamentliche Wissenschaft* (*ZAW*), *Journal of Biblical Literature* (*JBL*), and *Vetus Testamentum* (*VT*) may reach a wider public than if they were published in journals specializing in textual criticism.

9. Instituting of Projects

Specialization, as described above, always existed at a small scale, but in the past five decades it has proliferated exponentially. This increase coincided with the expansion of existing projects and the creation of new ones. Projects need specialized contributors, students or scholars, and one is either such a specialist before one joins a project or becomes one while working on the project.

Some such projects existed already fifty years ago (the Göttingen Septuaginta Unternehmen,[59] the Leiden Peshitta Institute (now in Amsterdam), the *Biblia Hebraica* series, the HUBP), while others rose from the ground with the expansion of universities, or with funds made available by universities or national or international funding agencies. I am certainly not aware of all the projects that exist today or have existed in the past half-century, but I will do my best.

---

57 On the computerized Scripture study alone, many monographs have been written and conferences have been held.

58 A good example is the encyclopedic handbook *THB* (*Textual History of the Bible*) that is used by specialists and nonspecialists alike.

59 Discontinued, but continued partly as a Psalter edition project, funded by the Academy at Göttingen, and the Robert Hanhart-Stiftung zur Förderung der Septuaginta-Forschung.

9.1   *Text Editions and Websites*

Pride of place goes to the classical text editions, Göttingen *Septuaginta Unternehmen*, the Leiden Peshitta Institute, *Biblia Hebraica* series, HUBP, Vetus Latina (Beuron), *Edición políglota sinóptica de 1 Reyes 1–11* (Julio Trebolle, Pablo Antonio Torijano Morales, and Andrés Piquer Otero). New text editions are undertaken by these projects: *HBCE* (*Hebrew Bible Critical Edition*); Hexapla Project; *CATSS* (*Computer Assisted Tools for Septuagint Studies*, Philadelphia – Jerusalem); *Biblical Online Synopsis* (Helsinki); *Daughter versions of Esther, Text of Joshua*, Salzburg University; *THEOT* (*Textual History of the Ethiopic Old Testament*); *Targum Institute* (targumm.nl); CAL–The Comprehensive Aramaic Lexicon; Eep Talstra Center for Bible and Computer, Amsterdam; the *J. Alan Groves Center for Advanced Biblical Research*, Pennsylvania. Websites include the Leon Levy Dead Sea Scrolls Digital Library[60]; Israel Museum[61]; and numerous websites on sources of the LXX[62]; numerous websites on Hebrew sources[63].

9.2   *Translations and Commentaries, Research Centers and Projects*

Bible d'Alexandrie, Septuaginta Deutsch, Septuagint Commentary Series (Leiden: Brill: 2005–), ed. M. V. Spottorno and N. Fernández Marcos, *La Biblia Griega – Septuaginta. Traducción española I–IV*, forthcoming.

Research centers and projects include *The Centre for Septuagint and Textual Criticism*, Leuven; *The Dominique Barthélemy Institute* for the History of the Text and Old Testament Exegesis, Fribourg; *Centre for the Study of the Bible*, Oriel College, Oxford; *The Ancient History Documentary Research Centre*, Macquarie University, Sydney (NT parallels for the LXX); *Targums WordMap*, Bar-Ilan University.

10.   **Explosion of Organizations, Conferences, and Publications**

Together with the explosion of projects, major sociological changes took place when specialized scholars organized themselves in professional organizations. I have witnessed this trend myself since 1969 when I joined the IOSCS

---

60   https://www.deadseascrolls.org.il/, last accessed October 25, 2023.
61   https://www.imj.org.il/en/wings/shrine-book/dead-sea-scrolls, last accessed October 25, 2023.
62   See Tov, *Textual Criticism of the Hebrew Bible*, ch. 8.11, http://oldtestamenttextualcriticism.blogspot.com/2011/, last accessed October 25, 2023.
63   See Tov, Textual Criticism of the Hebrew Bible, ch. 3.10; 5.7, http://oldtestamenttextualcriticism.blogspot.com/2011/, last accessed October 25, 2023.

(International Organization for Septuagint and Cognate Studies). This organization has existed since December 1968 and it holds annual meetings in conjunction with the SBL (Society of Biblical Literature) and triennially with the IOSOT (International Organization for the Study of the Old Testament). It publishes information, bibliography, a monograph series (*SCS*), and an annual *Bulletin (BIOSCS)*,[64] which in due course became a journal, the *Journal of Septuagint and Cognate Studies (JSCS)*.[65]

Similar organizations are: The International Organization for Targumic Studies (IOTS), that holds international meetings for research on Targum-related topics.[66] Unrelated to the IOTS, Brill publishes the journal *Aramaic Studies* (volumes 1–20; 2003–2022), formerly *Journal for the Aramaic Bible* (1999–2002), published by Sheffield Academic Press. Both journals contain many studies on Targum-related subjects. The International Organization for Masoretic Studies (IOMS), established in 1972, organizes meetings in conjunction with the SBL and IOSOT.

Each of these organizations holds annual, biennial, or triennial conferences at which papers are read. In addition, papers on textual matters are read within larger frameworks and at the many conferences dedicated to general and textual studies, such as the numerous conferences dedicated to the Dead Sea Scrolls and biennial conferences organized by *Septuaginta Deutsch* in Wuppertal, Germany.[67]

The many publications on textual matters were mentioned in the previous paragraphs. This abundance of publications exceeds many times the numbers of publications preceding the 1970s.

While the regular journals such as *VT*, *JBL*, *ZAW*, *DSD* continued to publish text-critical studies, two journals were established that are earmarked for textual criticism (in addition to journals dedicated to the LXX, the targumim, and the Dead Sea Scrolls): *Textus, A Journal on Textual Criticism of the Hebrew Bible*, was founded by the HUBP and published by Magnes Press for vols. 1–26 (1960–2016) and by Brill from there onwards (vols. 27–33; 2018–2024); and *TC: A Journal of Biblical Textual Criticism*, an online journal, vols. 1–28 (1996–2023).

The establishing of professional organizations, the abundance of projects, and the manifold professional meetings advanced textual scholarship. The

---

64 Volumes 1–43, 1968–2010.
65 To date, volumes 44–56, 2011–2023.
66 http://targum.info, last accessed October 25, 2023.
67 Published in *Die Septuaginta–Texte, Kontexte, Lebenswelten: Internationale Fachtagung veranstaltet von Septuaginta Deutsch (LXX.D), Wuppertal 20.–23. Juli 2006*, ed. M. Karrer and W. Kraus, WUNT 219 (Tübingen: Mohr Siebeck, 2008) and subsequent volumes.

more organizations there were, the more meetings were held, resulting in more papers being produced. This vicious circle of organizations and papers put pressure on scholars, young and old, to initiate new investigations and to prepare new research papers. All this did not exist before the 1970s. It was a boon for scholarship, although some colleagues complain that the proliferation of meetings and the urge to present papers at these meetings necessarily resulted in some immature or hastily written papers.

11. Trends and Fashions

Before the 1970s there were fewer trends and fashions in the research. Scholars followed their interests when writing their research papers, but they did of course react to each other's writings, especially in nineteenth-century Germany and in the United States. The generation of scholars with whom I studied in Israel, all born in Europe, spoke much about their practice of "philology," the all-encompassing treatment of the text, a term I have not heard much in the last fifty years. I try to be a philologist myself, that is, someone who derives from the text everything that's found in it.

In contrast to what came before, in the decennia since the 1970s one sees the development of trends and fashions in the topics to which scholars turn and on which they write. In a sense, the world has become one global scene, and scholarly developments in one country have influence internationally. Scholars cooperate easily via conferences, email, and by Zoom, and seminars that used to be given in Israel in Hebrew are now followed around the world in English (e.g., the Orion seminars). In this climate of global cooperation, it is easily understandable that new trends and fashions in research topics developed, for example, about:

New discoveries. Obviously, a new discovery such as that of the Hebrew, Greek, and Aramaic Scripture texts from the Judean Desert has attracted an unceasing flow of hundreds of publications. The same pertains to the Greek papyrus fragments from Egypt.

New research options. Already in 1970, in the third issue of the *BIOSCS*, Kent L. Smith wrote about the great possibilities of the computer for LXX studies.[68] Soon thereafter, data entry of the LXX was started and several research projects were initiated, among them *CATSS*, co-directed by Robert A.

---

68   K. L. Smith, "Data Processing the Bible: A Consideration of the Potential Use of the Computer in Biblical Studies," *BIOSCS* 3 (1970): 12–14.

Kraft and myself.[69] This new tool is used as a new search engine that is more effective than the existing printed concordance; the resulting series of computer-assisted studies based on these data in the field of the study of translation technique and interchanges between MT and the LXX are equally important.[70] In the field of Hebrew studies, clusters of studies were carried out on matters of orthography and vocabulary.

Kaige-Theodotion. After the discovery of the Greek Minor Prophets scroll from Naḥal Ḥever (8HevXII gr) that embodies an early revision of the LXX, Barthélemy suggested in 1963 that segments of the "LXX canon" also belonged to that revision. Ever since, many books have been written on this topic, conferences have been devoted to it, and this revision has become a major area of research.

Translation technique of the LXX. While some studies had been written in earlier decennia, in recent decades much work has been done in this area, especially by the Finnish school of research.[71] Study of translation technique was recognized as an important area in its own right, but especially so as a first step in the recognition of the text-critical evaluation of the LXX.

Variant Literary Editions. Many segments in textual witnesses that attest to literary stages in the development of the Scripture books different from those of MT have been dubbed "variant literary editions."

Translation Model. The theoretical translation model created by Gideon Toury[72] has inspired many a LXX scholar, especially Albert Pietersma.

12. The Advent of the Computer

The computer brought unparalleled advantages to textual studies, probably more than to other areas of investigation of the Hebrew and translated Bible, and thereby changed its character in many ways, though the basic task of textual criticism was not changed. It was realized at an early stage that computer

---

69 E. Tov and F. H. Polak, *The Parallel Aligned Text of the Greek and Hebrew Bible* (division of the *CATSS* database, codirected by R. A. Kraft and E. Tov); module in the *Accordance* and *Logos* computer programs, 2005 (with updates, 2006–).

70 E. Tov, "Achievements and Trends in Computer-Assisted Biblical Studies," in *Proceedings of the Second International Colloquium. Bible and Computer: Methods, Tools, Results, Jérusalem, 9–13 juin 1988*, ed. C. Muller, Travaux de linguistique quantitative 43 (Paris: Champion; Geneva: Sladkine, 1989), 33–60.

71 I. Soisalon-Soininen, A. Aejmelaeus, R. Sollamo.

72 G. Toury, *Descriptive Translation Studies – and Beyond*, revised edition (Amsterdam: Benjamins Translations Library, 2012).

projects could prepare digital versions of all the texts and that the availability of these texts, combined with dedicated lexicons and collections of variants, would create new options for textual studies.[73]

13. In Conclusion, A Better World for Textual Studies?

Yes, a better world. Thanks to the Dead Sea Scrolls, we possess many more data regarding the textual conditions in the last centuries BCE and the first century CE. This does not necessarily mean that we have more information regarding what the original texts of the Scripture books looked like. In my view, "the more we know, the less we know" since we now realize how complex the development of the Scripture books was between the time of their composition and the third–first centuries BCE. As in the past, scholars remain interested in the "original" text of Hebrew Scripture, and I do not think that this goal has changed. In my view, the lack of knowledge should call for more restraint and caution, but this is not always the case.

Looking back at the status of textual scholarship half a century ago, it is a better world now. Some concepts have changed. We know more, but we would be well-advised to emphasize what is still unknown. I do not know whether there are more persons involved, and not all of them come with the same linguistic training as in the past. However, we possess much more data, many more tools, we use computers, and there are meaningful projects.

---

[73] See some of my earlier studies: "A New Generation of Biblical Research," in *Proceedings of the First International Colloquium. Bible and Computer: The Text, Louvain-la-Neuve (Belgique) 2–3–4 septembre 1985* (Paris: Champion; Geneva: Sladkine, 1986), 413–43; "Computer Assisted Research of the Greek and Hebrew Bible," in *Computer Assisted Analysis of Biblical Texts: Papers Read at the Workshop on the Occasion of the Tenth Anniversary of the "Werkgroep Informatika," Faculty of Theology, Vrije Universiteit, Amsterdam, November 5–6, 1987*, ed. E. Talstra (Amsterdam: Free University Press, 1989), 87–99; "The Use of Computers in Biblical Research," in Tov, *Hebrew Bible, Greek Bible, and Qumran*, 228–46; "Electronic Tools for Biblical Study at Home, at the University, and in the Classroom," in *Computer Assisted Research on the Bible in the 21st Century*, ed. L. Vegas Montaner et al., Bible in Technology 8 (Piscataway, NJ: Gorgias, 2010), 45–60. For some of the disadvantages of the use of computers, see Tov, "Textual Criticism of the Hebrew Bible in the Digital Age."

Bibliography

Albright, William F. "New Light on Early Recensions of the Hebrew Bible." *Bulletin of the American Schools of Oriental Research* 140 (1955): 27–33.

Allen, Leslie C. "Some Types of Textual Adaptation in Ezekiel." *Ephemerides theologicae Lovanienses* 71 (1995): 5–29.

Baillet, Maurice, J. T. Milik, and R. de Vaux. *Les 'petites grottes' de Qumrân*. DJD III. Oxford: Clarendon, 1962.

Barthélemy, Dominique, et al. *Preliminary and Interim Report on the Hebrew Old Testament Text Project*. 5 vols. New York, N.Y.: United Bible Societies, 1974, 1979–1980.

--------. *Critique textuelle de l'Ancien Testament, 2. Isaïe, Jérémie, Lamentations*. Fribourg: Éditions Universitaires; Göttingen: Vandenhoeck & Ruprecht, 1986.

--------. *Critique textuelle de l'Ancien Testament, 3. Ézéchiel, Daniel et les 12 Prophètes*. Fribourg: Éditions Universitaires; Göttingen: Vandenhoeck & Ruprecht, 1992.

--------. *Studies in the Text of the Old Testament: An Introduction to the Hebrew Old Testament Text Project*. Winona Lake, IN: Eisenbrauns, 2012.

--------. *Critique textuelle de l'Ancien Testament, 5. Job, Proverbes, Qohélet et Cantique des Cantiques*. Fribourg: Éditions Universitaires; Göttingen: Vandenhoeck & Ruprecht, 2015.

Brooke, George J. "What is a Variant Edition? Perspectives from the Qumran Scrolls." In *In the Footsteps of Sherlock Holmes: Studies in the Biblical Text in Honour of Anneli Aejmelaeus*, edited by Kristin De Troyer et al., 607–22. Leuven: Peeters, 2014.

Cornill, Carl H. *Das Buch des Propheten Ezechiel*. Leipzig: Hinrichs, 1886.

Cross, Frank M. "A New Qumran Fragment Related to the Original Hebrew Underlying the Septuagint." *Bulletin of the American Schools of Oriental Research* 132 (1953): 15–26.

Cross, Frank M. "The Oldest Manuscripts from Qumran." *Journal of Biblical Literature* 74 (1955): 147–72.

--------. *The Ancient Library of Qumrân and Modern Biblical Studies*. London: Duckworth, 1958.

Crawford, Sidnie White. "The Jewish and Samaritan Pentateuchs: Reflections on the Difference (?) between Textual Criticism and Literary Criticism." *Hebrew Bible and Ancient Israel* 9 (2020): 320–33.

Debel, Hans. "'Greek Variant Editions' to the Hebrew Bible?" *Journal for the Study of Judaism* 41 (2010): 161–90.

Dijkstra, Meindert. "The Glosses in Ezekiel Reconsidered: Aspects of Textual Transmission in Ezekiel 10." In *Ezekiel and His Book: Textual and Literary Criticism and Their Interrelation*, edited by Johan Lust, 55–77. Leuven: University Press, 1986.

Ego, Beate. "1.3.3 Targumim." In *Textual History of the Bible, The Hebrew Bible*. Vol. 1A: *Overview Articles*, edited by Armin Lange and Emanuel Tov, 239–62. Leiden: Brill, 2016.

Eichhorn, Johann Gottfried. *Einleitung in das Alte Testament*. 3 volumes. Leipzig: Weidmann, 1780–1783.

Elgvin, Torleif. *The Literary Growth of the Song of Songs during the Hasmonean and Early-Herodian Periods*. Leuven: Peeters, 2018.

Finsterbusch, Karin. "Traditional Textual Criticism Reconsidered: MT (codex L)-Ezek 35, LXX (papyrus 967)-Ezek 35 and Its Hebrew Vorlage as Variant Editions and the Implications for the Search for the 'Original' Text." *Hebrew Bible and Ancient Israel* 9 (2020): 334–45.

Fohrer, Georg. "Die Glossen im Buche Ezechiel." *Zeitschrift für die Alttestamentliche Wissenschaft* 63 (1951): 33–53; *Beihefte zur Zeitschrift für die alttestamentliche Wissenschaft* 99 (1967): 204–21.

Fox, Michael V. *Proverbs: An Eclectic Edition with Introduction and Textual Commentary*. Atlanta, GA: The Society of Biblical Literature, 2015.

Gentry, Peter J. "Pre-Hexaplaric Translations, Hexapla, Post-Hexaplaric Translations." In *Textual History of the Bible, The Hebrew Bible*. Vol. 1A: *Overview Articles*, edited by Armin Lange and Emanuel Tov, 211–35. Leiden: Brill, 2016.

Gesenius, Wilhelm. *De Pentateuchi Samaritani origine indole et auctoritate commentatio philologico-critica*. Halle: Bibliotheca Rengeriana, 1815.

Goshen-Gottstein, Moshe H. "Hebrew Biblical Manuscripts: Their History and Their Place in the HUBP Edition." *Biblica* 48, no. 2 (1967): 243–90.

--------. *The Hebrew University Bible: The Book of Isaiah: Sample Edition with Introduction*. Jerusalem: Magnes, 1965.

Goshen-Gottstein, Moshe H., and Shemaryahu Talmon. *The Hebrew University Bible: The Book of Ezekiel*. Jerusalem: Magnes, 2004.

Graves, Michael. "1.3.5 Vulgate." In *Textual History of the Bible, The Hebrew Bible*. Vol. 1A: *Overview Articles*, edited by Armin Lange and Emanuel Tov, 278–89. Leiden: Brill, 2016.

Hausspie, Katrin. "Ezekiel." In *The Oxford Handbook of the Septuagint*, edited by Alison G. Salvesen and Timothy M. Law, 275–89. Oxford: Oxford University Press, 2021.

Hendel, Ronald S. "The Oxford Hebrew Bible: Prologue to a New Critical Edition." *Vetus Testamentum* 58 (2008): 324–51.

--------. *Steps to a New Edition of the Hebrew Bible*. Atlanta, GA: The Society of Biblical Literature, 2016.

Herrmann, J. "Stichwortglossen im Buche Ezechiel." *Orientalistische Literaturzeitung* 11 (1908): 280–82.

——. "Stichwortglossen im Alten Testament." *Orientalistische Literaturzeitung* 14 (1911): 200–204.

Hitzig, Ferdinand. *Die Prophetischen Bücher des Alten Testaments*. Leipzig: Hirzel, 1854.

Holmes, Samuel. *Joshua: The Hebrew and Greek Texts*. Cambridge: Cambridge University Press, 1914.

Kahle, Paul E. "Untersuchungen zur Geschichte des Pentateuchtextes." *Theologische Studien und Kritiken* 88 (1915): 399–439. Reprinted in Paul E. Kahle, *Opera Minora*, 3–37. Leiden: Brill, 1956.

van der Kooij, Arie. "De tekst van Samuel en het tekstkritisch onderzoek." *Nederlands Theologisch Tijdschrift* 36 (1982): 177–204.

Kuenen, Abraham. *An Historico-Critical Inquiry into the Origin and Composition of the Hexateuch*. London: Macmillan, 1886.

De Lagarde, Paul A. *Librorum Veteris Testamenti Canonicorum, pars prior, graece*. Göttingen: Dieterich, 1883.

Lange, Armin. "The Textual Plurality of Jewish Scriptures in the Second Temple Period in Light of the Dead Sea Scrolls." In *Qumran and the Bible: Studying the Jewish and Christian Scriptures in Light of the Dead Sea Scrolls*, edited by Nora Dávid and Armin Lange, 43–96. Leuven: Peeters, 2010.

Lilly, Ingrid E. *Two Books of Ezekiel: Papyrus 967 and the Masoretic Text as Variant Literary Editions*. Leiden: Brill, 2012.

Lofgren, Oscar. "Zur Charakteristik des 'vormasoretischen' Jesajatextes." In *Donum natalicium H.S. Nyberg oblatum*, 171–84. Uppsala: Almqvist & Wiksells, 1955.

Longacre, Drew. "Developmental Stage, Scribal Lapse, or Physical Defect? 1QIsa^a's Damaged Exemplar for Isaiah Chapters 34–66." *Dead Sea Discoveries* 20 (2013): 17–50.

Movers, Franz C. *De utriusque recensionis vaticiniorum Ieremiae graecae alexandrinae et hebraicae masoreticae indole et origine commentatio critica*. Hamburg: Fredericus Partner, 1837.

Müller, Reinhard, Juha Pakkala, and Bas ter Haar Romeny. *Evidence of Editing: Growth and Change of Texts in the Hebrew Bible*. Atlanta, GA: The Society of Biblical Literature, 2013.

Müller, Reinhard, and Juha Pakkala, eds. *Insights into Editing in the Hebrew Bible and the Ancient Near East: What Does Documented Evidence Tell Us about the Transmission of Authoritative Texts?* Leuven: Peeters, 2017.

Rabin, Chaim, Shemaryahu Talmon, and Emanuel Tov. *The Hebrew University Bible: The Book of Jeremiah*. Jerusalem: Magnes, 1997.

Rofé, Alexander. *The Religion of Israel and the Text of the Hebrew Bible: Corrections in the Biblical Texts in the Light of the History of the Religion of Israel*. Jerusalem: Carmel, 2018. [In Hebrew.]

Rost, P. "Miszellen, I. Ein Schreibgebrauch bei den Sopherim und seine Bedeutung für die alttestamentliche Textkritik." *Orientalistische Literaturzeitung* 6 (1903): 403–7, 443–46. *Orientalistische Literaturzeitung* 7 (1904): 390–93, 479–83.

Schenker, Adrian, ed. *The Earliest Text of the Hebrew Bible: The Relationship between the Masoretic Text and the Hebrew Base of the Septuagint Reconsidered*. Atlanta, GA: Scholars Press, 2003.

Shepherd, Michael B. "A Study in Variant Literary Editions." In *Textuality and the Bible*, 61–77. Eugene, OR: Wipf & Stock, 2016.

Smith, K. L. "Data Processing the Bible: A Consideration of the Potential Use of the Computer in Biblical Studies." *Bulletin of the International Organization for Septuagint and Cognate Studies* 3 (1970): 12–14.

Thenius, Otto. *Die Bücher Samuels erklärt*, edited by M. Löhr. Leipzig: Hirzel, 1898.

Tigay, Jeffrey H., ed. *Empirical Models for Biblical Criticism*. Philadelphia, PA: University of Philadelphia, 1985.

Talshir, Zipora, and Dalia Amara, eds. *On the Border Line: Textual Meets Literary Criticism*. Beer Sheva: Ben-Gurion University of the Negev Press, 2005. [In Hebrew.]

Tigchelaar, Eibert J. C. "Editing the Hebrew Bible: An Overview of Some Problems." In *Editing the Bible: Assessing the Task Past and Present*, edited by John S. Kloppenborg and Judith H. Newman, 41–65. Atlanta, GA: The Society of Biblical Literature, 2012.

Toury, Gideon. *Descriptive Translation Studies—and Beyond*. Revised edition. Amsterdam: Benjamins Translations Library, 2012.

Tov, Emanuel. "Achievements and Trends in Computer-Assisted Biblical Studies." In *Proceedings of the Second International Colloquium. Bible and Computer: Methods, Tools, Results, Jérusalem, 9–13 juin 1988*, edited by C. Muller, 33–60. Paris: Champion; Geneva: Sladkine, 1989.

--------. "The Background and Origin of the Qumran Corpus of Scripture Texts." In *Sacred Texts and Disparate Interpretations: Qumran Manuscripts Seventy Years Later: Proceedings of the International Conference Held at the John Paul II Catholic University of Lublin, 24–26 October 2017*, edited by Henryk Drawnel, 50–65. Leiden: Brill, 2020.

--------. "Computer Assisted Research of the Greek and Hebrew Bible." In *Computer Assisted Analysis of Biblical Texts: Papers Read at the Workshop on the Occasion of the Tenth Anniversary of the "Werkgroep Informatika," Faculty of Theology, Vrije Universiteit, Amsterdam, November 5–6, 1987*, edited by Eep Talstra, 87–99. Amsterdam: Free University Press, 1989.

--------. "Eclectic Text Editions of Hebrew Scripture." In *Textual Criticism of the Hebrew Bible, Qumran, Septuagint: Collected Essays, Volume 3*, 121–31. Leiden: Brill, 2015.

--------. "Electronic Tools for Biblical Study at Home, at the University, and in the Classroom." In *Computer Assisted Research on the Bible in the 21st Century*, ed. Luis Vegas Montaner et al., 45–60. Piscataway, NJ: Gorgias, 2010.

———. "The Greek Biblical Texts from the Judean Desert." In *Hebrew Bible, Greek Bible, and Qumran: Collected Essays*, 339–64. Tübingen: Mohr Siebeck, 2008.

———. "The Last Stage of the Literary History of the Book of Jeremiah." In *The Oxford Handbook of the Book of Jeremiah*, edited by Edward Silver and Louis Stulman, 129–47. New York, NY: Oxford University Press, 2021.

———. "Modern Editions of the Hebrew Bible." In *Textual Developments, Collected Essays, Volume 4*, 77–96. Leiden: Brill, 2019.

———. "A New Generation of Biblical Research." In *Proceedings of the First International Colloquium. Bible and Computer: The Text, Louvain-la-Neuve (Belgique) 2–3–4 septembre 1985*, 413–43. Paris: Champion; Geneva: Sladkine, 1986.

———. "A New Volume in the Biblia Hebraica Quinta Series: Genesis, by Abraham Tal." In *Like Nails Firmly Fixed (Qoh 12:11): Essays on the Text and Language of the Hebrew and Greek Scriptures Presented to Peter J. Gentry on the Occasion of His Retirement*, edited by Phillip S. Marshall, John D. Meade, and J. Kiel, 15–35. Leuven: Peeters, 2022.

———. "The Philosophy of the Biblia Hebraica Quinta Edition." In *La Bible en face. Études textuelles et littéraires offertes en homage à Adrian Schenker, à l'occasion de ses quatre-vingts ans*, edited by Innocent Himbaza and Clemens. Locher. Cahiers de la Revue Biblique 95 (2020): 19–39.

———. "'Proto-Masoretic,' 'Pre-Masoretic,' 'Semi-Masoretic,' and 'Masoretic': A Study in Terminology and Textual Theory." In *Textual Developments, Collected Essays, Volume 4*, 195–213. Leiden: Brill, 2019.

———. "Recensional Differences between the MT and LXX of Ezekiel." In *The Greek and Hebrew Bible: Collected Essays on the Septuagint*, 397–410. Leiden: Brill, 1999.

———. "The Search for an Original Text Form of the Hebrew Bible: Theory and Praxis." *Contributions to Biblical Exegesis and Theology*. Leuven: Peeters, forthcoming.

———. *Studies in Textual Criticism, Collected Essays*, Volume 5, 403–24. Leiden: Brill, 2024.

———. "The Textual Base of the Biblical Quotations in Second Temple Compositions." In *Textual Developments, Collected Essays, Volume 4*, 3–20. Leiden: Brill, 2019.

———. "Textual Criticism of the Hebrew Bible in the Digital Age: Advantages and Disadvantages of the Use of Digital Tools." *Biblicum Jassyense, Romanian Journal for Biblical Philology and Hermeneutics* 8 (2021): 5–14.

———. *Textual Criticism of the Hebrew Bible*. 4th edition, revised and enlarged. Minneapolis, MN: Fortress, 2022.

———. "The Use of Computers in Biblical Research." In *Hebrew Bible, Greek Bible, and Qumran: Collected Essays*, 228–46. Tübingen: Mohr Siebeck, 2008.

———. "The Use of the Septuagint in Critical Commentaries." In *New Avenues in Biblical Exegesis in Light of the Septuagint*. Vol. 1. of *The Septuagint in Its Ancient Context, Philological, Historical and Theological Approaches*, edited by Leonardo Pessoa da Silva Pinto and Daniela Scialabba, 41–58. Turnhout: Brepols, 2022.

Tov, Emanuel, and F. H. Polak. *The Parallel Aligned Text of the Greek and Hebrew Bible.* Division of the *CATSS* database, codirected by Robert A. Kraft and Emanuel Tov. Module in the *Accordance* and *Logos* computer programs, 2005; with updates, 2006–.

Ulrich, Eugene C. *The Dead Sea Scrolls and the Developmental Composition of the Bible.* Leiden: Brill, 2015.

Wellhausen, Julius. *Der Text der Bücher Samuelis.* Göttingen: Vandenhoeck & Ruprecht, 1871.

Wiener, Harold M. "The Recensional Criticism of the Pentateuch." *Biblical Studies* 70 (1913): 278–90.

Williamson, H. G. M. "Do We Need A New Bible? Reflections on the Proposed Oxford Hebrew Bible." *Biblica* 90 (2009): 153–75.

--------. "Scribe and Scroll: Revisiting the Great Isaiah Scroll from Qumran." In *Making a Difference: Essays on the Bible and Judaism in Honor of Tamara Cohn Eskenazi*, edited by David J. A. Clines et al., 329–42. Sheffield: Sheffield Phoenix Press, 2012.

PART IV

Modern Culture

The Gendering Garden: Narrative Creations of Adam and Eve as Cisgender Prefiguration in Biblical, Rabbinic, and Contemporary Young Adult Literature

Daniel Vorpahl

Creation's Binary Surface Structure

Within the contextual frame of Jewish tradition, the origin of humankind, including its sex, appears to be well-documented in the first three chapters of Genesis, the first book of the Torah. Nevertheless, the biblical depiction of the creation of earth and life by God serves as a starting point for a continuous tradition-historical reception of humankind's sex and gender identities and their social relations. Contemporary studies in the Hebrew Bible and its reception cannot only reconstruct branches of these traditions in terms of a chronology but can also reflect their transmission-dynamics and deconstruct cultural processes of the establishment of gender roles and identities within traditional narratives.

My paper undertakes this same hermeneutical adventure, deconstructing the narrative creation of humankind's sexes and genders in biblical, rabbinic, and young adult literature by reference to Genesis 1–3, the Palestinian midrash *Genesis Rabbah* (fifth century CE) and Deborah Bodin Cohen's volume of teenage tales, *Lilith's Ark* (2006). Since the scope of this study is restricted to these few selected source texts, I do not aim for a complete history of ideas. Rather, I target an insight into the literary relatedness and cultural dynamics of the reception and construction of sex/gender roles and identities within the Jewish tradition from antiquity until today. In addition, I aim to demonstrate to what extent the contemporary study of the Bible and its reception can enter into dialogue with poststructuralist theories and fruitfully contribute to highly topical gender-discourses.[1] In my approach, I understand deconstruction as a hermeneutical concept that aims to expose the constructiveness of social roles and identities that are literarily imparted as natural, or at least traditional. The

---

[1] The potential of ancient religious texts' contribution to current challenges of gender studies is also reflected by U. Auga, *An Epistemology of Religion and Gender: Biopolitics – Performativity – Agency* (New York, NY: Routledge, 2020), 68.

tools of this revealing concept emerge from a combination of close-reading biblical exegesis, socio-philosophical theories, and historical-critical literary reception studies.[2]

A general structure of the biblical creation story is apparent from Gen 1:1 until the first verses of Genesis 2. The repeated contrapositions of heaven and earth (Gen 1:1, 15, 17, 20, 26, 28, 30; 2:1, 4), light and darkness (1:4–5, 15–16), day and night (1:5, 14, 16, 18), morning and evening (1:5, 8, 13, 19, 23, 31), sea and land (1:10, 20, 22, 26, 28), earth and earthling (2:5, 7), and not least man and woman (1:27), imply that the whole world is structured by opposing or complementary pairs.[3] This pattern is framed by further iterations and compositional parallelisms in the verses' structure, especially in Genesis 2. At least the text's surface structure, the sing-song of its reading, bets on the harmony of binarity. And as the world is here initially created as a paragon of perfection, without wasting any words on destruction or death, it appears to be intended for the balanced equilibrium of one thing and the other. According to the surface structure and rhythm of Genesis 1, the world's logic seems to operate in binary patterns of thought. This impression is intensified by the continual repetition of the stated conceptual pairs.

What disappears from view thereby, is a third component that is in fact continuously involved as well as being related to all these pairs: the creator, God. As the center of the system of creation, God escapes the structurality of this system, being perceptively located outside of it, so that "the center is not the center,"[4] as the deconstructivist philosopher Jacques Derrida characterizes such phenomena. Beyond that, the creative deity in Genesis is not merely creating pairs, but rather bringing them into being by separating elements or entities into others. Taking a closer look at Gen 1:7–10 for example, we find God separating the water into one water above and one water below, then identifying the water above as heaven, while the water below is again separated from the newly appearing dry land. Indeed, we find here a distinction of dry land, sea and heaven (which then continues in Gen 1:20, 26, 28), and therefore a picture of a world that is more complex than the pair of above and below. Equally, it is continuously said that it became evening and it became morning (Gen 1:5,

---

[2] The development of biblical exegesis into reception studies, including discourse analysis and intertextuality, is expounded in the methodological chapter of my dissertation: D. Vorpahl, *Aus dem Leben des Buches Jona: Rezeptionswissenschaftliche Methodik und innerjüdischer Rezeptionsdiskurs* (Berlin: De Gruyter, 2021), 19–35.

[3] See also R. Brubaker, "Social Theory as Habitus," in *Bourdieu: Critical Perspectives*, ed. C. Calhoun et al. (Chicago, IL: Chicago University Press, 1993), 221.

[4] J. Derrida, "Structure, Sign and Play in the Discourse of the Human Sciences," in *Writing and Difference*, trans. A. Bass (London: Routledge, 1990), 279.

8, 13, 19, 23, 31), thus we have an awareness that the becoming itself is each time an entity of endless shades of dusk and dawn, framing a day with several further spaces of time.

A close reading of the biblical creation story thereby reveals that dualisms do not at all correspond with the complexity of life. The evening is not explained to its full extent by differentiating it from the morning, as it is also the end of a day, or the beginning of a night. Structuralism, beginning with the linguist Ferdinand de Saussure, argues that "no element can function as a sign without referring to another element which itself is not simply present."[5] But, as Jacques Derrida added, this "interplay of signification has [actually] no limit,"[6] but the "presence of an element is always a signifying and substitute reference inscribed in a system of differences and the movement of a chain."[7]

Nevertheless, the binary surface structure of the biblical creation story persists and has its tradition-formative impact. Within the Hebrew Bible alone, the reception of God as the creator of heaven and earth,[8] the contraposition of morning and evening,[9] or the perception of women and men as a correlated contrastive pair[10] are generally acknowledged among a whole "series of mythico-ritual oppositions."[11] In places where the philosopher Pierre Bourdieu in principle locates the embedding of the "opposition of the sexes,"[12] I recognize a structure of thinking that spawns the heteronormative binary of the human sexes and legitimizes its social gender expressions.

Binary Patterns of Thought in the Garden of Eden

My argument is that the creation story's binary surface structure also shapes the creation of humankind, in Gen 1:26–28 as in Gen 2:7–25, and subsequently dictates the rhythm of construction of a binary cis-gender culture and the

---

5   J. Derrida, "Semiology and Grammatology. Interview with Julia Kristeva," in *Positions*, trans. A. Bass (Chicago, IL: The University of Chicago Press, 1981), 26.
6   Derrida, "Structure," 281.
7   Ibid., 292.
8   See, e.g., Gen 14:19, 27:28, Exod 31:17, Deut 4:39, 1 Chr 29:11, Ezra 5:11, Ps 115:15, Isa 37:16, and Jer 32:17.
9   See, e.g., Deut 28:67, 1 Sam 17:16, 1 Kgs 17:6, 1 Chr 16:40, and Ps 30:6.
10 See, e.g., Gen 5:2, 24:16, 26:11, Lev 20:11, and Deut 22:5.
11 P. Bourdieu, *Masculine Domination* (Stanford, CA: Stanford University Press, 2001), 18.
12 Ibid.

establishment of heteronormativity within the Hebrew Bible and its subsequent traditions.[13]

This assumption rests on two premises. The first is that the biblical creation narrative is a sequence of divine speech acts according to the perceptual convention of the world in which the ancient Near Eastern recipients lived. God utters and designates what immediately comes into being, from heaven, over the line of the horizon, through the sea, until the shoreline and solid ground (Gen 1:3–10, 14–25). The performative utterances of God become manifestations of the transcendent word in the immanent world. The biblical creation story is hence an epitome of speech act theory according to J. L. Austin.[14] And in Genesis 1–2, performative utterances are established as an effective tool to create a fait accompli.

Austin's discovery of "the performative use of language,"[15] its ability to execute action instead of being only descriptive, provides the basis for the understanding of performativity as the core feature of gender, developed by Judith Butler.[16] Butler's theory that "the gendered body is performative" and "has no ontological status apart from the various acts which constitute its reality"[17] marks the second premise of my argument. In this analysis, performativity refers not to a singular 'act of performance,' but to "a reiteration of a norm or a set of norms"[18] that "produces the effects that it names."[19] The biblical creation story makes a major contribution to the normativization of such effects that were culturally internalized as expressions of gender.

In Gen 1:26–28, the binary pattern of thinking that I expounded at the outset of this article is apparent: God creates the earthling (האדם/*ha'adam*) likewise male (זכר/*zakhar*) and female (נקבה/*neqevah*, Gen 1:27). The following verse's commandment of multiplication (Gen 1:28) implies that these two variants of the human being are intended for sexual reproduction and could therefore consider themselves to be correlated biological sexes. Similar to the

---

13   See also C. L. Meyers, *Rediscovering Eve: Ancient Israelite Women in Context* (New York, NY: Oxford University Press, 2012), 60.

14   See J. L. Austin, *How To Do Things With Words: The William James Lectures delivered at Harvard University in 1955* (Oxford: Oxford University Press, 1976), 5–6.

15   J. H. Gill, *Words, Deeds, Bodies: L. Wittgenstein, J. L. Austin, M. Merleau-Ponty, and M. Polanyi* (Leiden: Brill, 2019), 24.

16   See J. Butler, *Gender Trouble: Feminism and the Subversion of Identity* (New York, NY: Routledge, 1999), 178–9.

17   Ibid., 173.

18   J. Butler, *Bodies That Matter: On The Discursive Limits of "Sex"* (New York, NY: Routledge, 1993), 12.

19   Ibid., 2.

separation of water into heaven, sea and finally land (Gen 1:7–10), one entity (water/human) is split into two forms (heaven and sea/male and female), with the final outcome of a new third entity (land/offspring), which corresponds to the more complex reality of life underneath the binary surface structure of creation as described above. But this complexity is camouflaged by the ascription of heteronormativity, as it is no longer God but humankind itself that becomes responsible for re-creation. The earthling's binarity is no longer a condition in a series of events of the creation, but becomes a performative identity, in particular if זכר (*zakhar*) and נקבה (*neqevah*) are translated, interpreted, or actually embodied as man and woman.

Although Gen 5:2 explicates that אדם (*adam*) is the generic term for both sex variants already in Gen 1:27,[20] for a number of verses the text speaks only about the primordial human *ha'adam* and *his* woman (*ishah*, Gen 2:25; 3:8, 17, 20; 4:1). This exemplifies that even the claim for "equality *as* woman in contrast to *the* man" must bow to the idea of a natural sex/gender binarity in a competitive and likewise "heteronormative fashion."[21] Moreover, the consequential rabbinic interpretation that the first human being was androgynous (GenR 8:1)[22] offers no way out of this binary pattern of thinking, as the term אנדרוגינוס (*androginos*) is nevertheless a binary composition, namely of the ancient Greek *andros* (man) and *gyne* (woman).

The second story of the earthling's creation in Gen 2:7–25 is no less binary. However, it is often emphasized that Genesis 2 focuses on the social coexistence of the human being instead on its reproduction.[23] In Gen 2:18, God declares that it is not good for the earthling to be on their own. But the inferred identification of the human as a social being disregards that God is not looking for companion for the earthling, but for exactly one equivalent counterpart (Gen 2:20). The creation story's binary pattern of thinking is also influential in this socially oriented creation of humankind, although in the everyday reality of ancient Israel the individual human being lived not as part of a couple but in close companionship with social circles of immediate family and extended kin, which merged together in nomadic tribal groups.[24] Indeed, even marriage

---

20   See also Meyers, *Rediscovering Eve*, 71.
21   Auga, *An Epistemology of Religion*, 59 (accentuations in the original).
22   See also Meyers, *Rediscovering Eve*, 73.
23   See R. A. Simkins, "Gender Construction in the Yahwist Creation Myth," in *Genesis: A Feminist Companion to the Bible*, ed. A. Brenner (Sheffield: Sheffield Academic Press Ltd, 1998), 44–5.
24   See N. P. Lemche, *Ancient Israel: A New History of Israel* (London: Bloomsbury T & T Clark, 2015), 26–7 and 98–102.

existed in numerous forms, including polygamy.[25] No less out of touch with this ancient ethnic group's reality is the statement that the man will leave his parents to cling to his wife (Gen 2:24), as the ancient Israel was a patrilocal culture.[26]

To acknowledge the mechanism of action evident in these binary thought patterns is mandatory to understand the societal model of a heteronormative cis-gender relation which gets its final shape in the further garden narrative. Each and any construction of dualisms generates a lack of differentiation and fuels simplification, which subsequently promotes the exercise of power, as one can solely act from just one of two opposing sides. To phrase it from a Bourdieuic angle: binary oppositions symbolize "hierarchical relations of difference,"[27] which correspond to a concept of power. And this is what we find in the garden narrative, at the latest in Genesis 3, but clearly already prepared in the chapter before.

After the manufacturing of the earthling (האדם/ha'adam) out of the earth (האדמה/ha'adamah) in Gen 2:7, a woman (אשה/ishah) is made out of the human being (האדם/ha'adam) and brought to it (Gen 2:22). Only now the species of the human being is differentiated into two sex/gender identities: woman (אשה/ishah) and man (איש/ish), whereby the former is derived from the latter, who is and remains identical with the primordial earthling (Gen 2:23). Both man's and woman's coming-into-being is dependent on the other's, as they only come into existence by being distinguishable from each other.[28] But unlike Derrida's deconstructivist approach,[29] the differentiating reference of *ish* and *ishah* is presented as binary and not unlimited, despite the fact that according to Gen 2:19–20, 23 they are likewise different from all other animals. The normativization of this binary gender model is then clearly recognizable when, in the rabbinic tradition, other sex/gender identities, such as *ailonit* or *saris*, are solely defined by their difference with respect to the female and male sex/gender identity (m. Nid. 5:9).

Distinguishing both creation narratives of humankind as the origin of a reproductive sex (Gen 1:27–28) and a social gender (Gen 2:7–25) cannot hide

---

25 See K. Southwood, "The Social and Cultural History of Ancient Israel," in *The Hebrew Bible: A Critical Companion*, ed. J. Barton (Princeton, NJ: Princeton University Press, 2016), 68–9.

26 See A. Kalmanofsky, *Gender-Play in the Hebrew Bible: The Ways the Bible Challenges Its Gender Norms* (London/New York, NY: Routledge, 2017), 36.

27 L. McCall, "Does Gender Fit? Bourdieu, Feminism, and Concepts of Social Order," *Theory and Society* 21, no. 6 (1992), 838.

28 See also Kalmanofsky, *Gender-Play*, 35.

29 See Derrida, "Structure," 292.

the fact that both are developed within binary patterns of thought, which gives rise to a "gender-role plan"[30] beginning with Genesis 2:22–24. Considering at least rudiments of binary gender equality within the garden narrative, it is often emphasized that in Gen 2:18, 20 the term עֵזֶר (*ezer*) "connotes a mentor-superior in the Bible rather than an assistant and is used frequently for the relation of God to Israel (and not for the relation of Israel to God)."[31] Linguistically, the fitting helper that God aims to provide for the earthling is indeed not intended to be a general servant but rather an equal partner in everyday life. But according to Amy Kalmanofsky, woman and man appear in Gen 2:24 to be even "more than complementary figures; they are [an] interchangeable … undifferentiated unit … not defined by hierarchy, but by symmetry."[32] Analogously, Ronald Simkins sees the gender-roles in Genesis 2 as not yet developed and differentiated, but being pronounced within a matrimonial structure.[33] And so does Kalmanofsky's image of the earthling and *his* woman as husband and wife incidentally confirm the impact of heteronormative binarity. But even with the best will, I cannot confirm her reading of a harmoniously social equality of man and woman in the manner initially purported by the term עֵזֶר (*ezer*).

Indeed, Gen 2:22–24 formulates no parallelisms at all: The earthling notes that the woman is taken from his flesh and bone. That is, it is not the other way around, nor is it recognized that both are made of the same flesh and bone. He receives the woman from God instead of being mutually introduced, and he recognizes and designates her as woman in deduced differentiation from himself. Also, it is stated that he will cling to her, while her will is not even articulated, until they finally unify symbolically into one flesh. This narration of the origin of binary genders and their relation is one-dimensional, "presented entirely from the masculine point of view; it is the man who decides that Eve is his soulmate and it is the male who searches for a partner, with no indication that the love he bears her is reciprocated,"[34] as Lisa Maurice puts it forthrightly. The relation of the first two humans, as described in Genesis 2, may indeed be neither explicitly hierarchical nor equal, but at the most complementary, in a

---

30   Simkins, "Gender Construction," 38.
31   T. Frymer-Kensky, "The Bible and Women's Study," in *Studies in Bible and Feminist Criticism* (Philadelphia, PA: The Jewish Publication Society, 2006), 168.
32   Kalmanofsky, *Gender-Play*, 36.
33   See Simkins, "Gender Construction," 45.
34   L. Maurice, "Tempting Treasures and Seductive Snakes: Presenting Eve and Pandora for the Youngest Readers," in *Gender, Creation Myths and Their Reception in Western Civilization: Prometheus, Pandora, Adam and Eve*, ed. L. Maurice and T. Bibring (London: Bloomsbury Academic, 2022), 76.

distinct one-dimensional way.³⁵ Subsequently, a rabbinic tradition even tells that the earthling requested the woman from God as his partner (GenR 17:4). So far, we can say that Gen 2:22–24 is not only binary and heteronormative but also androcentric, wherein, in my assessment, it becomes apparent how the creation story's binary patterns of thought fundamentally structure "the embodied gendered dialectic."³⁶

To maintain the social-relation-perspective within Genesis 2, it has to be observed that the human beings are not taken as a starting point to search for the configuration of social roles, but that the set-up of their social relation seems to be rather predefined by the principles of reproduction and androcentric satisfaction of needs. In fact, since the very beginning, the gender roles of the then-still-unnamed Eve and Adam have to fit in with a binary, limited, heteronormative relational model. As I will expand in the following section, this is an example of *epistemic violence* in the way that Ulrike Auga explains and uses the term.³⁷ Thereby, it is decisive that the compulsory provision of the knowledge of categorical role ascriptions for man and woman in Genesis 2–3 likewise hides and enhances the binarity of gender.

The Naturalization of Adam and Eve

The initial creational pattern of reproduction (Gen 1:27–28) and the circular reasoning that *ish* (man) and *isha* (woman) in Gen 2:23 are embodiments of *zakhar* (male) and *neqevah* (female) lead to the establishment of heterosexuality as the normative mode of life. From there the process of normativization continues through the assignment of gender roles to the first two human beings, namely as mother, wife, patriarch and breadwinner (Gen 3:16–20). These ascribed roles hide the binary scaffold that lies underneath and generates the basic rhythm for the composition of the whole song of gender binarity, whose melody has become established as our cultural soundtrack. A huge stake in this sociocultural process has the naturalization of heteronormative sex/gender binarity. It is majorly based on the fact that these role ascriptions

---

35 A cynical interpretation of the gender-inequality as prospects in regard to the imperfect worldly living conditions, contrary to the paradisiac circumstances in Gan Eden, is offered by Tikva Frymer-Kensky, saying the garden narrative simply announces "that gender inequality is the norm of the imperfect universe." Frymer-Kensky, "The Bible and Women's Study," 167.

36 B. Skeggs, "Context and Background: Pierre Bourdieu's Analysis of Class, Gender and Sexuality," *The Sociological Review* 52, no. 2 (2004), 22.

37 See Auga, *An Epistemology of Religion*, 53.

are an immediate part of the creation of woman and man as social variants of the earthling, fitting seamlessly with the two biological sexes who received the commandment of sexual reproduction. The historical context of this process is "a society that places a premium on procreation [and therefore] has to justify and naturalize the sexual act required to procreate and thereby naturalize heterosexuality."[38] When Genesis 2–3 ascribes the essence of two gender-identities (*ish* and *isha*) to the binary sex-entities (*zakhar* and *neqevah*) a socio-cultural process of naturalization is taking place, as explained by Pierre Bourdieu:

> Because the social principle of vision constructs the anatomical difference and because this socially constructed difference becomes the basis and apparently natural justification of the social vision which founds it.[39]

By the time that Eve (Gen 3:20) and Adam (Gen 4:25) are individually named, they already embody immovable gender roles. When Eve is named by the earthling as the "mother of all living" (Gen 3:20), it is a matter of *vaticinium ex eventu*, a literarily created destiny, as the woman was initially made to fulfill sexual reproduction with *ha'adam* (Gen 2:24), who will finally keep this term as his name (Gen 4:25).[40] The construction of the woman's body follows the target of reproduction, first formulated in Gen 1:27–28, and so does her punishment at the end of the garden narrative (Gen 3:16). The derivation of Eve's name finalizes this heteronormative naturalization of her gender identity, which is then body-visually reflected in the rabbinic literature by describing the woman as a constructed vessel for the storage of fetuses (GenR 18:3).[41] The woman's social role is thus completely deduced from the functional aim of her body's initial creation, which is not the case for the man's social role. Although he was initially made to cultivate the land (Gen 2:5, 15), which surely corresponds with Gen 3:17–19, the male earthling (*ha'adam*) was also charged to procreate (Gen 1:28). Vice versa both, female and male earthling, were initially made to rule the world, to dominate over the animals (Gen 1:28), and to generate food from the vegetation (Gen 1:29). But the binary gender distinction that

---

38   D. Guest, *Beyond Feminist Biblical Studies* (Sheffield: Sheffield Phoenix Press, 2012), 106.
39   Bourdieu, *Masculine Domination*, 11.
40   See Meyers, *Rediscovering Eve*, 72, and J. Gellman, "Gender and Sexuality in the Garden of Eden," *Theology & Sexuality* 12, no. 3 (2006), 323.
41   See also D. Vorpahl, "The Body as a Wonderland: Rabbinic Talk of the Human Body as a Sex/Gender Construction," in *Constructions of Gender in Religious Traditions of Late Antiquity*, ed. S. Sheinfeld and K. Ehrensperger (Lanham, MD: Academic Fortress, 2024), 257–280.

"constructs the body as a sexually defined reality"[42] founds a social order of masculine domination, which Pierre Bourdieu sees expressed in the gendered structures of labor division, space, and time.[43] These social structures are vindicated by circumstances that they actually create, namely by means of binary patterned identities of gender, which "is one of the most silent and invisible epistemological fundaments of knowledge."[44] That the described binary patterns of thought became a dominant form of thinking within the production of knowledge must be identified as an example of epistemic violence, according to Ulrike Auga.[45]

By negating the similarities and abilities that man and woman should share, and avoiding differences among men and among women,[46] but overemphasizing a sexual difference, while at the same time Adam is presented as the normative human being (*ha'adam*),[47] difference becomes the essence of female gender identity, as Simone de Beauvoir expressed in the title of her book *The Second Sex* (*Le Deuxième Sexe*, 1949). A rabbinic tradition then uses the woman's origin from the (male) earthling's body to argue that, contrary to the man, she shall need perfume, have a loud voice, and be stubborn (GenR 17:8). Beyond the biblical depiction, the rabbis not only describe the woman as essentially different, but further use this constructed difference to depict her as deficient, which in turn strengthens the normativity of the man. The one discrepancy between the prototypically imagined female and male body, namely the ability to ovulate, conceive and give birth, and breastfeed, is turned into Eve's prior role, at the latest by the end of Genesis 3. Although Carol Meyers reads the first part of Gen 3:16 not as a threat of "pangs in childbearing" but as an announcement for the woman's duty of work and pregnancy,[48] this means a double burden at best, in respect of the ancient Israelite's daily life reality, as explained in the following subchapter.

On the other hand, Adam is finally established as a cultural human being, responsible for breadwinning by agriculture. In contrast to the woman's duty,

---

42 Bourdieu, *Masculine Domination*, 11.
43 See ibid., 9–11.
44 Auga, *An Epistemology of Religion*, 53.
45 See ibid.
46 See McCall, "Does Gender Fit?," 849.
47 The normativization of maleness as the original form of the human being is then further established within the rabbinic tradition when male fetuses are declared to be fully developed after forty-one days, and female fetuses only after eighty-one days (m. Nid. 3:7), which continues in the higher social estimation of boys towards girls (b. Ber. 60a). See also Vorpahl, "The Body as a Wonderland," 260.
48 See Meyers, *Rediscovering Eve*, 89–91.

the man's is not bodily induced, as "the masculine order"[49] has no need for legitimation at all. The physical aspect of his duty's profile can be likewise fulfilled by the woman, as one needs no penis to cultivate land.[50] De facto the punishments of Gen 3:16–19 manifest gender prototypes of the ancient Israelite society: "the first man's role as a farmer and the first woman's role as a mother symbolize the appropriate behavior for all Israelite men and women."[51] Such prototypical gender-role-ascriptions must be clearly differentiated from the idea of so called "archetypes," which shall manifest "qualities and behaviors common to all men and women,"[52] as Amy Kalmanofsky explains in accordance with Carol Meyers. Because "gender has a cultural meaning which is ascribed to the human body, but not an inherent attribute of personhood or subjectivity,"[53] as Auga states according to Butler and Austin. There are no such things as natural gender identities but the social construct of a patriarchal, androcentric society in which the owning of land was normally not conceded to women, trapping them in economic dependence on men.[54] This is an example of power relations that are based on epistemic sovereignty, finding expression in a structural domination that Bourdieu would label as symbolic violence.[55]

Reproduction as Symbolic Capital

At least within the rabbinic tradition, agriculture is also regarded as a metaphor for procreation,[56] which comes as no surprise. Metaphors play a big part in processes of naturalization, as our "ordinary conceptual system, in terms of which we both think and act, is fundamentally metaphorical."[57] Metaphors are a linguistic tool for describing what we see or what we perceive without seeing, or sometimes of what we just assume by interpretation. When one comes

---

49 Bourdieu, *Masculine Domination*, 9.
50 For a list of text-related essentials for highland agriculture see Meyers, *Rediscovering Eve*, 81–2.
51 Simkins, "Gender Construction," 48.
52 Kalmanofsky, *Gender-Play*, 42.
53 Auga, *An Epistemology of Religion*, 61.
54 See Frymer-Kensky, "The Bible and Women's Study," 160. The single case of the daughters of Zelophehad in Num 27:1–8, who aim for a distributive share of their father's land and receive it because he had no sons, simply demonstrates the rarity of such exceptions.
55 See Bourdieu, *Masculine Domination*, 34–5.
56 See Simkins, "Gender Construction," 39, and Bourdieu, *Masculine Domination*, 13.
57 G. Lakoff and M. Johnson, *Metaphors We Live By* (Chicago, IL: The University of Chicago Press, 1980), 3.

to think of it, the earth (*ha'adamah*) gives birth to the earthling (*ha'adam*) by the impact of God (GenR 14:7–8; 17:8).[58] Then *ha'adam's* body gives birth to the woman (*ish*), again by the impact of God (GenR 17:8; 18:2). This essentially means that when the woman becomes Eve ("the mother of all living," Gen 3:20) and is afflicted with the maternal role, she actually receives this 'natural' destiny as a sort of male, but also divine, heritage.

Within the Bible, a picture language is kept alive, which sees the male semen as the source of life (Gen 3:15; Num 5:28; Pss 89:30, 37; 105:6), similar to a fruit's seed, while the woman's body is seen to function as soil or incubator,[59] as Ronald Simkins explains:

> The woman's role in procreation is metaphorically compared to the arable land's. Like the soil, a woman nurtures to full development the seed that is planted within her.[60] [But the] arable land is dependent upon the man to bring forth vegetation. It will remain a barren desert without the man to till it and sow seed in it. Similarly, the woman's ability to bear children is dependent upon her husband, who must first impregnate her.[61]

The garden narrative in particular spawned a number of such metaphors, whose symbolic meanings also transport cultural gender norms: the fruit (within European art history, often depicted as an apple), the serpent, or man and woman beneath a tree.[62]

Proceeding from Simkins' interpretation of a metaphorical parallelism between the man's sowing of seeds into the soil to produce vegetation and the similar act done to the woman's body to give birth to a child,[63] we may likewise adapt Pierre Bourdieu's use of the term capital to the concept of reproduction within the context of Ancient Near Eastern society.[64] This allows us to realize that reproduction work for a woman does not have the same value as for a man, as she "cannot escape the consequences of such capital when compared to other types of cultural capital."[65] According to his selective use of different

---

58 "[T]he creation of humans from dirt or clay is a common ANE metaphor. [...] In the Mesopotamian creation myths the fashioning of clay served as a metaphor for gestation during pregnancy." Simkins, "Gender Construction," 41.
59 See ibid., 46.
60 Ibid., 51.
61 Ibid., 49.
62 See ibid., 38 and Meyers, *Rediscovering Eve*, 63.
63 See Simkins, "Gender Construction," 51.
64 See McCall, "Does Gender Fit?," 841.
65 Ibid., 845.

forms of capital,⁶⁶ it seems misleading to identify reproduction as a *cultural* capital in the Bourdieuic sense, especially in light of the distinction between ancient societies and the modern ones that Bourdieu took into account. In the patriarchal ancient Israelite society, reproduction is not even just a physical capital, but also an economic one. Both values are in general ascribed to men, being successfully transformed into a symbolic capital, which Bourdieu uses to describe the social appreciation of an achievement or competence that cannot be proven.⁶⁷ Within the historical context of ancient Israelite society, biological fatherhood could not be proven, but abundance of especially male children had a positive influence on the social status of a man (Gen 15:1–6, 22:15–18) and the maintenance of his legacy.⁶⁸ Women on the other hand were expected to fulfil the social role of a mother in the face of an infant mortality rate of about fifty percent, which meant a continuous load of pregnancy, birth pang, feeding and childcare in view of enormous health hazards,⁶⁹ plus a continuous exclusion from socio-cultic activities (Lev 12:1–8). Carol Meyers qualifies this perspective by emphasizing that "women exercised managerial power"⁷⁰ in the household, and further argues that "both genders would find unending days of toil unwelcome. But women generally have positive feelings about producing offspring."⁷¹ Two pages later Meyers contradicts this gender-binary stereotype, probably unwittingly, by contextualizing that "[t]he more pregnancies a woman had, the greater her own risk of dying."⁷²

Given this social perspective of reproductive work, it must indeed be questioned, "whether gendered forms of capital, possessed by women, can in fact unequivocally function as profitable capital."⁷³ I would argue that within the patriarchal ancient Israelite society, reproduction became a symbolic capital for men, but not for women. This is due to its close connectedness to gender, which is itself an asymmetric form of symbolic capital hidden by naturalization.⁷⁴ With this in mind, Gen 3:16, 20 appears as a cultural inscription of social

---

66 See P. Bourdieu. "The Forms of Capital." In *Handbook of Theory and Research for the Sociology of Education*, ed. J. Richardson (New York, NY: Greenwood Press, 1986), 241–58.
67 See ibid., 245.
68 See Meyers, *Rediscovering Eve*, 97–8.
69 See ibid., 100.
70 Ibid., 97.
71 Ibid.
72 Ibid., 99.
73 McCall, "Does Gender Fit?," 846.
74 See Skeggs, "Context and Background," 23.

power relations within the female body.⁷⁵ Its reading as a natural essence of womanhood leads then to the ascription of women's social status in labor division, space, and time,⁷⁶ as Bourdieu states clearly:

> Far from the necessities of biological reproduction determining the symbolic organization of the sexual division of labour and, ultimately, of the whole natural and social order, it is an arbitrary construction of the male and female body, of its uses and functions, especially in biological reproduction, which gives an apparently natural foundation to the androcentric view of the division of sexual labour and the sexual division of labour.⁷⁷

The Rabbis' Binding of Eve

The first act of sexual reproduction within the Torah takes place in Gen 4:1 and is expressed with the term ידע (*yada*), to be literally translated as 'to know', which is a term used only infrequently in the Bible to refer to sexual intercourse. Wherever it is used in this sense within the Torah, it almost exclusively describes the male perspective of a heteronormative penetration of a woman (Gen 4:1, 17, 25; 19:5; 24:16). In the rest of the Bible, this usage is even less common, although occasionally adapted to a female perspective (Num 31:17; Judg 11:39). But the conventional use of the term ידע (*yada*) expresses perception and knowledge, which puts another complexion on its meaning in Gen 4:1, appearing to be an intellectualization of heteronormatively male penetration, if not even a parallelization of phallus and logos. This is all the more astonishing as the term ידע (*yada*) is seldomly used this way, while it appears as knowledge (*yada*) in the immediately preceding chapter, where it was the woman's intention to receive the knowledge of good and bad by eating from the forbidden fruit (Gen 3:5–6).

The conversation of woman and serpent that leads to the emancipatory act of picking and eating the fruit from the tree of knowledge of good and bad (Gen 3:6) reveals that the woman has already developed intellectual skills (Gen 3:1–5).⁷⁸ However, it is only the male earthling who names the animals (Gen 2:20), distinguishes the human being into man and woman by a performative utterance (Gen 2:23), and finally names Eve in Gen 3:20, which is an

---

75 Carol Meyers states that Gen 3:16 is "giving the man and henceforth all men mastery in marital sex – but not dominance in all aspects of life." Meyers, *Rediscovering Eve*, 96.
76 See Bourdieu, *Masculine Domination*, 9–11.
77 Ibid., 23.
78 See also Meyers, *Rediscovering Eve*, 80.

expression of cultural domination.[79] According to a rabbinic tradition passed down in the aggadic midrash *Genesis Rabbah* (fifth century CE), Adam was even the name giver of himself and God (GenR 17:4). But in the Torah's garden narrative the woman is not just his silent sidekick, but actually "the more active character."[80] In Gen 3:1–6 the woman's "high level of linguistic ability"[81] appears as a counterpart to the serpent's well-developed communication skills.[82] As the literary scholar Nehama Aschkenasy explains, the woman's reception of the tree as "desirable" (Gen 3:6) goes beyond simple observation, but shows that "her language is conceptual,"[83] analogously to her report that the serpent "beguiled" her (Gen 3:13): She "first creates the concept of seduction before she reports on the physical act of eating," while the man in Gen 3:12 "describes an automatic act of putting in his mouth something that was given to him."[84] Gerald Blidstein attributes this automatism as "typical husbandly fashion,"[85] setting a further example of stereotypical gender role ascription within the academic reception of the garden narrative.

Unlike her man, the woman acts independently and reflectively.[86] Her reflectivity strengthens the reading of the garden narrative as a story of emancipation and autonomous action, while in the rabbinic tradition the woman's punishment is even extended (GenR 17:8). Otherwise, GenR 17:2 compiles quotations of several rabbis, explaining that each man needs a wife for the sake of the good in his life, and to complete the heteronormative pair that the earthling initially is in the image of God according to Gen 5:1–2. But the rabbis have their own approach to the initial suitability of the woman as helper (עֵזֶר/*ezer*) of the earthling by focusing on the subsequent preposition כנגדו (*kenegdo*, "correlating to him") in Gen 2:18, interpreting this preposition as confrontational rather than analogical: "if one merits, she is a helper [*ezer*], but if not, she is against him [*kenegdo*]" (GenR 17:3). Instead of inevitably becoming a correlated counterpart, the woman appears here to be also a potential antagonist of

---

79   See Kalmanofsky, *Gender-Play*, 40.
80   Meyers, *Rediscovering Eve*, 59.
81   N. Aschkenasy, *Woman at The Window: Biblical Tales of Oppression and Escape* (Detroit, MI: Wayne State University Press, 1998), 126.
82   See D. Vorpahl, "A Donkey That Speaks Is a Donkey No Less: Talking Animals in the Hebrew Bible and Its Early Jewish Reception." In *Speaking Animals in Ancient Literature*, ed. H. Schmalzgruber (Heidelberg: Universitätsverlag Winter, 2020), 513–5.
83   Aschkenasy, *Woman at The Window*, 126.
84   Ibid., 127.
85   G. J. Blidstein, *In the Rabbis' Garden: Adam and Eve in the Midrash* (Northvale, NJ: Jason Aronson Inc., 1997), 44.
86   See Kalmanofsky, *Gender-Play*, 39.

the (male) earthling. But likewise, it expresses that the obligation is upon the man to merit how his woman deals with him. The converse argument then says that the woman's acting is a permanent re-acting to the man, which means a notable restriction of her autonomy of action.

This boundedness of woman and man is based on the hidden legitimacy of a binary pattern of thinking, whose androcentric direction leads to a general challenging of the woman's independence of mind and action. Therefore, rabbinic traditions deal with the question of what the man might be doing during the woman's conversation with the serpent (GenR 19:3). Instead of reflecting upon the serpent's general intention to talk to the earthling,[87] most scholars delve further into the question of the man's whereabouts, assuming that it is more expected of the serpent to talk to the man.[88] It is not that the whereabouts of the man in Gen 3:1–6 are not a matter of exegetical interest, but rather a reflection of greater amazement that the serpent addresses the woman instead of the man. Thus, this analysis speaks for the establishment of androcentric binary patterns of thought. This becomes even more obvious when the question is turned around, asking why God obviously addresses only the male earthling in Gen 3:9–12.

In consequence, the rabbis quoted in *Genesis Rabbah* explain the woman's autonomous acting in Gen 3:1–5 by the temporary absence of the male earthling, leaving the following statement that her man was "with her" (עמה/*imah*, Gen 3:6) when she shared the fruit astonishingly unrecognized.[89] The rabbis' assumptions are that the man either had fallen asleep after having sexual intercourse with his woman, or that meanwhile God gave him a tour of the entire world (GenR 19:3).

This reading is also influenced by a preceded discrediting of the female creature in general. According to GenR 18:2 God had initial doubts about which body part should become the source for the female earthling. A subsequent commentated series of items explains that the woman was not made from the head, so that she may not pridefully raise it, not from the eye, so that she may not look around coquettishly, not from the ear, so that she may not eavesdrop, not from the hand, so that she may not touch and steal, and not from the foot, so that she may not prowl (GenR 18:2). Following this, a number of biblical

---

87 See Vorpahl, "A Donkey That Speaks," 515–6.
88 See Kalmanofsky, *Gender-Play*, 36–7, and Blidstein, *In the Rabbis' Garden*, 21–2.
89 See also Blidstein, *In the Rabbis' Garden*, 21–2. Restrictively I have to emphasize that I do not share Blidstein's presupposition of a "bourgeoise" atmosphere in which "the serpent would never have dared approach her" if Adam would have been around to protect her, depicting Eve as the serpent's vulnerable prey (ibid., 22–3).

quotations are used to verify that these and other putative defects of character are nevertheless essential characteristics of women (GenR 18:2).

This method of elimination rather secondarily explains the creation of the woman from a human rib, while it primarily lists a number of stereotypical gender-role-ascriptions in association with a biological human body. By ascribing the danger of these embodied attributes to a primordial womanhood, these stereotypes are naturalized even beyond divine purpose. Beyond that, the female earthling's character traits are here tied to the male earthling's source material, which confirms that in the rabbinic episteme the woman's creation out of *ha'adam*'s flesh and bone (Gen 2:23) is not an accomplishment of equality but an embodiment of the hierarchical relation of a compulsory binary pair. Against the woman's autonomy of action in Gen 3:1–6, the rabbinic traditions in *Genesis Rabbah* carry out a binding of the primordial woman on male power.

Releasing Eve to a Cisgender Prefiguration

Rabbi Deborah Bodin Cohen understands her anthology *Lilith's Ark* (2006) explicitly as a continuation of the narrative tradition established within the classical rabbinic literature, addressing it to a Jewish teenage readership.[90] Bodin Cohen's self-sufficient genre association is based on the book's formation process: merging a sensitive Bible reading with traditional commentaries and historical details, recognizing gaps and tensions, filling them sensitively with her own and others' experiences and imagination.[91] By locating her book forthright standing in the tradition of midrash the author not only expresses her awareness of those ways of reading and the necessity to react to them. She also legitimizes her own literary innovation by reference to the continuity of this tradition, for herself and for her readership.[92] Likewise, she creates for them a literary area of freedom that is exempted from other authorities and offers space for subjectivization along one's own belief and power of imagination.

In the anthology's first story, *Eve: The Seeds of an Apple*, the author depicts the female earthling (consistently called Eve) in the Garden of Eden as a

---

90 See D. Bodin Cohen, *Lilith's Ark: Teenage Tales of Biblical Women* (Philadelphia, PA: The Jewish Publication Society, 2006), ix–x.
91 Compare Bodin Cohen, *Lilith's Ark*, ix–x, and Y. Hayim Yerushalmi, *Zakhor: Jewish History and Jewish Memory* (Seattle, WA: University of Washington Press, 1996), 17.
92 See D. Hervieu-Léger, *Religion as a Chain of Memory* (New Brunswick, NJ: Rutgers University Press, 2000), 142.

markedly active and fearless character whose male counterpart (consistently called Adam) emerges as remarkably patronizing and protective towards her. Primarily, these characterizations find expression in additional elaborations of the garden narrative. So does Adam constantly giving Eve unsolicited advice and instructions about living in the garden, based on his emphasized experiences as the first human being, which conflicts with Eve's self-confidence and curiosity. Instead, she begins to explore the garden on her own, to which Adam responds with disapproval, protest, and concern. But as he also refuses to join her scouting expeditions, it happens that the serpent meets Eve alone, several times in fact, before they talk about the tree of the knowledge of good and bad.[93]

Bodin Cohen thereby answers, with a narratively plausible clarification, the rabbis' prior question of how it came about that the serpent talks only to the woman. But, likewise, she presents indications in characters of the male and female earthlings that make it plausible that Adam would have been too prudent to speak to the serpent and that Eve dares to raise questions that Adam never would have asked. When she hears him talking to God and demands the same for herself, Adam insists upon speaking for both of them.[94] At this moment, Eve feels anger for the first time and follows the serpent's path once more, where she reaches the tree of knowledge and articulates her desire for wisdom.[95] Again, Eve's aim for knowledge is made narratively plausible.

In her version of the garden narrative, Bodin Cohen fleshes out Eve's relation with both the serpent and Adam into a processual web of relationships and thereby portrays the female earthling as a confident and self-reliant young person instead of a seducible and guilty primordial woman. Eve prowls around in the garden with her head held high, looking around, and eavesdrops upon Adam talking to God, which leads her to demand equal rights. Furthermore, she desires wisdom, which is why she touches and steals from the tree of knowledge. In fact, Bodin Cohen designs Eve's character and behavior in accordance with all the defective attributes that are ascribed to women in GenR 18:2. Yet she does so without condemnation.

Under the terms of the midrash, Adam must be accountable for Eve counteracting him, as he neither heard her out, nor gave serious consideration to her opinion and needs, as it says in GenR 17:3: "if one merits, she is a helper, but if not, she is against him." Bodin Cohen confronts this rabbinic tradition with Eve's autonomy of action. Pursuant to the contemporary genre of young

---

93 See Bodin Cohen, *Lilith's Ark*, 6–9.
94 See ibid., 9.
95 See ibid., 9–10.

adult literature, the Eve of *Lilith's Ark* is presented as a strong, emancipated female character facing a mansplaining counterpart within an androcentric environment. Thus, the author acknowledges the woman's autonomy of action in Gen 3:1–6, narratively strengthening Eve's subject formation and achievement of agency.[96]

When Eve finally takes a bite out of the fruit, Bodin Cohen describes its sweetness as an intense taste adventure, followed by the bodily reaction of Eve's puberty: "I felt my body grow and change. I developed curves, a thinner waist, and round breasts. I lifted my hands to my face. High cheekbones of womanhood had replaced the full face of a child."[97] Once young Eve has transformed into a woman, her aim shifts in a different direction than before: "Then I felt desire. I wanted a companion, a man, with whom I could explore the world."[98] Suddenly, heteronormative binarity appears in Bodin Cohen's story like a natural force that is essential to womanhood. Now Eve's "thoughts and perceptions are structured in accordance with the very structures of the relation of domination that is imposed on" her, and her "acts of cognition are, inevitably, acts of recognition, submission,"[99] according to Pierre Bourdieu.

With a second piece of the fruit, Eve returns to Adam, whose "jaw dropped"[100] at her sight, and she convinces him to eat from it as well by saying: "I am now a woman [...]. And you are just a boy. Eat the fruit, and we will become equals."[101] That Eve is now presenting Adam the prospect of equality, exegetically closes a blank space in the text of Gen 3:6, while it creates the impression of feminist agency within Bodin Cohen's narrative. But what kind of equality is held out in prospect here? It is an equality of bodily growth to an extent of sexual maturity with an aspiration for heteronormative coupling, as Bodin Cohen describes Adam eating the fruit and "[h]is chest grew wide and hairy, his arms thick and strong, and his face angular and handsome. I felt my body drawn to him,"[102] says Eve.

Bodin Cohen's description of physical transformation reproduces stereotypical body images in terms of a heteronormative differential feminism. Releasing Eve from an androcentric oppression, she turns her into a strong, confidently sexy cisgender prefiguration, with Adam as her masculine counterpart. And signifying Eve as cisgender at this point of Bodin Cohen's story gives credit to

---

96   See Auga, *An Epistemology of Religion*, 74.
97   Bodin Cohen, *Lilith's Ark*, 10.
98   Ibid.
99   Bourdieu, *Masculine Domination*, 13.
100 Bodin Cohen, *Lilith's Ark*, 10.
101 Ibid.
102 Ibid., 10.

the circumstance that after the consumption of the fruit she is not any kind of woman but precisely this heteronormative prefiguration. Bodin Cohen's version of the garden narrative is unmistakably framed by a heteronormative episteme of binary patterns of thought. Identifying the moment of knowledge with the bodily process of puberty is indeed an innovative interpretation, but, as a result, all previous autonomy and emancipation gets a veneer of childish revolt.

Looking at *Lilith's Ark* as young adult literature for a Jewish teenage readership, Bodin Cohen successfully turns the biblical tradition of the eating of the fruit into a mobilizing story about the individualization of adolescents.[103] She emancipates Eve from the rabbinic tradition, whose aggadic elaborations in return close the content gap in Gen 3:6 by telling that Eve either forced Adam with verbal aggression to eat from the fruit, or tricked him into its consumption by giving it to him as a juice or holding out the prospect of loneliness to him (GenR 19:5). The former explanation is based on the reading of Gen 3:17, where it is written that *ha'adam* was listening to the voice (קול/*kol*) of his woman and not to her words. This is pointed out by Gerald Blidstein, who adds to the rabbis' interpretation that the woman's "best weapons are tears and cries. [... So] Adam may simply have been overpowered by his wife's outburst, [... as] women neither reason nor cite Scripture – they weep and cry to gain their ends. And men succumb."[104]

What Blidstein frequently identifies as a "bourgeois" atmosphere with "fully defined and functioning"[105] roles already in the biblical text, does indeed repeatedly document Blidstein's own exemplariness for a modern, mansplaining expression of a heteronormative and androcentric, if not even misogynist episteme, based on profoundly internalized binary patterns of thought.

To overcome such ways of academic thinking, its essentialized categories of sex/gender have to be denaturalized.[106] But even then, their norms have to be unlearned, ascriptions of sex/gender identity have to be transformed into an open and dynamic understanding of subject formation and agency, as Auga outlines it.[107] To overcome the binary patterns of thought that structure the meaning which needs to be deconstructed, is a challenging but necessary step

---

103   See also Hervieu-Lèger, *Religion*, 159.
104   Blidstein, *In the Rabbis' Garden*, 50–51.
105   Ibid., 22.
106   See Auga, *An Epistemology of Religion*, 53.
107   See ibid., 72–74, and P. Bourdieu and L. J. D. Wacquant, *An Invitation to Reflexive Sociology* (Cambridge: Polity Press, 1992), 122.

in the pursue of this approach.[108] Therefore, binarity hast to be unmasked as a conceptual scaffold of thinking behind preconcepts of sex, gender roles, or heteronormative norms, but also religious or ethical beliefs in the dualities of good and bad, or right and wrong, which are all taken for granted. Binary patterns of thought do not correspond with the complexity of our world, especially not with all the tasks that we have to solve in the nearest future.

Bibliography

Aschkenasy, Nehama. *Woman at the Window: Biblical Tales of Oppression and Escape*. Detroit, MI: Wayne State University Press, 1998.

Auga, Ulrike. *An Epistemology of Religion and Gender: Biopolitics – Performativity – Agency*. New York, NY: Routledge, 2020.

Austin, J. L. *How to Do Things With Words: The William James Lectures delivered at Harvard University in 1955*. Oxford: Oxford University Press, 1976.

Biblia Hebraica Stuttgartensia/תורה נביאים וכתובים. Edited by Karl Elliger, Wilhelm Rudolph et al. Stuttgart: Deutsche Bibelgesellschaft, 2007.

Blidstein, Gerald J. *In the Rabbis' Garden: Adam and Eve in the Midrash*. Northvale, NJ: Jason Aronson Inc., 1997.

Bodin Cohen, Deborah. *Lilith's Ark: Teenage Tales of Biblical Women*. Philadelphia, PA: The Jewish Publication Society, 2006.

Bourdieu, Pierre. *Masculine Domination*. Translated by Richard R. Nice. Stanford, CA: Stanford University Press, 2001.

---------. "The Forms of Capital." In *Handbook of Theory and Research for the Sociology of Education*, edited by John G. Richardson, 241–58. New York, NY: Greenwood Press, 1986.

Bourdieu, Pierre and Loïc J. D. Wacquant. *An Invitation to Reflexive Sociology*. Cambridge: Polity Press, 1992.

Brubaker, Rogers. "Social Theory as Habitus." In *Bourdieu: Critical Perspectives*, edited by Craig J. Calhoun et al., 212–34. Chicago, IL: Chicago University Press, 1993.

Butler, Judith. *Bodies That Matter: On the Discursive Limits of "Sex"*. New York, NY: Routledge, 1993.

---------. *Gender Trouble: Feminism and the Subversion of Identity*. New York, NY: Routledge, 1999.

---

108   See J. Scott, "Deconstructing Equality-Versus-Difference: Or, the Uses of Poststructuralist Theory for Feminism," in *The Postmodern Turn: New Perspectives on Social Theory*, ed. S. Seidman (New York, NY: Cambridge University Press, 1995), 282–98.

Derrida, Jacques. "Semiology and Grammatology. Interview with Julia Kristeva." In *Positions*, translated by Alan Bass, 15–35. Chicago, IL: The University of Chicago Press, 1981.

---------. "Structure, Sign and Play in the Discourse of the Human Sciences." In *Writing and Difference*, translated by Alan Bass, 279–93. London: Routledge, 1990.

Frymer-Kensky, Tikva. "The Bible and Women's Study." In *Studies in Bible and Feminist Criticism*, 159–83. Philadelphia, PA: The Jewish Publication Society, 2006.

Guest, Deryn. *Beyond Feminist Biblical Studies*. Sheffield: Sheffield Phoenix Press, 2012.

Hayim Yerushalmi, Yosef. *Zakhor: Jewish History and Jewish Memory*. Seattle, WA: University of Washington Press, 1996.

Hervieu-Léger, Danièle. *Religion as a Chain of Memory*. New Brunswick, NJ: Rutgers University Press, 2000.

Gellman, Jerome. "Gender and Sexuality in the Garden of Eden." *Theology & Sexuality* 12, no. 3 (2006): 319–36.

Gill, Jerry H. *Words, Deeds, Bodies: L. Wittgenstein, J. L. Austin, M. Merleau-Ponty, and M. Polanyi*. Leiden: Brill, 2019.

Kalmanofsky, Amy. *Gender-Play in the Hebrew Bible: The Ways the Bible Challenges Its Gender Norms*. London: Routledge, 2017.

Lakoff, George, and Mark Johnson. *Metaphors We Live By*. Chicago, IL: The University of Chicago Press, 1980.

Lemche, Niels Peter. *Ancient Israel: A New History of Israel*. London: Bloomsbury T & T Clark, 2015.

Maurice, Lisa. "Tempting Treasures and Seductive Snakes: Presenting Eve and Pandora for the Youngest Readers." In *Gender, Creation Myths and Their Reception in Western Civilization: Prometheus, Pandora, Adam and Eve*, edited by Lisa Maurice and Tovi Bibring, 69–80. London: Bloomsbury Academic, 2022.

McCall, Leslie. "Does Gender Fit? Bourdieu, Feminism, and Concepts of Social Order." *Theory and Society* 21, no. 6 (1992): 837–67.

Meyers, Carol L. *Rediscovering Eve: Ancient Israelite Women in Context*. New York, NY: Oxford University Press, 2012.

Midrash Bereschit Rabbah/מדרש בראשית רבא. Critical Edition with Notes and Commentary. 3 volumes, edited by Julius Theodor and Chanoch Albeck. Jerusalem: Shalem Books, 1996.

Scott, Joan W. "Deconstructing Equality-Versus-Difference: Or, the Uses of Poststructuralist Theory for Feminism." In *The Postmodern Turn: New Perspectives on Social Theory*, edited by Steven Seidman, 282–98. New York, NY: Cambridge University Press, 1995.

Simkins, Ronald A. "Gender Construction in the Yahwist Creation Myth." In *Genesis: A Feminist Companion to the Bible*, edited by Athalya Brenner, 32–52. Sheffield: Sheffield Academic Press Ltd, 1998.

Skeggs, Beverley. "Context and Background: Pierre Bourdieu's Analysis of Class, Gender and Sexuality." *The Sociological Review* 52, no. 2 (2004): 19–33.

Southwood, Katherine. "The Social and Cultural History of Ancient Israel." In *The Hebrew Bible: A Critical Companion*, edited by John Barton, 54–85. Princeton, NJ: Princeton University Press, 2016.

Vorpahl, Daniel. "A Donkey That Speaks Is a Donkey No Less: Talking Animals in the Hebrew Bible and Its Early Jewish Reception." In *Speaking Animals in Ancient Literature*, edited by Hedwig Schmalzgruber, 509–25. Heidelberg: Universitätsverlag Winter, 2020.

---------. *Aus dem Leben des Buches Jona. Rezeptionswissenschaftliche Methodik und innerjüdischer Rezeptionsdiskurs*. Berlin: De Gruyter, 2021.

---------. "The Body as a Wonderland: Rabbinic Talk of the Human Body as a Sex/Gender Construction." In *Constructions of Gender in Religious Traditions of Late Antiquity*, edited by Shayna Sheinfeld et al., 257–280. Lanham, MD: Fortress Academic, 2024.

Disturbed Depths: The Aquatic Otherness of the Leviathan in *From Dust, A Flame*

Marissa Herzig

"The amalgamation of mutually incompatible meanings embodied even in one monstrous name, such as Leviathan, is beyond sorting out or resolving … Leviathan is part of creation; Leviathan is outside creation and a threat to it; Leviathan is the enemy nation; God crushed Leviathan's heads and killed it long ago; God will pierce Leviathan and kill it in the future; God plays with Leviathan; God sings Leviathan's praises. Biblical monsters bear no single meaning, no overall unity or wholeness. They are theologically unwhole-some. As such they stand for the haunting sense of precariousness and uncertainty that looms along the edges of the world, the edges of society, the edges of consciousness, and the edges of religious understanding and faith"
—T. Beal, *Religion and Its Monsters*

"What's a fire and why does it, what's the word?
Burn?
When's it my turn?
Wouldn't I love, love to explore that shore up above?
Out of the sea
Wish I could be
Part of that world"
—Alan Menken, Jodi Benson, John Musker, Ron Clements, *The Little Mermaid*

1. Introduction

In Rebecca Podos' recent Jewish[1] novel, titled *From Dust, A Flame* (2022), Malka, mother of the protagonist Hannah, summarizes *The Little Mermaid* in a flashback to her adolescent years. Malka claims that the mermaid Ariel "wanted to be human, and live on the land, and she did something about it."[2] While Podos equates Malka's yearning to flee her parochial hometown with Ariel's desire to flee the sea in *The Little Mermaid*, this quote reveals that to be human *is* to live

---

1 I define a Jewish novel as one that contains Jewish characters, folklore, religion, or culture, rather than one tied to an author's personal religious practices (although Podos herself is Jewish). Podos' novel touches on the golem, the Yiddish language, and Jewish holidays. Due to its preoccupation with Jewish subjects, this work can therefore be characterized as Jewish fantasy.
2 R. Podos, *From Dust, A Flame* (New York, NY: Balzer + Bray, 2022), 108.

on the land. Podos implies not only that water and humanity are in tension in Jewish literature but are actively in opposition. This disparagement of water often manifests in the figure of the Leviathan, who as an aquatic mythical creature in Jewish literature has consistently serves as a recurring metonymy to gesture more broadly to an association between monstrosity and water.

Yet the perception that marginalized bodies metaphorically and physically clash and collide with aquatic settings is far from limited to Jewish contexts. When examining the relationship between Black bodies and the weather in *In the Wake: On Blackness and Being* (2016), Christina Sharpe notes, "[in] what I am calling the weather, antiblackness is pervasive as climate. The weather necessitates changeability and improvisation; it is the atmospheric condition of time and place; it produces new ecologies."[3] While Sharpe astutely excavates the complicated relationship of racialized peoples to climate, there remains a distinct lack of scholarship on how Jewish bodies relate to the natural world. Although scholars Dee Dee Chainey and Willow Winsham have begun to excavate the generative space that water provides in folklore in *Treasury of Folklore, Seas, and Rivers: Sirens, Selkies, and Ghost Ships* (2021) it is in a European context, which does not account for divergences in Jewish literary representations. Jewish entanglements with water merit more attention, and my research aims to address this gap in the scholarship through a focus on water and transgression. Drawing on feminist posthumanist and ecocritical scholarship to examine how Rebecca Podos as a Jewish American woman author crafts nonhuman aquatic worlds as feminist spaces of agency, my intervention analyzes the ongoing fractures and limitations between Jewishness and the aquatic by comparing biblical and contemporary literary imaginings of the Leviathan as an Othered entity.

While Jewish scholarship has begun to address that water is represents a biblical threat to godly authority (see Mara Benjamin[4] and Rachel Haverlock[5]), it is worth reemphasizing that the common association of water and violence in Jewish literature stems from water's existence before creation in Genesis (Genesis 1:2). Genesis' characterization of water as a space of chaotic primordial evil is a threat to the dominant order, epitomized by the draconic Leviathan. Although the Leviathan appears in multiple other locations throughout the

---

3   C. Sharpe, *In the Wake: On Blackness and Being* (Durham, NC: Duke University Press, 2016), 106.
4   See M. H. Benjamin, "'There Is No Away:' Ecological Fact as Jewish Theological Problem." *Religions* 13, no. 4 (2022): 290.
5   See Havrelock, R. "Paradise on Earth," in *Seven Days, Many Voices: Insights into the Biblical Story of Creation*, ed. B. David (New York, NY: Central Conference of American Rabbis, 2017), 267–75.

Hebrew Bible from the Book of Job[6] to Psalms[7] and to the Book of Isaiah[8] among others,[9] my goal is not to catalogue these instances. This piece limits itself to Genesis 1:2 and 1:21 and its spiraling myths in order to focus on the pre-existing waters as signaling the sinister, transgressively liminal Leviathan. Thus, it is not simply water's existence before creation that fuels this monotheistic discomfort of the aquatic, but also because water is so strongly associated with the Leviathan, slyly suggesting that the Leviathan, too, could have existed before God.

To make space for a feminist posthumanist understanding of water in Jewish studies, I reckon with how this literal and metaphorical slipperiness of water permeates biblical anxieties about the aquatic in conversation with Podos' contemporary work. By recuperating nonhierarchical forms of relation, the Leviathan transcends humanism and reaches beyond the bounded human subject through the reimagination of cultural landscapes to create aquatic ontologies. Through the beginning of Genesis coupled with rabbinic reinterpretations, I will establish the aquatic as a threat to godly authority though the figure of the Othered, hypermaterialized Leviathan. Then, I will position Rebecca Podos' recent novel *From Dust, A Flame* (2022) as a contemporary retelling of the draconic, aquatic Leviathan, noting how anxieties about fluidity and the racialized, animalized nonhuman continue to the Jewish literary imagination. Podos' success as an author[10] interests me not only in that *From Dust, A Flame's* recent publication illuminates what is popular in twenty-first century Jewish fiction but also in its insistent marketing as a young adult novel. Podos did not construct her work for an academic audience, but her novel showcases broader cultural trends of how Jewish fiction continues to conceive of the Leviathan. In tracing the ambivalence regarding the aquatic in Jewish literature, I argue that contemporary Jewish authors tend to employ water and aquatic creatures to embody transgressive, liberatory epistemologies which deconstruct rigid boundaries of the human and nonhuman worlds. Ultimately, I contend that in *From Dust, A Flame*, the protagonist Hannah's

---

6   Job 3:8, 40:25–41:26.
7   Psalms 74, 104.
8   Isaiah 27:1.
9   Arguably Job 26:12, Psalm 89, and Isaiah 51:9–10 include the Leviathan, although the explicit terminology describes the similar and arguably draconic creature, Rahab.
10 Podos' debut work, *The Mystery of Hollow Places* (2016) was awarded the best Barnes & Noble Young Adult Book of the Year of 2016 and was chosen for the Junior Library Guild selection. Her second work, *Like Water* (2017), won the Lambda Literary Award for LGBTQ Children's and Young Adult works, illuminating that Podos was already an established and popular Young Adult (YA) author by time *From Dust, A Flame* was published.

vacillating shapeshifting that positions her between the category of the human and the aquatic reptile locates Hannah as a contemporary interpretation of the Leviathan.

2. Ambiguous Monstrosity: The Gendered Liminality of the Biblical Leviathan

The Leviathan's authority in the water and as a larger representation of aquatic authority, as well as the Leviathan's agency to exist without God, place tension and stakes upon its distinct depiction in Jewish storytelling. In *Pantheologies: Gods, Worlds, and Monsters*, Mary-Jane Rubenstein explains that God in western traditions "is said to be anthropomorphic, unchanging, rational, and masculine while the world is coded as animal-vegetal, changeable, irrational, and feminine."[11] If the antithesis of God is the natural world, then water, by opposition, becomes a feminine, godless, transgressive entity in western literary and cultural imaginations. If European Enlightenment thought configures the "Human" as a white, Christian, able-bodied, living man, then what counts as alive and dead and male and female are essential in constructing the unstable category of the human. Drawing on Luce Irigaray, Rubenstein explains that binaries in religious western monotheist traditions attempt to erase and yet inherently gesture "toward its feminized origins. Like the Oedipal child, the Western tradition aims to make its way from the dark, maternal womb space to the father's binding light—from paganism to monotheism, from the cave to the sky, from the dirt to the ideas."[12] This "dark, maternal womb space" illuminates how race, gender, water, and anxieties about life and death permeate discussions of the Other, which in Western European thought is consistently the nonhuman. I thus demonstrate that water in literature functions as a cultural shorthand to signify transgressive, non-living, nonhuman, feminine presences.

While the Leviathan is not explicitly or overtly female[13] the specters of femininity permeate monotheistic anxieties about the aquatic. On a basic Freudian note, humans are born in watery wombs. Black studies scholar Anissa Janine

---

11 M. Rubenstein, *Pantheologies: Gods, Worlds, Monsters* (New York, NY: Columbia University Press, 2018), 3.
12 Ibid., 7.
13 Nevertheless, the folktale retold by H. Schwartz, "The Water Witch" features the Leviathan as a supernatural entity who lends its aid to two children kept hostage by a water witch. The narrative's respect for Leviathan as opposed to the water witch seems to indicate that femininity trumps water as threat to patriarchal, godly order.

Wardi asserts "that our first experience of life is bathed in amniotic water at once highlights humans' intimate connection to water and, concomitantly, maternalizes water."[14] Wardi's focus here on the water as a necessity for human birth underscores that water and the womb go hand in hand.[15] In terms of the Leviathan, in *Monster Theory Reader*'s chapter "Of Swamp Dragons: Mud, Megalopolis, and a Future for Ecocriticism," Anthony Lioi notes that the Leviathan—this embodiment of water—is potentially tied to the "memory of the water dragon Tiamat, the mother goddess who is killed by her grandson Marduk in the Babylonian creation story, the Enuma Elish."[16] It is not a coincidence that in this pantheistic Babylonian creation myth, which monotheistic Judaism reacted against, that the two key creator gods were named "Tiamat and Apsu. The name Apsu, related to the Sumerian Abzu, suggests 'watery deep' or 'sweet water ocean.' Tiamat means 'sea'."[17] Tiamat, tied to the Hebrew word "tehom," meaning "deep" features in the second verse of Genesis in which "the earth was a formless void and darkness covered the face of the deep, while a wind from God swept over the face of the waters."[18] Not only does water exist before God's creation, but if the God of Israel formed to contrast a watery woman-like goddess, then it is reasonable to interpolate that water biblically serves as a trope of Otherness, whether that be femininity or otherwise. The Leviathan's legacy and link to Tiamat intimates potential existence before creation, which minimally associates the Leviathan with primordial chaos, an authority before and perhaps greater than the God of Israel. Much like Toni Morrison argues in *Playing in the Dark* that blackness props up whiteness in the American literary imagination, I contend that the Leviathan is the narrative tool to which the God of the Hebrew Bible defines itself in opposition. If the Bible, in essence, represents an anthology of what people believe God to

---

14   A. J. Wardi, "Blue Ecology and Resistance: Islands, Swamps, and Ecotones," in *Toni Morrison and the Natural World: An Ecology of Color* (Jackson, MS: University Press of Mississippi, 2021), 124.

15   Even in scientific discourse, this trope of water and wombs seems to continue to dominate popular conception of wombs far after the advent of psychoanalysis; see M. Odent, "Man, the Womb and the Sea: The Roots of the Symbolism of Water." *Pre- and Peri-Natal Psychology Journal* 7, no. 3 (1993): 187–93.

16   A. Lioi, "Of Swamp Dragons: Mud, Megalopolis, and a Future for Ecocriticism," in *The Monster Theory Reader*, ed. J. A. Weinstock (Minneapolis, MN: University of Minnesota Press, 2020), 443.

17   Beal, *Religion*, 16.

18   Genesis 1:2 (New Oxford Annotated Bible).

be,[19] then the Bible's consistent and defensive assertion of Leviathan as God's foil serves as an index to what represents the Other in the Bible.

By investigating the links between Tiamat and Leviathan as opponents of the Biblical monotheistic god, then the triangulation of Tiamat's femininity, the aquatic, and the draconic Leviathan begin to manifest. Lioi concretizes these connections by summarizing, "feminist theologian Catherine Keller demonstrates an enduring 'tehomophobia,' or fear of the sea and power of chaos, pervading Hebrew and Christian scripture, finally manifesting in the book of Revelation as the defeat of Satan-as-dragon and the drying up of the sea."[20] The entanglement of water, Leviathan, and femininity implies that much of what monotheism defined itself in opposition to was the feminine divine. In the *Dictionary of Demons in the Hebrew Bible*, Christoph Uehlinger illuminates that "Old Syrian seals (18th–16th century BCE) showing the weather-god killing a serpent, often in front of a goddess, are so numerous that there can be no doubt about their figuring the prototype of the Urgaritic Yammu/Leviathan conflict."[21] The manifestation of the goddess in conjunction with the Leviathan intimates that the two are entangled, and that the aquatic is tied to anxieties about female power. Finally, in *Genesis*, Robert Alter connects "the phonetic similarity between haway, 'Eve,' and the verbal root hayah, 'to live'. It has been proposed that Eve's name conceals very different origins, for it sounds suspiciously like the Aramaic word for 'serpent'."[22] This potential link between Eve and the serpent may appear superfluous to the conversations of the Leviathan and water, but if we remember that the serpent is the draconic specter of the Leviathan in the garden of Eden, then Eve's association with the draconic encourages a reading of the aquatic as feminine.

In Talmudic retellings of the Leviathan, rabbinic commentaries likewise capitalize on the threat of the feminine and reveal the more-than-material hyperembodiment of the Leviathan. In the Talmudic interpretation of Rabbi Judah, biblical and monster studies scholar Timothy Beal retells that there were allegedly originally two Leviathans, one male and one female, but "God castrated the male and killed the female, preserving her in salt."[23] The murder of the female not only excavates that femininity is unsurprisingly more

---

19 I am borrowing this definition from my former biblical literature professor, Dr. Stephen Cushman.
20 Lioi, "Of Swamp Dragons," 443.
21 C. Uehlinger, "Leviathan," in *Dictionary of Deities and Demons in the Bible* (*DDD*), ed. K. van der Toorn et al. (Leiden: Brill, 1995), 958.
22 R. Alter, *Genesis: Translation and Commentary* (New York, NY: W.W. Norton, 1996), 15.
23 Beal, *Religion*, 64.

Othered in Jewish patriarchal traditions, but also implies that the female is more of a threat because of her potential for procreation. In *A Jewish Bestiary*, Mark Podwal corroborates this rabbinic mythology, but adds that God only murdered the female Leviathan "when it seemed their offspring would destroy the entire world, God slew the female, salting her flesh for the messianic banquet."[24] While one wonders what untold violent deaths occurred to these offspring, this murder of the female Leviathan regardless reads as extremely physical, and does not simply end with her death, but insinuates that her murderers will preserve her corpse with salt, consuming it at their leisure as a celebration of a new world.

The Leviathan paradoxically links old generations and new worlds, for just as the Leviathan's material body can symbolize the new messianic age, Podwal also notes that rabbis have interpreted Adam and Eve's clothing as fashioned "from the skin of the slain Leviathan."[25] The Leviathan's material body marks metaphorical borders, whether that be from the Garden of Eden to a new, earthly existence, or from an earthly existence to a spiritual Messianic age. In "Monster Culture (Seven Theses)", Jeffrey Cohen delineates the power and infamy of the Leviathan to inscribe human boundaries:

> It is possible, for example, that medieval merchants intentionally disseminated maps depicting sea serpents like Leviathan at the edges of their trade routes in order to discourage further exploration and to establish monopolies. Every monster is in this way a double narrative, two living stories: one that describes how the monster came to be and another, its testimony, detailing what cultural use the monster serves. The monster of prohibition exists to demarcate the bonds that hold together the system of relations we call culture, to call horrid attention to the borders that cannot—must not—be crossed.[26]

Nonetheless, Beal asserts that the Leviathan as a threat to humanist and religious authority is not physical or communal, but philosophical and individual, for the Leviathan as a figure "is a revelation not of the wholly other but of a repressed otherness within the self. The monster, as personification of the *unheimlich* stands for that which has broken out of the subterranean basement or the locked closet where it has been banished from consciousness."[27]

---

24 M. Podwal, *A Jewish Bestiary: Fabulous Creatures from Hebraic Legend Et Lore* (University Park, PA: Pennsylvania State University Press, 2021), 36.
25 Ibid.
26 J. J. Cohen, "Monster Culture (Seven Theses)," in *The Monster Theory Reader*, ed. J. A. Weinstock (Minneapolis, MN: University of Minnesota Press, 2020), 46.
27 Beal, *Religion*, 8.

In equating the Leviathan with the subterranean, Beal furthers the association of the Leviathan with the monstrous, barely contained, Othered aquatic.

3. Rebecca Podos' Underwater Palace: Queering and Racializing the Leviathan

In *From Dust, A Flame*, Podos' preoccupation with river demons as antagonists functions as a cultural shorthand that reflects contemporary anxieties about reincarnations of the Leviathan. Podos' work begins with subverting limited constructions of Jewishness through the protagonist's Hannah's queer draconic and animalistic shapeshifting. Hannah, a queer teenage woman, begins to suddenly experience more-than-human transformations, leading her and her brother Gabe to their previously unknown Jewish family. They explore their Jewish and queer identities, but also attempt to solve the mystery of Hannah's transformations and their mother's sudden disappearance with the help of a young Jewish woman, Ari, who becomes Hannah's girlfriend at the end of the novel. The story alternates between Hannah's present adventure and her mother Malka's upbringing, in which she fell in love with a young man, Siman. Although Malka decides to run away with Siman, he tragically drowns near a river. Unbeknownst to Malka, a draconic water demon inhabits Siman's deceased body, convincing Malka to promise away her future child to him. Podos positions this water demon and Malka's vow to him as the reason for Hannah's shapeshifting. The story concludes by blaming the shapeshifting on this water demon, Jabez ben Ashmedai, to romanticize Hannah's newfound home as a space of domestic religious comfort (the last chapter even takes place at a Rosh Hashanah celebration). Podos bases her story on a Jewish folktale commonly referred to as "The Underwater Palace,"[28] for her water demon abducts Hannah's brother Gabe and her mother Malka to his subterranean castle.

Nevertheless, the tale "The Underwater Palace" has the potential to pave the way for a posthumanist epistemology. In this Prague story, which Podos explicitly retells in *From Dust, A Flame*, a young woman is engaged to a man whom she does not desire to marry. She has "another love, a secret love, who came to her one night a month as she stood on the bank of the river Vltava under a full moon."[29] The night before the wedding, she follows her lover, who turns out

---

28 For one retelling of this folktale, see H. Schwartz. *Leaves from the Garden of Eden: One Hundred Classic Jewish Tales* (New York, NY: Oxford University Press, 2010), 318–24.

29 Podos, *From Dust*, 152.

to be a water demon, under the river. The woman's aunt eventually discovers the Underwater Palace, and finds the woman happily married and pregnant, from which the aunt didactically concludes, "[s]he knew that some shedim do love, and observe the Sabbath, and even keep mitzvot. In short, shedim can be as complicated as people."[30] This water demon is clearly a replacement, a folkloric excuse to refuse this first man's hand in marriage. In essence, the water demon represents a transgressive femininity which refuses to comply with traditional patriarchal values. I maintain that this story and its retelling is a posthumanist one, for it is about a woman who employs the nonhuman, marginalized aquatic world to escape patriarchal, humanist norms.

Podos' own version of "The Underwater Palace" likewise affords posthumanist readings. Hannah observes that in Jabez ben Ashmedai's aquatic castle, "[w]ith no light source underwater besides the palace itself, it's impossible to tell what time it is up above."[31] In aquatic spaces, linear, normative, capitalist time is distorted, fuzzy, warped, and irrelevant. Nevertheless, this appearance of monochromatic darkness neglects how human-centered that perception is.[32] Even with that anthropocentric perception, there is potential in this limited awareness, for human "viewers are denied any sense of scale, perspective, or depth. The flat wall of blackness denies us any foundation, direction, or orientation toward a horizon. We hover, like the pelagic creatures, unmoored."[33] The lack of humanist hierarchy that darkness and water afford manifests directly in Hannah's sight, or lack thereof, since Podos' palace exists below the river bottom, "deep enough down that distant daggers of sunlight barely pierce the darkness."[34] Yet, Podos' ending to her own novel demonizes the nonhuman aquatic world by literally and figuratively expelling the nonhuman aquatic, which is epitomized by Hannah's final confrontation with the water demon. When Hannah says the water demon's real name, Jabez ben Ashmedai, she performs a quasi-exorcism:

> The sound he makes is of whining dogs and roaring beats, of gnashing teeth and claws scissoring through flesh, a wail of despair and fury all at once. It rises to a pitch that vibrates in my bones, sizzling my blood like a live wire dropped in water. Gabe claps his hands over his ears as we watch the sheyd disintegrate. His skin crackles and flakes. Fragments of his wings fall to the ground like dead,

---

30   Ibid., 153.
31   Ibid., 291.
32   S. Alaimo, "Violet-Black," in *Prismatic Ecology: Ecotheory beyond Green*, ed. J. J. Cohen (Minneapolis, MN: University of Minnesota Press, 2013), 236.
33   Ibid., 241.
34   Podos, *From Dust*, 275.

dried leaves, and his body shreds down to black bone, then withers to dust. At that moment, a sudden wind whips down the river, lifting the insect-like swarm that had been Jabez ben Ashmedai into the air, then into the yawning mouth of the box ... In an instant, the wavering light over the river dims, surges, and then winks out for good.[35]

The use of dogs, insects, wings and other nonhuman adjectives to describe this water demon highlights the how Othering and the nonhuman remain utterly entangled in humanist anxieties. The consistent racialization of the water demon, hyperexaggerated to the extent the narrator insists above that the water is not only racialized as externally dark, but also that internally "his body shreds down to black bone."[36] Even before Jabez ben Ashmedai reveals his true animalistic form, Podos racializes Siman's body post Jabez ben Ashmedai's demon possession. Podos describes that the demon's eyes in Siman's body appear as "dark as a coal room in a cold basement"[37] and as "black as the bottom of a very deep sea."[38] Podos potentially darkens Siman's body under Jabez ben Ashmedai's possession to signal to audiences that Siman's body remains under the control of the water demon, but at the cost of equating blackness and evil with water. Podos even playfully hints at the presence of the water demon in human form through his "Dark waves just curling out from under a fisherman's cap, and equally dark eyes."[39] Riffing off that hair and waves can undulate, Podos continues to racialize and darken Siman after the water demon inhabits his body, almost suggesting to audiences that they too can find demons if they look for physically dark features.

While this analysis may appear to exaggerate the significance of blackening Siman's body post-water demon possession, these tropes echo a long history of conflating marginalized and racialized people with the nonhuman world. I borrow from posthumanist scholar Zakkiyah Jackson who "reinterpret[s] Enlightenment thought not as black 'exclusion' or 'denied humanity' but rather as the violent imposition and appropriation—inclusion and recognition—of black(ened) humanity in the interest of plasticizing that very humanity, whereby 'the animal' is one but not the only form blackness is thought to encompass."[40] Under this logic of domination, just as whiteness and maleness

---

35 Podos, *From Dust*, 308.
36 Ibid.
37 Ibid., 230.
38 Ibid., 233.
39 Ibid., 169.
40 Z. I. Jackson, *Becoming Human: Matter and Meaning in an Antiblack World* (New York, NY: New York University Press, 2020), 3.

represent the static cultural conception of the "human," women and people of color are consistently associated with the nonhuman, whether that be nonhuman animals or the natural environment.[41] It is therefore worth pressing on the popular conflation of water and darkness and therefore blackness. The aquatic and dark demon clearly connects to Hannah's perception of evil in this scene, and even at its most mild portrayal, Podos portrays the ocean and water as philosophically and geographically isolating,[42] estranged,[43] and disorienting,[44] which anthropocentrically assumes that human contact is the only contact that matters. Moreover, the fiery title of the book itself indicates that oceanic ontologies are not welcome in this Jewish world.

It is therefore unsurprising that Podos configures Jewishness as land-based. While living in diaspora renders it more difficult to prescribe a specific nationalism, Podos seems to recognize the interplay between metaphorical roots when writing against watery, rootless existences. Reflecting on Jewishness, Hannah ponders, "I'd read about matrilineal descent in traditional Jewish law. It's still strange to think a thing like that could be planted in me at birth."[45] By constructing Jewishness as a seed, Podos portrays Hannah as a narrative plant.[46] Podos' land-based, rooted language to describe Jewishness seems to anticipate and write against a wandering watery existence. Even within the story, when Hannah's mother warns her to stay away from the river, Hannah abruptly halts to "dig my toes into the forest floor to slow myself, catch my sneaker on a root and go sprawling. I plant myself into the damp soil and the low ferns, skin scraping over half-submerged tree bark."[47] To defend against potential danger from the water, Hannah becomes plant-like. The language of the "forest," "root," "plant," "soil," and "ferns" are Hannah's safety against the dark, raging waters. Jewish ideological constructions of the land seem to form themselves in opposition to anxieties about a rootless, fluid existence, rather than from any inherent material connection with the land. This terrestrial response potentially anticipates how modern capitalism roots the land as central to vocation, ideology, and societal value, which renders water a slippery surface. Stacey Alaimo unearths that the "social construction of the ocean in industrial capitalism has been that of a 'vast void,' an 'empty transportation surface, beyond the

---

41 F. Probyn-Rapsey, "Anthropocentrism," in *Critical Terms for Animal Studies*, ed. L. Gruen (Chicago, IL: University of Chicago Press, 2018), 54.
42 Podos, *From Dust*, 76.
43 Ibid., 89.
44 Ibid., 180.
45 Ibid., 61.
46 Ibid., 69.
47 Ibid., 176.

space of social relations.'"[48] Posthumanist feminist scholar Astrida Neimanis also agrees that abstractly "water is deterritorialized, rendered 'placeless' ... abstract, isomorphic, measurable quantity', all reducible to that fundamental unit 'H2O'."[49] Podos perpetuates these stereotypes of blankness and bareness simply in naming the river "Hollow," which gestures to the alleged artificiality and emptiness of the aquatic. Hannah bemoans the "empty water,"[50] "empty fountains,"[51] and "room after room of nothing, nothing, nothing."[52] This alleged hollow, emptiness of the water not only disseminates colonialist ideologies, but interestingly contrasts with the distinct physical, material overabundant presence of the Leviathan.

Just as Leviathan lore maligns the Leviathan's over-embodied hypermateriality, the protagonist Hannah likewise negotiates what it means to be narratively and physically almost too physical. Hannah laments how she "live[s] in Gabe's unremarkable hand-me-downs to hide a body that I barely had control over, even before it started its nightly involuntary transformations."[53] Even before any supernatural occurrences claim the narrative, Hannah's character as a legacy of the Leviathan explores what it means to be overly-embodied, too present.

Hannah's liminal shapeshifting as not-quite-human not-quite-animal therefore situate her physically and metaphorically as a modern remnant of the Leviathan. Hannah's first transformation alters her round eyes to serpentine "impossibly golden eyes, and horizontal, knife-split pupils."[54] Far from a coincidence that serpents serve as the antithesis of godliness in Genesis, the snake as a symbol automatically locates Hannah's transformations as reptilian and contrary to divine authority. Hannah's second transformation replaces the serpentine eyes with "a wolf's vicious, curved ivory canines [that] sprout from my gums ... I scream at the sight of my reflection."[55] By pairing "vicious" and "scream" with an animalistic transformation, Podos perpetuates that animality opposes the human, and is worthy of fright. Far from uniform, Hannah's third transformation leaves "green-gold scales scattered across my body—a patch

---

48 Alaimo, "Violet-Black," 234.
49 A. Neimanis, *Bodies of Water: Posthuman Feminist Phenomenology* (London: Bloomsbury Academic, 2016), 19–20.
50 Alaimo, "Violet-Black," 298.
51 Ibid., 278.
52 Ibid., 293.
53 Ibid., 189.
54 Neimanis, *Bodies of Water*, 21.
55 Podos, *From Dust*, 25.

here, a stripe there."[56] These draconic and piscine scales, like the Leviathan, encase Hannah's body as nonhuman skin. Almost perpetuating anti-Semitic conceptions of demonic Jews, Hannah's subsequent alteration replaces scales for horns, leading Hannah to repetitively dissociate, "My body isn't my body, My body isn't my body, My body isn't my—."[57] In *Bodies of Water: Posthuman Feminist Phenomenology*, Neimanis asserts, "For us humans, the flow and flush of waters sustain our own bodies, but also connect them to other bodies, to other worlds beyond our human selves. Indeed, bodies of water undo the idea that bodies are necessarily or only human."[58] Hannah's posthumanist body reverses assumptions about a contained separation between water and the human, but also reveals the animalistic and nonhuman assumptions about water in the first place.

Just as water consequently deconstructs the human body as a definitive, limited category, meaning that watery ontologies shape body politics, Neimanis inversely remarks that "changing how we think about bodies means changing how we think about water."[59] The instinct to Other watery ways of being become narratively impossible, for just as Hannah cannot control her bodily changes, the narrative of the story continues to center her as a protagonist, which revises humanist separations of the aquatic. Indeed, the ensuing transformation from horns—which while demonic are not necessarily tied to the aquatic—to a dorsal fin definitively ties Hannah with the aquatic, non-human world. Hannah denigrates this dorsal fin as "mottled and wicked looking, just like the webbed needle-spines that run down a stonefish's back."[60] The lack of uniformity or consistency of the previous scales and the fins seem to contribute to the "wicked" appearance of the animalistic features.

In the most overt transformation, these dorsal spikes become wings, much like the draconic Leviathan.[61] Hannah laments that "The wings that have burst from my shoulder blades and through my tank top are a burnt-looking brown, stretched between impossibly delicate bones, like a fruit bat's. The skin is so thin that veins show through, spindly and black beneath the bathroom lights."[62] The colors of "brown" and "black" racialize this animalistic transformation, and the translucence of the wings literally offer neither a clear nor opaque

---

56 Podos, *From Dust*, 31.
57 Ibid., 59.
58 Neimanis, *Bodies of Water*, 2.
59 Ibid., 19.
60 Podos, *From Dust*, 59.
61 Ibid., 89.
62 Ibid., 90.

understanding of her liminal existence, which she interprets as "hideous wings."⁶³ Hannah's humanism equates these nonhuman transformations, which are admittedly not societally accepted, to assume that her "body does not look right. The sweatshirt protrudes nearly half a foot behind my shoulders, fabric bulging. I can't explain this away, and I definitely can't sit shiva with my bulked-up waist and jutting shoulder blades, not even in the most shadowy corner. I can barely sit."⁶⁴ Hannah's body's transformation renders her unable to fit into human normative bounds literally and figuratively. Similarly to how Hannah's body materially refuses to conform to human expectations, or to physically fit into human clothing, her inability to sit at a shiva defies not only human but specifically Jewish societal conventions.

Hannah's final transformation substitutes the noticeable wings with an amphibian tail. Hannah's tail combines a new animal part with her previous scales, since the tail was "a scaled, skinny whip like a lizard's that kinks and curls of its own accord ... easy enough to tuck and belt into my baggy-kneed boyfriend jeans."⁶⁵ Hannah's arguably queer fashion choices lend themselves to disguising her nonhuman tail, but the active language of "kinks and curls of its own accord" affords the tail a dissociated agency that distances the animal-like aspects of her body from herself. It is not simply that Hannah employs animalistic language to distance herself from these transformations, but that she distances herself from these transformations *because* they are animalistic in the first place.

The transformations between eyes, fangs, scales, horns, fins, wings, and a tail all add up to a draconic, aquatic animal which seems to heavily resemble biblical anxieties about the animalistic Leviathan. Indeed, Podos seems to inscribe all of these Leviathan-like characteristics onto the water demon, whose true name is Jabez ben Ashmedai. When he reveals his true appearance, Hannah describes him as "a horrific creature. Long, sharp limbs and clawed feet. Jagged wings unfolding from its back, two sets of them, blotting out the woods behind him. Horns rising up to stab the sky. It is hard angles and ragged edges and hot, stinking breath."⁶⁶ While Hannah employs the adjective "horrific," the description ironically mirrors her own individual transformations all wrapped up at one moment in one creature as a physical amalgamation and compilation of her metamorphoses. What is horrific to Hannah is the nonhuman body, which

---

63   Podos, *From Dust*, 91.
64   Ibid., 90.
65   Ibid., 177.
66   Ibid., 301.

she acutely experienced. This characterization of Leviathan-like entities as Other perpetuates biblical concerns that the watery, transgressive Leviathan will rise up and rebel against sanctioned, religious authority. Just as the water demon-as-Leviathan's wings obscure the woods behind him, so too does Podos apprehensively suggest that water could overtake the Jewish land.

Just as Hannah's transformations initially reshape the human body as entangled with the natural, non-human world, Podos seems to say that these transformations are unstoppable, ephemeral, and a part of Hannah's development as a queer character. Hannah narrates how "Ari grins and winks—*winks*—and I'm as helpless to stop the smile that steals across my face as I am to stop a damned thing about my body."[67] The "thing about my body," which alludes to Hannah's nonhuman shapeshifting, consequently ties a posthumanist embodiment to queer thought, which potentially either recuperates the posthumanist transformations or perpetuates queerness as Other. As a reminder that these animalistic transformations are associated with the aquatic, Podos' entire framing of the erotic is narratively submerged by the aquatic. When first introducing the main river, the Hollow, Hannah has her first moment of explicit sexual desire for Ari. Hannah sees Ari's wet form and ponders that Ari "might not be naked, but she's left her black T-shirt and pants slung over a branch that hangs over the skinny riverbank, and her racerback bra and boy shorts don't leave much to the imagination. The sight does strange and swooping things to my stomach."[68] Hannah's description explicitly conflates and links her erotic, transgressive queer[69] desire with the aquatic setting, especially when observing that "[t]he long stretch of her [Ari's] legs below her boy shorts glitters with river water."[70] Yet, Podos complicates this potentially queer posthumanist narrative with the normative, humanist conclusion at the end of the novel.

Although Podos links Hannah's bodily transformations to her exploration of her queer identity, Podos undercuts the posthumanist potential by maligning these transformations as a temporary curse from the water demon. After the water demon captures Gabe, Hannah's body returns to "normal,"

---

67   Podos, *From Dust*, 133.
68   Ibid., 139.
69   It is worth noting that even beyond queer desire, the aquatic is a space of the erotic in the book. For example, the real Siman and Malka's first real conversation was by that river, in which Siman spots Malka in her underwear (Podos, *From Dust*, 134). This erotic overtone to the aquatic is thematically intriguing, for one would expect love and sexuality to manifest in hot, fiery spaces. However, Podos clearly connects these themes spatially to the aquatic.
70   Podos, *From Dust*, 140.

implying a traditional notion of able-bodied human.[71] Hannah's allegedly cheery conclusion of reattaining her "normal" human body stipulates a disavowal of her nonhuman shapeshifting body, undermining Podos' glimpse of a dynamic posthumanist future. Far from static, feminist materialist scholar Stacey Alaimo defines the posthuman as "that which was and continues to be 'part of the world in its becoming'."[72] Part of why Hannah frequently refers to her bodily transformations as a "curse,"[73] and Ari refers to Hannah's body as "magic"[74] is because it is ever-changing and ever-evolving. Ari's potentially posthumanist outlook offers the possibility of not simply tolerating Hannah's transformations, but in appreciating the non-human differences and its potential. Nevertheless, Hannah dully and doubtfully declares, "[the] tail is gone. Nothing replaced it. Does this mean that the curse is gone? That my body is just my body again?"[75] By strictly reinforcing the dichotomy of the human and non-human through the extermination of the latter, Hannah participates in a troublesome narrative in which the "ocean has been portrayed as the earth's last frontier or wilderness, which, in terms of American mythology, positions it as the place for narratives of domination."[76] In conquering the internal nonhuman parts of herself, Hannah seamlessly moves to subdue the outward nonhuman water demon Jabez ben Ashmedai.

If Hannah's aquatic shapeshifting body celebrated the indefinable, unpredictable porousness of a posthuman world, then Hannah's eventual female human body reveals how patriarchal, ableist conceptions of the human sanction her material existence. Defying humanist understandings of the body, Hannah's continual animalistically aquatic transformations "present a challenge to three related humanist understandings of corporeality: discrete individualism, anthropocentrism, and phallogocentrism."[77] Similarly to Hannah, Gabe returns to socially accepted styles of clothing such that gone "were the guyliner and obnoxious couture clothing; he'd reverted to chinos and tees now that I was hornless, clawless, wingless."[78] This normative ending backpedals that Hannah's shapeshifting was an aberration not tied to a new posthuman

---

71   Podos, *From Dust*, 236.
72   S. Alaimo, "Oceanic Origins, Plastic Activism, and New Materialism at Sea," in *Exposed: Environmental Politics and Pleasures in Posthuman Times* (Minneapolis, MN: University of Minnesota Press, 2016), 115.
73   Podos, *From Dust*, 95; 130; 140; 184; 265; 273.
74   Ibid., 95.
75   Ibid., 236.
76   Alaimo, "Feminist Science Studies," 193.
77   Neimanis, *Bodies of Water*, 3.
78   Podos, *From Dust*, 309.

ontology or queerness, but tied to the malevolence of the water demon, which was evil by existing as watery, and watery by existing as evil.

Since Podos gestures to the biblical Leviathan through these aquatic metamorphoses, it is significant that Hebrew—the original language of the Bible—belongs to the villainous water demon rather than any of the protagonists. Whereas Jabez ben Ashmedai in Siman's body somewhat melodramatically calls Malka "ahuvati," which translates to "my love," Malka clearly contrasts this Hebrew with her nuclear family's Yiddish which the original, alive Siman would have heard.[79] As a re-storying of the Leviathan, it is ironic that Podos aligns Leviathan as Water Demon with godly Hebraic authority when the Hebrew Bible so insistently defines God in opposition to the aquatic Leviathan. Other than the term, "ahuvati," the water demon also claims that Gabe as Malka's child functions as a sacrifice even though he originally demanded a daughter since "Boy, girl, yeled, yalda—these words mean nothing, certainly not to one such as me."[80] The use of Hebrew, a distinctly gendered language, to subversively deconstruct gender as a category emphasizes the Leviathan's manifestation as Other. If gender is one of the most fundamental humanist constructs, in which women are positioned as nonhuman, that the modern Leviathan disregards gender constructs heightens the category of the monstrous aquatic as transgressive in the Jewish literary imagination.

4. Conclusion

My aim is not to single out Podos' contemporary work as an exception, but to illustrate how Jewish writers' feminism and racial politics could be ameliorated with a posthumanist praxis that deconstructs racial hierarchies and allows for more fluidity in practice and not just theory. Other contemporary Jewish women American authors, such as Naomi Novik in her retelling of Rumpelstiltskin in *Spinning Silver* (2018), Rena Rossner in her retelling of "The Goblin Market" in *The Sisters of the Winter Wood* (2018), and R.M. Romero in her similar retelling of "The Underwater Palace" in *The Ghosts of Rose Hill* (2022) all frame water and water creatures as wicked, perpetuating gendered and racial codes that flatten and limit Jewish identity.

The legacy and continued presence of the Leviathan as a transgressive figure provides a useful hermeneutic for reading the Other in Jewish literature, as anxieties about the racialized, feminized, queer aquatic are all encapsulated in the

---

79 Podos, *From Dust*, 229.
80 Ibid., 273.

alleged monstrosity of the Leviathan. The potential posthumanist porousness that the Leviathan affords helps to read against normative conventions of race, gender, sexuality and ability. The analysis demonstrates how the literary representation of the Leviathan serves to highlight not only the marginalization in the Hebrew Bible and in contemporary literature through the Leviathan's liminality and persistent materiality, but also through the Leviathan's potential to undo conventional constructions of Jewishness. Podos' centering of Hannah as a Leviathan-like entity through her queer aquatic shapeshifting begins to rewrite the historically vilified position of the Leviathan. Although Podos' ending does not push for a posthumanist future for Hannah in *From Dust, A Flame*, Podos' text and the biblical Leviathan myths highlight how the Leviathan as a figure and lens pushes us to reconsider how we configure Judaism in relation to the land and as opposed to the Othered aquatic.

Bibliography

Alaimo, Stacy. "Feminist Science Studies and Ecocriticism: Aesthetics and Entanglement in the Deep Sea." In *The Oxford Handbook of Ecocriticism*, edited by Greg Garrard, 188–204. Oxford: Oxford University Press, 2014.

--------. "Oceanic Origins, Plastic Activism, and New Materialism at Sea." In *Exposed: Environmental Politics and Pleasures in Posthuman Times*, 111–42. Minneapolis, MN: University of Minnesota Press, 2016.

--------. "Violet-Black." In *Prismatic Ecology: Ecotheory beyond Green*, edited by Jeffrey Jerome Cohen, 233–51. Minneapolis, MN: University of Minnesota Press, 2013.

Alter, Robert. *Genesis: Translation and Commentary*. New York, NY: W.W. Norton, 1996.

Barber, Elizabeth Wayland, and Paul T. Barber. *When They Severed Earth from Sky: How the Human Mind Shapes Myth*. Princeton, NJ: Princeton University Press, 2012.

Beal, Timothy K. *Religion and Its Monsters*. New York, NY: Routledge, 2002.

Benjamin, Mara H. "'There Is No Away:' Ecological Fact as Jewish Theological Problem." *Religions* 13, no. 4 (2022): 290.

Cohen, Jeffrey Jerome. "Monster Culture (Seven Theses)." In *The Monster Theory Reader*, edited by Jeffrey Andrew Weinstock, 37–56. Minneapolis, MN: University of Minnesota Press, 2020.

Coogan, Michael D., et al., ed. *The New Oxford Annotated Bible: New Revised Standard Version With The Apocrypha: An Ecumenical Study Bible*. Oxford: Oxford University Press, 2010.

Fernández, David A. *De Monstris: An Exhibition of Monsters and the Wonders of Human Imagination*. Toronto: University of Toronto Library, 2018.

Friedan, Ken. "Neglected Origins of Modern Hebrew Prose: Hasidic and Maskilic Travel Narratives." *AJS Review* 33, no. 1 (2009): 3–43.

Giggs, Rebecca. *Fathoms: The World in a Whale*. New York, NY: Simon and Schuster, 2020.

Havrelock, Rachel. "Paradise on Earth." In *Seven Days, Many Voices: Insights into the Biblical Story of Creation*, edited by Benjamin David, 267–75. New York, NY: Central Conference of American Rabbis, 2017.

Jackson, Zakiyyah Iman. *Becoming Human: Matter and Meaning in an Antiblack World*. New York, NY: New York University Press, 2020.

JPS Hebrew-English Tanakh: The Traditional Hebrew Text and the New JPS Translation. Philadelphia, PA: Jewish Publication Society, 2003.

King, Tiffany Lethabo. *The Black Shoals: Offshore Formations of Black and Native Studies*. Durham, NC: Duke University Press, 2019.

Lioi, Anthony. "Of Swamp Dragons: Mud, Megalopolis, and a Future for Ecocriticism." In *The Monster Theory Reader*, edited by Jeffrey Andrew Weinstock, 439–58. Minneapolis, MN: University of Minnesota Press, 2020.

Maisel, Grace, and Samantha Shubert. "My Friend, the Sea Monster." In *A Year of Jewish Stories: 52 Tales for Children and Their Families*, 73–6. New York, NY: UAHC Press, 2004.

Morrison, Toni. *Playing in the Dark: Whiteness and the Literary Imagination*. Cambridge, MA: Harvard University Press, 1992.

Neimanis, Astrida. *Bodies of Water: Posthuman Feminist Phenomenology*. London: Bloomsbury Academic, 2016.

Odent, Michel. "Man, the Womb and the Sea: The Roots of the Symbolism of Water." *Pre- and Peri-Natal Psychology Journal* 7, no. 3 (1993): 187–93.

Orlov, Andrei A. *Supernal Serpent: Mysteries of Leviathan in Judaism and Christianity*. New York, NY: Oxford University Press, 2023.

Podos, Rebecca. *From Dust, A Flame*. New York, NY: Balzer + Bray, 2022.

Podwal, Mark. *A Jewish Bestiary: Fabulous Creatures from Hebraic Legend Et Lore*. University Park, PA: Pennsylvania State University Press, 2021.

Probyn-Rapsey, Fiona. "Anthropocentrism." In *Critical Terms for Animal Studies*, edited by Lori Gruen, 47–63. Chicago, IL: University of Chicago Press, 2018.

Roorda, Eric. *The Ocean Reader: History, Culture, Politics*. Durham, NC: Duke University Press, 2020.

Rubenstein, Mary-Jane. *Pantheologies: Gods, Worlds, Monsters*. New York, NY: Columbia University Press, 2018.

Schwartz, Howard. *Leaves from the Garden of Eden: One Hundred Classic Jewish Tales*. New York, NY: Oxford University Press, 2010.

Sharpe, Christina. *In the Wake: On Blackness and Being*. Durham, NC: Duke University Press, 2016.

Uehlinger, C. "Leviathan." In *Dictionary of Deities and Demons in the Bible (DDD)*, edited by Karel van der Toorn, Bob Becking, and Pieter W. van der Horst, 956–60. Leiden: Brill, 1995.

Wardi, Anissa Janine. "Blue Ecology and Resistance: Islands, Swamps, and Ecotones." In *Toni Morrison and the Natural World: An Ecology of Color*, 124–53. Jackson, MS: University Press of Mississippi, 2021.

Beyond Religious and Secular: Biblical Intertextuality in Modern Mizrahi Literature

Alina L. Schittenhelm

Introduction

For a long time, Israeli literature tried to become a secular-national literature and to "free itself from the 'burden' of its religious past."[1] In this context, recent academia states a shift away from the biblical as a striking feature of modern Hebrew writing.[2] In contrast, Mizrahi literature as a subgenre of Hebrew literature, is characterized by the fact that it always drew from the holdings of Judaism, including numerous direct and indirect biblical quotations, religious symbols, or Jewish mysticism as well as hints to the popular literature of al-Andalus (Muslim Spain), or *piyyutim*. In various aspects Mizrahi writing represents a broad and present spectrum of biblical references in literature. Thus, Mizrahi prose and poetry refuses the dichotomies of the canon and has not sided with the ideal of either secular or religious. Against this backdrop the following paper argues that the biblical intertextuality by Mizrahi authors must be read as a complex interaction with Jewish traditions in modernity. For this purpose, three examples of popular works of recent years are analyzed.

The article sheds light on the place of the Jewish Bible in Hebrew literature by Mizrahi authors. It is devoted to examples which are of ambivalent biblical allusions. They bear witness to complex identifications. They do not necessarily testify to a religious positioning but to a social milieu and are used as figures of speech or cultural symbols. Almog Behar's *Tchahla ve-Hezkel* (2010), Sara Shilos' *Shum Gamadim Lo Yavou* (2005), and Shimon Adaf's *Mox Nox* (2011) are presented as spotlights of biblical intertextuality in modern Mizrahi writing. The authors belong to the second and third generation of Mizrahi literature in Israel and stand for a cross section of this writing. There are explicitly religious Mizrahi authors, as Haim Sabbato (b. 1952 in Cairo, Egypt) for example, whose

---

1   Sh. Pinsker, "'Never Will I Hear the Sweet Voice of God': Religiosity and Mysticism in Modern Hebrew Poetry," *Prooftexts* 30, no. 1 (2010): 131; A. Balaban, "Biblical Allusions in Modern and Postmodern Hebrew Literature," *AJS Review* 28, no. 1 (2004): 194; A. Shapira, "The Bible and Israeli Identity," *AJS Review* 28, no. 1 (2004): 26.
2   V. Shemtov, "The Bible in Contemporary Israeli Literature: Text and Place in Zeruya Shalev's 'Husband and Wife' and Michal Govrin's 'Snapshots,'" *Hebrew Studies* 47 (2006): 364.

literature and style is precisely influenced by *piyyutim*. Haviva Pedaya's (b. 1957 in Jerusalem, Israel) poetic work contains obvious cabbalistic and mystical elements. Authors such as Dan-Benaya Seri (b. 1935 in Jerusalem, Mandatory Palestine), and Mira Kedar (b. 1956 in Jerusalem, Israel) draw on biblical stories and language too. Besides that a turn toward religious poetry can also be observed in the 2010s.[3] Nevertheless, the selected works are more representative of modern Mizrahi literature and its relationship to religion, while the explicit religious authors have a rather limited impact. The books presented here are directing religious content at a predominantly secular audience and by that, they blur the dichotomy of secular and religious through a literary approach.

Even though Mizrahi literature is unique in Israeli literature in this respect, this perspective has hardly been considered so far. In the reception of Mizrahi literature, the ethnic tensions between Mizrahim and Ashkenazim and the experience of migration often overlay the religious implications. The following analysis attempts to connect the ethnic and biblical threads. Based on the three examples I want to illustrate a biblical continuity in Jewish writing and Israeli culture and discourses. With a certain freedom in dealing with the biblical texts as well as the intertwining of Jewish motifs with other cultural frameworks of the Arab world, modern Mizrahi fiction connects to Jewish textual traditions and draws a multifactored positioning. In this context the examples also raise the question of what role traditionalism (*Masortiyut*) plays for *Mizrahiyut* in Israel. The following analysis shows that the Bible has many faces, and its textual diversity is still visible in various forms.

Tchahla ve-Hezkel (2010)

Tchahla ve-Hezkel ("Rachel and Ezekiel," 2010) is an example of a striking reference to the Bible and its tradition in modern Mizrahi writing. In a high, artful language, which is somewhat difficult to access even for Hebrew readers, Almog Behar's (b. 1978 in Netanya, Israel) novel tells the story of an initially childless married religious couple, living in the poor quarters of Jerusalem. Hezkel first works as a printer, Tchahla is a housewife. The print shop in which Hezkel works produces religious literature as well as secular fiction, which gives him a mediated connection to non-religious poetry and literature. When Hezkel

---

3   Pinsker, "'Never Will I Hear the Sweet Voice of God'," 140.

gets fired, he starts to look for new employment. Through a chance encounter, he begins to write and present poetry himself at the café *Tmol Shilshom*.[4] In Hezkel's becoming an author, the story is reminiscent of a *Bildungsroman*. Central to the plot is that Tchahla and Hezkel, who met through a *shiddukh*,[5] struggle to communicate with each other. The book is characterized by silence as a theme and yet the language is the outstanding feature of the book. In the background, economic misery and poverty are always smoldering.[6]

The novel expresses its ambivalence towards religion even before the actual content begins: the book is dedicated to Sasson Somekh (1933–2019), an author, translator, outspoken secularist, and former Professor for Arabic Literature at the Tel Aviv University, as well as to Rabbi Ovadia Yosef (1920–2013), a Talmudic scholar, the spiritual leader of the Haredi SHAS party and the Sephardi chief Rabbi of Israel from 1973 to 1983. This seemingly contradictory paratext points to a certain spiritual and religious influence, but also to an intellectual, scientific, and worldly perspective, that Behar tries to merge.

The first sentence of the novel makes the setting of the plot apparent. Through the opening saying "הלכה למשה מסיני"[7] [*halakha lemoshe misinai*, "a law given to Moshe in/from Sinai"][8], a phrase used to describe oral laws in Jewish tradition, the context can be clearly placed in the field of Jewish practice. The action takes place between Jerusalem's narrow lanes, small synagogues, the couple's apartment, that of his teacher Ovadia, and the literary café *Tmol Shilshom*, which points to a contemporary plot. The number of characters is limited but most of them are explicitly religious, traditional protagonists, which can be seen in their everyday practices, the spaces where they act, but also in their language. This limited but spiritual and intellectual world is a place rarely visited by Hebrew literature.[9] Although the setting is specific, *Tchahla ve-Hezkel* tells a human story about relationships and loneliness, about understanding and misunderstandings, and about living together in a diverse immigration society.

---

4 The literary café *Tmol Shilshom* was opened in the heart of Jeruslaem in 1994 and has since hosted many writers, artists and literary events. See: https://www.tmol-shilshom.co.il/אודות, last accessed February 3, 2024.
5 Almog Behar, *Rachel and Ezekiel/ צ'חלה וחזקל* (Jerusalem: Keter Books, 2010), 15.
6 N. Baram, "Al 'Tchahla ve-Hezkel' le Almog Behar," ["About 'Rachel and Ezekiel' by Almog Behar"] *Afirion*, no. 119 (2011): 42–43.
7 Behar, *Rachel and Ezekiel*, 9.
8 Translation of all Hebrew quotes in this article are my own, unless indicated otherwise.
9 Baram, "Al 'Tchahla ve-Hezkel' le Almog Behar."

Tchahla ve-Hezkel is drawing from the Talmud, *piyyutim*, and the Hebrew Bible itself. Hezkel, who is not entirely distinguishable from the narrator,[10] discovers his talent to write. As he himself remarks, his writing is clearly based on his religious education and knowledge of the Jewish sources, prayers and *piyyutim*[11]: "Maybe if I also put together a few lines that I've heard in the prayers and that I know by heart, and insert some words of mine in between that come to my mind, I can also write words as a song and call it my song,"[12] he thinks.

Behar makes use of a complex syntax, which is not strictly a Tanakhic or Talmudic language, although the Jewish sources resonate in it. Throughout the book there are recitations of prayers traditionally said at the *Biyur Hametz* ceremony or the blessing on wine and grape juice, for example,[13] but also contemporary, vernacular language as well as Arabic sentences.[14] Besides the biblical verses and phrases, which are liberally incorporated in the book, the text contains intertextual references to other Mizrahi literature and research, such as Haviva Pedaya, Sasson Somekh, Ella Shohat, Sami Michael, and Erez Biton.[15] Behar uses them all quite freely, which underlines the crossovers in his work. The complexity of the various characterizations in Behar's book is expressed, for example, in a scene in which the protagonist is standing in line at the bank and at the train station. In these worldly places, his mind wanders. He recites *Shir Hashirim,* the book of Song of Songs, which is quoted with great regularity, and which he had to learn by heart, but after two lines he forgets the wording.[16] The motif of the forgotten text is repeated a few times in the book.[17]

Behar strews his novel with biblical verses as well as rabbinical idioms, a practice that reminds writers of the *Haskalah*. One example of biblical intertextuality in the text can be found in the topic of naming. As in other works by Mizrahi authors, Behar takes the names of the protagonists as an opportunity to link the migration narrative with biblical stories. On page 232 it is mentioned that the characters originally had other names when they arrived in Israel. Rabbi Ovadia, for example, was called Abdallah and his wife Mazal, Georgette. These names refer to an Arab (Iraqi) and North African, respectively

---

10   Behar, *Rachel and Ezekiel*, 58.
11   Ibid., 39–44.
12   Ibid., 43: [...], אולי גם אני אם אצרף שורות ששמעתי בתפילות ופסוקים שאני זוכר על-פה ואחבר ביניהם מעט מילים משלי שיעלו בראשי, אוכל לכתוב דברים צורת שיר ולומר זה השיר שלי.
13   Ibid., 36; 83.
14   Ibid., 243.
15   Ibid., 27–28; 41–42; 100; 171–72; 225; 228.
16   Ibid., 98.
17   Ibid., 34; 75.

French colonial (Moroccan), context. Behar addresses the fact that many immigrants, upon their arrival in Israel, had to shed their old names in favor of new Hebrew names. Names, like Georgette for example, had the fragrance of foreign countries attached to them and names like Abdallah were even more associated with the supposed new Arab enemies. Migrants in Israel therefore had to be "Hebrewized," which is what the Jewish-Hebrew names Mazal and Ovadia stand for. This theme is repeated earlier on page 203 of Behar's novel, where a Midrash on the book of Exodus, or Shemot, is indirectly quoted:

> ... How will you be prepared for miracles and wonders if you change your names and your languages and your clothes, for which the Israelites in Egypt were praised for not changing their names, nor changing their language, nor changing their clothes, nor did the Israelites in Babylon change their names, nor change their language, nor change their clothes, whereas you are the children of Babylon in Israel you changed your names and you changed your language and you changed your clothes, we changed our names and we changed our language and we changed our clothes ...[18]

This biblical intertextuality appears frequently in Mizrahi literature. Almog Behar, as well as the poet and activist Sami Shalom Chetrit (b. 1960 in Errachidia, Morocco) in his poem *Ele Shemot* ("These are the Names," 2003) for example, allude to the Exodus from Egypt in their wording.[19] The content, however, also refers to the Midrash Leviticus Rabbah 32, which lists four reasons for the liberation from Egypt: first, the Israelites did not changed their name, second, they kept their language, furthermore, they did not speak bad of others, and fourth, they were not sexually promiscuous. These reasons can also be found in the *Lekah Tov* written by the Talmudist Tobia ben Eliezer or the writings of Rabbi Eliyahu Habahur, who said that Israel did not change their name, their clothing, and their language in Egypt. In the figurative sense Behar, as well as Chetrit, retell the Israelite genealogy and point to a gap: those who came to Israel in the 1950s and 60s were forced to change their names and language.[20] By that the prevailing narrative in today's Israel rendered Georgette and Abdallah invisible and allowed only one narrow Jewish narrative. In other

---

18   Ibid., 203: [...] איך תהיו מוכנים לנסים ולפלאות אם אתם משנים שמותיכם ולשונותיכם ולבושיכם, שעל בני ישראל במצרים נאמר לשבח שלא שינו שמם ולא שינו לשונם ולא שינו לבושם, ואף בני ישראל בבבל לא שינו שמם ולא שינו לשונם ולא שינו לבושם, ואילו אתם בני בבל בישראל שיניתם שמותיכם ושיניתם לשונכם ושיניתם לבושכם, שינינו שמותינו ושינינו לשוננו ושינינו לבושנו [...]
19   S. Chetrit, שירים באשדודית [*Songs in Ashdodit*] (Tel Aviv: Andalus Publishing, 2003).
20   E. Schely-Newman, "Poetics of Identity: Mizrahi Poets between Here and There, Then and Now," in *Israel: A Diaspora of Memories*, ed. M. Baussant, D. Miccoli, and E. Schely-Newman, special issue of *Quest. Issues in Contemporary Jewish History* 16 (2019): 80.

texts, this experience is emphasized more clearly as a trauma of migration; in Behar's case it is more implied.

Many authors recalled the Exodus from Egypt as well as the Babylonian exile and the parable about the tower of Babel in the book of Genesis. Since these stories are dealing with themes such as migration, homeland, and language, they are frequently invoked in Mizrahi literature. The intertextuality is an approach to retell modern migration experiences in traditional images.[21] The literary scholar Avraham Balaban argues in this context that "despite losing its religious content, the biblical stories are still narratives that can be recycled and retold, or transferred ... to modern Israel."[22] Tying in with universal Jewish stories can be read as an attempt of the authors to make the memories relatable for non-Mizrahi Jews, for example, and to make themselves heard in Israeli society, which is still Ashkenazi-dominated. These selective motifs nevertheless highlight certain values from the canon. Here they fulfill a political purpose and parallel the immigration of Jews from the Arab world to Israel in the twentieth century. Several references to Babel can be also found in Shimon Ballas' early work *Hamaabara* (1964) or in Mona Yahia's *When the Grey Beetles Took Over Baghdad* (2000), for instance. Due to its geographical location, Babel was a particularly suitable reference for Iraqi writers.

Besides the ethnic gap, the theme that most characterizes Mizrahi literature is the complex relationship to Arabic as a culture and language. Apart from the Jewish influences, Arabic elements are also important for Behar's novel. The reference to Mizrahi history and discourse in the book is provided, among other things, by the historical Black Panthers group in Israel. Hezkel does not want to join the political movement of his friend, the "New Black Panthers"; politics does not seem to interest him very much.[23] The *Panterim Hashhhorim* [הפנתרים השחורים, *The Black Panthers*], to which reference is made here and whose name is directly linked to the Black Panther movement in the USA, was founded in 1971. The group's protests initially took place in Musrara, a former Palestinian neighborhood of Jerusalem. Later, numerous Mizrahi citizens across the country joined the protests. By August of the same year, the movement had held demonstrations throughout Israel with up to ten thousand participants. Their demands included the upgrading of Mizrahi housing, higher wages and improved working conditions, better and free access to

---

21   R. Kartun-Blun, "Isaaks Schrecken: Der Mythos der Opferung in der hebräischen Dichtung," in *Moderne Hebräische Literatur—Ein Handbuch*, ed. A. Feinberg (München: Richard Boorberg Verlag, 2005), 53.
22   Balaban, "Biblical Allusions in Modern and Postmodern Hebrew Literature," 203.
23   Behar, *Rachel and Ezekiel*, 69–70.

education and healthcare systems, and greater representation of Mizrahim in Israeli politics and public life.[24] The movement is referred to in the book as the "New Panthers," suggesting that there is continuity in the Mizrahi concerns. The evocation of the movement in the present points to the structural problems that have become entrenched since the original movement in the 1970s. Although Hezkel is not interested in a commitment to the group, he identifies with the Arab part of his personality. He for example, buys Umm Kulthum's Arabic music with the little money he has, or reads Mizrahi poetry, fiction, and research.[25] Furthermore the gradually revealed storyline that Hezkel has an Arab half-brother through his father, indicates a strong but complicated relationship with Arab culture. It is no coincidence that this story is also reminiscent of Abraham's son Ishmael with the Egyptian maid Hagar (Gen 16–17). It thus points to a natural closeness but also a remarkable distance between the unequal Arab and Jewish siblings. These remarks in the text point to the ambivalence that links Behar's book with the other works presented below.

Behar became known for his short story *Ana Min Al-Yahud* ("I am one of the Jews," 2005) in which Arabic as a culture and language comes to the forefront even more than in the novel. *Ana Min Al-Yahud* won *Haaretz*'s prestigious short story competition in 2005 and caused a stir among the Israeli public with its subject of the linguistic distress of the Mizrahim. The story, whose oxymoronic Arabic title irritated its Hebrew audience, addresses the loss of Jewish languages. The narrator, who miraculously forfeits his knowledge of Hebrew, suddenly lapses into his grandparents' Arabic diction. For the Israeli police this makes him indistinguishable from Palestinians. His attempts to reclaim his Israeli-Jewish identity on a linguistic level fail. Although he professes to be "one of the Jews" [أنا من اليهود, *ana min al-yahud*], he falls under a general suspicion precisely because of his language as a marker of non-belonging. As the story unfolds, the ominous "Dybbuk" of aphasia begins to infect other Israelis of different backgrounds, who also revert to the different accents of their ancestors. In confronting his parents and grandparents, who had laboriously broken away from Arabic, and resisting the virus, the narrator decides to remain silent. But even silence no longer represents a way out of his tragedy: he is nevertheless imprisoned and, as someone who is read as an Arab, particularly harassed. Through the impossibility of the narrator's return to his Israeli-Jewish identity,

---

24 J. Massad, "Zionism's Internal Others: Israel and the Oriental Jews," *Journal of Palestine Studies* 25, no. 4 (1996): 62; S. Chetrit, *Intra-Jewish Conflict in Israel: White Jews, Black Jews* (New York, NY: Routledge, 2010), 80–140; E. Shohat, "Sephardim in Israel—Zionism from the Standpoint of Its Jewish Victims," *Social Text* 19/20 (1988): 29–30.

25 Behar, *Rachel and Ezekiel*, 159–60.

Behar confronts his reading audience with the pain of the linguistic dilemma and the despair over the loss of the common Arab-Jewish heritage.[26]

Tchahla ve-Hezkel comes to a head with the planned pessah seder, which is intended to bring together the different positions to one holiday table, typified by the different invited protagonists. Behar's characters, however, are not completely absorbed by either the Jewish or the Arab culture and always remain in the in-between. *Tchahla ve-Hezkel* demonstrates an ambivalence between secular and religious, and between the Jewish and migrant identity, in a special way. Compared to other books in the genre, Jewish sources have a significantly higher relevance. More clearly than others, Behar chooses religion as a literary, thematic, and stylistic framework to narrate the identity conflict. The following paragraph introduces Sara Shilo's novel *Shum Gamadim Lo Yavou* in which this reference is chosen more restrained.

Shum Gamadim Lo Yavou (2005)

Sara Shilo's (b. 1958 in Jerusalem, Israel) award-winning novel *Shum Gamadim Lo Yavou* ("No Gnomes Will Appear," 2005) sheds light on an implicit approach to the Bible. The novel consists of individual monologues and became especially known for its striking language use, but in a different way than Behar's novel. The story is about a family in the Israeli periphery and is set in the early 1980s, shortly after the historic Knesset election of 1977. Shilo's and Behar's novels are comparable in their remoteness, however, the characters are not religious as in Behar's book. They therefore represent a different religious orientation. The plot of Shilo's novel, which has been translated into several languages, takes place in a *Masorti*, traditionalist-influenced surrounding, which is especially evident to Israeli and Hebrew readers. It can be assumed due to implications to the football club *Beitar Yerushalayim* or recurrently motioned assembly of the historically significant person of Rav Meir Kahane (1932–1990), the founder of the right-wing, religious party KAKH (כך). Kahane as well as the logo of his party, a "fist, yellow in a puddle of black"[27] that forms a Star of David, are described in Shilo's novel. Time references in the book are also often based

---

26   L. Levy, *Poetic Trespass: Writing between Hebrew and Arabic in Israel/Palestine* (Princeton, NJ: Princeton University Press, 2014), 296; R. Snir, "'Anā Min al-Yahūd': The Demise of Arab-Jewish Culture in the Twentieth Century," *Archiv Orientální* 74 (2006): 402–3.

27   S. Shilo, שום גמדים לא יבואו [*No Gnomes Will Appear*] (Tel Aviv: Am Oved, 2005), 250.

on Jewish holidays.[28] However, religiosity is more of a subplot that can easily be overlooked in the translations. Cultural knowledge is a precondition here.

Since most of Shilo's book is written in a supposedly lower language register, there is rather less reference to artistic biblical Hebrew phrasings. At first glance, the Hebrew in *Shum Gamadim Lo Yavou* seems to be a secularized slang or everyday language–the vernacular serves for communication and has no higher meaning. Nevertheless, the word "God" alone occurs almost a hundred times in Shilo's novel, and the first generation of immigrants also use spiritual Arabic terms or phrases, such as (*min*) *allah*[29], *inshallah*[30], or *ya rabb*.[31] Especially in the chapter of the two brothers, Dudi and Itzik, liberally biblical allusions can be found. They relate to the creation of the world by God,[32] the delivery of the Ten Commandments to Moses at mount Sinai,[33] to the Garden Eden, or to the story of Noah.[34] Here a selective choice of topoi and well-known biblical narratives is taken up. The main topic of the brothers' monologue is their complex relationship with each other, with God, and with the falconess Delilah, whom they raise to defend them from terrorists. The ease and confidence with which the protagonists in *Shum Gamadim Lo Yavou* use the biblical metaphors indicates a high intertwining of Jewish motifs in their daily lives and thinking. The narratives are presupposed to some extent.

> I have apologized to Herzl and King David and Abraham, Itzhak, Ya'akov and the four mothers, and also Hagar, whom I put with them, for how she was sent to the desert to die with Ishmael, and I also apologized to all IDF Soldiers ...[35]

In this quote, modern Zionist symbols are mixed with religious ones. The *Declaration of Independence* proclaimed Israel 1948 a democratic and Jewish state. The self-conception of the state has therefore always been theological.

---

28 Brit Mila (see Shilo, *Shum gamadim*, 35), Hanukka (50; 226), Shabbat (42; 46; 63; 107; 150; 157; 162; 172; 179; 182; 202; 204; 233; 252), Pessah (18; 87; 93; 150; 157; 207), חד גדיא/Had Gadia (251–252), Yom Kippur (28; 114; 118). Author's note: In the German translation, Lag Baomer is replaced several times by Pessah, presumably for the benefit of a better understanding of the audience (see Shilo, *Shum gamadim*, 28; 157, 207).
29 Shilo, *Shum gamadim*, 27; 37.
30 Ibid., 18.
31 Ibid., 12–13; 47–50.
32 Ibid., 107.
33 Ibid., 96.
34 Ibid., 128.
35 Ibid., 134: [...] ביקשתי סליחה מהרצל ודויד המלך ואברהם יצחק יעקב וארבע אמהות, וגם את הגר שמתי אתם ביחד על איך שזרקו אותה במדבר למות עם ישמעאל, וגם ביקשתי סליחה מכל חיילי צה"ל [...].

There is no formal separation between state and religion in Israel's legal and political system to this day. Religion is intertwined at all levels of governance and society.[36] As a result, faith in the public sphere and political rhetoric is indeed more dominant in comparison to other Western countries. In literature, biblical narratives have long served to unite the spiritual past with the political present. The Bible nurtured a national romanticism which served as a proof of the historical continuity between land and people.[37] Since Palestine's topography was full of symbolic attributions, the Bible also lent an influential intertext for imagining or describing a Jewish state by Hebrew writers in the twentieth century.[38] As mentioned above, dealing with the topics of migration and exile in Hebrew literature also promoted the reference to canonical imagery. In the quotation out of Shilo's novel, the Bible functions as a cultural metaphor. The biblical genealogy stands side by side with secular, patriotic tokens such as Theodor Herzl or the Israeli Army. Jewish textual tradition is here meant as a cultural, nationalist symbol. The series in Dudi's apology points to the entanglement of the Jewish textual traditions in the Israeli statehood and everyday culture. As in this quotation, the Bible functions as a political and thus Zionist narrative in Israeli literature.[39] Even though the references are quite mediated, the Israeli cultural context enters through the biblical intertextuality in Shilo's novel and help to situate the plot in a very specific cultural and literary tradition.

The biblical allusions in the text are used quite freely, as Itzik's following comparison of the cinema with paradise shows:

> Believe me Dudi, when you go into the movie you're not in the world anymore. It's paradise, I swear paradise. [...] Only that the guard of the paradise is Shushan, the son of a bitch, not such an angel.[40]

The cinema serves as a heterotopia to the neglected neighborhood in Shilo's text. For the disillusioned Itzik and his little brother Dudi, it is an exceptional refuge and a transcendent place. For them, film is the only way to encounter Western culture and opens up a foreign world that exceed the closed space of

---

36 R. Halperin-Kaddari and Y. Yadgar, "Between Universal Feminism and Particular Nationalism: Politics, Religion and Gender (in)Equality in Israel," *Third World Quarterly* 31, no. 6 (2010): 905.
37 Shapira, "The Bible and Israeli Identity," 11.
38 Shemtov, "Bible in contemporary Israeli Literature," 364.
39 Ibid., 363.
40 Shilo, *Shum gamadim*, 128: .תאמין לי דודי, שאתה נכנס לסרט אתה כבר לא בתוך העולם
גן-עדן זה, בחיי גן-עדן. [...] רק שהשומר של הגן-עדן זה שושן הבנזונה, לא איזה מלאך.

their own milieu and cramped surrounding: "Movies are mandatory, without [them] you'd die here."[41] The positive biblical metaphor, however, is disrupted. The cinema does not quite correspond to paradise on earth. Shushan is not an "angel," as he catches the children trying to squeeze into one pair of pants as "on the ark of Noah" to hide and save one entrance fee. Dudi and Itzik have a complicated relationship with religion and feel abandoned by God. The cinema nevertheless opens a sphere of the fantastic for the brothers and suggests that imagination alone enables the protagonists to overcome their geographical marginality and limited perspectives.[42]

Rabbinical quotes can also be found in the novel. Their high-flown Hebrew stands out clearly. The literary scholar Vered Shemtov notes that the role of the Bible in Hebrew literature has changed. She argues that biblical intertextuality in contemporary fiction is less common than it was in the past and therefore is often very striking in the texts.[43] This is especially true for the rabbinic quotations in this book. It is important to point out here that these sayings are used by the probably Ashkenazi manager of the factory,[44] in which the oldest brother Kobi works. Regarding the wave of layoffs ordered by the local authority, the factory manager quotes Mishna Pirkei Avot: "Beware of the authorities" [הֱווּ זְהִירִין בָּרָשׁוּת, m. Avot 2:3][45], and enlists Kobi in his plan. The sayings are expressed in a business-related conversation. They are used to describe a certain work ethos, to moralize hard work and sacrifice and, not least, to end the meeting. Since Ashkenazi figures in Mizrahi literature are usually characterized in a rather secular way, and because Kobi adds, that the wording of his boss makes him feel like "you're back in school,"[46] the quotes can be interpreted as a statement of authority which establish the hierarchy between the two characters. They irritate by not confirming the lower language of the previous chapters. By that the rabbinical sayings attest to an intellectual approach and educational horizon that the proletarian Mizrahi characters, despite their traditional background, do not seem to have. Nevertheless, the quotes are taken out of their spiritual context and seem to be used more like proverbs than as religious wisdom. Kobi's alienation is also reinforced in another scene

---

41 Ibid., 168.
42 Y. Oppenheimer, "Representation of Space in Mizrahi Fiction," *Hebrew Studies* 53 (2012): 350–51.
43 Shemtov, "Bible in contemporary Israeli Literature," 364–66.
44 Shilo, *Shum gamadim*, 147–50.
45 Ibid., 147.
46 Ibid., 150.

in which he says the *Kaddish* for his father. The corresponding bow he casually describes as doing a "yes with the head."[47]

The main protagonists in Shilo's novel are the elder daughter, Etti, and the mother, Simona. The father is completely absent due to his sudden death. Contrary to the patriarchal and orientalist stereotype, Mizrahi writing often rather testify to a female dominance in families, multifaceted and dynamic relationships between women, and initiation stories of upstanding girls. Authors like Ronit Matalon (1959–2017), Orly Castel-Bloom (1960), Dudu Bussi (1963), Sami Berdugo (1970), Dorit Rabinyan (1972), and Shilo show widowed, divorced, single, working, loving, rising, but also broken women. Interesting in relation to gender and Bible is also, that the brothers in Shilo's novel name their beloved falcon after Delilah, Shimshon's lover in the book of Judges,[48] who in Jewish tradition is mostly interpreted rather negatively as a non-Jewish *femme fatale*. The falcon turns out to be male and is therefore killed. The aforementioned reference to Hagar, the Egyptian maid and Abraham's concubine, also ties in with this. Interestingly, Castel-Bloom, an author of Egyptian origin, also evokes the image of the female demon Lilith from the book of Isaiah in her novel *Dolly City* (1992), as well as in the short story *Ummi Fi Shurl*.[49] Lilith and Delilah here epitomize women who refuse to be defined by men. Both are hardly present figures in the Bible but are personified with the danger of the beauty as well as with the evil. Here, reference is made to a mode of resistant femininity that can be traced in other aspects in Mizrahi fiction as well. Analyzing Mizrahi literature through the lens of gender likewise reveals no distinct positioning in the spectrum of religiosity and secularism, but rather a broad spectrum of female characters with confident decisions for and against traditionalism but also uncertainties about faith.

Shilo chooses a peripheral place instead of a holy place, such as Jerusalem in Behar's novel, for her action. The protagonists even seem alienated from the sacred sites, as can be seen, for example, in the fact that Etti does not seem to develop any connection to the nationally relevant sights during a school trip to Jerusalem and is only interested in the radio tower.[50] This shows how biblical places, which are also ordinary places in today's Israel, are opened up for non-religious interpretations in Israeli literature. As argued, *Shum Gamadim Lo Yavou* nevertheless takes place in a *Masorti* surrounding. In this way, the novel

---

47　Ibid., 162.
48　Shilo, *Shum gamadim*, 94.
49　Z. Ben-Yoseph Ginor, "Involuntary Myths: Mania, Mother, and Zion in Orly Castel-Bloom's 'Ummi Fi Shurl'," *Prooftexts* 25, no. 3 (2005): 247–48.
50　Shilo, *Shum gamadim*, 228.

depicts a milieu that is rare in canonical Hebrew literature, but which reveals a very specifically Mizrahi-Israeli space. Dudu Bussi's book *Ima Mitgaagaat Lamilim* ("Mom is Longing for Words," 2006), for example, but also Shimon Adaf's novel *Mox Nox*, analyzed below, refer to a similar environment.

Mox Nox (2011)

Shimon Adaf's (1972 in Sderot, Israel) œuvre consists of detective novels, poetry, short stories, science fiction, and fantasy. More or less obvious references in the texts suggest that the main characters are usually Mizrahim.[51] Adaf's writing is moreover known for strong mystical and mythical undertones and references to multiple texts and languages.[52] *Mox Nox* ("Night is Soon to Come," 2011) is Adaf's fifth novel and the counterpart to his previous novel, *Kfor* ("Nuntia," 2010), a religious dystopia and *Arim Shel Mata* ("Undercities," 2012), which he published afterwards. The series *Kfor*, *Mox Nox* and *Arim Shel Mata* can be read as a trilogy on the subject of religion, but *Mox Nox* is considered one of Adaf's more accessible and realistic books.[53] As Shilo's *Shum Gamadim Lo Yavou*, *Mox Nox* won the prestigious Sapir Prize in 2012. In the context of this analysis, the chosen novel represents an intermediate form: it takes an explicit approach to religious identity. It refers to a similar social and spatial remoteness as Shilo's book, but faith is, as in Behar's novel, much more present for the Mizrahi identity of the characters. At the same time, biblical quotes are encrypted, modified, and used sparingly, significantly less than in Behar's book. In Adaf's book, *Mizrahiyut* is primarily presented as a question of religion and class. *Kfor*, which is also accounted in the analysis at the end of the chapter, in turn refers strongly to the tradition of *piyyutim*.

Mox Nox is divided into two parallel narratives, between which there is no chronological alternation. It consists of 51 short chapters, constantly moving back and forth between the past and the present. The first autobiographically inspired story part is about a teenager from a religious family. It is set in the

---

51   Sh. Adaf and Y. Schwarz, "החיפוש אחר שורשי הדמיון," ["The Search for the Roots of Imagination,"] *Haaretz*, August 17, 2011, https://www.haaretz.co.il/misc/2011-08-17/ty-article/0000017f-dbf8-d3ff-a7ff-fbf8e7060000, last accessed February 3, 2024; D. Lemberger, "Contacts and Discontinuities: Changing Aspects in Shimon Adaf's Work," *Hebrew Studies* 55 (2014): 329.

52   Y. Dekel, "The Place, Makom, Nonplace: Between Netivot and Tel Aviv in Shimon Adaf's Panim Zeruvei Hamah (Sunburnt Faces)," *Shofar* 36, no. 3 (2018): 61.

53   L. Volach, "'Mox Nox' by Shimon Adaf: His Most Accessible Novel," *walla.co.il*, August 10, 2011, https://e.walla.co.il/item/1848635, last accessed February 3, 2024.

southern periphery, from which it is essential to "get out."[54] It is important to mention here that the nameless place is labeled as an *Ayara*. This indicates that it is a former development town, which replaced the Israeli immigrant camps from the early fifties onwards.[55] *Shum Gamadim Lo Yavou* also plays in an *Ayara*. Karen Grumberg points out that especially places like these, which have no political or cultural significance, invite their inhabitants to hold on to traditions and customs.[56] Therefore, the location is constitutive for the plot and the religious identification in the book. The second narrative strand takes place a few years later. The adult protagonist now lives in southern Tel Aviv, works as an author, and holds literary workshops. Tel Aviv is a completely different place that suggests centrality and participation. Like Hezkel and Etti, the main protagonist here is concerned with gaining a voice. He finds it in writing although his books do not seem too successful or accessible.[57] Here, too, the author echoes in the protagonist himself.

One of the main themes is the fragility of religious identity. In the first storyline the narrator describes the events of a summer in which the protagonist works in a kibbutz factory for dried fruits, where his father is also employed.[58] The sixteen-year-old is only moderately suited to the work in the factory, but he requires the money to buy books.[59] The most significant issue presented is that the nameless boy decides to detach himself from faith and his surroundings, represented by the religious, irascible father figure: "ברחתי מבית הכנסת מפני זעם אבי" ["I fled the synagogue from my father's anger"][60], the protagonist notes. He gradually stops praying and instead devotes himself to the Latin language and ancient philosophy as well as philosophy of the enlightenment.[61] Although the kibbutz is a distinctly Ashkenazi and secular place, the loss of faith is attributed to the bookstore and the town rather than the kibbutz. In the kibbutz, the Mizrahi characters are workers and therefore excluded from the actual idealistic space.

---

54 Sh. Adaf, מוקס נוקס [*Mox Nox*] (Or Yehuda: Kinneret/ Dvir, 2011), 172.
55 O. Yiftachel, "Social Control, Urban Planning and Ethno-Class Relations: Mizrahi Jews in Israel's 'Development Towns,'" *International Journal of Urban and Regional Research* 24 (2000): 418–26.
56 K. Grumberg, *Place and Ideology in Contemporary Hebrew Literature* (Syracuse, NY: Syracuse University Press, 2011), 3–4.
57 Adaf, *Mox Nox*, 233.
58 Ibid., 10.
59 Ibid., 32–33.
60 Ibid., 8.
61 Ibid., 11; 33; 41.

The protagonist escapes to the library, to the bookshop and spends a lot of time learning Latin grammar. This thread unfolds the relationship with his father. Referring to earlier poems by Adaf, Dorit Lemberger notes that the image of the cruel father and the intergenerational conflict due to disagreement over religious issues is a reappearing subject in Adaf's work. Lemberger compares this literary image to Gen 22,[62] the divine command toward Abraham to sacrifice his son Isaac–a recurring motif in Hebrew poetry.[63] In fact, the conflict with the father, who embodies religiosity, is central to the book. The motif is implicit, but here, too, the father virtually sacrifices the relationship to his family for his piety. All children, but also his wife, explicitly or inwardly turn away from him. The biblically negotiated bond between humankind and God becomes a negotiation of the relation between people in Adaf's novel. In an interview from 2012, the author defines his own relationship to Judaism as follows:

> Nowadays I am not religious in the institutional sense, but it is something I cannot escape from. All my aesthetics pass through the Jewish world. I am a machine built by Jewish engineers and the chief engineer was my father. My main dialog is with the Mishnah, the Talmud and the Rambam, and I move between great love and loathing for this. When you grow up in a strict religious home, the Halacha is the first thing you hate.[64]

Mox Nox largely dispenses with theological questions. Judaism is traced through symbols as prayers, the synagogue as a place of action, ritual objects, and religious clothing (*kippah, tallit, tefillin*). Biblical intertextuality is highly implicit. In very abstract and coded scenes, however, the protagonist reflects on the creation of the world, for example, or makes linguistic reflections on rabbinic, Latin and Hebrew vocabulary.[65] However, Jewish culture becomes more present through the language used. The *Masorti* milieu of the book influences linguistic processes in terms of word choice, syntax, and morphology.

---

62 D. Lemberger, "Questioning Boundaries of Language and the World: Ambivalence and Disillusionment in the Writings of Shimon Adaf," *Hebrew Studies* 56 (2015): 278.
63 Kartun-Blun, "Isaaks Schrecken: Der Mythos der Opferung in der hebräischen Dichtung."
64 E. Eliyahu, "שמעון אדף על הרגע שבו סופר נולד", ["Shimon Adaf about the Moment a Writer Was Born,"] *Haaretz*, December 25, 2012, https://www.haaretz.co.il/gallery/literature/2012-12-25/ty-article/0000017f-ee2b-d3be-ad7f-fe2bca910000, last accessed February 3, 2024: אני לא דתי היום במובן הממסדי, אבל זה משהו שאני לא יכול לברוח ממנו. כל האסתטיקה שלי עוברת דרך העולם היהודי. אני מכונה שבנו מהנדסים יהודים והמהנדס הראשי היה אבא שלי. עיקר הדיאלוג שלי הוא עם המשנה, התלמוד והרמב"ם, ואני נע בין אהבה עצומה לזה ובין תיעוב גדול. כשאתה גדל בבית דתי נוקשה אז ההלכה זה הדבר הראשון שאתה שונא.
65 Adaf, *Mox Nox*, 144; 246.

Biblical vocabulary appears occasionally in the form of idioms or proverbs and specific verb conjugations. Chapter eight, for example, begins with a biblically inspired phrase: "חמתו של אבי בערה בו להשחית" ["My father's anger burned within him (to the point of destruction)"; Esther 1:12][66], which appears in a similar form in the book of Esther, when Vashti refuses to appear before the king Ahasuerus. In the same dialog, the protagonist also uses the biblical saying: "על אפך ועל חמתך אני אלך" [כִּי עַל-אַפִּי וְעַל-חֲמָתִי]; "Even if it makes you angry"; Jer 32:31][67] towards his father. The proverb quoted on page 135, "שהמושל ברוחו וכובש את יצמו, for example, refers also in the context of anger to rabbinical literature.[68] The quote echoes a formulation in Rabbi David Kimchi's commentary on Kings 1:2: "ומושל בנפשך וכובש את יצרך" ["And a ruler in your soul and conquers your desire"; RADAK on 1 Kings 2:2]. Religious language is used throughout the novel, but characterizes in particular the description of the father.

In her research dealing with the speech of Mizrahim in Israel, the linguist Yehudit Henshke establishes the concept of *Ivrit Masoratit* ["traditional Hebrew"]. Henshke argues, that a widespread traditionalism among Mizrahim, is reflected as a sociolinguistic feature in the "language of the Israeli periphery."[69] Henshke's concept therefore refers to the living environment of Mizrahim in Israel and thus the plot location of all three novels. *Masorti*, Henshke says, as it is closely associated with Mizrahi, thus includes a significant component of linguistic and cultural continuity. The religious idiom hence encompasses the cultural space of its speakers as a contemporary Israeli identity. The language which is closely linked to the places symbolizes a shared Mizrahi memory of customs, feelings, values, and beliefs.[70] It is therefore not surprising that many Jewish, Middle Eastern religious and textual traditions are interwoven in contemporary Mizrahi fiction. Omnipresent proverbs, metaphors, creeds, and words from the semantic field of the biblical traditions shape the language of the protagonists in Mizrahi literature and poetry and in the Israeli periphery, which they map. The wording characterizes the social, spiritual, and political milieu. The intertextuality with the Bible contributes to

---

66   Ibid., 32.
67   Ibid., 33.
68   Ibid., 135.
69   Y. Henshke, "Israeli, Jewish, Mizrahi or Traditional? On the Nature of the Hebrew of Israel's Periphery," *Journal of Jewish Studies* 68, no. 1 (2017): 147–56.
70   Y. Henshke, "On the Mizraḥi Sociolect in Israel: A Sociolexical Consideration of the Hebrew of Israelis of North African Origin," *Journal of Jewish Languages* 1, no. 2 (2013): 222–23.

the definition of the literary world and the environment in this literature. This turns rabbinical and biblical language into a modern artistic and political tool.

The ongoing search for the relationship between the world and language is a central theme throughout Adaf's writing.[71] *Mox Nox* mixes a colloquial Hebrew, a high-level religious speech, and the Latin language (in Hebrew transcription). The book's title, an expression that in Latin means "night is soon to come," and its meaning of "the matter is expedited" or "something approaches the matter," points to ambiguities. The linguistic diversity and the crossovers refer to the experience of disassociation and fragmentation of Mizrahim in Israel. However, Adaf's story shifts not only between languages but also between times and spaces: the protagonist „simultaneously belongs and does not belong" to neither of the two settings.[72] Adia Mendelsohn-Maoz notes in this context, that by replacing the Zionist ideal of a stable identity with a process of "becoming" and the absence of a set home and temporality, the book "presents an aesthetic alternative that deliberately resists any fixed notion of space and identity."[73] Lemberger also claims appropriately, that the hybridity in Adaf's work enables him to overcome the particularism of identity politics. By confounding the readers expectations, he steps out of the representative mode and asks universal questions.[74] Adaf's work thus opens options in-between.

Both Adaf and Behar grew up in a traditional environment. The spotlights on their work show that their literary project is clearly based in the culture of traditional Sephardic Judaism. Behar's style and language refer to liturgical poetry, the *Halakha* and the *Midrash*. Their writing is an exceptional example of the presence of ancient texts in modern Hebrew writing. As in Behar's novel, *piyyutim* play a central role in Adaf's dystopia *Kfor*, which combines science fiction and fantasy with a deep grounding in Judaism. In the book itself *piyyutim* are presented as the right to express oneself.[75] The plot centers on investigation of people reciting religious poems without having passed the corresponding exam–likewise contagious phenomenon, for which there is initially no kosher medicine.[76] The misappropriation of the liturgy leads to misery.[77] Gideon Katz states, that the recurs on *Piyyut* in *Kfor* "reinforces the

---

71 Lemberger, "Ambivalence and Disillusionment in the Writings of Shimon Adaf," 293.
72 A. Mendelsohn-Maoz, "Shimon Adaf and the Peripheral Novel," *Journal of Jewish Identities* 7, no. 2 (2014): 9.
73 Ibid., 11.
74 Lemberger, "Contacts and Discontinuities," 329.
75 Sh. Adaf, כפור [*Nuntia*] (Or Yehuda: Kinneret/ Dvir, 2010), 147.
76 Ibid., 181–82.
77 Ibid., 160.

image of Judaism as a semi-lost entity."[78] Although Adaf's dystopia "focuses on the life of an Orthodox community and describes the life and faith of its inhabitants," Katz argues that the reference to *piyyutim* hint "at another kind of Judaism, dissimilar to both the Judaism of the Diaspora and to the Israeli stereotype of the ultra-Orthodox."[79] The reference to *piyyutim* at this point is thus not only Jewish, but Mizrahi Jewish. As a similar practice in the Ashkenazi tradition was lost over time, the liturgical poems have shaped Sephardic culture in particular.[80] In her book *Return of the Lost Voice*, the author and scholar Haviva Pedaya herself discusses the influence of *piyyutim* on Israeli culture. She notes a secularized opening in the cultural field from the 1980s onwards.[81] According to Pedaya, the search for identity in the Israeli context can also be cited as a reason for the turn to *piyyut* in pop culture.[82] Adaf's and Behar's work are impressive examples of this development, as they deal precisely with these questions. The religious intertextuality moreover contributes to the specific context of the literature, adds depth to the language and characters, as well as layers of meaning to the text. In relation to the question posed in this article, the reference to *piyyutim* can be defined as a feature of Mizrahi writing.

Conclusion

Israelis of Mizrahi background are, according to public opinion, on average more religious than Ashkenazim, Jews of European descent. All three books point to this cultural localization in different ways. Many studies do indeed show a widespread traditionalism among Mizrahim.[83] Yet, some also argue that the increased identification with Judaism is to be understood precisely

---

78 G. Katz, "Beyond the Religious-Secular Dichotomy: Looking at Five Israeli Dystopias," *Israel Studies Review* 30, no. 2 (2015): 106.
79 Ibid.
80 H. Pedaya, שיבתו של הקול הגולה: זהות מזרחית: פואטיקה, מוזיקה ומרחב [*Return of the Lost Voice*] (Tel Aviv: Hakibbuz Hameuhad, 2016), 82.
81 Ibid., 40–77.
82 Ibid., 122.
83 A. Asher and A. Keissar-Sugarmen, *A Portrait of Israeli Jews: Beliefs, Observance, and Values of Israeli Jews, 2009* (Jerusalem: Israel Democracy Institute/AVI CHAI-Israel, 2012), 30; N. Lewin-Epstein and Y. Cohen, "Ethnic Origin and Identity in the Jewish Population of Israel," *Journal of Ethnic and Migration Studies* 45, no. 11 (2019): 2126–29; Sh. Fischer, "Two Patterns of Modernization: An Analysis of the Ethnic Issue in Israel," *Israel Studies Review* 31, no. 1 (2016): 80; N. Mizrachi, "Sociology in the Garden: Beyond the Liberal Grammar of Contemporary Sociology," *Israel Studies Review* 31, no. 1 (2016): 39–40.

as a reaction to an anti-Arabic marginalization in Israel.[84] The thesis here, however, is not that biblical intertextuality affirms this attribution, but on the contrary—that references to Jewish tradition can be read as an opposition to Zionist ideals of secularization and equalization and as a confident attempt of self-constitution. A number of scholars have argued that the dichotomy of religious and secular is a Western pattern that was adopted in the pre-state era and Israeli Zionism.[85] Traditionalism, in contrast, can be seen as one path in between the poles of religiosity and secularism—as a way of dealing with religion in the modern age.[86] *Masorti* identity does not turn its back on religion and tradition—but rather conveys a sense of compatibility. The analysis here has shown a dialog with the attribution and a broad range in relation to literature.

The reference to the Hebrew Bible in Jewish and Israeli literature is marked by different phases. Especially since the *Haskalah* the Bible has been considered as an important wellspring of inspiration for Jewish prose as a whole.[87] The literary scholar Gershon Shaked states that through an open, secular, and sometimes subversive reading of the Bible, Hebrew literature becomes a "modern midrash."[88] All three novels, *Tchahla ve-Hezkel*, *Shum Gamadim Lo Yavou*, and *Mox Nox* can be described as such. Of course, non-Mizrahi writers also dealt with religious content and symbolism, Shmuel Yosef Agnon (b. 1887 in Buczacz, Galicia/Austro-Hungarian Empire, d. 1970 in Rehovot, Israel) being perhaps the best-known example. However, Mizrahi literature is characterized by the fact that it has defied general conventions and has always been ambivalent. Ballas' work *Hamaabara*, which can be described as the first Mizrahi

---

84 Fischer, "Two Patterns of Modernization," 76–79; E. Shohat, "Rupture and Return—Zionist Discourse and the Study of Arab Jews," *Social Text* 21, no. 2 (75) (2003): 52; Y. Shenhav, *The Arab Jew—A Postcolonial Reading of Nationalism, Religion and Ethnicity* (Stanford, CA: Stanford University Press, 2006).

85 Fischer, "Two Patterns of Modernization;" Y. Shenhav, "How Did the Mizrahim 'Become' Religious and Zionist? Zionism, Colonialism and the Religionization of the Arab Jew," *Israel Studies Forum* 19, no. 1 (2003): 73–87; Y. Yadgar, "Gender, Religion, and Feminism: The Case of Jewish Israeli Traditionalists," *Journal for the Scientific Study of Religion* 45, no. 3 (2006): 353–70; E. Shohat, "Rupture and Return;" N. Leon, "The Secular Origins of Mizrahi Traditionalism," *Israel Studies* 13, no. 3 (2008): 22–42; Z. Shavit and Y. Shavit, "Israeli Culture Today: How Jewish? How Israeli?," in *Handbook of Israel: Major Debates*, ed. E. Ben-Rafael et al. (Berlin: De Gruyter, 2016), 22–38.

86 Leon, "The Secular Origins of Mizrahi Traditionalism," 33; Fischer, "Two Patterns of Modernization;" Lewin-Epstein und Cohen, "Ethnic Origin and Identity in the Jewish Population of Israel," 2133.

87 G. Shaked, "Modern Midrash: The Biblical Canon and Modern Literature," *AJS Review* 28, no. 1 (2004): 44.

88 G. Shaked, *Modern Hebrew Fiction* (London: Toby Press, 2008), 61.

novel in Israel, for example, already contained direct quotations from *piyyutim*, although secularization was particularly demanded during this time. Both on the linguistic and on the religious level, Mizrahi literature cannot be rigidly defined. While Hebrew literature has tried to reposition itself as secular, examples as analyzed above show that the Bible is a cornerstone of Israeli and Jewish identity.[89] By an open and interpretative approach, Mizrahi authors testify to the ongoing dialog with the Bible in Jewish tradition—but also offer new directions for reflecting it. The three works show how dynamic Judaism is and how hard it can be, to assign identities to two poles.

Meanwhile, several authors with a Mizrahi background have questioned the monolithic ideals. Adaf, Behar, and Shilo were just three examples of different approaches regarding religion. Of course, this cannot be an overall judgment of all Mizrahi literature, but the examples should emphasize the diversity of dealing with the Bible as a Jewish textual source and a cultural background for Israeli society. They show how Mizrahi literature responds to the prevailing dichotomies in Israeli society. The analysis has illustrated that the Hebrew Bible continues to be, and in a variety of ways, an important cultural and literary source for modern Hebrew literature and that Mizrahi authors are not deterred from referring to it. The *Tanakh*'s richness and the art of its language continue to influence Hebrew writing of all kinds to this day. It is an important poetic inspiration for Israeli writers, and, not least, for their means: today's modern Hebrew language. In contrast to the general abandonment of references to the Bible in Hebrew literature, which was also noticeable in the impoverishment of language,[90] all three novels suggest, what Gershom Sholem claimed 1926 in his famous letter to Franz Rosenzweig; that the modern Hebrew language is inseparable from its religious well in the Tanakh. The books are characterized by sophisticated crossovers between the biblical, rabbinic, modern Hebrew, and the Arabic language. Their multilingualism creates a unique literary language in modern Mizrahi literature. The Bible as well as the rabbinical sources provide, as we have seen in Adaf's novel, numerous figures of speech and idioms. Behar's novel was used to show how the biblical allusions generate meaning and give density to the text. The Bible offers symbols, metaphors, and points of reference for Jewish identities and Hebrew writing, which is evident in Shilo's work.[91] Mizrahi literature thus offers a compromise between modernity and traditionalism, both in terms of content and language.

---

89   Shapira, "The Bible and Israeli Identity," 17.
90   Ibid., 26.
91   Balaban, "Biblical Allusions in Modern and Postmodern Hebrew Literature," 191; Shemtov, "Bible in Contemporary Israeli Literature," 371.

It is important to point out the peculiarity and differences at this point. This development cannot be reduced to a stylistic device but also reflects social trends and the resurgent role of religion in Israeli society.[92] However, analyzing Mizrahi literature in the context of this topic, also runs the risk of perpetuating stereotypes. The reference should therefore not be read merely as an affirmation, but rather as a complex engagement with a modern Jewish identity or even as an attempt to counteract the hegemony and its narratives. Modern Mizrahi literature thus blurs the distinction between the secular and the religious and helps to expand Judaism from different perspectives.

Bibliography

Adaf, Shimon. מוקס נוקס [Mox Nox]. Or Yehuda: Kinneret/ Dvir, 2011.

--------. כפור [*Nuntia*]. Or Yehuda: Kinneret/ Dvir, 2010.

Adaf, Shimon, and Yigal Schwarz. "החיפוש אחר שורשי הדמיון." ["The Search for the Roots of Imagination."] *Haaretz*, August 17, 2011. https://www.haaretz.co.il/misc/2011-08-17/ty-article/0000017f-dbf8-d3ff-a7ff-fbf8e7060000, last accessed February 3, 2024.

Asher, Arian, and Ayala Keissar-Sugarmen. *A Portrait of Israeli Jews: Beliefs, Observance, and Values of Israeli Jews, 2009*. Jerusalem: Israel Democracy Institute/AVI CHAI-Israel, 2012.

Balaban, Avraham. "Biblical Allusions in Modern and Postmodern Hebrew Literature." *AJS Review* 28, no. 1 (2004): 189–203.

Baram, Nir. "Al 'Tchaḥla ve-Ḥezkel' le Almog Behar." ["About 'Rachel and Ezekiel' by Almog Behar."] *Afirion*, no. 119 (2011): 42–43.

Behar, Almog. צ'חלה וחזקל [*Rachel and Ezekiel*]. Jerusalem: Keter Books, 2010.

Chetrit, Sami Shalom. *Intra-Jewish Conflict in Israel: White Jews, Black Jews*. New York, NY: Routledge, 2010.

Dekel. "The Place, Makom, Nonplace: Between Netivot and Tel Aviv in Shimon Adaf's Panim Zeruvei Hamah (Sunburnt Faces)." *Shofar* 36, no. 3 (2018): 60–77.

Eliyahu, Eli. "שמעון אדף על הרגע שבו סופר נולד." ["Shimon Adaf about the Moment a Writer Was Born."] *Haaretz*, December 25, 2012. https://www.haaretz.co.il/gallery/literature/2012-12-25/ty-article/0000017f-ee2b-d3be-ad7f-fe2bca910000, last accessed February 3, 2024.

Fischer, Shlomo. "Two Patterns of Modernization: An Analysis of the Ethnic Issue in Israel." *Israel Studies Review* 31, no. 1 (2016): 66–85.

---

92 Pinsker, "Religiosity and Mysticism in Modern Hebrew Poetry," 140.

Ginor, Zvia Ben-Yoseph. "Involuntary Myths: Mania, Mother, and Zion in Orly Castel-Bloom's 'Ummi Fi Shurl'." *Prooftexts* 25, no. 3 (2005): 235–57.

Grumberg, Karen. *Place and Ideology in Contemporary Hebrew Literature*. Syracuse, NY: Syracuse University Press, 2011.

Halperin-Kaddari, Ruth, and Yaacov Yadgar. "Between Universal Feminism and Particular Nationalism: Politics, Religion and Gender (in)Equality in Israel." *Third World Quarterly* 31, no. 6 (2010): 905–20.

Henshke, Yehudit. "Israeli, Jewish, Mizrahi or Traditional? On the Nature of the Hebrew of Israel's Periphery." *Journal of Jewish Studies* 68, no. 1 (2017): 137–57.

--------. "On the Mizraḥi Sociolect in Israel: A Sociolexical Consideration of the Hebrew of Israelis of North African Origin." *Journal of Jewish Languages* 1, no. 2 (2013): 207–27.

Kartun-Blun, Ruth. "Isaaks Schrecken: Der Mythos der Opferung in der Hebräischen Dichtung." In *Moderne Hebräische Literatur—Ein Handbuch*, edited by Anat Feinberg, 53–72. München: Richard Boorberg Verlag, 2005.

Katz, Gideon. "Beyond the Religious-Secular Dichotomy: Looking at Five Israeli Dystopias." *Israel Studies Review* 30, no. 2 (2015): 92–112.

Lemberger, Dorit. "Contacts and Discontinuities: Changing Aspects in Shimon Adaf's Work." *Hebrew Studies* 55 (2014): 329–54.

--------. "Questioning Boundaries of Language and the World: Ambivalence and Disillusionment in the Writings of Shimon Adaf." *Hebrew Studies* 56 (2015): 265–94.

Leon, Nissim. "The Secular Origins of Mizrahi Traditionalism." *Israel Studies* 13, no. 3 (2008): 22–42.

Levy, Lital. *Poetic Trespass: Writing between Hebrew and Arabic in Israel/Palestine*. Princeton, NJ: Princeton University Press, 2014.

Lewin-Epstein, Noah, and Yinon Cohen. "Ethnic Origin and Identity in the Jewish Population of Israel." *Journal of Ethnic and Migration Studies* 45, no. 11 (2019): 2118–37.

Massad, Joseph. "Zionism's Internal Others: Israel and the Oriental Jews." *Journal of Palestine Studies* 25, no. 4 (1996): 53–68.

Mendelsohn-Maoz, Adia. "Shimon Adaf and the Peripheral Novel." *Journal of Jewish Identities* 7, no. 2 (2014): 1–13.

Mizrachi, Nissim. "Sociology in the Garden: Beyond the Liberal Grammar of Contemporary Sociology." *Israel Studies Review* 31, no. 1 (2016): 36–65.

Oppenheimer, Yochai. "Representation of Space in Mizrahi Fiction." *Hebrew Studies* 53 (2012): 335–64.

Pedaya, Haviva. שיבתו של הקול הגולה: זהות מזרחית: פואטיקה, מוזיקה ומרחב [*Return of the Lost Voice*]. Tel Aviv: Hakibbuz Hameuhad, 2016.

Pinsker, Shachar. "'Never Will I Hear the Sweet Voice of God': Religiosity and Mysticism in Modern Hebrew Poetry." *Prooftexts* 30, no. 1 (2010): 128–46.

Schely-Newman, Esther. "Poetics of Identity: Mizrahi Poets between Here and There, Then and Now." In *Israel: A Diaspora of Memories*, edited by Michèle Baussant, Dario Miccoli, and Ester Schely-Newman. Special issue of *Quest. Issues in Contemporary Jewish History* 16 (2019): 72–91.

Shaked, Gershon. *Modern Hebrew Fiction*. London: Toby Press, 2008.

--------. "Modern Midrash: The Biblical Canon and Modern Literature." *AJS Review* 28, no. 1 (2004): 43–62.

Shalom Chetrit, Sami. שירים באשדודית [*Songs in Ashdodit*]. Tel Aviv: Andalus Publishing, 2003.

Shapira, Anita. "The Bible and Israeli Identity." *AJS Review* 28, no. 1 (2004): 11–41.

Shavit, Zohar, and Yaacov Shavit. "Israeli Culture Today: How Jewish? How Israeli?" In *Handbook of Israel: Major Debates*, edited by Eliezer Ben-Rafael, Julius H. Schoeps, Yitzhak Sternberg, and Olaf Glöckner, 22–38. Berlin: De Gruyter, 2016.

Shemtov, Vered. "The Bible in Contemporary Israeli Literature: Text and Place in Zeruya Shalev's 'Husband and Wife' and Michal Govrin's 'Snapshots'." *Hebrew Studies* 47 (2006): 363–84.

Shenhav, Yehouda. "How Did the Mizrahim 'Become' Religious and Zionist? Zionism, Colonialism and the Religionization of the Arab Jew." *Israel Studies Forum* 19, no. 1 (2003): 73–87.

--------. *The Arab Jew—A Postcolonial Reading of Nationalism, Religion and Ethnicity*. Stanford, CA: Stanford University Press, 2006.

Shilo, Sara. שום גמדים לא יבואו [*No Gnomes Will Appear*]. Tel Aviv: Am Oved, 2005.

Shohat, Ella. "Rupture and Return—Zionist Discourse and the Study of Arab Jews." *Social Text* 21, no. 2 (75) (2003): 49–74.

--------. "Sephardim in Israel—Zionism from the Standpoint of Its Jewish Victims." *Social Text* 19/20 (1988): 1–35.

Snir, Reuven. "'Anā Min al-Yahūd': The Demise of Arab-Jewish Culture in the Twentieth Century." *Archiv Orientální* 74 (2006): 387–424.

Volach, Lilach. "'Mox Nox' by Shimon Adaf: His Most Accessible Novel." *walla.co.il*, August 10, 2011. https://e.walla.co.il/item/1848635, last accessed February 3, 2024.

Yadgar, Yaacov. "Gender, Religion, and Feminism: The Case of Jewish Israeli Traditionalists." *Journal for the Scientific Study of Religion* 45, no. 3 (2006): 353–70.

Yiftachel, Oren. "Social Control, Urban Planning and Ethno-Class Relations: Mizrahi Jews in Israel's 'Development Towns'." *International Journal of Urban and Regional Research* 24 (2000): 418–38.

List of Contributors

Rosalie Gabay Bernheim
is a final-year doctoral researcher at the School of Modern Languages, University of St Andrews. Her research focuses on representations of the body in pre-modern Jewish and Christian texts, with a particular emphasis on bodily fluids such as menstruation and lactation. In addition to her primary research, Rosalie has a keen interest in the dynamics of medieval Christian-Jewish relations. Her doctoral thesis, titled "Believing in Blood: Menstruation, Menopause, and Jewish-Christian Relations in Medieval Religious Texts," offers a comparative analysis of how Jewish and Christian texts perceive, interpret, and value the menstrual cycle, highlighting its role as a key identity marker within both religious traditions.

Amy Fedeski
is the Alfred and Isabel Bader Postdoctoral Fellow in Jewish History at Queen's University. Amy completed her PhD, "What We Want To Do As Americans": Jewish Political Activism and United States Refugee Policy, 1969–1981, at the University of Virginia's Corcoran Department of History. She holds a BA (Hons) History and Politics from the University of Sheffield and an MPhil American History from Selwyn College, University of Cambridge.

Benjamin Fisher
is Professor of History at Towson University, and the author of *Amsterdam's People of the Book: Jewish Society and the Turn to Scripture in the Seventeenth Century* (2020). He researches Jewish-Christian relations and the history of Jewish engagement with the Bible, and has been a research fellow at the Harvard Center for Jewish Studies and the Oxford Centre for Hebrew and Jewish Studies.

Marissa Herzig
is an English PhD candidate at the University of Toronto whose research focuses on the nonhuman in Jewish folklore. She is a Junior Fellow at Massey College, part of the Jewish Studies collaborative programme, and her dissertation primarily examines retellings of the golem and dybbuk from the lens of disability studies, critical race theory, and gender and sexuality studies.

Yuval Katz-Wilfing

has researched and taught about rabbinical literature and Jewish life in the University of Vienna and the Austrian Academy of Sciences. He is the CEO of the Austrian Committee for Christian-Jewish Co-operation and is regularly lecturing and writing about inter-religious dialogue from a Jewish perspective. His main academic interests relate to the history of ideas, identity construction, soul concept, conversion, and interreligious dialogue.

Armin Lange

is Professor for Second Temple Judaism at Vienna University's Department for Jewish Studies as well as a corresponding member of the Austrian Academy of Sciences. His research specialises in ancient Judaism, the Dead Sea Scrolls, the textual criticism of the Hebrew Bible, ancient antisemitism, and the cultural and religious histories of antisemitism. He has published widely on all of these research areas. He is the executive organiser of the Salo W. and Jeannette M. Baron Awards for Scholarly Excellence in Research of the Jewish Experience and series editor of *Baron Lectures: Studies on the Jewish Experience*.

Kerstin Mayerhofer

holds an PhD in Jewish Studies from the University of Vienna. Kerstin's PhD dissertation offered a comprehensive history of the motif of Jewish 'male menstruation' as a medieval entanglement of sexism and antisemitism. Kerstin has since been conducting research on pre-modern sexism, antisemitism, and racism, on the conceptualisation of the Jewish body, and on gender(s) and sexualitie(s) in Judaism. Kerstin is currently a post-doctoral assistant at the University of Vienna's Department of Jewish Studies and series editor of *Baron Lectures: Studies on the Jewish Experience* (since 2021).

Michael Segal

is the Father Takeji Otsuki Professor of Biblical Studies at the Hebrew University of Jerusalem and Editor of the Hebrew University Bible Project. He is the author of *The Book of Jubilees: Rewritten Bible, Redaction, Ideology and Theology* (2007); *Dreams, Riddles, and Visions: Textual, Contextual, and Intertextual Approaches to the Book of Daniel* (2016); *The Twelve Prophets: The Hebrew University Bible Edition* (with S. Talmon; 2024); and numerous other studies.

Lawrence H. Schiffman

is the Judge Abraham Lieberman Professor of Hebrew and Judaic Studies at New York University and Director of the Global Network for Advanced Research in Jewish Studies. His publications include *From Text to Tradition: A*

History of Second Temple and Rabbinic Judaism (1991); *Reclaiming the Dead Sea Scrolls* (1995); *Qumran and Jerusalem: Studies in the Dead Sea Scrolls and the History of Judaism* (2010) and more than 200 articles on the Dead Sea Scrolls and Rabbinic Judaism.

Alina L. Schittenhelm

is a PhD candidate at the University of Potsdam and an ELES research fellow. Her PhD project focuses on topographies and gender in modern Mizrahi literature. In 2023, she completed a research stay at the literature department of Tel Aviv University. Alina holds a MA in Jewish Studies, and a BA in Jewish Studies and Philosophy from the University of Potsdam. Her research interests include the Hebrew language and Hebrew literature, as well as Israel and Mizrahi Studies.

Ora (Rodrigue) Schwarzwald

is a linguist and professor emerita at the department of Hebrew and Semitic Languages, Bar Ilan University. She is a member of the Academy of the Hebrew Language, an academic correspondent of the Real Academia Española, and president of the Ladino Academy in Israel. Her Research areas include modern Hebrew and Judeo-Spanish (Ladino). She has published several books and numerous scientific articles, edited several books, the journal *Hebrew Linguistics*, and is currently the editor of *Ladinar*.

Emanuel Tov

is the J.L. Magnes Professor of Bible at the Hebrew University in Jerusalem, where he has taught since 1974. He specialises in the textual criticism of Hebrew and Greek Scripture as well as in the Qumran Scrolls. He was the editor-in-chief of the Dead Sea Scrolls Publication Project. He has written 17 books, edited more than fifty, and published more than 350 research papers. In 2023, he was awarded the Salo W. and Jeanette Baron Awards for Scholarly Excellence in Research of the Jewish Experience.

Daniel Vorpahl

holds a PhD in Jewish Studies and works transdisciplinary in between this field and Religious Studies, Gender Studies, and Comparative Literature. Currently working as a research assistant for Hebrew Bible and Its Exegesis at the University of Potsdam, their interests of research involve the literary construction of gender and its religious relatedness in (post-)biblical, rabbinic, children's and young adult literature, and discourse analytical reception studies on biblical themes.